EXECUTRY TAX PLANNING

EXECUTRY TAX PLANNING

(The impact of death on all major taxes with particular reference to Scotland)

By

H. Reynold Galbraith

Solicitor (Dual Qualified in Scotland and in England & Wales), BL. (Glasgow), MA (Kent), SSC, Partner, Donaldson Alexander Russell & Haddow, Solicitors, Glasgow.
Former Diploma Tutor in Wills, Trusts, Executries and Tax at the University of Glasgow and Glasgow Graduate School of Law;
Author of Scottish Trusts: A drafting Guide
General Editor of Green's Scottish Trusts and Succession Service

Published in 2009 by
Thomson Reuters (Legal) Limited
(Registered in England and Wales,
Company No 1679046.
Registered office and address for service
100 Avenue Road, Swiss Cottage,
London, NW3 3PF) trading as W. Green

Typeset by LBJ Typesetting Ltd, Kingsclere
Printed and bound in Great Britain by
Athenaeum Press Ltd, Gateshead

ISBN 978-0-414-01736-8

A catalogue record for this title is available
from the British Library

PREFACE

Our new Constitution is now established, and has an appearance that promises permanency; but in this world nothing can be said to be certain, except death and taxes.[1]

When someone dies in Scotland, the duties imposed by Scots law on executors are many and varied. The bereaved will generally employ a professional, usually a legal practitioner, to carry out these duties. One of the duties, and one, which is often pushed to the side or "outsourced", relates to the executors' duties in connection with taxation. This is unfortunate because the practitioner is ideally placed to carry out these duties, not only for the great advantage of the executors and the beneficiaries but also for the practitioners' firm in well-earned fees! The genesis of this modest text stems from this.

At the root of it is the duty of the executors to make all necessary tax returns, to settle tax due and ingather any assets owing to the executry.

Taxes on personal incomes were first introduced by William Pitt in 1799, to pay for the Napoleonic War. At that time, Britain's financial problems were in dire straits and in his December budget of 1798 Pitt introduced a new graduated income tax. This began with a tax on incomes of £60 and which rose by degrees until it reached 10 per cent on incomes of over £200. Pitt believed that this income tax would raise £10 million but in fact in 1799 the yield was just over a paltry £6 million!

The real "breakthrough", though, was the creation of deduction at source. This nifty method of tax gathering ensured the long-term success of income tax. In 1907, the new Liberal government introduced differential income tax rates, with a higher rate for unearned incomes. This was a direct punishment on that section of society, whom the Liberals considered "public enemy number one", namely those who lived on unearned income, such as rents, dividends or interest! The Liberals alleged that those rentiers were "the direct cause of poverty"! The long, hard struggle between "labour" and "capital" so ensued, with a contemporary periodical commenting that there was no section of the globe in which invested capital stood in so much peril as in Britain.

Tax on capital gains, though, was quite another story. Unbelievably, it was not until 1962, when the stock market, which had risen threefold between 1953 and 1959, became a "happy hunting ground for speculators", that a tax on (only) short-term gains was first introduced. It seems astonishing today that it took the regime so long to close this loophole, particularly when tax on investment income was so high. Instead, from 1958 to 1975, there was, in addition to high income tax rates, some form of control on dividends, to keep the growth of rentiers' income in step with that of "labour".

---

[1] Attributed to Benjamin Franklin in a letter to Jean-Baptiste Leroy.

However, Benjamin Franklin's aphoristic utterance over 200 years ago seems more than ever relevant today. Tax in one form or another occupies much of our time and thinking—with good reason, since the UK has arguably the most complex tax history in the world.

Since 1930, there have been more than eight amending systems, let alone tax rates. This relentless (and indeed remorseless) quest for the holy grail of the perfect tax system has been for two main reasons (other than the obvious one of increasing revenue for the state): the aspiration to encourage companies to invest and the desire to tax the rich.

The rationale for this modest text, which, in a sense, combines the twin facets of Franklin's aphorism, is, basically, to assist busy practitioners to find the information for all (or at least the most common) aspects of executry tax in Scotland in the one place and to assist in enabling the executors to discharge their duties concerning tax.

It is believed that the last textbook relating to tax specifically in Scotland is Jones and Mackintosh, *Revenue Law in Scotland*.[2]

The *Report by the Research Working Group on the Legal Services Market in Scotland*[3] found that one of areas reserved to qualified solicitors in Scotland by the Solicitors (Scotland) Act 1980 was the preparation of executry documents. In general only solicitors could offer this work for payment.

> "However, when reference was made to the conveyancing or executry monopolies that solicitors enjoyed, there was very often a gross misunderstanding of solicitors' 'monopoly' in these areas. In executry services, for example, application for confirmation of executors was the only reserved area while all other services were unreserved."

Perhaps the law and practice of taxation is one aspect which the legal profession is in danger of completely losing to other practitioners, mainly to the accountancy professions. However, in a recent article,[4] a leading Scottish Newspaper indicated that the Institute of Chartered Accountants in Scotland had received permission to carry out executry and probate work south of the border and that it was thought that application would shortly be made for approval in Scotland. However, these other professions seem to be trained in English law and the many and superior aspects of Scottish executry practice may be in danger of disappearing altogether. Some may argue that the battle had been lost by Scottish solicitors before it started. On the other hand it could be argued that Scottish solicitors should not fear competition!

A leading Scottish newspaper, the *Scotland on Sunday*, in a recent article on the effects of the downturn on the Scottish house price market constantly referred to the English expression "probate".

At the time of writing (January 31, 2009), the Scottish National Party has the largest number of seats in the Scottish Parliament, albeit without

---

[2] Martyn Jones and Simon Mackintosh, *Revenue Law in Scotland* (Butterworths, 1986).
[3] Scottish Executive, *Report by the Research Working Group on the Legal Services Market in Scotland*, (Edinburgh, 2006).
[4] *Scotland on Sunday*, April 13, 2008.

an overall majority! The Scottish Parliament under Labour or SNP seems happy to accept English terminology. National taxation, perhaps fortunately, at present is outwith the scope of the Scottish Parliament. Many people would view the prospect of a Scottish Parliament having extended, not to say full, taxation powers with bemusement if not outright panic!

It is thought that this text may be of particular use to the practitioner in a smaller firm, possibly one who carries out a certain amount of executry work but who in the past has shied away from executry tax work. Much of the work is carried out using software programmes and there is a dearth of texts on the simple procedures.

It may also be of interest to other professionals who now carry out or are to be involved in the periphery of executry tax work, such as accountants, financial advisors and banks. It is to be hoped that it will be of interest to law students in the (fond) hope that the downward quality of young persons entering the profession in Scotland can be halted if only slightly.

It is suggested that of particular benefit to practitioners will be the section on post-death planning which, with the formation of trusts, is coming to form an increasing part of the practitioner's work.

By far the highest potential for claims against practitioners stems from tax matters. The author's view is that there is a difficulty of perception in the profession in Scotland on tax. There is an almost universal failure to deal properly with tax matters in the profession. The reasons for this could form a separate text in itself. Generally speaking, the work is not "rocket science" but the consequences of failure can be severe.

There are a number of excellent works in England but there appears to be a dearth of books specifically devoted to executry tax planning in Scotland. This text is therefore a diffident attempt to redress the balance of advantage, which our English counterparts have enjoyed for some years.

The period in the run-up to finalisation of this book has seen a quite spectacular and often bizarre *volte face* by Her Majesty's Revenue and Customs ("HMRC") to reverse one of the main planks of its budget. The pre budget statement of October 24, 2008 also contained some shocks, some of which will be referred to later in the text. In spite of, or despite this, the section on tax treatment of executries and the problem-solving sections may also be of assistance to chartered accountants both in Scotland and in the rest of the UK. It is also hoped this volume will be of use to students generally and particularly those on post-qualifying diploma courses.

TAX LAW REWRITE PROJECT

The other matter which has occurred in the past few years is the Tax Law Rewrite Project. The aim of the Project is to rewrite the UK's primary direct tax legislation to make it clearer and easier to use, without changing the law. The project's work is overseen by a Consultative Committee and a Steering Committee. To date the project has delivered the following:

- The Capital Allowances Act 2001 (effective from April 2001)

- The Income Tax (Earnings and Pensions) Act 2003 (effective from April 2003)
- The Income Tax (Pay as You Earn) Regulations 2003 (effective from April 2004)
- The Income Tax (Trading and Other Income) Act 2005 (effective from April 2005)
- The Income Tax Act 2007 (effective from April 2007)

Obviously the last three acts directly concern the topics of this text.

Unfortunately, during the period while this is underway, the practitioner must check if the original Act, which may be the ICTA, is still in force and try to find where it has been re-enacted. Predictably, mistakes were made in this redrafting.[5]

The Income Tax Act 2007, also known as ITA, received Royal Assent on March 20, 2007 and takes effect from April 6, 2007.[6] It covers inter alia:

- basic provisions about the charge to income tax, income tax rates, the calculation of income tax liability and personal reliefs;
- specific rules about trusts, deduction of tax at source, manufactured payments and repos, the accrued income scheme and tax avoidance; and
- general income tax definitions.

GENERAL PLAN OF THE TEXT

With a view to assisting the use of the text for reference there are dividers dividing the book in to the three main sections:

- Tax matters up to date of death;
- Tax during administration period; and
- Tax post administration

Within each of the sections, there is a chapter devoted to the particular tax and its particular relevance to whether it is up to date of death, during administration or post administration. There is no sustained attempt at making chapters a particular length and some, e.g. the chapter on post-death variation runs to many pages, while that on council tax may be less than a page! However this arrangement, it is suggested, will enable the busy practitioner to easily locate the section, which concerns him.

Chapter One introduces taxation generally.

Chapter Two provides the context of the law of succession in Scotland. Reference is also made to s.29 of the Family Law (Scotland) Act 2004

---

[5] See HMRC, Tax Law Rewrite Project.

[6] The Act, the Explanatory notes and the Table of Origins and Destinations have been published on the OPSI website at *http://www.opsi.gov.uk/acts/acts2007a.htm* [accessed April 29, 2009]. The reader can also access these by selecting the relevant links in the Rewritten Legislation page at *http://www.hmrc.gov.uk/rewrite/acts-and-regs.htm* [accessed April 29, 2009].

with reference to claims by cohabitants on intestacy of cohabitants. Although not directly relevant, it was considered that it might be of assistance to non-legal practitioners and also practitioners alike to consider, since the provisions of the Family Law (Scotland) Act giving rights to cohabitants on intestacy must be factored into any consideration of any executry tax planning.

Chapters Three and Four deal respectively with income tax and capital gains tax up to date of death. Chapter Three also includes suggestions as to the "Herculean " task of abstracting information from banks, building societies and public bodies.

Chapter Five attempts to cover the question of inheritance tax up to date of death and the submission of the appropriate returns on death. Although it is appreciated that the section on inheritance tax returns will only actually be made during the "administration period", i.e. after death, it seems logical to place it in the section "up to death". This Chapter also touches on transfers made during lifetime and the vexed question of gifts with reservation.

The important tax, pre-owned assets tax, is dealt with in **Chapter Six** and **Chapter Seven** covers stamp duty. This is often overlooked in executry practice but it can be important. For completeness there is a short section on Council Tax in **Chapter Eight**.

There is no respite for the busy practitioner! Having barely drawn breath at completing the tasks mentioned in the first section, he or she must immediately address tax matters in the administration period as set out in the second section. The second section on tax during the administration period begins with income tax during the administration period in **Chapter Nine**. Here an example of how scheduling the payment to beneficiaries is given and it is shown how tax can be saved. This is supplemented by the case study "The Two Picasso Cartoons" which is reproduced in the Appendix. **Chapter Ten** deals with capital gains tax during the administration period. Since the rate of capital gains tax has been lowered to 18 per cent this can be an extremely important matter given that the alternative may be to pay inheritance tax at 40 per cent.[7] **Chapter Eleven** covers inheritance tax itself. No reference is made to pre-owned assets tax in this section and short chapters, i.e. the chapters on stamp duty and council tax are very short, i.e. **Chapters Twelve and Thirteen,** to reflect the fact that this does not often come into executry tax planning, and this brings the second section to a close.

The third section deals with post-death tax planning and in some ways it is the most important in that it deals with post-death variations and its impact on the various taxes, mainly on inheritance tax but also on income tax and capital gains. Stamp duty is also covered.

It has been decided to split this third section into two parts. **Part One** deals with the position where variation has not taken place and **Part Two** deals with the situation where it has. There is a short introductory, namely, **Chapter Fourteen. Chapters Fifteen, Sixteen and Seventeen** deal with post administration without variation as it affects income tax, capital gains tax and inheritance tax, respectively. **Chapter Eighteen** attempts to mop up pre-owned assets tax, stamp duty and council tax.

---

[7] Under inheritance tax.

Chapter Nineteen, by far the longest chapter, introduces the part dealing with post-death variation and changes the emphasis by dealing with inheritance tax first. **Chapters Twenty and Twenty One** deal with the impact of post-death variation on capital gains tax and income tax respectively. **Chapter Twenty Two** deals briefly with the stragglers, i.e. pre owned assets tax, stamp duty and council tax.

The penultimate **Chapter Twenty Three** deals with avoiding negligence claims and final chapter, **Chapter Twenty Four** deals with future trends. It also makes some predictions as to the future of trusts, which are now the subject of ongoing reports by the Scottish Law Commission. Please note that the important tax, namely value added tax (VAT), will not be covered.

Tax Facts

Sometimes a practitioner will experience not so much difficulty as wasting time in quickly and efficiently finding the basic facts about, for example, the amount of income tax allowances. This may involve several clicks to reach the correct web page. To assist in this there is a tax facts section near the start of the text, which attempts to provide a note of all principal tax rates, exemptions, time limits for submission and of course, penalties. These are organised under the headings of the various taxes, e.g. income tax, capital gains, etc.. However, they are also reproduced for the individual taxes at the start of the relevant chapter. While this, on the face of it, may seem like an unnecessary duplication, nevertheless, it is suggested that it may cut down the time having to turn to the section at page xxv to access the relevant section.

It might be that I am criticised for spending so much space on the question of penalties. However, I believe it is justified given the introduction by HM Revenue & Customs of a new range of penalties and indeed a new philosophy behind them.

A Word about Styles

This is a matter which has caused much soul searching. Attempts to trace ownership of styles have largely failed. The author freely admits he has drawn on styles culled from textbooks, the Law Society Diploma materials in which he was involved on the periphery, his own firm's styles and others. He is reminded of an anecdote told to him by one of his former principals. This older solicitor recalled the days when solicitors went out of the office for their coffee to one of the many coffee houses in Glasgow and his view concerned the use of umbrellas. The older solicitor's view, which seemed to be common, was that if you contributed one umbrella at the start of the season to the favoured coffee house umbrella stand, then you were entitled to take one from the stand whenever you needed one. The author respectfully considers that he has contributed styles to the profession over the years at seminars and therefore feels that he is entitled . . . !

Terminology

A sustained attempt is made to use Scottish terminology. English and other readers will appreciate, e.g. that a testator is the person making the will; truster is a settler; a liferent trust is an interest in possession trust; a will in Scotland can be a "will", a settlement, a testamentary settlement and a trust disposition and settlement; a fiar is a remainder-man and so on. I have been tempted to use the expression "appoint" or "powers of appointment", meaning to transfer or give trustees authority to transfer, or select and transfer on the theory that it is a lost cause! It is in the magical land of the pre-owned assets tax ("POT" or "POAT") where Scots are most subjected to anglicisation. POT covers three categories of property, which the legislation describes as land, chattels and intangibles property. I will attempt to use the correct Scottish terms for the last two of these, namely corporeal moveables and incorporeal movable property.

However, I have preferred the more usual and Scottish meaning wherever possible. It is a source of concern that English terminology should be used in Scotland including by the Scottish Government! Probably this trend has been hastened by the passing of "English" Finance Acts!

It is also a matter of concern that the idea should be given general credence to the fallacy that English and Scots law and practice as regards executry law are similar. Postings on the Trust Discussion Forum seem to give weight to this misapprehension. This is a dangerous assumption and should be guarded against, especially by those involved in executries who do not have a background in Scots law. It would seem from recent pronouncements of Her Majesty's Treasury that they take the view that the law and practice are similar. It is thus not xenophobia or crankiness to belabour the use of Scottish terminology; the problem is that taking the example culled from trust law, the use of "English" expressions engenders a belief for example, that Scottish trust law is just a "translation" of English trust law. This can be extremely dangerous.

In Scotland the law of trusts developed separately. Scots law is based not on the dualism of legal and equitable ownership nor on obligations enforceable in equity; there is no distinction of law and equity in Scotland. It is based on the principle of property being vested in trustees as legal owners subject to the burden of their holding and administering it for the trust purposes, for the benefit of persons who have claims on the trust estate. Another problem occurs mainly with younger practi-tioners who seem more than keen to use English expressions. This is understandable with members of the accountancy professions but beg-gars belief with legally qualified ones.

CIVIL PARTNERSHIP ACT

On the topic of terminology, with the passing of the Civil Partnership Act as amended by the Family Law (Scotland) Act 2006, it is necessary to deal with not only surviving spouses but also surviving civil partners. While this text will not go into the matter in full detail and with a view to avoiding cumbersome clauses, the expression "surviving spouse" will, unless the context so stipulates, mean either surviving spouse or civil partner. In certain cases it may be relevant to include "co-habitee". Generally unless otherwise stated "he" will include "she" and so on.

I have been, and expect to be, criticised for the fragmented nature of the book and for including matters which do not at rest glance seem relevant to the topic. It could and has been argued that matters such as stamp duty and pre-owned assets tax should not necessarily find a place in a textbook on executry tax planning. However, I accept and welcome this criticism. My defence is that I intend the text to be of assistance to practitioners; one of the problems facing practitioners is to be able to find articles or matters of interest quickly and this has been the rationale for inclusion. In addition, deeds of variation are a fruitful source of setting up trusts. As I explain, a claim for professional negligence may (and rightly) fall on a practitioner who fails to bring to the attention of a surviving spouse, executors, trustees or indeed the truster or testator the utility of a mini-discretionary trust as an IHT-saving vehicle. It goes without saying that trust practitioners ignore at their peril the possible impact for clients of the pre-owned assets tax.

THE SCOTTISH LEGAL COMPLAINTS COMMISSION (SLCC)

The Scottish Legal Complaints Commission, which is to be based in Edinburgh, became operational on October 1, 2008. The Commission is a new, independent, complaints-handling body; it has been given powers to deal with unresolved complaints. The Scottish Justice Secretary, Mr Kenny Macaskill, announcing the appointment, stated:

> "Complaints handling is not just about dealing with things that go wrong, but ensuring that things go right. The commissioners will help to build a culture of learning from complaints through their oversight and promotion of standards. This focus on the quality of service will undoubtedly benefit both consumers and the profession alike."

In some ways it is beneficial for both solicitors and their clients to have complaints taken out of the hands of the Law Society. The problem was one of perception. The public view was that the Law Society "would look after their own". The perception of the practitioner was that the Society spent too much time safeguarding the public and not the very people who they represented!

It is not entirely clear how this will work in practice and this may only develop through time. In a helpful article, "'Gateway' opens its doors",[8] Craig Watson writes:

> "The Commission will act as a gateway for all complaints against lawyers, and by mediating, resolving or determining complaints about service and sifting out those that are frivolous, vexatious or without merit. Conduct matters will be passed on to the professional organisations, though the Commission will oversee the way conduct complaints are handled as well as taking over the Scottish Legal Services Ombudsman's current overseeing powers."

---

[8] Craig Watson, "'Gateway' opens its doors" (2008) 53(9) J.L.S. 34.

The plan is that the Commission will consider complaints about service where the work, which was the subject of the complaint, was instructed after October 1, 2008. The Law Society will still deal with complaints relating to "service" business instructed before October 1. A one-year time limit for making complaints will apply when the Commission is fully operational. No doubt this one-year limit will be increased!

The Law Society will still handle professional misconduct matters, with prosecutions still going before the independent Scottish Solicitors' Discipline Tribunal (SSDT).

A new complaint has also been created, which is to be known as: "unsatisfactory professional conduct". This will be the responsibility of the Law Society to adjudicate upon. "Unsatisfactory professional conduct" is defined as conduct falling short of professional misconduct. The Law Society are to be entitled to make one or more of a mandatory censure, a fine of up to £2,000 and compensation to the aggrieved complainer of up to £5,000. This, it is understood, may be for each ground of complaint which is upheld. It may also compel the practitioner to undergo training.

The cost of this new Commission will inevitably be financed by members of the legal profession in Scotland and an estimate of the amount due from each solicitor has been fixed at £275 for the year 2009/2010 (for solicitors with three or more years' experience).

It had been naively thought that this would lead to a reduction in costs for the Law Society. However, in a letter to members,[9] the President, Richard Henderson CB, wrote:

> "It was however anticipated that the Society's complaints work (and therefore costs) would reduce when the Commission opened. Unfortunately, however, this is not to be the case for at least another year. Although the Complaints Commission opened its doors on 1st October 2008, it has stated its intention to deal only with work where a solicitor is instructed on or after that date. In consequence, the Commission is unlikely to investigate many complaints in its first nine months of operation (their budget for which is £2.6m). The budget was approved by the Scottish Parliament before the limited initial remit was announced. Statute now prevents changes to the budget and requires the Society to collect the levy from the profession.
>
> Nonetheless, due to the transitional arrangements of the Commission, the Society's obligation in terms of complaints handling will not reduce as expected and the financial costs to the profession of the Society's complaints handling remain largely . . ."

PENALTY REGIME

Over the years, HM Revenue & Customs have frequently indicated their intention to make the UK tax system simpler and more consistent. Legislation has introduced penalties to help those taxpayers who try to

---

[9] Dated September 16, 2008.

comply. The corollary to this is that they will be more severe on those who do not. At first the new penalties are aimed at mistakes on returns and documents for inter alia capital gains tax, income tax and corporation tax and will affect returns and other forms for return for periods starting on or after April 1, 2008, which are due to be filed on or after April 1, 2009.

There will be a quite conscious attempt to penalise those who do not take reasonable care and the penalties will be higher if the error is deliberate. Disclosing errors to HMRC early will substantially reduce any penalty due. HM Revenue & Customs have given guidance on the question of "taking reasonable care" and regard will be had to arrangements for systems in place which if followed, could reasonably have been expected to produce an accurate basis for the calculation of tax due and despite this inaccuracies arose which result in a misstatement.

A FAIRER TAX FOR SCOTLAND

The Scottish Government recently promulgated a consultation document entitled "A Fairer Local Tax for Scotland". Broadly speaking this proposes a local income tax and is to replace what is described as "an unfair council tax". The proposals include tax-free personal allowance matching the UK personal allowance levels and a three per cent rate applied to the income presently subject to basic and higher rates of UK income tax. There are to be exemptions for saving and investment income and a tax for second homes.

The document goes into considerable detail. It does seem that there is support in certain quarters based mainly on the premise that it will make the executive more accountable.

Submissions have been sought from parties and perhaps one of the most trenchant has come from the Institute of Chartered Accountants of Scotland, who are reported in the *Scotland on Sunday*[10] and express the fears:

> "[T]hat the proposed system would place a huge and costly burden on employers and create cross-border tensions. It raises questions over the operation of the tax including the ability of H M Revenue & Customs to collect it."

At the very least it is suggested that most residents in Scotland would view the prospect of yet another tax, even a beneficial one, with bemusement if not outright panic and alarm!

"Danger Warning!!"

These will recur throughout the text and it is hoped that they will provide a warning to the busy practitioner of a smoking bomb! **"Attentions"** are meant to be a slightly less degree of ignition!

---

[10] *Scotland on Sunday*, July 13, 2008.

Post-Death Tax Planning

The author is greatly indebted to Ralph Ray both for his excellent work, "Post-Death Planning: Variations and Disclaimers",[11] and for his many articles and texts on the subject.

Thanks

It is not easy to "take up a literary career" at any time but particularly so if you only start in your mid sixties and have to juggle it with the demands of a busy city legal practice and teaching commitments. It is greatly helped, however, if you have assistance from people who are very generous with their time. In this connection, I would like to take this opportunity to thank all my colleagues at Central Law Training and on the Post Qualifying Diploma. In particular, I would like to record my thanks to the late Loudon Downs, to Beth Hamilton, and John Kerrigan for their support and assistance over the years. Special thanks are also due to Jim Ferguson for all his help and patience over the years and also for checking tables. I would also like to thank Lorna Harper, Ashley Rickards and Alastair Galbraith for their help in typing, proof reading the text and compiling tables. I owe an immense debt of gratitude to my colleagues and friends at Greens, in general, not only for their miracle work in transforming my disconnected ramblings in the text but also for their support and encouragement over the years but in particular to Mrs Jill Hyslop, my publisher, for her constant encouragement, advice and support.

Apology

At the risk of offending readers of the fairer sex, particularly the many extremely talented individuals involved in this branch of the profession's work, I must confess to often using the expression "he", "him" or "his" when, of course, I should correctly have used the expressions "she/her/hers".

Disclaimer

Please note that this publication is intended principally as a guide for qualified professionals engaged in the practice of law, accountancy and financial services. While it is to be hoped that general readers will find it interesting and of use, it should be emphasised that as regards this latter class, it is for general guidance only for individual readers and does NOT constitute accountancy, tax, investment or other professional advice. Neither the publishers nor the author can accept any responsibility or liability for loss, which may arise from reliance on information contained herein. It goes without saying tax law, the law and practices by government and Her Majesty's Revenue & Customs are constantly changing. There is no substitute for consulting a suitably qualified

---

[11] Ralph Ray, "Post-Death Planning: Variations and Disclaimers", *Tolley's Tax Digest*, Issue 19, May 2004.

lawyer, accountant, tax specialist, independent financial adviser or other professional adviser. In addition, the taxpayer's own situation may vary and the professional adviser will be able to give specific advice based on the personal circumstances.

I am dealing with UK taxation only and any references to "tax" or "taxation" in this Tax Guide, unless the contrary is expressly stated, refers to UK taxation only. Please note that references to the "UK" do not include the Channel Islands or the Isle of Man. Foreign tax implications are beyond the scope of this Tax Guide.

All mistakes in the text and in the law, which it is attempted to be as at January 31, 2009, are mine.

Rennie Galbraith
Glasgow, March 1, 2009

TABLE OF CONTENTS

Chapters

PART ONE: PERIOD UP TO DEATH

TABLE OF ABBREVIATIONS

AA	Age Allowance
ACT	Advance Corporation Tax
APA	Additional Personal Allowance
AIE	Assumed income entitlement (TA 1988 s.696(3B))
BRI	Income which is taxed at the basic rate
CGT	Capital Gains Tax
ESC	Extra Statutory Concession
FA	Finance Act
FID	Foreign Income Dividend
HMRC	Her Majesty's Revenue & Customs
ICTA 1988	Income and Corporation Taxes Act 1988[2]
IHT	Inheritance Tax
IHTM	Inheritance Tax Manual
ISA	Individual Savings Account
IT	Income Tax
IHTA	Inheritance Tax Act 1984
ITA 2007	Income Tax Act 2007
ITEPA 2003	Income Tax (Earnings and Pensions) Act 2003
IR	Inland Revenue
IRC	Inland Revenue Commissioners
ITTOIA	Income Tax (Trading and Other Income) Act 2005
The Law Society	The Law Society Of Scotland
LIFO	Last in First out
LRI	Income which is taxed at the lower rate
Ltd	Limited
MCA	Married Couples Allowance
NRSFRI	Non-Repayable Schedule F Rate Income
NRB	Nil rate band
NS	National Savings
OEIC	Open Ended Investment Company[4]
PA	Personal Allowance
Para	Paragraph
PAYE	Pay As You Earn
PAYE Regs	IT (Employments) Regulations (SI 1993/744)
PEP	Personal Equity Plan
PEP Regs	Personal Equity Plan Regulations (SI 1989/469)
PET	Potentially Exempt Transaction
Pt	Part
RPI	Retail Price Index
s.	Section
SA	Self Assessment

---

[1] Sometimes referred to as The Taxes Act 1988 or TA 1988 and even more rarely as the Taxation Act 1988.

[2] Sometimes Scottish OEICs are referred to flippantly as McOEICs.

Sch.	Schedule
SDMA 1891	Stamp Duties/Management Act 1981
SDRT	Stamp Duty Reserve Tax
SI	Statutory Instrument
SLCC	The Scottish Legal Complaints Commission
SLDT	Scottish Solicitors' Discipline Tribunal
SP	Inland Revenue Statement of Practice
TA 1988	Income and Corporation Taxes Act 1988
TCGA 1992	Taxation of Chargeable Gains Act 1992
TESSA	Tax Exempt Special Savings Account
TNRBA	Transferred Nil Rate Band Allowance
TMA 1970	Taxes Management Act 1970
TR	Taper Relief
WBA	Widows Bereavement Allowance

ADDENDUM—BUDGET 2009

As this text goes to press, information in respect of the Budget 2009 is available and is as summarised as follows:

Income Tax

With regards to income tax, certain changes are to operate from April 6, 2009, April 6, 2010 and April 6, 2011 respectively.

As from October 6, 2009, the Chancellor has raised the ISA limit to £10,200 for those aged 50 or more. From April 6, 2010 this will apply to all savers irrespective of age.

From April 6, 2010, income which is in excess of £150,000 is to be taxed at a staggering 50 per cent, apart from dividends that fall within this band, which will be taxed at 42.5 per cent. **This was a year earlier than expected and at a rate higher than the rate of 45 per cent, which had been proposed**. As if this was not bad enough, individuals with net income of £100,000 will lose £1 of personal allowance for every £2 by which their income exceeds this limit. The other matter is that the favourable treatment of taxation of rent from holiday lettings is to be abolished. From April 6, 2010, taxpayers who are fortunate enough to receive income of over £100,000 will gradually have their personal allowance eroded. What is to happen is the basic personal allowance will be reduced by up to 100 per cent, at the rate of £1 for every £2 of income above £100,000. It is estimated that at the present level of £6475, the whole allowance will vanish at £112,950. Although HM Revenue & Customs do not actually emphasise this aspect, it is that for the income ranging from £100,000 to £112,950 the actual rate of income tax may be up to a staggering 60 per cent!

From after April 6, 2011 the rate of relief on pension contributions is to be restricted.

Although it is not strictly relevant to the text, from April 6, 2010 the rate applicable to Trusts will rise from 40 per cent to 50 per cent with a dividend rate of 42.5 per cent.

For the year from April 6, 2009, the personal allowance at age under 65 is £6,475; for age 65–74, £9,490; and for those aged 75 and over is £9,640.

Married couples' allowance, i.e. for those aged less than 75 and born before April 6, 1935, is no longer applicable. There is a 10 per cent starting rate for savings income only with a limit of £2,440 for 2009–2010. The proviso is if the taxpayers' taxable non-savings income is above this limit then the 10 per cent savings rate will not be applicable. The 10 per cent dividend ordinary rate and the 32.5 per cent dividend upper rate are not affected. The married couples' allowance, however, for aged 75 and over is £6,965 and the minimum amount is £2,670. Income limit for age related allowances is £22,900.

With regards to the rates on income tax, the starting rate for 10 per cent is nil to £2,440, the basic rate at 20 per cent is now from nil to £37,400 and the higher rate of 40 per cent is over this limit.

> *Attention !!*
>
> *Married couples' allowance is only available where one of the spouses (or civil partners) was born pre-April 6, 1935.*

Capital Gains Tax

For individuals for the year from April 6, 2009 is £10,100 and for Trusts £5,050. The rate remains at 18 per cent.

Stamp Duty Land Tax

On transfer of land and buildings, until December 31, 2009 is nil in respect of residential up to £175,000 and on non-residential up to £150,000. It is 1 per cent in respect of residential properties over £175,000 and under £250,000. Regarding non-residential, it is for £150,000 to £250,000.

It then goes up to 3 per cent residential over £250,000 to half a million pounds and a similar amount for non-residential. Over one million pounds for both residential and non-residential is a staggering 4 per cent.

From January 1, 2010 the rates will be:

Rate	Residential—Non Disadvantaged Area £	Residential— Disadvantaged Area £	Non Residential £
	Consideration	Consideration	Consideration
Nil	0–125,000	0–150,000	0–150,000
1%	125,000–250,000	150,000–250,000	150,000–250,000
3%	250,001–500,000	250,001–500,000	250,001–500,000
4%	Over 500,000	Over 500,000	Over 500,000

TAX FACTS FOR THE YEARS ENDING

Income Tax Facts for the Years Ending April 5

IT	Income Tax Allowances	Tax Code	2008 £	2009 £	2010 £	2011/12
1	Aged under 65 years	L	5,225	6,035[1]	6,475	See below*
2	Aged 65 to 74 (income not over Income limit)	P	7,550	9,030	9,490	
3	Aged over 75 (income not over Income limit)	T	7,690	9,180	9,640	

IT	Income Tax Allowances	Tax Code	2008 £	2009 £	2010 £
	Married Couples/Civil Partners Minimum allowance (one born before April 6, 1935 but aged under 75) at 10%	V	2,440	2,540	2,670
	Married Couples/Civil Partners allowance (aged under 75) at 10% (one or other born before April 6, 1935)	T	6,285	6,535	N/A
	Married Couples/Civil Partners allowance (aged 75 or over) at 10%% (one or other born before April 6, 1935)	T	6,365	6,625	6,965
	Income limit for age related allowances reduced by 50% where one spouse born before April 6, 1935		20,900	21,800	22,900
	Minimum amount of married couple's allowance		2,440	2,540	
	Blind person's allowance		1,730	1,800	1,890
	Rent a room allowance	4,250 (£2,150 if letting jointly).	4,250 (£2,150 if letting jointly).		

- Tax relief for the married couple's allowance is at 10 per cent.

---

[1] This was increased to compensate for the loss of the 10 per cent starting rate.

- There will be a new 10 per cent starting rate for savings income only, with a limit of £2,320 (2008/2009). If the deceased tax-payer's taxable non-savings income is above this limit, then the 10 per cent savings rate will not be applicable. There are no changes to the 10 per cent dividend ordinary rate or the 32.5 per cent dividend upper rate.
- Watch out in the case of the married couples allowance: it is the eldest of the two spouses who qualifies the couple.

Income Tax Rates and Taxable Bands

		2008	2009	2010	2011/12
Dividend rate	10%				
Upper Dividend rate	32.5%				See below*
Savings Rate	10%	£0 to —			
New savings rate	10%		Up to £2,320[2]		
Starting Rate 10%	10%	£0–£2,230 (on all income)	£2,320 (only applies where taxable non-savings is under £2,320)	£2,440	
Basic Rate on earned and property income	22%	£2,231–£34,600			
	20%		£0 – £34,800		
Basic rate on savings income					
Higher Rate 40%		Over £34,600	Over £34,800	£37,400	
Pre-owned assets tax		As for income	As for income		
Must notify new sources of income by October 5 following the end of the year of assessment					
Submission of returns					
Paper only					

---

[2] If the savings income is above this the 10 per cent savings rate will not be applicable!

	2008	2009	2010	2011/12
By October 31 following the end of the year of assessment				
Online by January 31 following the end of the year of assessment				
Penalties				
Failure to submit on time	£100	£100	£100	
Continued failure				
Commissioners may authorise up to	£60 per day	£60 per day	£60 per day	
Or up to the amount of the outstanding tax.				
Payment is normally due by January 31 after end of year of assessment[3]				

Attention!!

Income tax is payable under the Taxes Management Act 1970 as amended. The date for payment is January 31 following the end of the tax year. Interim payments to account are to be made on January 31 during the tax year and on July 31 following the end of the tax year. No payments are required if the amount due is less than £500 (to be increased to £1,000 for the tax years 2009/2010 and subsequently). If the proportion the amount of tax, which must be outstanding before a taxpayer is required to make a payment on account of income tax under s.59A of the Taxes Management Act 1970, bears to the assessed amount is less than 1 to 5, no payments are required. So if more than 80 per cent of the assessed tax is met by income tax deducted at source no payments on account are required. The final payment of income tax is due under the Taxes Management Act 1970 as amended The balance of tax due for the year of assessment after deducting payments to account, etc. is due on January 31 following the year of assessment. A surcharge of five per cent may be made after February 28 with a further surcharge after July 31.

---

[3] TMA 1970 s.59B.

Danger Warning!!

In his pre-Budget statement on Monday, November 24, 2008, the Chancellor of the Exchequer, The Right Honourable Alistair Darling, announced plans to introduce a new 45 per cent tax rate for high earners and other changes to the way income tax is paid. From April 2011, taxpayers earning more than £150,000 a year are to have a new tax rate of 45p in the £1. Apparently, this will impact on the top one per cent of incomes. In addition, he is to change the personal allowances of high earners to end what he describes as "the anomaly of these being worth twice as much to high-rate taxpayers as those who pay basic-rate tax". The personal allowance, £6,035, is the amount of earnings on which no tax is payable. All taxpayers have the same allowance. From April 2010, taxpayers earning between £100,000 and £140,000 would have their personal allowances halved so they received the same benefit as those earning less. For taxpayers earning more than £140,000 he will withdraw the allowance entirely. He also announced plans to make permanent this year's increase in the income tax personal allowance of £120 a year for basic rate taxpayers.

Capital Gains Tax Facts for the years ending April 5

	2008	2009
The Annual Exempt Amount (AEA)	£9,200 for individuals executries (first 3 years) and £4,600 for some trustees	£9,600 for individuals executries (first 3 years) and £4,800 for some trustees
CGT Tax Rates		
Individuals	10%, 20% or 40%	18%
Trusts and estates	40%	18%
Exemptions		
Individuals and estates***	£9,200	£9,600
Trusts	£4,600	£4,800
Chattels (proceeds) 5/3 of excess gain chargeable	£6,000	£6,000
Date Return to be made		
Date payment to be made	To be paid (along with any balance of income tax due on January 31 following the end of the tax year	

	2008	2009
Penalty for late payment and time limits for sub-mission		
Broadly speaking as for income tax		

Inheritance Tax

On death	From £0–£312,000 (after April 5, 2008)	nil
	£312,000—no upper limit	40%
Lifetime rates	From £0–£312,000	20%
	£312,000—no upper limit	

Inheritance Tax Facts

	Gross Transfers on death
Period	Nil Rate Band
2007/08[4]	£300,000
2008/09[5]	£312,000
2009/10[6]	£325,000
2010/11[7]	£350,000

Principal Exemptions

During lifetime	
Annual Exemption	£3,000 (may be carried forward to succeeding year only to the extent unused)
Small Gifts	£250 per donee. If the gift exceeds this none of it is exempt

---

[4] FA 2005 s.98.
[5] FA 2006 .s155.
[6] FA 2006 s.155.
[7] FA 2007 s.4.

During lifetime	
Gifts out of income	If made out of income which has been taxed and donor left with sufficient to live on. Usually a pattern of expenditure is sought.
Gifts in consideration of marriage	From £1,000 to £5,000 depending on relationship to prospective bride or groom.
Disposition for maintenance under s.11 IHTA	Exempt
On Death as well	
Gifts to spouse	Exempt (provided she has UK domicile if not restricted to £55,000)
Gifts to charities(UK)	Exempt.
Any portion of the nil rate band which is not used at a taxpayer's death can be transferred to the executors of his/her surviving spouse or civil partner for the purposes of IHT charge on the death of the survivor on or after October 9, 2007.	

	Delivery dates
Chargeable lifetime transfers	Later of 12 months after transfer took place and three months after the date when the accountable party became liable.
PETs[8] which have become chargeable	12 months after the month in which the death took place.
Gifts with reservation which are chargeable on death	12 months after the month in which the death took place.
Transfers on death	Later of 12 months after the month in which the death took place.

Penalties

If a late account is received and proceedings before the Special Commissioners to obtain it have not already been taken	A penalty of £100* is due.

---

[8] Potentially Exempt Transfers.

If the account is more than six months late	The penalty is £200.
* If the account is more than 12 months late *	The penalty increases to a maximum of £3,000.
* If the actual tax liability is less than these figures, the penalty cannot be more than the amount of the tax due.	

Inheritance Tax Facts for the years ending April 5

	Rates
Gross Transfers on death	40%
Gross Transfers on lifetime transfers	20%
	Gross Transfers on death
Period	Nil Rate Band
2007/08[10]	£300,000
2008/09[12]	£312,000
2009/10[14]	£325,000
2010/11[16]	£350,000

Any portion of the nil-rate band which is not used at a taxpayer's death can be transferred to the executors of their surviving spouse or civil partner for the purposes of IHT charge on the death of the survivor on or after October 9, 2007.

> *Attention!!*
>
> *Chargeable transfers other than on death which are made between April 6 and September 30 are assessable for payment on April 30 in the following year. Between October 1 and April 5 tax is due six months after the end of the month in which the chargeable transfer is made. Inheritance tax on*

---

[9] FA 2005 s.98.
[10] FA 2006 s.155.
[11] FA2006 s.155.
[12] FA 2007 s.4.

> *transfers on death are to be made at the earlier of six months after the end of the month on which the death occurs and delivery of the IHT 400 or 200 by the executors. Tax or additional inheritance tax becomes payable on death on chargeable transfers and PEPS within seven years of death.*
>
> *The failure to deliver the inheritance tax return within 12 months of the death, unless tax is less than £100 or there is a reasonable excuse, will make the executor liable for an initial penalty of £100 or the amount of tax payable if less and a further penalty of £60 where the penalty is determined by court or special commissioners for each day in which the failure continues. If the failure continues after six months after the date on which the account is due and proceedings are not commenced, a further penalty of up to £100 or the amount of tax payable if less will apply. If the failure continues for one year after the end of the period in which the amount is due a penalty not exceeding £3,000 will apply.*

Pre-Owned Assets Tax

As for Income Tax.

The election for having the charge treated as INHERITANCE TAX must be made before January 31 in the year following the first year of assessment, e.g. if the taxpayer becomes liable to the income tax charge for 2006–2007, he has until January 31, 2008 to make the election.

If the deceased dies part way through the tax year, before they have made the election?	He is liable for income tax on the benefit derived from the pre-owned asset from April 6 in the first year of assessment up to date of death. The executors are not able to make an election after the date of death and the estate will be liable to pay the income tax due up to that date (provided it is not below the *de minimis* limit). This will be a debt on the estate for inheritance tax. The charge of course ends the death of the taxpayer.
If the taxpayer dies before the start of the tax year when the charge to income tax on pre-owned assets comes into force?	As above the charge ends with death.

Stop Press

From **March 1, 2009**, the interest rate applying to the continued use of corporeal or incorporeal moveables formerly owned, under the pre-owned asset rules, is 4.75 per cent. This is a reduction from the previous rate of 6.25 per cent

Stamp Duty Land Tax

Land dealings	From March 23, 2006	
Residential Property		
Non-disadvantaged areas	Up to £125,000	Nil
	£125,001–£250,000	1%
	£250,001–£500,000	3%
	£500,001 upwards	4%
Disadvantaged areas.	Up to £150,000	Nil
Stamp duty land tax is not charged on residential transactions in disadvantaged areas if the price of the property is less than £150,000.		
	£150,001–£250,000	1%
	£250,001–£500,000	3%
	£500,001 upwards	4%
Non-residential properties (or mixed), disadvantaged and non-disadvantaged	Up to £150,000	Nil
	£150,001–£250,000	1%
	£250,001–£500,000	3%
	£500,001 upwards	4%
Danger Warning!!	**After September 2, 2008 and before December 31, 2009**	
	Up to £175,000	Nil
Exemptions		
These do not require to be notified.	• No chargeable consideration	
	• Transactions between spouses/civil partners on separation, divorce or annulment as a result of a court order, or by virtue of an agreement in the course of the annulment, separation or divorce	
	• Conveyance of assets by executors to beneficiaries of a will or on intestacy unless for consideration	

Land dealings	From March 23, 2006	
	• Variation of will within two years of the death providing not for consideration, other than the making of another variation in return	
From March 12, 2008 no longer necessary for the purchaser to self-certify that the transaction is exempt in order for the transaction to be registered		
Submission of tax	Generally interest runs from 30 days after the expiry of 30 days after date of completion	
Penalties for failure to deliver stamp duty land tax return	• £100 if delivered within three months	
	• Otherwise the discretionary trust rules will apply £200	
	• If not delivered within 12 month, penalty up to amount of tax chargeable	

Stamp duty/stamp duty reserve tax on the transfer of shares and securities

Rate	0.5%	
Penalties	Generally penalty and interest runs from 30 days after the expiry of 30 days after date of completion.	
	If the document is less than one year late the maximum penalty will be an amount equivalent to the duty or £300, whichever is less.	
	If the executor's document is more than one year late the maximum penalty is an amount equivalent to the duty or £300, whichever is more.	

Important Dates

January 31	Last date to file self assessment electronically,
	balancing payment, and
	first payment to account of tax due for current year.
	Captial gains tax due for preceding year.
February 28	Automatic 5% surcharge on any tax outstanding.
February	Consider if payments to account should be made to beneficiaries before April 6.
April 6	Start of new tax year.
July 31	Second payment to account due. Further automatic 5% surcharge on any tax outstanding.
October 31	Last date to file self assessment by paper.
November 1	Remember to start (if not already done) to gather and keep information for next year's return.
Inheritance Tax	Six months after the end of the month of death or chargeable transfer.
For chargeable lifetime transfers between April 6 and September 30	30 April in the following year.

Stop Press!!

The government have announced their intention to increase personal allowance and basic rate bands for 2009/2010, to £6,475 and £37,400 respectively. This effects the changes made in May 2008 (when the personal allowance was increased "retrospectively" to compensate those who had lost out from the abolition of the 10 per cent starting rate band). Consequently, the higher rate income tax threshold is to be increased from £40,835 to £43,875 next April. As proposed in Gordon Brown's last Budget as Chancellor in March 2007, other income tax bands and allowances will merely increase by inflation in April 2009. Full details of the new rates for 2009/2010 announced in the Pre-Budget Report are set out in the Tax Facts section.

The bad news is that the **personal allowance will be withdrawn around** April 2010, when a new system of personal allowance withdrawals will begin for those fortunate taxpayers with total income over £100,000.For every £2 of income in excess of £100,000; £1 of personal allowance will be lost. For example, an individual with income of £102,000 will lose £1,000 of their personal allowance. This process will continue until the individual has lost half of their personal allowance, thus creating a band of income from £100,000 to around £106,700. This will equate to a **marginal income tax rate of 60 per cent!**

The remaining half of the individual's personal allowance will be withdrawn, i.e. £1 reduction for every £2 over the limit when their income exceeds £140,000, using the same process as set out above and thus creating another band of income from £140,000 to around £146,700 when their PA may disappear entirely, with a marginal tax rate of up to 61.5 per cent!

TABLE OF CASES

TABLE OF STATUTES

TABLE OF STATUTORY INSTRUMENTS

PART ONE

PERIOD UP TO DEATH

Chapter One

INTRODUCTION AND EXECUTRY TAX GENERALLY

"CONFIRMATION is the ratification by a competent court of an appointment of executor, made either by the deceased or by the court, and constitutes a title to take possession of, administer and dispose of the estate of the deceased contained in an inventory given up by the executor, and upon which the confirmation precedes."[1]

INTRODUCTION

The origins of executries in Scotland go back many hundreds of years. **1–01** Currie identifies the Probate and Legacy Duties Act 1808 (s.149) as one of the early references to confirmation.[2] Until the Succession (Scotland) Act 1964 came into force, the commissary courts dealt solely with moveable estate. Heritable property devolved to heirs and was dealt with in an entirely different manner whose genesis stemmed from the feudal system of land tenure in Scotland. Before the passing of the Abolition of Feudal Tenure (Scotland) Act 2000 (which came into force on November 28, 2004), practically all land in Scotland was held under feudal tenure. In theory land was vested in the Crown, and the Crown passed ownership to its immediate vassals, known as "superiors". They in turn could pass on ownership to their "vassals". It originated in the need for military support but was replaced by a pecuniary payment in more modern times.

After 1964, s.14(1) of the Succession Scotland Act 1964 provided that information could be obtained for the whole estate "without distinction between moveable and heritable property".

While the law relating to commissary matters is well documented, the early history of the law of succession is hidden in the mists of time.

Scholars agree that prior to the Reformation in 1560 succession was dealt with by canon law and the administration of estates was dealt with by officials of the Roman Catholic Church. In 1560 an Act removed these duties and passed authority to commissary courts, which were the forerunners of the modern sheriff court commissary departments.

The Office of Executor

Currie indicates that the office of an executor is an administrative **1–02** appointment; it is not to be regarded as a benefit.[3] It is quite clear that there is a differentiation between executor and beneficiary. There is a

---

[1] James G. Currie and Eilidh M. Scobie, *The Confirmation of Executors in Scotland* (Edinburgh: W. Green & Son Ltd, 1965).
[2] Currie and Scobie, *The Confirmation of Executors in Scotland*, 6th edn (Edinburgh, W. Green & Son, 1965) p.1.
[3] Currie and Scobie, *The Confirmation of Executors in Scotland*, 6th edn (Edinburgh, W. Green & Son, 1965) p.9.

misconception among members of the public that an executor cannot be beneficiary. In practical terms, while this might be preferable for many reasons, the reality is that in most cases an executor will be a beneficiary and probably a principal beneficiary such as a spouse or child.

The executor's function as stated is an administrative one and he or she requires to carry out the instructions of the testator. These directions will be found in the will or may devolve through intestacy.

In a very real sense the executor stands in the shoes of the deceased and as such becomes due to the deceased's creditors and a creditor to the debtors of the deceased. The duties and liabilities of an executor are dealt with in detail in the excellent edition of *Currie on Confirmation of Executors in Scotland* by E.M. Scobbie.[4]

Scope of this Part

1–03 This part of the text attempts to deal with the period from April 5 when the deceased last made a tax return up to the date of death. In most cases where the death in the tax year occurs some time after April 5 it is likely that the tax return will be for the period from April 6 before the death up to the date of death. In these cases it may be that the tax return has been made. For example, if a person dies in the autumn of 2008 there is a better chance of a tax return having been made up to April 5, 2008 than if the person died in, say, May of 2008. In many cases the returns may be well behind and the executor is faced with the prospect of dealing with the tax year *or years* from April 6 up to the date of death.

WHAT IS THE ADMINISTRATION PERIOD?

1–04 Scots practitioners have an advantage over their English counterparts in that they have help in the form of a statutory definition of the period of administration. Section 702 of the TA 1988 provides that:

Application to Scotland

702.—For the purpose of the application of this Part to Scotland—

(a) any reference to the completion of the administration of an estate shall be construed as a reference to the date at which, after discharge of, or provision for, liabilities falling to be met out of the deceased's estate (including, without prejudice to the generality of the foregoing, debts, legacies immediately payable, prior rights of surviving spouse or civil partner on intestacy and legal rights of surviving spouse or civil partner or children), the free balance held in trust for behoof of the residuary legatees has been ascertained;

(b) for paragraph (b) of section 697(1) the following paragraph shall be substituted—

"(b) the amount of any of the aggregate income of the estate for that year to which a person has become entitled by virtue of a specific disposition";

---

[4] Currie and Scobie, *The Confirmation of Executors in Scotland*, 8th edn (Edinburgh, W. Green & Son, 1995).

(c) "real estate" means heritable estate; and
(d) "charge on residue" shall include, in addition to the liabilities specified in section 701(6), any sums required to meet claims in respect of prior rights by surviving spouse [or civil partner] or in respect of legal rights by surviving spouse or civil partner or children.

In some ways this reference underlines the straightforwardness of Scots procedure over English; it is possible in six lines of statute to summarise the end of the administration period as:

"[A]ny reference to the completion of an estate shall be construed as a reference to the date at which, after discharge of, or provision for, liabilities falling to be met out of the deceased's estate (including . . . debts, legacies immediately payable, prior rights of surviving spouse on intestacy and legal rights of surviving spouse or children), the free balance held in trust for . . . the residuary legatees been ascertained."

English practitioners may require to refer to HMRC's *CG Manual*:

"CG30813—Personal representatives: residue: providing funds
Residue is only ascertained when the personal representatives have both established the net worth of the estate and provided the liquid funds to pay liabilities and pecuniary legacies. Once that point is reached residue is ascertained and it is irrelevant that the assets have not been distributed."

"CG30943—Personal representatives: beneficial ownership: when residue ascertained
The leading case providing authority for this principle is *CIR v Sir Aubrey Smith* 15TC661. In that case Lord Hanworth MR said at the bottom of page 675, top of page 676:

'The question is, in all cases: has the administration of the estate reached a point of ripeness at which the executor can infer an assent; at which the executor can infer that the residuary estate has been ascertained and that it is outstanding and not handed over merely for some other reason.'"

An attempt was made under the Tax Rewrite programme to define the **1–05** "administration period" for English Practitioners.

Income Tax (Trading and Other Income) Act 2005 (c.5)

Part 5 Miscellaneous Income

Chapter 6 Beneficiaries' Income from Estates in Administration

Types of Estate Income

Meaning of "the administration period" and "the final tax year"

653.—(1) In this Chapter "the administration period", in relation to the estate of a deceased person, means the period beginning with the deceased's death and ending with the completion of the administration of the estate.

    (2) In the application of subsection (1) to Scotland, the reference to the completion of the administration is to be taken as a reference to the date at which, after discharge of, or provision for, liabilities falling to be met out of the deceased's estate, the free balance held in trust for the residuary legatees or for the persons with the right to the intestate estate has been ascertained.

    (3) In this Chapter "the final tax year" means the tax year in which the administration period ends.

This perhaps does not get them much further. Indeed it could be argued by the foregoing that all the legislature has done is to obfuscate what was a perfectly good definition in ICTA 1988.

A helpful definition is given in the popular English textbook *Wills, Administration and Taxation Law and Practice*[5]:

> "It is generally accepted that completion of the administration occurs on the date the residue is ascertained for distributions."

The actual returns themselves will be covered in the relevant Chapters. It seems appropriate at this stage to deal with certain matters which are common to most returns.

WHEN TO MAKE THE TAX RETURN

Self-Assessment

1–06   Although it may not seem like it, self-assessment is a relatively new concept for the United Kingdom. It came into operation in April 1997. The principal forms have undergone many changes since their inception but broadly speaking, the completed form consists of a short tax form and additional schedules to deal with differing types of income.

These must be returned to HM Revenue & Customs (if the executors decide to do it themselves) before January 31 following the end of the fiscal year, failing which a fixed penalty of £100 will be levied. If it is not submitted six months after that a further £100 will be levied. HMRC have the power to levy up to an extra £60 per day. In addition interest will be charged if any tax is outstanding after the date of payment and after January 31 a five per cent levy may be applied if still outstanding after February 28, to be increased to 10 per cent if still outstanding after July 31. Obviously it will be necessary to produce the information as soon after April 5 as possible.

It used to be the case that if the taxpayer wishes HM Revenue & Customs to assess the return it must be submitted before September 30 following the end of the year of assessment. Now, generally speaking, they will check all returns.

---

[5] John Barlow, Lesley King and Anthony King, *Wills, Administration and Taxation Law and Practice*, 9th edn (London: Thomson Sweet & Maxwell, 2008).

It is important at the outset to identify those dates which are critical, e.g. when the deceased's tax return must be submitted and working back from that date when all the tax details have to be included. An attempt has been made to identify and list those at the start of the book in the Tax Facts Section and at the start of each Chapter but it is important that the practitioner includes these in his diary, online calendar, bringforward system or other reminder system. Principally he should identify when any deadline is approaching. Paper self-assessment tax returns must be filed by October 31 this year. HM Revenue & Customs have reminded executors that paper returns submitted after October 31 could incur a £100 penalty. The deadline for filing online returns remains January 31. Any tax due has to be paid by January 31, whether the return is filed on paper or online.[6]

Late Returns

If the return is sent in late it will incur a penalty. If it is only slightly late, say less than 24 hours, there should be no penalty. The *Steeden v Carver*[7] case confirmed that a late return will escape a penalty provided that it is less than 24 hours late.   **1–07**

There was a well-documented occurrence of HMRC software failing recently. Interestingly it seems that it was only the HMRC return software which failed. Returns submitted using private software were not affected.

In an article Keith Gordon[8] gives the following example:

> "Joe had a proprietary tax return package and could have (and would have) filed his client's return at about 5pm on 31 January 2008. However, at 4.30 he learnt from the HMRC website that there were problems and that executors were being given an extra 24 hours to file returns.
>
> Accordingly, Joe made the conscious decision to file the return on Saturday 2 February and deal with another pressing matter in the meantime.
>
> In such circumstances, Joe would have a reasonable excuse throughout Friday 1 February 2008 (given the apparent extension given to all returns per the HMRC website). Therefore, following *Steeden v Carver*, Joe should not be subject to a penalty.
>
> Furthermore, he would, in my view, have had a reasonable excuse for not compromising his weekend and would have had a reasonable excuse at least through to midnight on Sunday 3 February. Thus, Joe could have relied upon *Steeden v Carver* at least until Monday 4 February."

Danger Warning!!

If HMRC issue a penalty notice and the executor has a reasonable excuse, whilst the executor may be advised to pay the penalty, he should immediately exercise the right to challenge it.

---

[6] HMRC reported that up to August 17, 2008, 2,102,716 self-assessment returns were filed, of which over 44 per cent were filed online: *HMRC News Release*, August 19, 2008.
[7] *Steeden v Carver* (1999) SpC 212.
[8] Keith Gordon, "Penalties for late tax return", *Taxation* (February 28, 2008).

How to Prove Return has been Made

1–08 Solicitors and others require some degree of certainty that a return has been received timeously not merely to avoid a penalty but also to identify when the "window" for enquiry will expire. Some years ago, HM Revenue and Customs stopped issuing receipts for hand-delivered returns. Legally, posting a return and obtaining proof of posting will satisfy in most cases. This should be the preferred option. However, when a deadline approaches, some practitioners prefer to deliver by hand or employ professional couriers. In a response to the Tax Faculty, HMRC indicated:

> "In view of this, we are issuing guidance to our staff that in the event of an agent challenging a penalty notice on the basis that the return had in fact been lodged, we should accept any reasonable evidence the agent has that the return was filed on time. It is not possible to be prescriptive as to what evidence we will accept as this may vary between agents. However, the key message is that we are looking to take a reasonable view. We hope that this allays any concerns likely to be caused by our offices not giving receipts."

It is well worth taking some time to ensure that there is evidence of lodging by post office, proof of posting or file entries regarding hand delivery.

WHERE TO MAKE THE TAX RETURN

1–09 If, as often happens, no documentation is produced by the executors this can cause a certain amount of difficulty. Generally, the tax office, which dealt with the deceased's tax affairs, should be contacted as soon as possible after death. Sometimes it is not always straightforward to find the tax district dealing with the deceased's tax affairs. Details of the deceased's tax office, national insurance number and tax reference can be obtained from the executry papers supplied to the executor by the family such as notice of coding P45, self assessment and so forth. Accountants or one of the many tax agencies may have been dealing with the deceased's tax affairs and they can supply the information along with a copy of the deceased's last tax return and schedules.

If these steps do not yield the information, the following steps may be taken.

- If the deceased was an employee or received superannuation payments from a former employer, ask them to supply the information for the tax office and the reference.
- If the deceased was self-employed, contact the tax office nearest to the place of business. Alternatively, contact the tax office nearest the deceased's home address, giving details of date of birth and national insurance number.

For reasons of economy it is likely that the executor will be writing or faxing. Clients sometimes have difficulty in realising that it is much more cost effective to write rather than to telephone. Some districts do not seem to be able to deal with letters rather than telephone calls. For this reason it is as well to follow the initial letter up soon after with a reminder sending a copy of the first letter. The problem here is that if the practitioner is unable to obtain the information by letter, it may be that a beneficiary will, in exasperation, telephone or call at the tax office and be given the information immediately, which the executor had asked for some weeks earlier. Credibility can be lost unless matter is pressed!

The office should be advised of the death and asked for a copy of the deceased's last tax return. If this is available a completed form 64–8 should be sent.

The main purpose, of course, in writing and intimating the 64–8 form is to attempt to have HMRC deal with the executor directly as agents for the executors. Sometimes it happens that the information which the executor requested from HMRC, such as a copy of the deceased's last return or other documentation, is not available. It may be that one or more reminders are sent and the executors or clients become restive with the practitioner for what they perceive as his failure to obtain the information.

As stated above, nothing, of course, can be more heartbreaking than for the clients to telephone HMRC directly only to receive the information immediately over the phone and a copy of the documentation, which the executor has been endeavouring to obtain for weeks if not months, sent to them by first class post!

DEALING WITH HMRC

In an amusing article, "Let's not be beastly to HMRC (well, not all the **1–10** time)", Simon Sweetman[9] looks at tax enquiries from "the other side of the fence". He points out that tax officers are often frustrated by the length of time it can take them to deal with enquiries.

In a routine enquiry he discovered, admittedly in the context of dealing with small businesses, that "the first complete reply [from the HMRC] in the average enquiry is 90 days". Officers often consider that there exists a culture of obstruction and, non-cooperation amongst professionals and their powers are insufficient to deal with this.

Inspectors feel frustrated by the system, with some of them feeling that the new powers HMRC are taking are still insufficient or that the requirements for record-keeping are not stringent enough and penalties for poor record-keeping are not enforced.

Generally, officers of HM Revenue & Customs are very helpful. Like most of us they are at times (chronically) overworked. Sometimes misunderstandings may occur. These may be the fault of the executor; at other times they may be the fault of HMRC. When these occur and with a view to avoiding problems it may be helpful to bear in mind certain matters. If the executor ignores letters from HMRC, this may be viewed as obstruction and may result in the issue of formal notices, which will carry penalties. This in turn may affect the ultimate percentage of

---

[9] Simon Sweetman, "Let's not be beastly to HMRC (well, not all the time)", *Taxation* (July 7, 2008).

penalty levied. If possible reply quickly, if only to acknowledge it. Please remember that, while it is correct to be helpful, just because an inspector asks for something, it does not mean he is entitled to it!

INCORRECT RETURNS AND PENALTIES

1-11   As predicted, HMRC implemented their consultation document reviewing their powers on penalties. The Chancellor had indicated that the Finance Act 2007 Sch24 was to be extended to form a single penalty regime for incorrect returns across all the taxes, levies and duties administered by HMRC. The philosophy was that the penalty would be fixed by such elements as the amount of tax understated, the nature of the behaviour giving rise to the understatement and the extent of disclosure by the executor. Moreover the use of suspended penalties will be extended. For incorrect returns, the measure is expected to be in force for return periods commencing on or after April 1, 2009 where the return is due to be filed on or after April 1, 2010.

New penalties for failure to notify will be in effect for failure to meet notification obligations, which arise on or after April 1, 2009. The new provisions for incorrect returns will provide for penalties in line with Sch.24. In an extremely helpful article,[10] which should be compulsory reading for all engaged in this work, Mike Truman reviews the relevant sections of the *Compliance Handbook*, in which HM Revenue & Customs have set out guidance on how the new penalty rules (in FA 2007 Sch.24) should be applied:

> "The level of penalties for errors on tax returns is currently a matter that is very open to negotiation, because statute law defines the maximum penalty but does not define the minimum. It is probably true to say that penalties tend to cluster around the 20% to 50% level, but good negotiating skills and experience in the field can be very effective. For returns submitted after 5 April 2009, the penalty regime is completely different, and it remains to be seen how effective negotiation will be. And although that starting date is still some months away, the records which are going to form the basis of those returns, and in which the errors are likely to be made, are being kept now, recording current transactions."

The entire scope of penalties and a full treatment of the extent of Sch.24 of the Finance Act 2007 is outwith the scope of this text but the following is a brief summary. There will be no penalty where an executor simply makes a mistake. However, there will be a penalty of up to 30 per cent, 70 per cent and 100 per cent for failure to take reasonable care, a deliberate understatement and a deliberate understatement with concealment respectively. Reasonable care involves good record-keeping, asking for advice if something is not clear, keeping accurate records to ensure returns are correct and confirming and if necessary persisting in ascertaining what the correct factual position is when it is not clear.

---

[10] M. Truman, "Hot Stuff", *Taxation* (September 17, 2008).

Probably the most important thing is to immediately advise HM Revenue & Customs when the executor has made a mistake.

Danger Warning!!

Do not wait until you have a chance to review the file for any other mistakes, but tell HMRC immediately you discover a mistake. Any penalty will be substantially reduced where a timeous disclosure is made, i.e. take active steps to put right the problem, more so if this is unprompted. In addition where the disclosure of failure is made without prompting the penalty could be reduced to nil.

Please note that if a full admission is made when provoked by a challenge, HM Revenue & Customs will reduce the penalty by up to 50 per cent. It probably goes without saying that if reasonable care is not taken the errors will be penalised, and the penalties will be higher if the error is deliberate. Disclosing errors to HMRC will substantially reduce any penalty due. It will also be important to be able to make obvious that record-keeping and systems are in place. HMRC will seriously penalise anyone who tries to cover up errors. **1–12**

Danger Warning!!

Where a return is incorrect because a third party has deliberately provided false information or deliberately withheld information from the executor, with the intention of causing an understatement of tax due, there will be a new provision allowing a penalty to be charged on the third party, such as solicitors, making the return. HMRC wish to standardise the new rules for all taxes.

In categorising liability for penalties the principle is that mistakes are first dealt with where reasonable care has been taken, where the mistake was careless but not calculated, where it was calculated but not covered up and where it was both calculated and covered up; where reasonable care is employed there is likely to be no penalty.

The following table attempts to clarify matters. **1–13**

Category of error	Minimum penalty after investigation by HMRC	Minimum penalty (unsolicited by HMRC)	Maximum penalty
Careless	15%	0%	30%
On purpose	35%	20%	70%
Hidden	50%	50%	100%

Obviously, the actual legislation and decided cases comprise the definitive source of law. Nevertheless and particularly with tax law, it is extremely useful to have guidance on how HM Revenue & Customs intend to interpret it. "However, some of the provisions included in the Compliance Handbook, which was made available online in April 2008, are not entirely reassuring."[11] Obviously, a higher standard is to be required from professionals than from the lay executor.

In their website HMRC indicate the intention to introduce "a simpler and more consistent penalty system for tax errors". The expression "reasonable care" is used repeatedly by HMRC, for example:

> "Under the new system if *the executor* takes reasonable care to get the *executor's* tax right, we will not penalise *the executor*, even if the *executor* makes a mistake."

The new system of penalties applies, for the purposes of this text, initially to income tax (including self assessment), and capital gains tax. It will apply for these taxes to errors in tax returns or other documents, for periods starting on or after April 1, 2008, due to be submitted on or after April 1, 2009. Obviously returns for the 2007–2008 period, like self assessment returns, are subject to the existing penalties.

The new penalties for tax errors will be extended to most other taxes, levies and duties, for periods commencing from April 1, 2009, where the return is due to be submitted from April 1, 2010.

1–14   All this is well and good but we can only speculate what will (and is likely to) happen when HMRC is at fault. It is understood that the HMRC computer dealing with self assessment tax returns helpfully "crashed" on January 31, 2008,which coincidentally was the day on which practically all returns were due to be submitted. In an excellent article Keith Gordon[12] wrote:

> "At the time of the first computer 'outage', there was very little information available to assist the adviser trying to get a client's return in before the deadline. However, later that afternoon, an announcement was posted on the HMRC website giving executors (and their advisers) an extra 24 hours to file their returns, without penalty."

However, it is understood that a further problem occurred the next day, i.e. Friday, February 1, 2008! Clearly it is important to avoid a penalty. Nothing can be worse that having to explain to a client who receives notice directly of a £100 penalty. (Technically, the penalty can be avoided simply by paying all the tax by the due date. However, that can be a high-risk strategy because the penalty is not actually avoided, merely capped at £nil. If there is an adjustment to the tax liability, for example following an enquiry, the penalty will similarly increase, subject to the limit of £100.)

---

[11] M. Truman, "Hot Stuff", *Taxation* (September 17, 2008).
[12] K. Gordon, "Penalties for Late Tax Returns", *Taxation* (February 28, 2008).

> *DANGER WARNING!!*
>
> *Submitting a return late gives HMRC an extra period in which to open an enquiry into the tax return. For example, a 2006/2007 return due on January 31, 2008 but delivered on February 20, 2008 can be selected for an enquiry at any time before May 1, 2009.*

Matters were not helped when HM Revenue & Customs indicated the view that, notwithstanding the computer problems at HMRC and notwithstanding the public announcements of an informal extension to the filing period, they would automatically issue penalty notices on February 2 for returns not filed on time but would receive representations made against such penalties sympathetically!

The Golden Rule

Every executor is entitled to have a self assessment penalty waived if the 1–15 executor has a reasonable excuse for being late (Taxes Management Act 1970 s.93(8)):

> (8) On an appeal against the determination under section 100 of this Act of a penalty under subsection (2) or (4) above, neither section 50(6) to (8) nor section 100B(2) of this Act shall apply but the Commissioners may—
>> (a) if it appears to them that, throughout the period of default, the taxpayer had a reasonable excuse for not delivering the return, set the determination aside; or
>> (b) if it does not so appear to them, confirm the determination.

Contrary to anything promulgated on the HMRC website or elsewhere, it does not matter what software (if any) was being used. If, objectively, there is a good excuse for being late, that should suffice.

If HMRC cannot be persuaded that a reasonable excuse exists then one can appeal to the General or Special Commissioners.

> *Attention!!!*
>
> *HMRC have announced that a new form is to be made available for taxpayers to claim reasonable excuse against a penalty for the late filing of a paper tax return for 2007/2008. The claim can be made in situations where the attempted electronic filing was unsuccessful. The procedure will be monitored by HMRC in the run-up to the January 31, 2009 filing deadline and further guidance may be issued.*[1]

Remission of Penalties on Deceased Estates

HMRC recently confirmed that charging executors with penalties 1–16 incurred by the deceased is incompatible with human rights legislation. They say they will write to executors who offer to pay penalties to the effect that penalties would be repaid should the Department or the courts decide penalties arising from the default of a deceased should not be imposed on the deceased's personal representative.

The Tax Law Rewrite Project

1-17 The Tax Law Rewrite Project, which was referred to in the Preface, aimed to rewrite the UK's primary direct tax legislation to make it clearer and easier to use, without changing the law. The project's work is overseen by a Consultative Committee and a Steering Committee. To date the project has delivered the following:

- The Capital Allowances Act 2001 (effective from April 2001);
- The Income Tax (Earnings and Pensions) Act 2003 (effective from April 2003);
- The Income Tax (Pay as You Earn) Regulations 2003 (effective from April 2004);
- The Income Tax (Trading and Other Income) Act 2005 (effective from April 2005); and
- The Income Tax Act 2007 (effective from April 2007).

Obviously the last three concern us.

1-18 Unfortunately during this period the practitioner must check if the original Act, which may be the ICTA, is still in force and try to find where it has been re-enacted. Predictably, mistakes were made in this redrafting.[13]

The Income Tax Act 2007, also known as ITA, received Royal Assent on March 20, 2007 and takes effect from April 6, 2007.[14] It covers inter alia:

- basic provisions about the charge to income tax, income tax rates, the calculation of income tax liability and personal reliefs;
- specific rules about trusts, deduction of tax at source, manufactured payments and repos, the accrued income scheme and tax avoidance; and
- general income tax definitions.

As Emma Chamberlain and Chris Whitehouse in their text *Inheritance Tax Planning with Precedents*[15] state:

"[M]atters are not helped by the tax rewrite project which has now sorted out [!] income tax and is now embarking on a rewrite on Corporation Tax. The voluminous outpouring of this undoubtedly

---

[13] See HMRC, *Tax Law Rewrite Project*.

[14] The Act, the Explanatory Notes and the Table of Origins and Destinations have been published on the OPSI website: *http://www.opsi.gov.uk/acts/acts2007a.htm* [accessed April 11, 2009]. The executor can also access these by selecting the relevant links in the Rewritten Legislation: *http://www.hmrc.gov.uk/rewrite/acts-and-regs.htm* [accessed April 11, 2009].

[15] Emma Chamberlain and Chris Whitehouse, *Inheritance Tax Planning with Precedents* (Thomson Sweet and Maxwell, January 2008).

well-motivated body is a cause for despair. Here is a real case where less could well be more. Alternatively, as Dame Edna Everage is reputed to have remarked of a particularly prolific author 'slow down Melvin we can't keep up with the executor'."

There is something bizarre in attempting to make tax legislation comprehensible. The authors of the above book draw on the case of New Zealand, which followed a different and much more successful policy of genuine simplification. The New Zealand tax authorities dealt with policy areas and then attempt to write them in good English!

Problems have occurred in rewriting, particularly in the context of trusts. There are three definitions of "settlement" and five definitions of "truster" or "trustee". There is a different wording in respect of residence for both income tax and capital gains tax and for trustee residence for inheritance tax purposes.

PRE-OWNED ASSETS TAX[16]

There was a considerable furore when this tax was introduced for the tax **1–19** year from April 6, 2005. More detail will be given in a later Chapter. Broadly, an annual income tax charge applies to an individual who enjoys an asset which he either previously owned or financed, and the asset is not within the scope of inheritance tax (IHT). The main source of the consternation was the apparently retrospective nature, since it concerned transactions which have occurred since 1986. However, although it is complicated, it has turned out to be something of a damp squib. The overwhelming areas where it might be relevant fall within the inheritance tax rules regarding gifts with reservation. However, it should not be overlooked since the consequences to the executor and to the practitioner could be disastrous!

HM Revenue & Customs Website

A considerable amount of time and expertise has been expended on the **1–20** HM Revenue & Customs website: *http://www.hmrc.gov.uk* [accessed April 12, 2009], most of which has been well spent! The busy practitioner should invest some time to familiarise himself with this, particularly the "find a form" function, which should be compulsorily "bookmarked" or added to "favourites"! There are one or two slight problems, e.g. if the form "IHT 403" is entered it will show a link to "IHT 400". It is necessary to enter this link to find all the supplementary forms.

---

[16] FA 2004 Sch.15.

Chapter Two

SUCCESSION

"And those who mourn with heavy hearts."[1]

2–01　Before considering the substantive aspects of executry tax planning it may be helpful to summarise the Scottish Law of Succession and the question of legal rights as at the time of writing.[2] The Scottish Law Commission has been considering this and it is likely that changes will be put before the Scottish Government in the near future.

It is usual to consider intestate succession[3] first, since an understanding of certain rights such as legitim, *jus relicti* and *jus relictae* can assist in determining how spouses, civil partners and children may actually claim on testate succession.

Intestate estate is defined in the Succession (Scotland) Act 1964 as the deceased's estate not disposed by will. A will may be (and is frequently) not only the usual testamentary settlement but can extend to other deeds which affect succession such as survivorship destinations in dispositions, which are very common, and marriage contracts and nominations, which are not.

Dealing with intestate estates, therefore, the first right, namely, the housing and furniture and plenishings prior rights, are due out of the intestate estate. Next, the cash sum prior right is due out of the intestate estate left after the previous two prior rights. Legal rights of legitim and *jus relicti* or *jus relictae* are due out of the net moveable intestate estate, i.e. the estate remaining after all the prior rights. The rules relating to the free estate apply to the net intestate estate left after "inheritance tax and other liabilities of the estate having priority over legal rights, the prior rights of the surviving spouse or civil partner and rights of succession". Subject to the question of claiming legal rights, the rules of intestate succession apply only where there is no will.

2–02　Furthermore, the rules set out in the Succession (Scotland) Act 1964, as amended, apply only to an estate governed by Scots law. In general, succession to movables is dealt with by the law of the domicile of the deceased at death while succession to heritable property depends on the law of the country in which they are situated.

As stated, the Succession (Scotland) Act 1964 as amended deals with the law of succession. The prior rights of a surviving spouse or civil partner are three in number; the dwelling house right under s.8 of the Succession (Scotland) Act 1964, the furniture and plenishings right also under s.8 and the cash sum under s.9. Probably the most important is the rights of the surviving spouse in the dwelling house right and furniture.

---

[1] Hymn 279 C4.
[2] December 22, 2008.
[3] Scottish Law Commission, *Discussion Paper on Succession* (Scot Law Com. No.136, August 2007).

Prior rights of surviving spouse, on intestacy, in dwelling house and furniture

8.—(1) Where a person dies intestate leaving a spouse, and the intestate estate includes a relevant interest in a dwelling house to which this section applies, the surviving spouse shall be entitled to receive out of the intestate estate—

(a) where the value of the relevant interest does not exceed £30,000 or such larger amount as may from time to time be fixed by order of the Secretary of State—

(i) if subsection (2) of this section does not apply, the relevant interest;

(ii) if the said subsection (2) applies, a sum equal to the value of the relevant interest;

(b) in any other case, the sum of £30,000 or such larger amount as may from time to time be fixed by order of the Secretary of State;

Provided that, if the intestate estate comprises a relevant interest in two or more dwelling houses to which this section applies, this subsection shall have effect only in relation to such one of them as the surviving spouse may elect for the purposes of this subsection within six months of the date of death of the intestate.

(2) This subsection shall apply for the purposes of paragraph (a) of the foregoing subsection if—

(a) the dwelling house forms part only of the subjects comprised in one tenancy or lease under which the intestate was the tenant; or

(b) the dwelling house forms the whole or part of subjects an interest in which is comprised in the intestate estate and which were used by the intestate for carrying on a trade, profession or occupation, and the value of the estate as a whole would be likely to be substantially diminished if the dwelling house were disposed of otherwise than with the assets of the trade, profession or occupation.

(3) Where a person dies intestate leaving a spouse, and the intestate estate includes the furniture and plenishings of a dwelling house to which this section applies (whether or not the dwelling house is comprised in the intestate estate), the surviving spouse shall be entitled to receive out of the intestate estate—

(a) where the value of the furniture and plenishings does not exceed £8,000 or such larger amount as may from time to time be fixed by order of the Secretary of State, the whole thereof;

(b) in any other case, such part of the furniture and plenishings, to a value not exceeding £8,000 or such larger amount as may from time to time be fixed by order of the Secretary of State, as may be chosen by the surviving spouse;

Provided that, if the intestate estate comprises the furniture and plenishings of two or more such dwelling houses, this subsection shall have effect only in relation to the furniture and plenishings of such one of them as the surviving spouse may elect for the purposes of this subsection within six months of the date of death of the intestate.

(4) This section applies, in the case of any intestate, to any dwelling house in which the surviving spouse of the intestate was ordinarily resident at the date of death of the intestate.

(5) Where any question arises as to the value of any furniture or plenishings, or of any interest in a dwelling house, for the purposes of any provision of this section the question shall be determined by arbitration by a single arbiter appointed, in default of agreement, by the sheriff of the county in which the intestate was domiciled at the date of his death or, if that county is uncertain or the intestate was domiciled furth of Scotland, the sheriff of the Lothians and Peebles at Edinburgh.

(6) In this section—

(a) "dwelling house" includes a part of a building occupied (at the date of death of the intestate) as a separate dwelling; and any reference to a dwelling house shall be construed as including any garden or portion of ground attached to, and usually occupied with, the dwelling house or otherwise required for the amenity or convenience of the dwelling house;

(b) "furniture and plenishings" includes garden effects, domestic animals, plate, plated articles, linen, china, glass, books, pictures, prints, articles of household use and consumable stores; but does not include any article or animal used at the date of death of the intestate for business purposes, or money or securities for money, or any heirloom;

(c) "heirloom", in relation to an intestate estate, means any article which has associations with the intestate's family of such nature and extent that it ought to pass to some member of that family other than the surviving spouse of the intestate;

(d) "relevant interest", in relation to a dwelling house, means the interest therein of an owner, or the interest therein of a tenant, subject in either case to any heritable debt secured over the interest; and for the purposes of this definition "tenant" means a tenant under a tenancy or lease (whether of the dwelling house alone or of the dwelling house together with other subjects) which is not a tenancy to which the Rent and Mortgage Interest Restrictions Acts 1920 to 1939 apply.

2–03 The surviving spouse or civil partner is entitled to receive the deceased's interest, whether as owner or tenant, in any dwelling house in which the surviving spouse or civil partner was ordinarily resident at the date of the deceased's death. The deceased's interest in the dwelling house is subject to any debt secured over it. Where the value of the deceased's interest exceeds £300,000 the survivor's entitlement is to that amount of money rather than the interest itself. Where the surviving spouse or civil partner is entitled to cash (up to £300,000) in lieu, if the interest forms parts of a larger property used for carrying out a trade, profession or business and the estate as a whole would be substantially reduced in value by splitting off the dwelling house. Very occasionally the deceased will have had an interest in two or more dwelling houses in which the surviving spouse or civil partner was ordinarily resident. In that case the survivor may choose provided this is done within six months.

Where the intestate estate includes the furniture and plenishings of a dwelling house in which the surviving spouse or civil partner was ordinarily resident at the date of the deceased's death (whether or not the dwelling house is also part of such estate) the surviving spouse or civil partner is entitled to such furniture and plenishings up to the value of £24,000.

Prior right of surviving spouse to financial provision on intestacy

9.—(1) Where a person dies intestate and is survived by a husband or wife, the surviving spouse shall be entitled to receive out of the intestate estate—

  (a) if the intestate is survived by issue . . . the sum of £4,000 or such larger amount as may from time to time be fixed by order of the Secretary of State, or

  (b) if the intestate is not survived by issue . . . the sum of £8,000 or such larger amount as may from time to time be fixed by order of the Secretary of State,

together with, in either case, interest at the rate of four per cent per annum or, at such rate as may from time to time be fixed by order of the Secretary of State, on such sum from the date of the intestate's death until payment:
Provided that where the surviving spouse is entitled to receive a legacy out of the estate of the intestate (other than a legacy of any dwelling house to which the last foregoing section applies or of any furniture and plenishings of any such dwelling house), he or she shall, unless he or she renounces the legacy, be entitled under this subsection to receive only such sum, if any, as remains after deducting from the sum fixed by virtue of paragraph (a) of this subsection or the sum fixed by virtue of paragraph (b) of this subsection, as the case may be, the amount or value of the legacy.

(2) Where the intestate estate is less than the amount which the surviving spouse is entitled to receive by virtue of subsection (1) of this section the right conferred by the said subsection on the surviving spouse shall be satisfied by the transfer to him or her of the whole of the intestate estate.

(3) The amount which the surviving spouse is entitled to receive by virtue of subsection (1) of this section shall be borne by, and paid out of, the parts of the intestate estate consisting of heritable and moveable property respectively in proportion to the respective amounts of those parts.

(4) Where by virtue of subsection (2) of this section a surviving spouse has right to the whole of the intestate estate, he or she shall have the right to be appointed executor.

(5) The rights conferred by the Intestate Husband's Estate (Scotland) Acts 1911 to 1959 on a surviving spouse in his or her deceased spouse's estate shall not be exigible out of the estate of any person dying after the commencement of this Act.

(6) For the purposes of this section—

(a) the expression "intestate estate" means so much of the net intestate estate as remains after the satisfaction of any claims under the last foregoing section; and

(b) the expression "legacy" includes any payment or benefit to which a surviving spouse becomes entitled by virtue of any testamentary disposition; and the amount or value of any legacy shall be ascertained as at the date of the intestate's death.

2–04 "Furniture and plenishings" are defined in the 1964 Act so as to cover the full range of household contents, but money, heirlooms and any article or animal used by the deceased for business purposes are excluded. As with the dwelling house right, if the intestate estate comprises furniture and plenishings of two or more dwelling houses the survivor has six months in which to select which furniture and plenishings to take. Interestingly the right to the dwelling house and the right to the furniture and plenishings are independent so that the furniture and plenishings of a different house may be selected from that for the dwelling house right!

After the prior rights in s.8 are satisfied the surviving spouse or civil partner is entitled to a fixed sum of £42,000 if the deceased is survived by issue or £75,000 if there are none.

Where there is not enough to meet this, the whole balance goes to the surviving spouse or civil partner. Where, however, the remaining intestate estate is more than this it is met out of heritable and moveable property in proportion to enable the corresponding balance for the calculation of legal rights, these of course being due only out of net moveable estate.

The legal rights of the surviving spouse or civil partner are known as *jus relictae* for a widow or *jus relicti* for a widower and the legal rights of any issue is known as legitim. Where the deceased left *both* a surviving spouse or civil partner *and* issue, the legal rights of the surviving spouse or civil partner amount to one-third of the net moveable intestate estate; the issue take another third between them. If there is a surviving spouse or civil partner *but no issue*, the legal rights of the surviving spouse or civil partner amount to one-half of the net moveable intestate estate. If there are issue but no surviving spouse or civil partner, the issue's legal rights are one-half of the net moveable intestate estate shared between them.

2–05 "Net moveable intestate estate" is defined as the moveable intestate estate less debts chargeable against the moveable intestate estate and the amount of the surviving spouse's or civil partner's prior rights.

"Issue" in the context of legitim is not restricted to the deceased's surviving children. The concept of infinite representation was introduced by s.11 of the Succession (Scotland) Act 1964.

The legitim fund is divided into equal shares at the level *where there is one surviving descendant* and each surviving descendant takes a share; the issue of each predeceasing descendant also take a share.

After satisfying any claims for prior and legal rights the remainder of the net intestate estate, taking heritage and moveables together, devolves in accordance with the rules in s.2 of the 1964 Act which contains a statutory list of those entitled to succeed in order of preference. Representation of predeceasers by their issue is applied throughout the list, except in relation to a direct ascendant or a spouse or civil partner of the deceased. Adopted children are treated as the children of the adopter for all succession purposes. Surviving issue of a predeceasing child of the deceased take the share the child would have taken had he or she survived. Failing issue, where the deceased is survived by a parent or parents and also by brothers and sisters, the surviving parent or parents are entitled to one-half of the free estate and the brothers and sisters to the other half. If the deceased is survived by a sibling but predeceased by both parents, or survived by at least one parent but not by siblings, the surviving sibling(s) or parent(s) respectively succeed to the whole free estate. Siblings of the whole blood are preferred to siblings of the half blood. Again, surviving children of a predeceasing sibling represent their parent. In the absence of any issue, siblings (or their issue) or parents, the succession passes to the surviving spouse or civil partner.

Obviously the rules require both assets and debts to be classified as **2–06** heritable or moveable and there is a good deal of complex law on what property is heritable or moveable for the purposes of succession, e.g. timber, minerals and crops. Some forms of property, heritable securities for example, are treated as moveable for general succession purposes but are regarded as heritable in the creditor's estate for the purpose of calculating legal rights. Debts have to be set off against assets to calculate the net estate. Generally, heritable debts have to be set against heritable property and moveable debts against moveable property. However, if there is insufficient property of one kind, the balance of the debt has to be set against the other kind. Some debts may have to be apportioned between the two categories of property and only certain debts are deductible for legal rights purposes.

Example

John Wormwood dies intestate on April 5, 2008, survived by his wife, Absinthe and his mother Heather. His estate consists of the following assets:

- *a villa in Morningside worth £600,000;*
- *furniture, plenishings and personal effects, etc. valued at £64,000; and*
- *stocks and shares worth £560,000. The total is £1,224,000.*

He leaves no issue and is survived by his wife and his mother. The widow's prior rights are:

- *£300,000 as the house is worth more than that sum;*

- *£24,000 of furniture and plenishings; and*
- *£75,000 as the cash sum.*

After the first two prior rights have been taken the remaining heritable estate is £300,000 and the remaining moveable estate is £600,000. The cash sum is taken as to £50,000 out of moveables and as to £25,000 out of heritage. The net moveable estate for legal rights purposes therefore amounts to £550,000, of which the widow is entitled to half, i.e. £275,000.

The next problem turns on the following sections of the Family Law (Scotland) Act 2006:

Financial provision where cohabitation ends otherwise than by death

28.—(1) Subsection (2) applies where cohabitants cease to cohabit otherwise than by reason of the death of one (or both) of them.

   (2) On the application of a cohabitant (the "applicant"), the appropriate court may, after having regard to the matters mentioned in subsection (3)—

     (a) make an order requiring the other cohabitant (the "defender") to pay a capital sum of an amount specified in the order to the applicant;

     (b) make an order requiring the defender to pay such amount as may be specified in the order in respect of any economic burden of caring, after the end of the cohabitation, for a child of whom the cohabitants are the parents;

     (c) make such interim order as it thinks fit.

   (3) Those matters are—

     (a) whether (and, if so, to what extent) the defender has derived economic advantage from contributions made by the applicant; and

     (b) whether (and, if so, to what extent) the applicant has suffered economic disadvantage in the interests of—

       (i) the defender; or
       (ii) any relevant child.

   (4) In considering whether to make an order under subsection (2)(a), the appropriate court shall have regard to the matters mentioned in subsections (5) and (6).

   (5) The first matter is the extent to which any economic advantage derived by the defender from contributions made by the applicant is offset by any economic disadvantage suffered by the defender in the interests of—

     (a) the applicant; or
     (b) any relevant child.

   (6) The second matter is the extent to which any economic disadvantage suffered by the applicant in the interests of—

     (a) the defender; or
     (b) any relevant child,

is offset by any economic advantage the applicant has derived from contributions made by the defender.

(7) In making an order under paragraph (a) or (b) of subsection (2), the appropriate court may specify that the amount shall be payable—

(a) on such date as may be specified;
(b) in instalments.

(8) Any application under this section shall be made not later than one year after the day on which the cohabitants cease to cohabit.

(9) In this section—
"appropriate court" means—

(a) where the cohabitants are a man and a woman, the court which would have jurisdiction to hear an action of divorce in relation to them if they were married to each other;
(b) where the cohabitants are of the same sex, the court which would have jurisdiction to hear an action for the dissolution of the civil partnership if they were civil partners of each other;

"child" means a person under 16 years of age;
"contributions" includes indirect and non-financial contributions (and, in particular, any such contribution made by looking after any relevant child or any house in which they cohabited); and
"economic advantage" includes gains in—

(a) capital;
(b) income; and
(c) earning capacity;

and "economic disadvantage" shall be construed accordingly.

(10) For the purposes of this section, a child is "relevant" if the child is—

(a) a child of whom the cohabitants are the parents;
(b) a child who is or was accepted by the cohabitants as a child of the family.

Application to court by survivor for provision on intestacy

29.—(1) This section applies where—

(a) a cohabitant (the "deceased") dies intestate; and
(b) immediately before the death the deceased was—

(i) domiciled in Scotland; and
(ii) cohabiting with another cohabitant (the "survivor").

(2) Subject to subsection (4), on the application of the survivor, the court may—

(a) after having regard to the matters mentioned in subsection (3), make an order—

(i) for payment to the survivor out of the deceased's net intestate estate of a capital sum of such amount as may be specified in the order;

(ii) for transfer to the survivor of such property (whether heritable or moveable) from that estate as may be so specified;

(b) make such interim order as it thinks fit.

(3) Those matters are—

(a) the size and nature of the deceased's net intestate estate;

(b) any benefit received, or to be received, by the survivor—

(i) on, or in consequence of, the deceased's death; and

(ii) from somewhere other than the deceased's net intestate estate;

(c) the nature and extent of any other rights against, or claims on, the deceased's net intestate estate; and

(d) any other matter the court considers appropriate.

(4) An order or interim order under subsection (2) shall not have the effect of awarding to the survivor an amount which would exceed the amount to which the survivor would have been entitled had the survivor been the spouse or civil partner of the deceased.

(5) An application under this section may be made to—

(a) the Court of Session;

(b) a sheriff in the sheriffdom in which the deceased was habitually resident at the date of death;

(c) if at the date of death it is uncertain in which sheriffdom the deceased was habitually resident, the sheriff at Edinburgh.

(6) Any application under this section shall be made before the expiry of the period of six months beginning with the day on which the deceased died.

(7) In making an order under paragraph (a)(i) of subsection (2), the court may specify that the capital sum shall be payable—

(a) on such date as may be specified;

(b) in instalments.

(8) In making an order under paragraph (a)(ii) of subsection (2), the court may specify that the transfer shall be effective on such date as may be specified.

(9) If the court makes an order in accordance with subsection (7), it may, on an application by any party having an interest, vary the date or method of payment of the capital sum.

(10) In this section—

"intestate" shall be construed in accordance with section 36(1) of the Succession (Scotland) Act 1964 (c.41);

"legal rights" has the meaning given by section 36(1) of the Succession (Scotland) Act 1964 (c.41);

"net intestate estate" means so much of the intestate estate as remains after provision for the satisfaction of—

(a) inheritance tax;
(b) other liabilities of the estate having priority over legal rights and the prior rights of a surviving spouse or surviving civil partner; and
(c) the legal rights, and the prior rights, of any surviving spouse or surviving civil partner; and

"prior rights" has the meaning given by section 36(1) of the Succession (Scotland) Act 1964 (c.41).

Administration of Justice Act 1982: extension of definition of "relative"

30.—In section 13 of the Administration of Justice Act 1982 (c.53) (supplementary provisions and definitions in relation to Part 2), in the definition of relative, after paragraph (b) insert—

"(ba) any person, not being the civil partner of the injured person, who was, at the time of the act or omission giving rise to liability in the responsible person, living with the injured person as the civil partner of the injured person; . . ."

Section 29, while quite revolutionary, is not without its problems! It gives **2–07** rights to co-habitants in succession in Scotland. Indeed it has been roundly criticised by many experts in the field.

Co-habitants can either be opposite sex or same sex. The opposite sex co-habitation is similar to aspects of marriage and would include such aspects as sexual and emotional relations, shared financial relationships and social acceptance as a couple. It would also exhibit the element of stability.

Same sex co-habitation would exhibit the same aspects as if parties were living together as civil partners.

Section 25 (subs.2) is the one which has caused most concern. In many ways, and as publicly stated by Profession Joe Thomson on numerous occasions, it does not really make sense. The co-habitant has been defined at s.25 (subs.1) but s.25(2) then provides a further criteria for determining whether a person is a co-habitant for the purposes of ss.26–29. The court is to take cognisance of the length of the period during which they lived together, the nature of the relationship and the nature of any financial arrangements. There is no minimum period for co-habitation before the co-habitants can exercise their right under s.29. It should be noted that the rights only arise on intestacy. It should also be noted that the right to apply for a share in the deceased's estate only arises if the deceased has died intestate. As previously stated a surviving spouse or civil partner has no legal rights on intestacy. The co-habitant can make a will without making any provision for a surviving co-habitant.

It is also the case that the surviving spouse or civil partner *does not* **2–08** *have to be living with the deceased before they have prior rights.* A surviving co-habitant's right is *entirely dependent* on residence with the deceased at death. The court can make an order for payment of a capital sum or transfer of heritable or moveable property, he can also specify the date when it should be paid in instalments and the date when any property should be transferred.

The application should be made within six months beginning with the day on which the deceased died and can only come out of net intestate estate which is defined by s.29(10) as so much of the intestacy estate as remains after provision is made for the satisfaction of inheritance tax, debts and funeral expenses, and prior legal rights of a surviving spouse or civil partner. It takes precedence over the claim of children or issue to legitim or otherwise. The court under s.29(3) must take into account the size and nature of the intestate estate, any benefit received by the surviving co-habitant previously or otherwise, the nature and extent of any other rights and any other matters which it considers appropriate.

Section 29 (subs.4) provides that the surviving co-habitant shall not be entitled to any more than if there had been a surviving spouse or civil partner of the deceased.

It is likely that the Scottish Law Commission will make recommendations with regard to this section.

In the meantime it is likely to play havoc with winding up estates where there was the possibility of the deceased being in a cohabiting relationship at the date of death!

Chapter Three

INCOME TAX TO DATE OF DEATH

"Round and round
I started in the Revenue in 1953 at a time when we counted
post over seven days although it had become fourteen by the
time I escaped in 1978 (it was form 5/Cl by the way). I was
involved in setting up Centre I which was built on a moor
such as Shakespeare had in mind in Macbeth. However, I
am writing to the executor to tell a story, which was going
the rounds not long after East Kilbride opened. There was
an endless belt in the tower block which was designed to
take post etc. from floor to floor. One put an electronic tag
on an item which automatically spat it out at the appropri-
ate place. It was soon realised that if something came in
which was too difficult or too troublesome to deal with it
could be put out of harm's way by placing it on the belt
without any floor tag. There were apparently thousands of
items going round and round but no-one outside Head
Office in London could authorise switching it off to retrieve
them and no-one on the spot was prepared to stick his neck
out and explain the problem.
Perhaps they are all still there."[1]

TAX FACTS

Income Tax Facts for the Years Ending April 5

3–01

IT	Income Tax Allowances	Tax Code	2008 £	2009 £	2010 £	2011/12
1	Aged under 65 years	L	5,225	6,035[2]	6,475	See below*
2	Aged 65 to 74 years (income not over income limit)	P	7,550	9,030	9,490	
3	Aged over 75 years (income not over income limit)	T	7,690	9,180	9,640	

---

[1] T. Batchelor, *Taxation* (November 23, 2006) quoted from a letter from a reader.
[2] This was increased to compensate for the loss of the 10 per cent starting rate.

> **Danger warning!!**
>
> *The allowances at 2 and 3 reduce where the deceased's income is above the income by £1 for every £2 of income above the limit. They will never reduce below the personal allowance.*

IT	Income Tax Allowances	Tax Code	2008 £	2009 £	2010 £
	Married Couples'/Civil Partners' minimum allowance (one born before April 6, 1935 but aged under 75) at 10%	V	2,440	2,540	2,670
	Married Couples'/Civil Partners' allowance (aged under 75) at 10% (one or other born before April 6, 1935)	T	6,285	6,535	6,965
	Married Couples'/Civil Partners' allowance (aged 75 or over) at 10% (one or other born before April 6, 1935)	T	6,365	6,625	6,965
	Income limit for age-related allowances reduced by 50% where one spouse born before April 6, 1935		20,900	21,800	22,900
	Minimum amount of married couple's allowance		2,440	2,540	
	Blind person's allowance		1,730	1,800	1,890
	Rent a room allowance		4,250 a (£2,150 if letting jointly).	4,250 a (£2,150 if letting jointly).	

- Tax relief for the married couple's allowance is at 10 per cent.
- There will be a new 10 per cent starting rate for savings income only, with a limit of £2,320 (2008/2009). If the deceased taxpayer's taxable non-savings income is above this limit, then the 10 per cent savings rate will not be applicable.
- There are no changes to the 10 per cent dividend ordinary rate or the 32.5 per cent dividend upper rate.
- Watch out in the case of the married couple's allowance—it is the eldest of the two spouses who qualifies the couple.

Income Tax Rates and Taxable Bands

		2008	2009	2010	2011/12
Dividend rate	10%				
Upper Dividend rate	32.5%				See below*
Savings Rate	10%	£0 to—			
New savings rate	10%	Up to £2,320³			
Starting Rate: 10%	10%	£0—£2,230 (on all income)	£2,320 (only applies where taxable non-savings is under £2,320)	£2,440	
Basic Rate on earned and property income	22%	£2,231—£34,600			
	20%			£0—£34,800	
Basic rate on savings income					
Higher Rate: 40%		Over £34,600	Over £34,800	£37,400	
Pre-owned assets tax		As for income	As for income		
Must notify new sources of income by October 5 following the end of the year of assessment					
Submission of returns					
Paper only					
By October 31 following the end of the year of assessment					
Online by January 31 following the end of the year of assessment					
Penalties					
Failure to submit on time		£100	£100	£100	
Continued failure: Commissioners may authorise up to (or up to the amount of the outstanding tax):		£60 per day	£60 per day	£60 per day	

³ If the savings income is above this the 10 per cent savings rate will not be applicable!

INCOME TAX RATES AND TAXABLE BANDS

Attention!!

Income tax is payable under the Taxes Management Act 1970 as amended. The date for payment is January 31 following the end of the tax year. Interim payments to account are to be made on January 31 during the tax year and on July 31 following the end of the tax year. No payments are required if the amount due is less than £500 (to be increased to £1,000 for the tax years 2009/2010 and subsequently). If the proportion the amount of tax, which must be outstanding before a taxpayer is required to make a payment on account of income tax under s.59A of the Taxes Management Act 1970, bears to the assessed amount is less than 1 to 5, no payments are required. So if more than 80 per cent of the assessed tax is met by income tax deducted at source no payments on account are required. The final payment of income tax is due under the Taxes Management Act 1970 as amended. The balance of tax due for the year of assessment after deducting payments to account, etc. is due on January 31 following the year of assessment. A surcharge of five per cent may be made after February 28 with a further surcharge after July 31.

When is Income Tax Paid?

3–02   The date for payment of tax is January 31 following the year of assessment. At that time, there are two interim payments. These both occur in the year of assessment on January 31 and July 31, thus if the taxpayer wishes to deal with the tax year to April 5, 2009, his tax thereon is due at January 31, 2010. However, interim payments are due on January 31, 2008 and July 31, 2008. Tax under IPEPA 2003 on employment and pension income is deducted under the PAYE system.

LEGISLATION

3–03   The Income Tax Act 2007 is part of the Law Rewrite Programme and deals with income tax in the UK. It begins with an "overview" of the legislation which deals with income tax as follows.

- Income Tax (ITEPA 2003): this Act deals with charges to tax on employment income, pension income and social security income.
- Income Tax ITTOIA 2005: this deals with charges to tax on trading income, property income, savings and investment income and some other miscellaneous income.
- The Income Tax Act 2007 (which contains the other main provisions about income tax).
- There are also provisions about income tax elsewhere, for example in Pt 18 of ICTA (double taxation relief), CAA 2001 (allowances for capital expenditure) and Pt 4 of FA 2004 (pension schemes, etc.).

The Income Tax Act 2007 has 17 Parts which deal with basic provisions about income tax, the annual nature of income tax (the rates at which income tax is charged (Ch.2) and the calculation of income tax liability (Ch.3). Part 3 is about executors' personal reliefs including personal allowances (Ch.2).

These Acts, namely the Income Tax Act 2007, the Income Tax (ITEPA 2003) and the Income Tax ITTOIA 2005, will be the ones which concern us in this Chapter and the other sections of the this text concerning income tax.

Income Tax Allowances

The Chancellor announces the rates of allowances at the Pre-Budget **3–04** Report, which precedes the start of the tax year to which they relate. Pre-Budget Report takes place in November or December.

Taxable Bands

The Chancellor announces the taxable bands and the rates of tax at the **3–05** Budget Report, which precedes the start of the tax year to which they relate. Generally speaking, the Budget takes place in March.

Attention!!

In a unique statement recently, the Chancellor, the Right Honourable Alistair Darling, announced changes to the Budget after the Budget had been submitted to Parliament. The announcement was made in May 2008 following representations, many from his own party, to help low-income tax payers affected by the abolition of the 10 per cent starting rate of income tax. The personal allowance for the 2008–2009 tax year was increased by £600 from £5,435 to £6,035. However, to avoid higher-rate taxpayers benefiting from this, the Chancellor was to reduce the basic rate limit by £1,200 from £36,000 to £34,800. In effect higher-rate executors would see no difference in the amount of tax they pay!

Introduction

It is the executor's duty to make all necessary returns of (inter alia) tax **3–06** up to the date of death, ingather any repayment and settle any tax due.

Generally speaking, the returns with which the solicitor has to deal will be of the more straightforward kind, perhaps consisting of a simple repayment claim or self-assessment. He is unlikely to be called on to deal with a deceased who is a Lloyd's underwriter or is involved in esoteric investments such as futures, arbitrage or the like!

It is worth stating that, with (and perhaps because of) new technology, it is often not so much difficult so much as extremely tiresome to obtain the information to compile the return. Often it may take weeks (or indeed months) to obtain such elementary matters as tax certificates for interest deducted (and this is from the larger banks)! A person may have not one or two accounts but routinely as many as half a dozen, e.g. a current account, a savings or deposit account, one or more ISA accounts, a high interest account and another account whose title is often associated with a precious metal! This often causes difficulty at the point when the bank or building society, when presented with confirmation and the appropriate discharge forms, will, often with a sense of a job well done, issue one cheque for the total of these many and varied accounts. The practitioner is faced with the unenviable task of identifying the different amounts and linking these with the figures supplied as estate at date of death, i.e. sum at credit of capital and accrued interest to date of death and whether this was gross or after tax. If it is gross, it should be shown in the inventory as net (except for ISAs and the like) as this may involve additional IHT.

These problems can be minimised by trying to obtain the information at as early a stage as possible. A typical letter might be along the following lines:

Letter to bank

Our reference: c/lion   *If calling please ask for Mr Cheetham*

September 2, 2008

The Manager
Bank of Pixieland
701 Great Trumptington Road
GLASGOW
G1 2X

Dear Sir,

Mrs Fiona Primrose's Executry

We act for the executors of the late Mrs Fiona Rosemary Cowslip or Primrose, Retired Investment Banker, 22 Daisy Road, Newton Mearns, who died at Glasgow on August 11, 2008.

Amongst the deceased's effects, we discovered reference to an account with the executor represented by roll number D/123456 account number 00100001.

Please furnish us with the following writs or information:

1. *A note of the amount at credit of the account(s) at date of death.*
2. *A note of the interest accrued to date of death and whether this was gross or net.*
3. *Any papers, writs or other accounts you hold for behoof of the said deceased. If you hold any other accounts please let us have the same information for them.*
4. *A note of any interest(s) for the period from April 6, 2008 to date of death.*
5. *A note of any standing orders or direct debits.*
6. *The relative forms for signature by the executors to encash the account(s) when confirmation has been obtained.*
7. *Please also let us have a note of the interest paid or payable to the account during the fiscal year from April 6, 2007 to April 5, 2008.*

It is particularly important that you clearly identify if any of the accounts are ISAs or TESSAs.

Finally, please note to send any statements to us (not to the house) meantime.

Yours faithfully

Please note that some banks like to have an extract of the death **3–07** certificate or a certified copy thereof. Please note to confirm if you are sending a copy stipulate that it is a copy of the extract.[4]

The practitioner should attempt these tax returns himself. Sometime the deceased will have employed a chartered accountant or other tax advisor to prepare his or her tax returns; it may often seem easier to prepare the tax return "in-house" than to become involved in supplying the accountants or others with the wealth of seemingly unnecessary information which their software system demands. However, it is the practitioner's duty in those cases to supply the information as quickly as possible.

It may also be appropriate to write to the executor or the person instructing you along the following lines:

February 7, 2009

Gordon Caraway Esq
6 Sweet Violet Lane
Barrhead
Galsgow

Dear Mr Caraway

Your late mother's tax return

We are about to start work on your mother's Tax Return to date of death. We note that we appear to be missing one or two documents and information.

We need if possible your mother's P60 or P45 if she left employment during the year. If your mother was in employment it would be helpful to have the P11D showing taxable benefits and a note of the State Pension and any benefits.

Investment income such as bank or building interest is also needed. The banks have not yet been able to supply us with this information and in addition any dividends or distributions in connection with shares or unit trusts would also be helpful.

If your mother had a life assurance policy or bond some of the benefits from this are taxable and if a chargeable events certificate has been received it would be helpful for us to have this also.

Finally, any rental income which your mother received is needed and if she paid into a private pension scheme or had any disposal of capital assets such as shares or heritable property it would be helpful if we could be advised of these.

---

[4] Section 53(3) of the Registration of Births, Deaths and Marriages (Scotland) Act 1965 makes it an offence to pass as genuine any copy or reproduction.

It would be helpful if the original papers could be sent to us. Generally speaking the more information you can provide the better. Please note that there is a final deadline for this and the Revenue have powers to levy penalties for late submission.

We will endeavour to meet deadlines but as you will appreciate if we are not in possession of the documentation this may prove difficult.

With kind regards and best wishes.

Yours sincerely

PRELIMINARY

3–08 It is important to advise HMRC of the death *and* your interest, for example, as agents for the executors. The office to contact is the one which deals with the deceased's tax affairs during his lifetime. It goes almost without repeating that receiving mail addressed to the deceased often causes upset to the relatives. The tax office, its address and the deceased's tax reference and national insurance number are usually obtainable from the papers which the relatives may pass to the executor, such as a notice of coding or a payslip from the deceased's superannuation. Failing that, the executor may write to the former employer or, if the deceased was self-employed, the tax district nearest his principal place of business. Failing all that, the executor may write to the tax office nearest the deceased's home address.

THE KEY TO SUCCESS

3–09 At the outset, the practitioner should obtain and complete a 64-8 form, have the executor sign it and send it off to HMRC, and thereafter send it to the tax office as soon as possible. In theory this should allow HMRC to exchange and disclose information about the deceased and to deal with them on matters within the responsibility of HM Revenue & Customs. In theory this form is not really appropriate to executries, but it is as well to have it since H M Revenue & Customs may use its non production as an excuse not to deal with the professional advisor!

Form 64–8

HM Revenue & Customs

Authorising your agent

Please read the notes on the back before completing this **authority.** This authority allows us to exchange and disclose information about you with your agent and to deal with them on matters within the responsibility of HM Revenue & Customs (HMRC), as specified on this form. This overrides any earlier authority given to HMRC. We will hold this authority until you tell us that the details have changed.

I, *(print your name)*

GUSTAVUS RUINE

of *(name of your business, company or trust if applicable)*

1000 PETAL STREET, GLASGOW

authorise HMRC to disclose information to

(agent's business name) GRABIT & RUINE

I agree that the nominated agent has agreed to act on my/our behalf, and the information is correct and complete. The authorisation is limited to the matters shown on the right-hand side of this form.

Signature *see note 1 overleaf before signing*

G Ruine.

Date　1 MARCH 2009

Give your personal details or Company registered office here

Address

Postcode

Telephone number

Give your agent's details here

Address

1000 PETAL LANE

GLASGOW

Postcode

Telephone number

Agent codes (SA/CT/PAYE)

Client reference

For official use only

SA	☐ / /	COTAX	☐ / /
NIRS	☐ / /	EBS	☐ / /
COP	☐ / /	VAT	☐ / /
NTC	☐ / /	COP link	☐ / /

64-8

Please tick the box(es) and provide the reference(s) requested *only* for those matters for which you want HMRC to deal with your agent.

Individual*/Partnership*/Trust* Tax Affairs ☐ * select
**delete as appropriate* (including National Insurance)

Your National Insurance number *(individuals only)*
☐☐ ☐☐ ☐☐ ☐☐ 　*If you are self employed tick here* ☐

Unique Taxpayer Reference *(if applicable)*
☐☐☐☐☐☐☐☐☐☐ 　*If UTR not yet issued tick here* ☐

If you are a Self Assessment taxpayer, we will send your Statement of Account to you, but if you would like us to send it to your agent instead, please tick here ☐

Tax Credits ☐

Your National Insurance number *(only if not entered above)*
☐☐ ☐☐ ☐☐ ☐☐

If you have a joint Tax Credit claim and the other claimant wants HMRC to deal with this agent, they should sign here
Name

Signature

Joint claimant's National Insurance number
☐☐ ☐☐ ☐☐ ☐☐

Corporation Tax ☐
Company Registration number
☐☐☐☐☐☐☐☐

Company's Unique Taxpayer Reference
☐☐☐☐☐☐☐☐☐☐

NOTE: Do not complete this section if you are an employee. Only tick the box if you are an employer operating PAYE

Employer PAYE Scheme ☐
Employer PAYE reference

VAT ☐ *(see notes 2 and 5 overleaf)*
VAT registration number
☐☐☐☐☐☐☐☐☐ 　*If not yet registered tick here* ☐

HMRC 02/09

1 Who should sign the form

If the authority is for	Who signs the form
You, as an individual	You, for your personal tax affairs
A Company	The secretary or other responsible officer of the company
A Partnership	The partner responsible for the partnership's tax affairs. It applies only to the partnership. Individual partners need to sign a separate authority for their own tax affairs
A trust	One or more of the trustees

2 What this authority means

- **For matters other than VAT or Tax Credits**

We will start sending letters and forms to your agent and give them access to your account information online. Sometimes we need to correspond with you as well as, or instead of, your agent.

For example, the latest information on what SA forms we send automatically can be found on our website, go to **www.hmrc.gov.uk/sa/agentlist.htm** or phone the SA Helpdesk on **0845 9 000 444.** You will not receive your Self Assessment Statements of Account if you authorise your agent to receive them instead, but paying any amount due is your responsibility.

We do not send National Insurance statements and requests for payment to your agent unless you have asked us if you can defer payment.

Companies do not receive Statements of Account.

- **For VAT and Tax Credits**

We will continue to send correspondence to you rather than to your agent but we can deal with your agent in writing or by phone on specific matters. If your agent is able to submit VAT returns online on your behalf, you will need to authorise them to do so through our website. For joint Tax Credit claims, we need both claimants to sign this authority to enable HM Revenue & Customs to deal with your agent.

3 How we use your information

HM Revenue & Customs is a Data Controller under the Data Protection Act 1998. We hold information for the purposes specified in our notification to the Information Commissioner, including the assessment and collection of tax and duties, the payment of benefits and the prevention and detection of crime, and may use this information for any of them. We may get information about you from others, or we may give information to them. If we do, it will only be as the law permits.

We may check information we receive about you with what is already in our records. This can include information provided by you, as well as by others, such as other government departments or agencies and overseas tax and customs authorities. We will not give information to anyone outside HM Revenue & Customs unless the law permits us to do so.

This authority does not allow your agent to request personal information held about you under the subject access provisions of the Data Protection Act 1998.

Further information can be found on our website, **www.hmrc.gov.uk**

4 Multiple agents

If you have more than one agent (for example, one acting for the PAYE scheme and another for Corporation Tax), please sign one of these forms for each.

5 Where to send this form

When you have completed this form please send it to:
HM Revenue & Customs, Central Agent Authorisation Team, Longbenton, Newcastle upon Tyne, NE98 1ZZ.
There are some exceptions to this to help speed the handling of your details in certain circumstances.
If this form:

- accompanies other correspondence, send it to the appropriate HM Revenue & Customs (HMRC) office
- is solely for Corporation Tax affairs, send it to the HMRC office that deals with the company
- is for a Complex Personal Return or Expatriate customer, send it to the appropriate CPR team or Expat team
- accompanies a VAT Registration application, send it to the appropriate VAT Registration Unit
- has been specifically requested by an HMRC office, send it back to that office.

This should be, and often is, sufficient for HM Revenue & Customs to deal with the practitioner. However, in a recent article in *Taxation*,[5] the author Robert Clubb identified some difficulties. The main examples in this helpful and often amusing article related to such matters as: centralised processing of forms 64-8 not always being efficient; HMRC being selective about information they copy in to agents; and unnecessary duplication. A consistent approach from HMRC would be helpful:

> "One of the routines that causes so much frustration to agents and should be so simple for HMRC to get right is the processing of forms 64–8. Agents often spend copious amounts of time chasing and re-submitting these forms, not to mention those occasions where the agent discovers that, after many years, without explanation, authority for them to act has disappeared into HMRC's equivalent of the Bermuda Triangle."

It is clear that it may not be sufficient to send the 64–8 to the deceased's tax office but to send a copy or copies to other offices who it is considered may have an interest, e.g. Centre One and HM Revenue & Customs trusts and estates.

In recent times HMRC will often now send a letter to the agents acting for the deceased. The letter will be from the appropriate department and will enclose a Form R27. It may also include an "Authority to Disclose Information Form", also for completion. See below for examples of these forms.

---

[5] R. Clubb, "Tactical misinformation", *Taxation* (April 9, 2008).

Page 1 of Form R27

HM Revenue & Customs

Potential repayment to the estate

Please use these if you write or call. It will help to avoid delay.

Your reference

Our reference

/

National Insurance number

| A B | 1 2 | 3 4 | | 5 6 | C |

If you need more help or advice call

Name —————————

Phone —————————

Office address/date stamp

Estate of the late _____ Mrs Rose Lane

I have sent you this form so that I can finalise the tax position up to the date of death. If you are dealing with the deceased's estate please complete this form. If you are not, please give it to the person who is. They will normally be called the Personal Representative or Executor and may be a solicitor or accountant. **It is important that this form is completed and signed personally by the Personal Representative** and not by an agent or professional adviser acting on their behalf.

Completing the form

Page 1 You must complete **Details about the estate and period of administration** in every case.

Page 2 You must complete **Details about income and allowances** in every case **unless** you have already sent me a Self Assessment Tax Return or R40 claim form covering the period 6 April to the date of death, or you want to complete one now (in which case please tick the box at the top of page 2 that applies and I shall send one). The details that you give on page 2 will help me to work out the final tax liability.

Page 3 It is possible that there may be a repayment of tax. To enable me to make any repayment due, you must complete **Claim to Repayment** in every case unless you have already sent me a Self Assessment Tax Return or R40 claim form covering the period 6 April to the date of death.

Page 4 You must complete **the Declaration** in every case.

You should only complete **Repayment nomination** if you are the person entitled to receive any repayment which may be due, but you want to have the repayment paid direct into your bank or building society account or you want to nominate someone else to receive the repayment on your behalf.

Details about the estate and period of administration

IMPORTANT - Do not send the will, probate, confirmation or letters of administration with this form. If I need to see any of them I will ask.

Tick as appropriate

Did the deceased leave a will? Yes ☑ No ☐

If 'Yes', does it provide for all or some of the assets to be held in trust? Yes ☐ No ☑

Do you expect the estate to receive any untaxed income, or to sell any assets from the estate during the period of administration? Yes ☑ No ☐

Have you obtained or intend to obtain ~~probate~~, confirmation or ~~letters of administration~~? Yes ☑ No ☐

If 'Yes', please enter

• the date it was obtained or is due to be obtained | 25 / 12 /2008 | • the net value of the deceased's estate *(this will be shown on the probate)* | £ 134,000 |

If 'No' and the value of the estate is likely to be more than £5,000, please explain in the box below why you are not obtaining probate, confirmation or letters of administration. Use a separate sheet if you need more space.

Authority to Disclose Information

This authority allows us to exchange and disclose information on your behalf, with your agent and to deal with them on matters within the responsibility of HM Revenue and Customs (HMRC). We will hold this authority until you tell us the details have changed.

This overrides any earlier authority given to HMRC, such as form 64-8, that ceases on death.

I (Print your name)
CHARLES STEELE
Representing (Name of Deceased)
MRS ROSE LANE
Capacity in which you sign e.g. Executor/Personal Representative
EXECUTOR
National Insurance number of Deceased
AB 123456C
Authorise HMRC to disclose information to (name of agent)
CHEETHAM & STEELE
Signature
Date   15th June 2008

Give your personal details here
Address   The Ilk
Milngavie
Postcode   G11 2AA
Give your agents details here
Address Cheetham & Steele
1 Blank Street
Glasgow
Postcode
Telephone number: 0141-000-0000
Agent codes (SA/CT/PAYE)
Client reference S/RL

3–10   The R27 Form is an attempt to work out the position quickly, presumably for executries where the estate is simple. It seeks and is headed "potential repayment to the estate". The form is well designed and easy to read and initially provides boxes to tick. It then requests details of income and totals only. There is also included a repayment claim form and authority to pay agents.

The problem, however, is that the form is only of use where the deceased's tax affairs are relatively simple. It will probably not preclude the necessity in less simple or indeed complicated cases for the submission of a full self-assessment form. To this extent it may involve the executors in additional work, indeed almost duplication of effort.

The Authority to Disclose Information form is basically a mandate to allow HMRC to exchange and disclose information on behalf of the executors with agents. This is to be welcomed since, as previously mentioned, the 64–8 is not really designed to deal with a situation when an executry arises. Thus it seems pointless and indeed stupid to ask for the executor's tax district and national insurance number!

3–11   From time to time HM Revenue & Customs have said that agents who used the online agent authorisation (64-8) service may experience some delay in processing the application and updating HMRC records. They usually hope to have it cleared up quickly and not require to submit a duplicate authorisation request.

They are in fact "undertaking a fundamental review of all of our processes for agent authorisation" and say they will "be consulting with agent representatives about this and will be able to provide further details by the end of the year".[6]

The tax office will ask if it is intended to obtain confirmation, to complete a tax return for the period in which the death occurred and, possibly for earlier years, to send any business accounts not previously sent in for years up to the date of death if the deceased was self employed. An R187 form may be submitted to the executor if HM Revenue & Customs think that the deceased's affairs were straightforward.

This form may save time and obviate the necessity for a full return. It is not necessary to await confirmation before completing this form. However, it may be that if a tax return form, whether repayment or self-assessment is needed, it is introducing an unnecessary step and considerable expense to the executor.

METHODOLOGY

3–12 Clearly, a sustained treatment of the income tax system of the United Kingdom is not possible in a volume of this kind. It is hoped, however, to identify and to make the basic rules relevant for tax returns up to date of death. However, the Income Tax Act 2007 gives a series of steps to identify and calculate income tax.[7]

---

[6] *http://www.hmrc.gov.uk* [accessed April 20, 2009].
[7] Income Tax Act 2007 (c.3).

CALCULATION OF INCOME LIABILITY

"To find the liability of a person ['the executor'] to income tax for a **3–13**
tax year, take the following steps.

Step 1

Identify the amounts of income on which the [executor] is charged
to income tax for the tax year. The sum of those amounts is 'total
income'. Each of those amounts is a 'component' of total income.

Step 2

Deduct from the components the amount of any relief under a
provision listed in relation to the [deceased] taxpayer in section 24
to which the [executor] is entitled for the tax year . . . The sum of
the amounts of the components left after this step is 'net income'.

Step 3

Deduct from the amounts of the components left after Step 2 any
allowances to which the [deceased] taxpayer is entitled for the tax
year under Chapter 2 of Part 3 of this Act or section 257 or 265 of
ICTA (individuals: personal allowance and blind person's allowance).

Step 4

Calculate tax at each applicable rate on the amounts of the
components left after Step 3. See Chapter 2 of this Part for the rates
at which income tax is charged and the income charged at particular
rates.

Step 5

Add together the amounts of tax calculated at Step 4.

Step 6

Deduct from the amount of tax calculated at Step 5 any tax
reductions to which the [deceased] is entitled for the tax year under
a provision listed in relation to the [deceased] in section 26. See
sections 27 to 29 for further provision about the deduction of those
tax reductions.

Step 7

Add to the amount of tax left after Step 6 any amounts of tax for
which the [executor] is liable for the tax year under any provision
listed in relation to the [executor] in section 30.

The result is the [executor's] liability to income tax for the tax
year."[8]

We will now examine each of these in more detail.

---

[8] Income Tax Act 2007, s.23.

STEP 1

Find Total Income

3–14   Identify the amounts of income on which the deceased taxpayer is
charged to income tax for the tax year. The sum of those amounts is
"total income". Each of those amounts is a "component" of total
income, namely, dividend, savings and non-savings. This may be the
most complicated, time consuming and often frustrating part of the
exercise.

Sometimes the deceased will have his paperwork in order and the
family or the executors will present themselves with:

- form P60;
- form P45—if the executor has been sent one;
- pension statements;
- interest statements from banks and building societies; and
- dividend vouchers.

Often (usually) they will not and the practitioner will have to resort to
other methods of finding the documents or information needed. It may
be useful to examine other documents. The list of the deceased's assets,
which the practitioner may have received from the executors, and the
Confirmation, which the executor obtains in due course, will indicate the
sources of the executry income. Prior to April 5, 1996 a copy of the
deceased's last tax return or repayment claim would have helped to
confirm the sources. If the executors did not have a copy of the return or
claim, they would have been able to obtain a copy from the tax office,
provided a note of the district and reference was available. The details of
the tax office are shown on Coding Notices and Assessments.

3–15   A copy of the deceased's SA100 and schedules thereto will not yield
details of the sources of income since the SA100 only provides totals.
However, usually a statement or analysis of income will be prepared and
the totals transferred to the SA100. A copy of this statement can be
utilised to check and confirm the sources.

While this information-gathering period is taking place it is strongly
recommended that a process is devised whereby the information as it
comes in is "captured" in a manner which is easily referred to.

If access to a "spreadsheet programme" is available on computer, one
method of dealing with this information, which may well come in at
different times and in different formats, will be to produce a table. The
table is produced on a spreadsheet as follows. The letters of the
alphabet, i.e. A to Z on the left-hand side, form the first column. The
column headings form the top "row". The column headings will be, for
example, under the period to date of death, e.g. from April 6, 2007 to
December 31, 2007 (date of death). Under this, the document is divided
into sub-columns in connection with dividend rate at 10 per cent,
ordinary rate at 22 per cent (20 per cent for the period from April 6,
2008), net and gross and then gross, net and tax for the 20 per cent.

3–16   The item of estate, say the Royal Bank, is inserted at the figure R as
shown.

Example

Francis Meadow Speedwell

Take the case of the unfortunate Francis Meadow Speedwell, Number 10 Dandelion Grove, Milngavie, a retired financial consultant, aged 68, who died on August 30, 2008. He had substantial investments, bank and building society accounts, a property, Number 7 Cowslip Cottages, Port Mistletoe, which he rented out. He also carried out a small amount of consultancy work (Financial Solutions). He leaves a widow, Mrs Penelope Marsh Marigold or Speedwell, aged 63, and two children, Poppy and Bluebell.

His income for the period from April 6, 2008 to date of death on August 30, 2008, which is obtained after many letters, faxes, emails and telephone calls, is shown in Table 1 below.

After a few weeks and more letters to and from banks, pension funds, etc. the document may look something like Table 2.

The completed note for up to date of death is shown in Table 3.

The other point is that all untaxed interest, e.g. pension and bank interest which is not taxed can be shown in bold.

The advantage of this is that when the executor comes to do the executry tax return these cells can be copied and transferred to a fresh set at the right but this time headed from August 31, 2008 to April 5, 2009 which will constitute the basis for the first executry tax return. This can be repeated ad infinitum and it ensures that individual sources of income in general and untaxed interest in particular are not overlooked.

Table 1: Speedwell Number Two—Francis M. Speedwell's Executry—Statement of Income

		for period 6/4/08 to 20/8/08 (date of death)							for period 21/8/08 to 05/04/09	
		Dividends at 10% net	Non dividend income at 20% net	tax	gross	Non Savings at 20% net	tax	gross	Dividends at 10% net	Non dividend income at 20% net
Achmilla plc	superannuation					£ 3,400.00	£ 600.00	£ 4,000.00		
B										
C										
D										
Egg			£ 43.20	£ 10.80	£ 54.00					
F										
G										
H										
Imperial Holdings		£ ?								
J										
K										
L										
M										
National Savings	income bonds (paid) gross				£ 500.00					
O								£ 4,600.00		
Pension (Gross)										
Q										
Royal Bank	Current Account		£ 340.00	£ 85.00	£ 425.00					
	Deposit Account		£ ?							
S										
Tesco plc		£ 700.00								
U										
V										
W										
X										
Y										
Z										

Table 2: Speedwell Number Two—Francis M. Speedwell's Executry—Statement of Income

		for period 6/4/08 to 20/8/08 (date of death)							for period 21/8/08 to 05/04/09		
		Dividends at 10% net	Non dividend income at 20% net	tax	gross	Non Savings at 20% net	tax	gross	Dividends 10% net	Dividends at 10% net	Non dividend income at 20% net
Achmilla plc	superannuation					£3,400.00	£600.00	£4,000.00			
B											
C											
D											
Egg			£43.20	£10.80	£54.00						
Financial Solutions	Consultancy work							?			
G											
H											
Imperial Holdings		£43.00									
J											
K											
L											
M	income bonds (paid) gross										
National Savings					£500.00						
O											
Pension (Gross)								£4,600.00			
Q											
Royal Bank	Current Account		£340.00	£85.00	£425.00						
	Deposit Account		£?								
S											
Tesco plc		£700.00									
U											
V											
Whitby Building Society			£33.50	£8.38	£41.88						
X											
Y											
Z											

Table 3: Speedwell Number Three—Francis M Speedwell's Executry—Statement of Income

for period 6/4/08 to 20/8/08 (date of death)

		Dividends at 10% net	Non dividend income at 20% net	tax	gross	Non Savings at 20% net	tax	gross
Achmilla plc	superannuation					£ 3,400.00	£ 600.00	£ 4,000.00
B								
C								
D								
Egg			£ 43.20	£ 10.80	£ 54.00			
Financial Solutions	Consultancy work				Nil			
G								
H								
Imperial Holdings		£ 43.00						
J								
K								
L								
M								
National Savings	income bonds (paid) gross				£ 500.00			
O								
Pension (Gross)								£ 4,600.00
Q								
Royal Bank	Current Account		£ 340.00	£ 85.00	£ 425.00			
	Deposit Account		£ 700.00	£ 175.00	£ 875.00			
S								
Tesco plc		£ 700.00						
U								
V								
Whitby Building Society			£ 33.50	£ 8.38	£ 41.88			
X								
Y								
Z								

Summary 04/08–08/08

Dividends	£ 743.00					
Taxed Interest		£ 1,116.70			£ 500.00	
Untaxed Interest						
State Pension (Gross)						
Other Pension						£ 4,600.00
					£3,400.00	

for period 21/8/08 to 05/04/09

Dividends at 10% net	Non dividend income at 20% net

Total Income

Total income is the sum of the tax payer's income from all sources after **3–17** deducting allowable expenses which is chargeable to income tax. These sources of income will be determined from Pt 2 of the ITTOIA Act 2005 as profits from the trade profession or vocation, Pt 3 as property income from rents, Pt 4 as savings and investments income and Pt 5 as other income such as other annual income not chargeable to tax otherwise and under the Income Tax (Earning & Pensions) Act 2003. It is likely that it will be mainly Pt 4 and under ITEPA 2003 Act which the practitioner will be concerned with.

Obviously total income includes sums received gross such as trading income and rent and the grossed up amounts of sums, which will frequently be as regards banks, building societies and so forth received net of tax. Bank interest generally has tax deducted at 20 per cent and dividends at 10 per cent. Salaries or superannuation may have tax deducted under the PAYE scheme. It will be necessary therefore to gross up sums of interest received net of tax and this is simply carried out by the following calculation. The practitioner should multiply the net sum by 100 over 100 minus the tax rate, e.g. if tax has been deducted and £320 is received net of tax then £320 represents 80 per cent of the gross figure since 20 per cent has already been deducted. To find out what 100 per cent is the executor simply divides 80 to find one per cent and then multiplies by 100 to find 100 per cent.

This simple step is appropriate whatever rate of tax has been **3–18** deducted, e.g. take the case of a liferentrix who received £8,000 in the tax year to April 5, 2008. The income is all bank interest or government stocks and tax at the basic rate of 20 per cent has already been deducted. To calculate the beneficiaries' statutory income, the income is grossed up to £10,000, i.e. 8,000 x 100 over 100 minus 20 = £10,000. The £10,000 will be returned by the deceased as part of gross income but of course £2,000 has already been deducted and this is shown as a tax credit in calculating the return.

Depending on the deceased's tax payer's situation one of the following will apply:

- if he is a non tax payer or pays tax at a lower rate he may be entitled to a repayment; or
- if he pays at the standard rate then the effect of this will be neutral assuming that the additional amount is not taken into a higher bank; or
- if he is already in the higher tax rate it will be necessary to pay probably another 20 per cent or 25 per cent if the Chancellor's pre budget proposals are enacted.[9]

Dividends of course are treated in a different manner; they are received with a 10 per cent tax credit which is not recoverable.

Certain matters require special attention.

---

[9] Additional tax on dividend income is also to be expected for higher executors.

Taxable and Exempt Income

3–19 As stated the list of the deceased's assets, which is received from the executors or the deceased's family, will indicate the sources of the deceased's income, but a copy of his last tax return or repayment claim may help to confirm the sources. If the executors do not have a copy of the return or claim, the executor should be able to get a copy from the tax office, provided the executor has a note of the tax reference, which is shown on Coding Notices and self-assessment tax calculation or statement of account. If the deceased is outwith the self-assessment system the information will be quite comprehensive. However, if the deceased was within the self-assessment scheme, the returns now show only the totals for each type of income. It may be possible to get hold of the deceased's workings from the executors and obtain details of the deceased's taxable assets. The tax return and the schedules comprise an extremely useful source of information for the executry practitioner. Having dealt with this and as details of the estate are received from banks, building societies, stockbrokers and others, it is vital to have regard to untaxed taxable income. More mistakes are caused by this than anything else. Practitioners fail to identify these sources of income and they are not returned to HMRC at the appropriate time, and worse still tax is not retained to cover this.

Danger Warning!!

More problems are caused by the failure to identify untaxed interest at the outset. It is vitally important to make the distinction between income which is exempt from tax and income which is paid gross but is taxable.

In any event, having identified the sources of income and inserted them in your spreadsheet check list, any income which is not taxable should be identified, such as:

- SS Child Benefit;
- SS Attendance Allowance;
- SS Pensioners' Christmas Bonus;
- First six months' SS Incapacity Benefit;
- SS Housing Benefit;
- SS Sickness Benefit;
- Some SS Income Support;
- Armed Forces' Wounds and Disability pensions;
- War Widows' pensions;
- Disability or injury pensions of police and fire-fighters;
- First £70 interest on NS ordinary accounts (interest paid on other accounts is not exempt);
- Increase in value of NS Savings Certificates[10];
- NS Premium Bond prizes;

---

[10] These are not strictly interest in the strict legal sense of the word although they are commonly (mistakenly) called "interest".

- Interest on TESSA (Tax Exempt Special Savings Accounts) to April 5, 1999 or earlier death;
- Income of PEPs (Personal Equity Plans) to April 5, 1999 or earlier death—unless the amount of interest withdrawn in the tax year is more than £180;
- Income[11] from Individual Savings Accounts to date of death[12];
- Bonuses and profits on qualifying life assurance policies;
- Capital part of a purchased life annuity;
- Save As The executor Earn account bonuses;
- Profit-related pay and shares from Profit Sharing Schemes;
- Interest on damages for personal injuries;
- Interest from Save As The executor Earn certified contractual savings schemes;
- Loan interest paid by a member of a credit union to the union;
- Housing benefit;
- Income support, unless the claimant is on strike;
- Pension Credit;
- Social fund payments;
- Attendance allowance;
- Child benefit, guardian's allowance and one parent benefit;
- Child dependency additions paid with widowed mother's allowance, retirement pension and incapacity benefit;
- Disability living allowance;
- Disablement benefit, constant attendance allowance and exceptionally severe disablement allowance;
- Lower rate short-term incapacity benefit and transitional awards of incapacity benefit;
- Maternity allowance;
- Severe disablement benefit;
- War disablement pension, including allowances; and
- War orphan's pension, war widow/widower's pension.

Other types of income, which are exempt from tax, include:

- damages awarded for personal injury;
- interest awarded by a court on damages for personal injuries;
- jurors' financial loss allowance, if the juror is an employee;
- long service awards to employees;
- luncheon vouchers, up to the value of 15p per day;
- certain pensions. Voluntary pensions which are not connected to a past employment and to which the executor contributes annually are exempt. Disability pensions of members of the armed forces are exempt. Any pension awarded to an employee on retirement because of an injury at work is exempt;
- insurance benefits paid to a person who is sick, disabled or unemployed to meet her/his financial commitments, for exam-

---

[11] Not on dividends of UK equities.

[12] It is sometimes difficult for laymen and some banks and building societies to understand that this interest is gross only until the date of death. After that, the ISA falls and the interest on the investment is taxable in the normal way.

ple, benefits paid under mortgage protection insurance, permanent health insurance, payment protection (creditor) insurance and long-term insurance;
- strike pay and unemployment pay from trade unions;
- earnings when the person is working abroad;
- employment rehabilitation allowance;
- employment training allowance;
- the youth training scheme allowance, unless the trainee has employee status;
- fares to school;
- educational maintenance allowance;
- school uniform and clothing grants;
- student grants, including the parental contribution and scholarships;
- hospital patient's travelling allowance;
- premium bond prizes and winnings from gambling, for example, football pools, horse racing and the National Lottery;
- home improvement, repair and insulation grants;
- Working Tax Credit and Child Tax Credit; and
- rent a room scheme—some of the income is exempt.

These sums should be clearly identified and care should be taken that tax is not paid on them. It may seem trite to mention this but it is surprising how many times HMRC require to strike out items from the above which are included in a tax return.

Taxable Income Paid Gross

3–20   This is the one which causes most difficulty, i.e. omitting an item paid gross particularly from a government source. Having identified the sources of income, which are not taxable, note these, which are taxable but are paid gross without deduction of tax, such as:

- SS Retirement pensions;
- SS Widows' pensions;
- SS Incapacity Benefit after the first six months;
- SS Income Support to unemployed and strikers (TA 1988 s.151);
- Statutory Sick Pay (TA 1988 s.149);
- Interest on NS Investment accounts above the limit;
- Interest on NS Income Bonds;
- Interest on NS Capital Bonds;
- Interest on Government stocks on NS Register;
- Interest on 3.5 per cent War Stock, 2.5 per cent Consolidated Stock and other stocks paid gross on the Bank of England Register. Most Bank of England stocks, usually referred to as "gilt-edged" stocks are routinely paid gross, unless the owner, for whatever reason, stipulates that they are to be paid net (of tax at 20 per cent);
- Rental income from heritable property; and
- Trading income.

Many of these will continue to produce income in the executry until the assets are realised or transferred. The income will have to be assessed in the executry tax return, the time for submitting which the practitioner should have inserted in his diary. If the deceased's business is not terminated at death, the executors will also receive some trading income, which they must return for assessment.

Income which is taxable includes:

- some social security benefits and pensions;
- employment related allowances and benefits;
- some earned income;
- some fringe benefits, for example, company cars;
- some occupational pensions;
- interest on some types of savings;
- income support paid to people who are on strike;
- industrial death benefit;
- invalid care allowance;
- retirement pension;
- statutory maternity pay;
- statutory sick pay;
- jobseeker's allowance;
- widowed mother's allowance;
- widow's pension; and
- higher-rate short-term and long-term incapacity benefit.

The other type of untaxed income is interest and one which is often overlooked is that arising under the accrued income scheme.

Accrued Income Scheme

Introduction

The scheme allocates the interest between buyer and seller in regard to **3–21** certain purchase and sales of certain kinds of shares.[13] The Accrued Income Scheme determines how HM Revenue & Customs treat any interest earned in the period spanning the date of sale of government fixed interest and certain other fixed interest securities for tax purposes. Executors may be affected by the scheme if they transfer securities (or have securities transferred to them).

When interest-bearing securities such as British Government Securities (gilts), local authority bonds or company loan stock are sold the contract note (sale agreement) will specify who is entitled to the next interest payment. In most which are *cum-divided* sales, the buyer will receive the next interest payment, and the transfer price will have been increased to reflect the value of that payment. In *ex-dividend* sales, the next interest payment will be paid to the seller and the transfer price will have been reduced to take that into account.

Please note that the scheme applies to interest-bearing marketable bonds and loan stock; it does not apply to ordinary or preference shares

---

[13] Strictly speaking reference should be made to "stock". Traditionally, Bank of England and certain other stocks were referred to as "stock" and the price was quoted per £100. Now the expression "shares" is used to include stock and shares.

in a company, units in a unit trust, National Savings Certificates or bank deposits.

There are exemptions if the total holding of securities (not just the ones transferred) is small enough to be under the nominal value of the total holdings, i.e. under £5,000 at any time in the tax year in which the next interest due date falls, and the previous tax year.

Accrued Income Scheme Example

3–22 *On March 30, 2007 Robert Herb sells £4,000 8.5 per cent Treasury Stock 2010 (this pays interest on January 16 and July 16). On April 10, 2007 Robert used the proceeds to buy £6,800 five per cent Treasury Stock 2014. He held no other securities at any time. The March 30, 2007 transfer falls in the tax year to April 5, 2008, when the nominal value of the total holding of securities never exceeded £5,000. However, the next interest payment on the sold securities is July 16, 2008, which is in the tax year to April 5, 2009. Because Robert had bought £6,800 five per cent Treasury Stock in that tax year, on April 10, 2007, he exceeded the limit and the Accrued Income Scheme applied to the March 31, 2007 sale.*

As stated, the scheme allocates the interest between buyer and seller. The seller is taxed on the income from interest which has accrued up to the date of transfer; the buyer is taxed on the income accruing from the date of transfer. Generally shares are bought and sold through a stockbroker, who will supply the executor with a contract note which shows any accrued interest.

Treatment of Interest

3–23 This depends on whether the deceased (or the executors) was a seller or a buyer.

Seller

Cum-dividend sales (which most will be). If accrued interest is added to the price received, tax will be due on that amount.
Ex-dividend sales. If accrued interest is deducted from the price, the executor receives a deduction for that amount against the next payment of interest.

Buyers

Cum-dividend purchases. If accrued interest is added to the price a deduction is received for that amount against the next payment of interest.
Ex-dividend purchases. If accrued interest is deducted from the price the executor pays, tax is paid on that amount.

Example

This example shows the calculations for the transactions in the immediately preceding example.

On March 31, 2007 Robert sold £4,000 nominal value of 8.5 per cent Treasury Stock 2010, which paid interest on January 16 and July 16. The contract note shows that £71 accrued interest has been added to the sale price. Tax is due on this amount, possibly at 20 per cent but depending on Robert's income.

The next payment of interest on the sold securities is on July 16, 2008 (the tax year April 6, 2008 to April 5, 2009). HMRC will tax Robert on the £71 in that tax year. When his tax return is completed for the year ended April 5, 2009 it must include the £71 to any other interest received during the year.

Not wishing to simplify his tax affairs, on April 10, 2008 Robert buys £6,800 five per cent Treasury Stock 20012 which pays interest on March 7 and September 7. The contract note shows that £27 accrued interest has been included in the total price he paid. Accordingly, he will receive tax relief on this amount.

The next interest payment is on September 7, 2008 (the tax year April 6, 2008 to April 5, 2009). There is £170 interest paid on September 7, but HMRC will only tax him on £170 − £27 = £143. When the tax return for the year ended April 5, 2009 is submitted it is necessary to reduce the £170 interest receipt by the £27 relief for accrued income.

Danger Warning!!

If two or more transactions are made in the same kind of security with the same related interest payment, the results of those transactions must be combined to give a net charge to tax, or relief from tax, for that interest payment. This is the only time that the results of transactions are added together.

The accrued income scheme will be referred to again in the section dealing with executry income tax returns.

Characteristics of Interest

A well-respected legal authority describes interest as "the return or **3–24** compensation for the use of or retention by one person of a sum of money belonging to or owed to another". We also have judicial definitions for guidance. For instance, in the case of *Westminster Bank Ltd v Riches* (28 TC 159), Lord Wright said that:

> "[T]he essence of interest is that it is a payment which becomes due because the creditor has not had his money at the due date. It may be regarded either as representing the profit he might have made if he had had the use of the money, or, conversely the loss he suffered because he had not that use. The general idea is that he is entitled to compensation for the deprivation".

This theme was expanded upon in *Re Euro Hotel (Belgravia) Ltd* (51 TC 293). Mr Justice Megarry stated that as a general rule, there are two requirements to be satisfied for a payment to be interest. First, there must be a sum of money by reference to which the payment is to be ascertained; secondly, that sum of money must be due to the person entitled to the alleged interest.

It is clear from these cases that entitlement is an essential feature of interest. An entitlement to interest arises under common law where there is an express agreement to pay interest or such agreement can be inferred from the circumstances.

What Happens if the Executor Discovers that the Deceased has not Declared Income?

3–25   Sometimes the practitioner will discover that the deceased, for whatever reason, did not include untaxed income from various sources. It may be that the executor has included income from these sources in the return to the date of death and HM Revenue & Customs (as yet!) have only raised an assessment for that year and not noticed that the sources (including rental from property) were not included in the deceased's previous return. HM Revenue & Customs have three years from the end of the year in which the final return was submitted in which to raise assessments for earlier years. Without pausing to draw breath, this should be intimated to HMRC. The executor is bound to deliver as true and faithful an account of the estate as he can and this must include ensuring that the liabilities of the deceased are stated as clearly as the assets. The executor has to arrange for the tax affairs of the deceased to be settled and this must include any earlier years which are misstated or understated. To conceal information from the person charged with settling those liabilities could (and probably should) lead to prosecution. It is clearly different where the executor is unaware of income, but that is not the case here. Advice not to include might create a reference to NCIS, with all that might include.

It need hardly be stated, but if the executor declines to instruct the practitioner not to so intimate to HMRC, the practitioner must robustly advise him that this is potentially tax evasion on the part of the executor and the practitioner should consider his position. The practitioner may wish to add (particularly if the practitioner is keen to occupy the high moral ground—always a good place for a professional to be) that as a matter of personal honesty and standards, lying is an impossible position for a professional person to adopt and is unworthy of consideration.

Clearly what should have been done was to indicate in the "white space" on the last page of the SA 100 that there may have been sums received in previous years and that full details of these will be submitted when known. As information becomes known or estimates become available these should be intimated to HMRC and tax tendered as appropriate. If not then it is likely that HMRC will penalise him, if and when the true position becomes known to them.

Danger Warning!!

In addition it could be argued that these penalties are personal to an executor or trustee, i.e. they are not a legitimate expense against which the individual is entitled to be indemnified.

Allocation of Income between Deceased and Executors

Income of the deceased is allocated according to the dates on which it is **3–26** payable or credited.

Interest on bank and building society accounts, fixed interest stocks and National Savings investments must be apportioned for inheritance tax on a daily basis, but the apportionment does not apply for income tax. This is sometimes difficult for the lay client to understand! The basis of assessment is the receipt of the interest before or after death. The full amount of the interest, including the amount accrued to death, forms part of the executry income at the next interest date or at the closing of the account, if earlier. Please note that the next interest date and the closing date may not be in the same fiscal year, in which case interest must be split.

The exceptions to this rule are the interest earned on TESSAs, ISAs and PEPs up to death. HM Revenue & Customs allows the tax exemption to apply to that accrued interest. Of course they must be shown in the inheritance tax inventory gross.

Government Stocks

The interest is assessed according to the date on which payment is due. **3–27** The interest accrued to death for IHT is also subject to income tax, but the IHT paid on it is deductible in the calculation of the beneficiary's liability to higher rate IT on it.

Dividends/Distributions (from unit trusts/OEICs)

Dividends are allocated according to the date on which they are payable, **3–28** thus an uncashed dividend at date of death forms part of the deceased's income and a dividend payable after death forms part of the executry income.

Dividends added to an *ex-dividend* quotation for IHT are treated as capital for IHT, because they form part of the deceased's assets (IHTA 1984 s.5), but they are part of the executry income for income tax.

If interest or a dividend falls due for payment on the date of death it should be treated as the deceased's income. TA 1988 s.695(1) provides that the administration of an estate commences "on the death of a deceased person", but *Bryan v Cassin* (1942) 24 TC 468 provides that the executry income starts on the day after death.

Wages and Salaries

The "receipts basis" applies and therefore the final balance to death **3–29** (which was not paid to the deceased) should in theory form part of the executry income. In practice the balance is treated as the deceased's income. The practitioner should ask the employers for a P60 certificate of the total income from April 5 and the income tax paid on it. The practitioner should also check with them whether the certificate includes the final balance.

Pensions

The "accruals basis" applies and therefore the balance to death should **3–30** be included in the deceased's income.

Deceased's Statutory Income and tax Deducted at Source

3–31 The following points should be noted for calculation of income:

Trade or profession. Death is a cessation of the business for tax. The profit to death will have to be calculated in a Profit and Loss Account, which in most cases will be prepared by the deceased's accountant. A sole trader's (untaxed) income will continue into the executry unless the business is terminated at death.

Wages, salaries and occupation pensions (including any unpaid balance) and the IT deducted are vouched by the P60 certificate.

Social security pensions are paid gross including any unpaid balance.

Interest paid gross may have been received from NS products, Government stocks on the NS Register, rent, etc.

STEP 2

3–32 Deduct from the components the amount of any relief under a provision listed in relation to the executor in s.24 of the 2007 Act to which the executor is entitled for the tax year. The sum of the amounts of the components left after this step is the "net income".

Certain matters constitute deductions from total income. The effect of these is sometimes to take sums out of the tax calculation completely so that the income is not treated as the tax payer's. Examples of this are few but the important ones are interest payments on qualifying loans, for example a loan to buy a partnership, which are allowable.[14] There are certain other examples such as payments to trade unions (s.24) and certain payments to pensions.

There are special provisions for gifts to charities and gift aid. These are deducted from the total income.

STEP 3

3–33 Deduct from the amounts of the components left after Step 2 any allowances to which the executor is entitled for the tax year under Ch.2 of Pt 3 of the 2007 Act or ss.257 or 265 of ICTA (individuals: personal allowance and blind person's allowance).

Personal reliefs are deductible at Step 3. These reliefs depend not so much on the type of income but the personal circumstances of the deceased tax payer. Every taxpayer is entitled to a personal allowance of £6,035 in 2008/2009, £6,475 for 2009/2010. This is increased in the case of someone over 65, but under 75 years of age, and is £9,030, £9,490 for 2009/2010. This is increased yet again for persons aged 75 years or over to £9,180.

These allowances are only available for persons on lower incomes. The figure for 2008/2009 is £21,800, £22,900 for 2009/2010 and if the net income exceeds that the allowances are correspondingly reduced but never below the personal allowance limit.

---

[14] ITA 2007 s.383.

It should be noted that spouses and of course civil partners are **3–34** generally treated as single separate entities with their own personal allowances. However, married couples where at least one of the parties to the marriage was born before April 6, 1935 are entitled to an additional allowance. For the year 2008/2009 married couples allowance is £6,535 for the over 65 and £6,625 for the over 75 although this is reduced where income again exceeds the limit of £21,800.

It should be noted that this applies to civil partnerships and new marriages. Please watch out that it is always the claim of the party *who is older* who receives the allowance although in fact they may elect to set against the higher income. Sometimes practitioners must guard against a tendency to "misogyny" by assuming it will be the husband who is the elder!

Marginal Age Relief

During the fiscal year to April 5, 2009 age allowances are reduced by £1 **3–35** for every £2 of income over £21,800 until allowance is reduced to the PA of £6,035. During the reduction, the individual receives "Marginal Age Relief". Interestingly the income during the margin is effectively taxed at a higher rate, potentially up to 30 per cent!

The age qualification applies if the birthday is within the fiscal year, even if it is after death.

The personal allowance should be allocated to the income which is taxed at the highest rate so that the PA receives the full benefit at 20 per cent. (Any PA unused at death is not transferable to the executors or to the surviving spouse, but see under Married Couple's Allowance.) Obviously the executors are not entitled to any personal allowance.

The married couple's allowance is routinely allocated to the husband, but the wife may claim half of the basic allowance without the husband's consent, provided she claims before the fiscal year starts.

The whole of the married couple's allowance may be transferred by **3–36** joint consent to the wife if intimation is lodged before the fiscal year starts, but the husband retains the balance of any allowance due at a higher rate for one of the spouses being over 65.

If the husband's income falls within the margin the AA is first reduced to the basic PA then the higher MCA is reduced to the basic allowance. The wife's income is not taken into account, even if the allowance is given on her age or is transferred to her because the husband's income is too low to use it

STEP 4

Calculate tax at each applicable rate on the amounts of the components **3–37** left after Step 3 of Ch.2 of the 2007 Act for the rates at which income tax is charged and the income charged at particular rates.

The rates of tax at Step 4 depend on the actual type of income being taxed. It is necessary, therefore, to identify the various categories. There are three categories in effect, as follows:

Non-saving income: which is not separately defined in ITA 2007 but broadly covers earnings, pensions, taxable social security benefit, trading profits and income from property. Normally it is received gross apart from earnings which may well have tax deducted under the PAYE system.

Savings income: this is defined in ITA 2007 at s.18 and broadly it covers bank and building society interest. This is generally taxed at basic rate tax and will often have the tax deducted. It may be that a deceased tax payer who is not liable to pay tax because his income is too small can reclaim some of his tax deducted.

Dividend income: which is defined in ITA 2007 at s.19. Dividends are received with a 10 per cent tax credit which is not recoverable even if the deceased is not a tax payer. These amounts of course have to be grossed up if they are net. The gross amount is then included and the tax payer receives credit for any tax already deducted and for the dividend tax credit.

3–38   Section 16 of the ITA 2007 deals with the different types of income and the order in which they are taxed; thus dividends are treated as the highest part of a tax payer's income. Next comes savings income and finally other income. The non-dividend/non-savings income, e.g. rental income, is consequently always taxed first.

The rates charged on dividends differ from the rates charged on savings and other income. For the current year 2008/2009 the non-dividend income has a starting rate of 10 per cent. However, this only covers savings incomes and covers the first £2,230. There follows a basic rate of 20 per cent and this covers £2,231–£36,000. The higher rate of 40 per cent covers £36,000 and above. It should be noted that the starting rate is only available on the savings income.

Danger Warning!!

Please note that if the savings income is taxed after non-savings income the starting rate of 10 per cent will not be available where a tax payer has non-savings income in excess of £2,230.

3–39   Any grossed up dividend, that is to say dividends plus the 10 per cent tax credit, which falls within the basic rate tax band is taxed at 10 per cent. If the grossed up dividend falls within the higher rate band it is taxed at 32.5 per cent, which is also known as the dividend upper rate.

Bank and building society interest was taxed at the basic rate until April 5, 1996 and at the lower rate thereafter, but may have been received gross if the deceased's total income was certified as being within the personal allowance.

Dividends are taxed at the lower rate as explained below.

Dividend Tax Rates 2007–2008

3–40   There are two different Income Tax rates on UK dividends. The rate paid depends on whether the deceased's overall taxable income (after allowances) falls within or above the basic rate Income Tax limit.

The basic rate Income Tax limit is £34,600 for the 2007–2008 tax year.

Dividend income in relation to the basic rate tax band	Tax rate applied after deduction of, e.g. personal allowance and any blind person's allowance
Dividend income which falls below the £34,600 basic rate tax limit	10%
Dividend income above the £34,600 basic rate tax limit	32.5%

It does not matter whether the dividends emanate from a company, unit trusts or open-ended investment companies, as all dividends are taxed the same way.(But bear in mind that "interest distributions" from unit trusts and open-ended investment companies are taxed at the rates for savings income—see below.)

Tax on Savings Income

There are three different Income Tax rates on savings income: 10 per **3–41** cent, 20 per cent or 40 per cent. The rate(s) the deceased pays depends on his overall taxable income.

Special Types of Dividends

In addition to ordinary dividends from UK companies, stock (scrip) **3–42** dividends from UK companies, for which the tax credit is 10 per cent, should be recognised. If an Enhanced Scrip Dividend is received, the market value of the shares on their first trading day is treated as being the net dividend, which is grossed up at 10 per cent to calculate the deemed tax credit.

Taxation of Pensions under PAYE

We are familiar with the arrangements for taxation of wages and salaries **3–43** under Schedule E through PAYE.

The same arrangements apply to the taxation of occupational pensions under the PAYE Regulations. The Regulations provide that retirement is not a cessation of employment. If the employer pays emoluments after death, he must deduct tax.

It is a fallacy to think that the amount of income tax paid must be correct if it is assessed under PAYE. The reality is that repayments are frequently due in life under PAYE and are usually due on death.

The IR issues a Coding Notice to the taxpayer and his employer/ **3–44** pension payer. Coding Notices may be used by the IR for recovering small amounts of IT due for a previous year.

The main purposes are to record the entitlement to allowances and to bring untaxed income into the calculation of the IT by deducting it from the allowances. The untaxed income of pensioners consists of the SS pension and any taxable interest received on NS products, as already noted. After the untaxed income is deducted from the personal allowance a four-figure sum is usually left (after making the deductions). The last digit of it is omitted to make the tax code number. A single letter is added to the code number to indicate the entitlement to allowance or rate of tax, for example:

- L: Basic Personal Allowance only;
- H: Basic Personal Allowance and Married Couple's Allowance or Additional Personal Allowance;
- P: Singe Age Allowance aged 65–74;
- V: Basic rate executor, aged 65–74 and entitled to Age Allowance and Married Couple's Allowance;
- NT: No tax payable;
- BR: Basic Rate tax only;
- DO: All earnings at Higher Rate;
- K: Deductions exceed allowances. The excess is to be taxed as income.

If a pensioner has two occupational pensions, the allowances are allocated to the main pension. The whole of the second pension is taxed at the basic rate.

STEP 5

3–45 Add together the amounts of tax calculated at Step 4. It should be borne in mind that where different types of income are taxable, dividends always form the highest allotted part of the income of the deceased tax payer.

Example

Take the case of Jonathan Ragwort, who has income (earned) of £150,000 per annum. He also receives net interest of £32,000 which grossed up will be £40,000. He also receives a dividend from Pansy Plc of £90.00 with a £10 tax credit.

The earned income will be the first part of his income. Part of it will not be liable to tax at all because he has a personal allowance. The balance will be taxed partly at the basic rate and partly at the higher rate. The savings income will be taxed next. It is likely that it will all fall into the higher rate band and he will liable to pay tax at 40 per cent on the £40,000. He will of course have had the benefit of the 20 per cent tax deducted at source and will therefore only have to pay additional 20 per cent! The dividend is in fact to be taxed last and he will have to pay an additional 20 per cent on all of it. As stated the dividend is taxed last and will all fall into the higher rate tax band. As it turns out he is liable to tax at 32.5 per cent on it but he has the benefit of the whole 10 per cent tax credit.

3–46 If he did not have any earnings earned, that is to say non-savings income, the interest then would be taxed first. As before some of it would not be liable to tax because of the personal allowance. The next tranche would be taxed at the 10 per cent starting rate available and the balance at basic rate. The dividend would be taxed at the dividend ordinary rate and he would have no further liability to tax. He might be entitled to a small refund on the portion or part of the savings income which fell into the starting rate band.

Example

Frederick Foxglove on the other hand has interest of £900 which is grossed up to be £1,125. He also has a dividend of £18,000 with a £200 tax credit. It is likely he will be able to recover all the tax already paid on the interest, i.e. £225, but the dividend tax credit is not repayable.

Reference is made to the example towards the end of the Chapter of Miss Wednesday Next to show how other items interact with a slightly more complicated example.

STEP 6

Deduct from the amount of tax calculated at Step 5 any tax reductions to **3–47** which the executor is entitled for the tax year under a provision listed in relation to the executor in s.26 of the 2007 Act.

Sections 27 to 29 contain for further provision about the deduction of those tax reductions. They concern such matters as certain business reliefs and those relating to maintenance payments. Section 27 deals with the order of deducting these.

STEP 7

Add to the amount of tax left after Step 6 any amounts of tax for which **3–48** the executor is liable for the tax year under any provision listed in relation to the executor in s.30 of the 2007 Act. The result is the executor's liability to income tax for the tax year.

In summary the matters which the practitioner needs to focus on are as follows:

- the character of income;
- whether it is taxable or not;
- when it will be taxed;
- calculation of the tax; and
- when the tax is payable.

REVENUE ENQUIRIES

It sometimes occurs that after the death and following upon the issue of **3–49** Confirmation, HM Revenue & Customs may initiate an enquiry into the tax affairs of the deceased. The powers for this are contained in s.28A(1) and (2) of the Taxes Management Act 1970. This can prove a time-consuming and sometimes pointless, but always expensive, exercise and will generally involve obtaining bank statements going back several years and details of other information. If it occurs, it is clearly important that obtaining the information is addressed as soon as possible. Specialised help should be sought at the earliest possible time if it appears complicated. When the information is available, it should be passed to the appropriate branch of HM Revenue & Customs. This will generally be a compliance section of a local area. When the enquiry is completed, the executor and his practitioner will be advised of the position. It may be that an amendment is required to a return as a result of the enquiry. Alternatively, no amendment may be required. In the former case, there is a right of appeal within 30 days of the date of the notice. This appeal must be in writing and should state the grounds for the appeal on Form SA536. It is also possible to ask to postpone payment of any tax. If the basis on which to settle the appeal is not agreed, it will generally be considered by independent appeal commissioners. There is a Revenue leaflet entitled, "Tax Appeals. A Guide to Appealing against Decisions of the Inland Revenue on Tax and Other Matters". This can be viewed at the Revenue's website at *http://www.hmrc.gov.uk* [accessed April 20, 2009].

How to Recognise when a Repayment of Tax is Due

3–50 We have been dealing with payment of tax up to the date of death. However, often the converse will be the case! Indeed it may be possible to identify not only if a repayment is due for the current year but also for the recent preceding years as well. It is possible to go back six years before the year in which the date of death occurred. A repayment will be due when income is taxed above the correct rate. The Personal/Age Allowance must be taken up by taxable income, which is not taxed. The lower rate band must be taken up by income, which is taxed at 20 per cent. Each of the bands must be filled with income taxed at the appropriate rate. The following tests will indicate whether a repayment is due.

PAYE Coding

Checking PAYE Coding Notices

Cracking the code

3–51 A tax code is used by an employer or those paying superannuation to determine the amount of tax to deduct from pay or superannuation. If they have the wrong tax code the executor will pay too much or too little tax. It is typically made up of one letter and several numbers, e.g. 128L or K389. The executor can get a good idea of what the deceased's (or what HM Revenue & Customs think the) income is from the coding. If the tax code is a number followed by a letter the executor multiplies the number in the executor's tax code by 10; this gives the total amount of income which the executor can earn in a year before paying tax; the letter shows how the number should be adjusted following any changes to allowances announced by the Chancellor.

It is worth while taking some time to become acquainted with the meaning of these letters. Common tax code letters are explained below.

Code	Reason for use
L	for those eligible for the basic personal allowance (this is also used as an emergency tax code)
P	for persons aged 65 to 74 and eligible for the full personal allowance

Code	Reason for use
V	for persons aged 65 to 74, eligible for the full personal allowance and the full married couple's allowance (for those born before April 6, 1935 and aged under 75) and estimated to be liable at the basic rate of tax
Y	for persons aged 75 or over and eligible for the full personal allowance
T	if there are any other items HMRC needs to review in the deceased's tax code
K	when the executor's total allowances are less than the deceased's total "deductions"

If the tax code has two letters but no number, or is the letter "D" followed by a zero, it normally indicates that the deceased had two or more sources of income and that all of the deceased's allowances have been applied to the tax code and income from his main employment or pension.

BR	Is used when all the income is taxed at the basic rate—formerly 22 per cent. From April 6, 2008 the basic rate is 20 per cent (most commonly used for a second employment or pension)
DO	Is used when all the deceased's income is taxed at the higher rate of tax—currently 40% (most commonly used for a second employment or pension)
NT	Is used when no tax is to be taken from the deceased's income or pension

3–52 If the deceased had two employment incomes or pensions, it is likely that all of the second income will be taxed at the basic or higher rate—depending on how much the deceased earned. This is because all of the allowances will have been used against the income from the main employment or pension.

The employer will use an emergency tax code where, for example, a taxpayer starts a new employment or pension and the pay is above the PAYE threshold or if the deceased did not give his new employer a P45 when starting a new employment. An emergency tax code is also used in certain special cases, for example if the taxpayer gives the employer a P45 after May 24 but it applies to a previous year.

If there is no higher rate liability, is the income below the threshold for Marginal Age Relief? If the income is within the margin, an exact calculation will be required, because the AA and higher MCA reduce with each £2 of income.

3–53 To summarise therefore: a four-figure sum is usually left after making the deductions. The last digit of it is omitted to make the tax code number. As stated, a single letter is added to the code number to indicate the entitlement to allowance or rate of tax, for example:

- L: Basic Personal Allowance only;
- H: Basic Personal Allowance and Married Couple's Allowance or Additional Personal Allowance;
- P: Singe Age Allowance aged 65–74;
- V: Basic rate executor, aged 65–74 and entitled to Age Allowance and Married Couple's Allowance;
- NT: No tax payable;
- BR: Basic Rate tax only;
- DO: All earnings at Higher Rate;
- K: Deductions exceed allowances. The excess is to be taxed as income.

3–54 The PAYE system will only work effectively if the Coding Notices are accurate. The restriction of the MCA is particularly confusing. The full allowance is given, but it has to be restricted by a deduction to ensure that the relief is given at the appropriate rate. The amount of the restriction will depend whether the executor's marginal rate of tax is at the basic or higher rate.

Elderly executors may not have the ability, or more likely the inclination, to check their codes and may forget to intimate a change of circumstances to the Revenue, with the result that errors may not be corrected, such as:

- an entitlement to AA or marginal AA following a reduction of the taxed investment income. The revenue should recognise an entitlement to AA following an increase in the statutory income limit, but they may fail to amend the coding; Action: check that the allowance is appropriate for the executor's age and income;
- a deduction for untaxed income from a source that no longer exists. Action: check that a deduction is still appropriate;
- a deduction for untaxed income, which exceeds the income being received following a reduction in the interest rate. Action: check that the amount of the deduction is correct;
- a deliberate withholding of allowances by HM Revenue & Customs as a result the deceased's failure to submit a Tax Return. Action: write to HM Revenue & Customs.

Allowances at Death Under PAYE

3–55 Is sufficient income paid gross to cover the Personal/Age Allowance? (For example, from state pension or occupational pensions and NS interest.) If not, a repayment at 20 per cent will be due on the excess of the allowance, provided there is sufficient other income available to cover the excess.

If only savings are available, the repayment will be at 20 per cent. Repayments are frequently due to an elderly wife with a non-contributory state pension because her age allowance substantially exceeds her restricted state pension. If the taxable income paid gross exceeds the Personal/Age Allowance, tax will be due at 20 per cent on the excess.

Personal/Age Allowance

3–56 If the occupational pension does not take up the whole of the appropriate tax band, is there sufficient non-savings income to cover the balance of it? Where the rates were different, i.e. non savings at 22 per cent and savings at 20 per cent, a repayment at two per cent (22 per cent minus 20 per cent) will be due. Since April 6, 2008 these rates are the same and this would only apply to periods pre-April 6, 2008.

Basic Rate Band

Repayments may be due as a result of errors in PAYE coding as noted above arising from a failure to intimate a change of the executor's circumstances or a deliberate reduction of allowances by the HMRC. **3–57**

Higher and Basic Rate Band

A repayment on income taxed under PAYE will be due at death (unless the death is at the end of the fiscal year) because the full PA/AA and MCA are due for any part of the tax year of death (however short), but the PAYE system allocates only an equal proportion of the year's allowances at each payment of salary, wage or pension. See Derby's example. **3–58**

Examples of Repayment Calculations

Example: Mrs Marjoram

Mrs Raina Marjoram died on March 7, 2009. Her income consisted of dividends gross of £540 and bank and building society income of £2,530; this was after deduction of tax at 20 per cent of £632.50. She also had a state pension amounting to £5,274. At her date of death she was widowed and aged 79. **3–59**

The non-savings income, i.e. the state pension of £5,274 absorbs the first £5,274 of her allowance of £9,180.

The rest is dedicated to the non-dividend savings income of £3,163 and the balance of £744 to the dividend income. This latter is in fact lost because the tax on this is not repayable.

It can be seen at a glance therefore that the entire tax on the non-dividend income, i.e. £632.50 will be repayable.

It should be noted that this is on a relatively modest estate and a modest income.

Example: John and Mary

John has not yet retired and has a gross income of about £25,000. He dies of a heart attack on May 31, 2008 aged 63, survived by his wife Mary, aged 61. **3–60**

John's total income to the date of his death is less than his Personal Allowance of £6,035 and therefore all the income tax deducted or credited as paid on his salary and savings income is repayable. The Married Couple's Allowance is not available since neither of the spouses were born before April 6, 1935.

Mary is not entitled to age allowance because she is not yet 65. She may receive the SS Widow's Pension, unless she is already receiving a Retirement Pension on her own contributions, in which case she will get nothing more.

Example: Derby and Joan

Derby had a gross income of over £22,000 in 2008/2009, consisting of a state pension and an occupational pension taxed under PAYE and savings income. His wife, Joan, had a non-contributory state pension and a modest **3–61** *amount of investment income. Joan died in May 2008 aged 76. Derby was heartbroken and died on October 6, 2008 aged 74 years and nine months.*

Joan is entitled to the higher Age Allowance (£9,180), which fully covers her state pension (£5,012) and her investment income. The pension paid would be about £200, leaving a balance of age allowance. All the income tax paid on her savings income to the date of her death is repayable.

Derby was only entitled to the basic Personal Allowance and Married Couple's Allowance in 2008/2009, because his income was over the limit for Marginal Age Relief. In 2008/2009 his income was about £11,000 to the date of his death. He is entitled to the higher Age Allowance of £9,180 because his 75th birthday would have occurred during the fiscal year of his death. He is also entitled to the higher MCA based on Joan's age during the fiscal year.

If the deceased has paid too much tax under this temporary code, the executor will get a refund.

Transferring the Married Couple's Allowance or the Blind Person's Allowance

3–62   The deceased executor's spouse or civil partner might have been claiming Married Couple's Allowance or Blind Person's Allowance. If there was not enough income in the year they died to use up all the allowance, the survivor can ask HM Revenue & Customs to transfer the balance left to them. They do this by completing a Form 575 Notice of transfer of surplus Income Tax allowance.

Processing a Repayment Claim

3–63   If the deceased was in business on his own account, his accountant should be asked to adjust the income tax to death. Self-employed persons have been assessed on a current year basis since April 6, 1996 in anticipation of self-assessment from April 6, 1997. The income tax due for 2007/2008 was payable on January 31, 2008 and July 31, 2008.

If the deceased was in partnership, the partnership deed may have to be checked to see whether the remaining partners can insist on a continuation. If additional income tax is due, it will be a debt on the estate.

If the deceased was receiving untaxed income or was liable for income tax at the Higher Rate, he may have been completing a tax return each year. HM Revenue & Customs may ask the executors to complete a full return.

3–64   If the deceased was receiving regular repayments, a form for the next claim should have been issued with the last repayment and may be used.

The Inspector will require for the repayment:

- the claim form which may be either a form R27, a form R40 or a self-assessment tax return signed by (usually) one of the executors; and
- a mandate signed by the executors authorising payment to the firm, failing which the repayment cheque will be made payable to the executors. The Repayment Claim form and the self-assessment tax return incorporate a mandate.

Apart from the Form 64–8 the following may not need to be sent until requested:

- Sufficient vouchers to cover the amount of tax repayable. HM Revenue & Customs may not need these to be sent but they should be available in case they are needed to vouch the claim.
- The executor may have to obtain formal tax deduction certificates from banks and building societies. If a tax return is required, all the income must be vouched.
- The Confirmation, so that the Inspector can check that the assets at death agree with the sources of income in the last tax return. A Certificate of Confirmation of the amount repayable is not usually accepted.
- Mandate Form 64–8 to allow the Inspector to issue copies of any assessments and other notices to the executor.
- Often now HM Revenue & Customs issue a Form 27, which is similar to a repayment claim and is suitable for more straightforward repayment claims. Unfortunately, this sometimes means that the executor is involved in an extra form!

Form R27

When HMRC are advised of a death, they will normally send Form R27: **3–65** potential repayment to the estate to the executors. They say that they will try to send it to the "professional" executor, if known, but generally they may send it to the deceased's address or to the first-named executor. It is important for the practitioner to write to HM Revenue & Customs so that the widow or spouse is not troubled by receipt of correspondence from HMRC which often causes much grief to the bereaved. The form includes a repayment claim which must be claimed within five years from January 31 following the end of the tax year it relates to.

Form R40

The deceased may have regularly used Form R40 to claim back tax **3–66** deducted from their bank or building society interest. If they did, the executor can use this form straight away to claim any repayment due for the period to the date of death. As stated, HM Revenue & Customs may also require Form 27 to be completed, but not p.2, the section on income and allowances. In their website HMRC state:

> "It takes us some time to finalise the person's tax position, so please allow four weeks after the [executor] sent us the form before contacting us about the repayment."

Completing a Self-Assessment Tax Return

The deceased might have normally completed a tax return. The executor **3–67** can complete one for the period from the start of the tax year to the date of death. HMRC will send a self assessment form or it can be downloaded from the website. HMRC may also require Form R27 to be completed but not page 2, the section on income and allowances. HMRC have a helpful guide, "Completing a tax return on behalf of someone who has died".[15]

It is possible to go back six years over and above the existing year.

TAXATION OF INVESTMENT BONDS MATURING ON DEATH

3–68 These types of investments are very popular. They can be "tailored" almost to meet the individual requirements and personal investment/risk profiles of investors. Most of these investment bonds are written as non-qualifying single-premium life policies. They are normally effected as single premium life assurance policies. As such, they enjoy a different tax treatment from other investments. This can lead to some valuable tax-planning opportunities for individuals. The favoured tax treatment stems from the "chargeable event" rules. The company pays tax on income and capital gains accrued within its funds. HMRC take the view that payment of this tax equates to the taxpayer having paid capital gains tax and basic rate income tax; accordingly there is no further personal liability to capital gains tax or basic rate income tax on the proceeds from the executor bond. However, the tax paid is not able to be reclaimed by basic-rate or non-taxpayers. "Non-qualifying" means that the profits of the policy do not qualify for exemption under TA 1988 Sch.15. If a chargeable event occurs, and a gain is realised, a taxpayer may be liable to higher rate income tax. A "chargeable event" generally arises on the death of the person whose life is assured.

Investment Bonds have to be distinguished from Personal Portfolio Bonds in which the bondholder can control the way in which the bond is invested. Personal Portfolio Bonds are now subject to an annual charge on a deemed gain of 15 per cent unless the bondholder's choice is restricted to "acceptable investments" as defined in the regulations.

The arrangements for taxation of ordinary Investment Bonds depends whether the bond is with a UK company or an offshore company as follows.

3–69 If the bond is with a UK company basic IT is paid by the company and the bondholder pays higher rate IT if there is a chargeable event such as the maturity of the bond, an assignation or the withdrawal of more than five per cent of the initial investment.

If the bond is with an offshore company, there is no charge until the chargeable event and then the bondholder pays at his marginal rate.

In each, the company has to advise the bondholder of the amount of the taxable gain made on the chargeable event.

If the estate contains an investment bond, which becomes repayable on death, the valuation letter received from the insurance company will intimate that the death was a chargeable event and will calculate the chargeable gain, which the company has to report to the Revenue. This terminology is confusing and suggests that there could be a capital gains tax liability, whereas the chargeable gain is in fact subject to income tax.

---

[15] See *www.hmrc.gov.uk/sa/behalf-who-has-died.htm* (accessed June 17, 2009).

Generally, if the policy rights were vested in a taxpayer immediately **3–70** before the chargeable event (the death), the amount of the gain will be deemed to be part of his income for the year in which the event happened (i.e. the deceased's income to date of death and not the executry income). If the bond had matured or had been surrendered by the deceased before his death, the gain would have formed part of his income of that year.

If the policy rights were vested in the executors immediately before the chargeable event, the amount of the gain will be deemed to be part of the income of the deceased's estate. This provision would apply, for example, if the policy did not mature at death and was surrendered by the executors. In those circumstances the gain will be deemed to have borne IT at the basic rate, so that the executors do not have to pay any IT on the gain. The deemed IT credit is not repayable and the gain must be apportioned among the beneficiaries in a way that is just and reasonable.

The significance of these provisions is in the certification of the beneficiaries' income from the estate. Non-taxpayers will not be able to recover the IT deemed to have been paid. Those on lower and basic rates will have no more to pay, but the higher rate paying beneficiary will have to pay extra IT on his share of the gain.

The surrender of a bond by executors will be a rare event. If the bond **3–71** did not mature on death it will probably be a bond on joint lives maturing on the death of the surviving spouse. In that event the first death is not a chargeable event and no IT is then payable.

The whole profit on investment bonds in excess of the initial investment is taxable. The profit, including the withdrawals made during the life of the bond, is spread over the life and the proportion applicable to the final year is added to the investor's income as the top slice of his income for the calculation of the rate of tax, which is then applied to the full profit.

If part of the slice falls within the basic rate band, no additional IT is due on the part within the basic rate. This is known as "top slicing relief". If the investor already pays IT at the higher rate, no relief will be due and the whole profit will be subject to IT.

Withdrawals made during the life of the bond are also exempt from higher rate IT if they do not exceed five per cent of the initial investment until the whole of the initial investment has been withdrawn (usually after 20 years at five per cent). Larger percentages may be withdrawn tax-free if they do not bring the investor within the IT higher rate band or if less than five per cent has been withdrawn in earlier years and the average withdrawals to date do not exceed five per cent a year.

Chargeable Events

A liability to Higher Rate Income Tax may arise if a chargeable event **3–72** occurs, a chargeable event gain or "profit" arises in the event of the bondholder's death, or if the deceased withdrew more than five per cent per policy year of the amount which he had paid into the bond.

This five per cent withdrawal allowance is cumulative, and any unused part can be carried forward to future years, subject to the total cumulative five per cent allowance amount not exceeding 100 per cent of the amount the deceased paid into the bond.

When a chargeable event thus occurs, the company sends details of the chargeable event gain to the Revenue. They also send details to the executor. These details are used to calculate whether there is any Higher Rate Income Tax to pay. Gains may also affect the executor entitlement to Higher Personal Allowance (Age Allowance). As Basic Rate Income Tax is treated as already paid, the maximum rate of Income Tax which may become payable is the difference between the Higher Rate of Income Tax and the Basic Rate of Income Tax.

3–73   A chargeable event will occur on the death of the life assured. In this situation, the tax treatment is the same as if the bond had been finally cashed in immediately before death. Any gain or "profit" is calculated on the cashing-in value rather than the total amount which is actually paid on the death claim.

Any tax liability on withdrawals is calculated on the amount withdrawn in excess of the accumulated five per cent allowances. The gain or "profit" which is taxed is the amount of this excess which falls into the higher rate tax bracket when added to the deceased's taxable income for the tax year in which the policy anniversary, following the excess, falls.

"Top-slicing relief" may reduce the tax liability on any excess. To work out the profit slice, the excess is divided by the number of complete years which the bond has been held, or since the last chargeable event, if less. The amount of the profit slice is then added to the executor's taxable income. Any part of the profit slice which falls into the higher rate tax bracket is taxable at the difference between Higher Rate of Income Tax and the Basic Rate of Income Tax. The total tax due is calculated by multiplying this amount of tax on the profit slice by the number of complete policy years which the bond has been held (or by the number of complete policy years since the last chargeable event, if less). Top-slicing can reduce the executor's tax liability if none of the executor's taxable income, before the profit slice, would have been subject to higher rate tax.

Tax liability on final cashing in

3–74   Any tax liability on final cashing in or death is based on the gain or "profit" (if any) which the Bond has made. This profit is the amount the executor receives when the executor cashes in the executor bond plus all previous withdrawals, less the total amount the executor has paid in plus any excesses over the accumulated five per cent allowances. Top-slicing relief then applies on final encashment as follows. The Revenue divides the profit by the number of complete policy years which the bond has been held to give the profit slice. The profit slice is added to the executor's taxable income, and any part which falls into the Higher Rate Income Tax bracket becomes liable to tax at the difference between the Higher Rate of Income Tax and the Basic Rate of Income Tax. The total amount of tax due is calculated by multiplying the amount of complete policy years which the bond has been held.

Example: investment bonds

3–75   *A. Mateur, who regarded himself as a professional financial adviser, invested £10,000 in a single premium investment bond with the Ripoff Insurance Company (a UK company). The bond was written as a non-*

qualifying life policy. He arranged to take withdrawals of five per cent (£500) as tax-free income because he was then a higher rate executor. The payments were tax-free because they represented repayments of his capital.

Five years later, disillusioned by the lack of growth in his bond, he surrendered it and invested the proceeds in the purchase of a red vintage sports car in an attempt to regain his lost youth. Unfortunately he died two months later within the same fiscal year.

The surrender of the bond was a chargeable event giving rise to the following chargeable gain:

Proceeds of surrender	*£11,500*
Less original investment	*£10,000*
	£ 1,500
Withdrawals during life of bond	
5 years @ £500	*£ 2,500*
Chargeable gain	*£ 4,000*

Applying top-slicing over the five-year life of the bond produces a net chargeable gain of £800 (£4,000 5), which is added to his gross income to establish any higher rate liability. If Mr Mateur's income exceeded the Basic Rate limit by, say, £500 after adding the £800, the £300 would be relieved of any additional IT, but the £500 would be subject to income tax at the Higher Rate. The tax due would be £500 x 5 (the bond's life) = £2,500 x 17 per cent—£425.

If Mr Mateur had not surrendered his bond, his death would have been the chargeable event and the chargeable gain would have fallen into his income to the date of his death under s.547(1)(a). If IT is payable on the chargeable gain at death, it will be a debt on the estate for calculation of the IHT.

The following is a slightly more complex example of income tax liability.

Example: Miss Wednesday Next

Wednesday Next, a hard-worked market gardener, died on October 10, 2008 **3–76** *aged 58. After diligent enquiry and despite the obstruction of various agencies, the solicitors charged with winding up her estate find as follows:*

- *Her share of profits for the tax year 2008/2009 amounted £60,000.*
- *She received, during the period from April 6, 2008 to date of death, interest from the Thursday Building Society of £6,000.*
- *A Dividend of £990 was paid to the account from Friday Investment Trust Plc on October 2, 2008.*
- *A dividend of £1,000 was paid to her account from the Saturday Investment Trust Plc on October 11, 2008.*

The dividend of £1,000 from Saturday Investments is income during the course of the administration.

1	Calculate Total Income	
	Trading profit	£60,000.00
	Interest—grossed up	
	£6,000 × 100/80	£7,500.00
		£67,500.00
	Dividend—Grossed up	
	£990 × 100/90	£1,100.00
		£68,600.00
2	Deduct allowable reliefs	nil
		£68,600.00
3	Deduct Personal Allowance	(£5,435)
		£63,165.00
4	Tax on net income	
	The trading income is dealt with first	
	These receipts are greater than the starting rate band, accordingly none of the savings income will be taxed at the starting rate.	
	Everything except the dividend income will be taxed at the basic rate (20%) or the higher rate (40%)	
On the first	£36,000 at 20%	£7,200.00
On the remaining	£26,565 (£60,000.00 + £7,500.00 − £5,435) at 40%	£10,626.00
		£17,826.00
	The dividend income of £1,100 is taxed as the highest part of the deceased's income at 32.5%	£357.75
		£18,183.50
	However Wednesday has a tax credit of	
	10% on the dividend (£110) and a tax credit on the building society interest of £1,500!	£1,610.00
5	The tax due by the executors is:	£16,573.50

Please note that this is the figure which should be claimed as a debt due against the estate for IHT purposes. Often, when the inventory is being compiled it is appropriate to include an estimate of the tax due or indeed the tax repayment. It is important to advise HMRC at the earliest opportunity of the revised figure.

Compensation for Loss of the 10 per cent Tax Band

The Chancellor has announced his proposals to compensate those **3–77** affected by the loss of the 10 per cent starting rate tax band for earned and pension income. The proposal is to increase the basic personal allowance (tax-free income) for those under 65 by £600 to £6,035 (from £5,435). This is equivalent to a tax saving of £120 per year (£600 at 20 per cent) for a basic rate executor. The points to note are as follows:

1. Workers under 65 on income roughly between £7,000 and £9,000 per annum are still likely to pay more tax this year than they did in 2007/2008, though the tax rises are reduced by the new proposals. For example, an individual on an income of £7,455, who would only have paid tax at 10 per cent last year, would still pay about £40 more in tax and national insurance this year.
2. As personal allowances and tax bands are usually increased each Budget, the losses to low income executors relative to other tax payers are much higher. If the personal allowance and starting rate band had been increased as usual, low income tax payers could have expected to pay less tax in 2008/2009. On this basis taxpayers earning about £7,500 could be considered still to be losing out by £100 or more per year
3. For employees, the increase in the personal allowance is expected to take effect in September. This is to allow coding notices to be amended. The result will be a "catch up" rebate of £60 of tax in the September pay packet, and after that a reduction of £10 per month for the rest of the tax year.
4. People over 65 do not come within the scope of this "compensation" package. This is because increased allowances for this age group were introduced from April 2008.
5. Higher rate tax payers will not gain any advantage because the point at which higher rate tax is paid will be reduced. Tax of 40 per cent will now be due when income for those under 5 reaches £40,835 (£6,035 personal allowance plus £34,800 basic rate band). Under the original Budget proposals it would have been £41,435.
6. The 10 per cent savings rate may be of use to a few more people aged under 65. For the savings rate band to apply, total income, including savings, must be below the personal allowance plus £2,320. This is now £8,355 for those under 65. (For comparison the limits are £11,350 for those aged 65 to 74 and £11,500 for those aged over 75.)

Attention!!

Sometimes it is possible to ascertain from the tax coding or elsewhere that the deceased was entitled to a tax repayment possibly going back several years. This can occur most frequently if the tax coding shows the deceased as unmarried or under age or otherwise.

Chapter Four

CAPITAL GAINS TAX TO DATE OF DEATH

"Unless there's action, all is vain; faith proves itself in deeds."[1]

4–01 Capital Gains Tax Facts for the Years Ending April 5

	2008	2009
The Annual Exempt Amount (AEA)	£9,200 for individuals executries (first 3 years) and £4,600 for some trustees	£9,600 for individuals executries (first 3 years) and £4,800 for some trustees
CGT Tax Rates		
Individuals	10%, 20% or 40%	18%
Trusts and estates	40%	18%
Exemptions		
Individuals and estates***	£9,200	£9,600
Trusts	£4,600	£4,800
Chattels (proceeds) 5/3 of excess gain chargeable	£6,000	£6,000
Date Return to be made		
Date payment to be made	To be paid (along with any balance of income tax due on January 31 following the end of the tax year)	
Penalty for late payment and time limits for submission		
Broadly speaking as for income tax		

---

[1] CH (Church Hymnary) 4—Hymn 710.

> **Danger Warning!!**
>
> **The exemption for executry estates only lasts for the three fiscal years from and including the year in which the deceased passed away.**

THE LEGISLATION

The legislation is contained in the Taxation of Chargeable Gains Act **4–02** 1992 ("TCGT 1992").[2]

INTRODUCTION

Capital gains tax ("CGT") was first introduced in 1965 on capital gains **4–03** made on the disposal of assets by individuals, executors and trustees. The basis of CGT is that it is paid when a chargeable person disposes of chargeable assets; this gives rise to the chargeable gain unless an exemption or a relief is applicable. As with most taxes CGT is charged on a "current year basis", that is to say the tax will arise and be assessable during the tax year from April 6 to April 5.

CAPITAL GAINS TAX

The deceased's executors will be liable for tax on any capital gains **4–04** realised during the period to the date of death. This is reported under the normal self-assessment rules, but the time limit for assessment is restricted to three years after January 31 following the year of assessment in which the death occurred (Taxes Management Act 1970 s.40(1)).

Assessment on personal representatives

40.—(1) For the purpose of the charge of tax on the executors of a deceased person in respect of the income, or chargeable gains, which arose or accrued to him before his death, the time allowed by sections 34, 35 or 36 above shall in no case extend more than 4 years after the end of the year of assessment in which the deceased died.

(2) In a case involving a loss of tax brought about carelessly or deliberately by a person who has died (or another person acting on that person's behalf before that person's death), an assessment on his personal representatives to tax for any year of assessment ending not earlier than six years before his death may be made at any time [not more than 4 years after the end of] the year of assessment in which he died.

---

[2] All references in this Chapter are to this Act.

(3) In this section "tax" means income tax or capital gains tax.

(4) Any act or omission such as is mentioned in section 98B below on the part of a grouping (as defined in that section) or member of a grouping shall be deemed for the purposes of subsection (2) above to be the act or omission of each member of the grouping.

The annual exemption is £9,600 for 2008/2009. Capital gains of up to the amount of the annual exemption may be realised tax-free each tax year. Executry estates also have their own annual exemption in the tax year of the death and the following two tax years. Taper relief and indexation were abolished in the budget of 2008. Capital losses are, in the first instance, automatically set off against gains arising in the same tax year. Any surplus is carried forward for set off against future gains. Generally speaking, capital losses may not be carried back. However on death, where obviously it is not possible to carry the loss forward, it may be carried back. In the general case losses must be realised by April 5, 2009 in order to be set off against 2008/2009 capital gains. If the losses incurred in the period reduce the net capital gains of the period below the level of the annual exemption then some of this exemption is effectively lost. Where losses have been set off against gains eligible for taper relief (pre-April 5, 2008), that relief has effectively been wasted. Hence, the timing of the disposal of any assets standing at a loss should be considered very carefully, bearing the above points in mind.

While the method of taxing capital gains, as well as taper and indexation, was abolished, an example has been produced for the previous regime as follows.

Rate of CGT (For years prior to 2008/2009)

4–05 Chargeable gains were taxed at income tax rates. An individual's net chargeable gains for the year are treated as the top slice of income in computing CGT. CGT was charged at the starting rate (10 per cent), lower rate (20 per cent), or higher rate (40 per cent).

Example

In 2006/2007, James Helleborine had earned income of £4,300. He had no other income but has incurred a chargeable gain of £40,000 (after deduction of the annual CGT exemption—see below).

James has no liability to income tax because his income is below the personal allowance threshold of £5,224—therefore the 10 per cent band is available. CGT is:

£2,230 @ 10% = £215
£17,850 @ 20% = £3,570
Capital gains tax payable is £3,785

If James' income for the year was £10,000 (i.e. all of the 10 per cent band used by his earned income) then all of the chargeable gain of £40,000 would be taxable at 20 per cent—£4000 CGT payable.

If his income for the year was £50,000 then all of the chargeable gain of £40,000 would be taxable at 40 per cent—£8,000 CGT payable.

If his income is below the 40 per cent income tax threshold but the chargeable gain pushes him above the 40 per cent threshold then some of the gain will be taxed at 20 per cent and some at 40 per cent. His CGT liability will therefore range from £4,000 to £8,000.

For an individual the first tranche of gain in a fiscal year is free of CGT. This annual exempt amount is indexed linked and is currently £9,200 for 2007/08 (£8,800 for 2006/2007). Husband and wife are each entitled to a separate annual exemption.

CHANGES FOR 2008/2009

For the tax year 2008/2009 there is a single rate of capital gains tax at 18 **4–06** per cent. This applies to individual executors, trustees and executors. The 18 per cent does not does not affect the income tax rates.

For disposals on or after April 6, 2008 and held over gains coming into charge on or after April 6, 2008 taper relief will no longer be available (even if assets were held before this date) and the chargeable gain will be liable to tax at the new rate of 18 per cent (subject to the deduction of allowable losses, any other reliefs and the annual exemption).

For disposals on or after April 6, 2008 indexation allowance will no longer be available in computing the gain arising. This change will only affect assets which were acquired before April 6, 1998.

As a result of these changes, individuals disposing of assets on or after April 6, 2008 will work out the tax due as follows (please note that the example uses the 2007/2008 annual exemption allowance—"AEA"—for illustrative purposes).

Example

In 1994 Mr Oregano purchased a holiday home for £100,000. He sells it in July 2008 for £250,000. The capital gains tax due is calculated by deducting the purchase cost of £100,000 from the sale proceeds of £250,000 to give a gain of £150,000. Assuming he has no other capital gains in the tax year 2008/2009 and leaving to one side the purchase and sale expenses, he can deduct from this the full annual exemption of £9,200 giving a chargeable gain of £140,800. That gain is taxed at 18 per cent giving tax payable of £25,344.

Capital Gains Tax (CGT)

The Chancellor confirmed the new standard rate of 18 per cent, coupled **4–07** with the withdrawal of indexation allowance and taper relief for individuals and trustees, with effect from April 6, 2008. Other reliefs, such as those relating to principal private residences, losses brought forward, Enterprise Investment Scheme and Venture Capital Trusts, and business asset rollover relief, will continue to be available. Assets acquired before March 31, 1982 will be deemed to have had a cost equivalent to their market value at that date.

In certain circumstances, the CGT base cost of an asset is tied to its value ascertained for inheritance tax ("IHT") purposes. A correction made necessary by the IHT changes noted below means this rule will not apply where the value does not have to be ascertained for IHT purposes on the death of an individual.

The Annual Exempt Amount ("AEA") will be increased for 2008/2009 to £9,600 for individuals and £4,800 for some trustees.

CAPITAL GAINS TAX TO DATE OF DEATH

Preliminary

4–08 Capital Gains Tax liability arises where chargeable assets are disposed of by a taxable person giving rise to a chargeable gain unless a relief or exemption applies. Death per se does not give rise to CGT liability— TCGA 1992 s.62(1)—which may be considered under three separate headings:

    1. disposals made by the deceased up to date of death;
    2. disposals by the executors during period of administration; and
    3. disposals to beneficiaries of assets they have received from the deceased's estate.

Disposals Made by the Deceased up to Date of Death

4–09 The deceased may have made disposals upon which capital gains tax arises and which liability has not been discharged prior to date of death. The executors must ensure that a full capital gains tax return is made for the period from the preceding April 6 to date of death and for any previous year for which liability has not been agreed. They must calculate the liability according to the following principles and pay the tax at the appropriate rates. Conversely, they must investigate whether this can be reduced by any unrelieved losses.

Death: general provisions

62.—(1) . . .
    (2) Allowable losses sustained by an individual in the year of assessment in which he dies may, so far as they cannot be deducted from chargeable gains accruing in that year, be deducted from chargeable gains accruing to the deceased in the 3 years of assessment preceding the year of assessment in which the death occurs, taking chargeable gains accruing in a later year before those accruing in an earlier year.
    (2A) Amounts deductible from chargeable gains for any year in accordance with subsection (2) above shall not be so deductible from any such gains so far as they are gains that are treated as accruing by virtue of section 87 or 89(2) (read, where appropriate, with section 10A).
    (3)–(10) . . .

In addition, existing losses disappear at death. Where an individual is terminally ill unrelieved losses can be preserved by transferring such assets to a spouse on a no gain/no loss basis.

    Where the disposal is less than the acquisition value, relief can be obtained on that loss (s.16); loss is set off initially against gains in the same year, thereafter against future gains. Obviously this may not be relevant in an executry situation. The deceased cannot carry his losses forward. Section 62(2), however, permits losses sustained in the period from April 6 to date of death to be set off against chargeable gains of the deceased in the preceding three years, taking the latter year first. In addition losses sustained on the disposal of certain shares in trading companies can be set off against liability to income tax. Please note losses carried forward or back are deducted only as necessary to reduce the year's gain to the exempt amount. Any capital gains tax thus repayable will be an asset of the estate.

Capital losses can normally only be set against gains arising in the **4–10** same year of assessment or, if in excess of any such gains, carried forward. However, TCGA 1992 s.62(2) provides that capital gains tax losses arising in the year of death may be "carried back"; these losses may be set off against gains arising in the deceased's lifetime, but only during the previous three years of assessment. The losses are to be set off against more recent years before earlier years. The example below illustrates this.

Example—Carry back of capital losses

During the period from April 5, 2008 to November 25, 2008, when she died, Lily Valley was unfortunate in the timing of her portfolio review. Her executors found that in that period she had made capital losses of £19,000. In the year before she had made gains which after annual exemption amounted to £21,000. Tax had been paid on these gains. The executors successfully apply for this loss to be carried back and a CGT repayment arises to the estate. The bad news is that this repayment will be an asset of the estate for inheritance tax purposes!

Attention!!

The deceased and executor are treated as separate persona; any losses of the deceased unused at death cannot be carried forward to offset against gains realised by the executor. Likewise, any losses realised by the executor cannot be carried back to offset against gains prior to death.

Method

The investigation of capital gains tax to date of death is perhaps one of **4–11** the most difficult and most often ignored aspects of executry work. The dilemma of whether to commit disproportionate resources of time and effort into investigation must be addressed. In many cases it will be fairly obvious that the deceased held no shares, or more commonly, that his level of shareholding did not come up to taxable levels, e.g. small holdings acquired in public utility privatisations. Often it will be obvious if he did make chargeable gains and fairly exhaustive enquiries should be made of his broker and/or bankers. The executor will, as a matter of course, be obtaining a copy of his most recent tax returns from the Inland Revenue and it might be appropriate to ask for these going back at least three years. The sources of income are not, however, shown in self-assessment returns, only the totals of each type of income. The supplementary pages for CG will disclose the chargeable gains made during the year. Clues can also be obtained from a cessation of dividend payments. Often elderly people, in an "attempt to simplify" their financial affairs, sell shares and put the proceeds into, say, a building society. They may have been persuaded by a "Financial Advisor" to sell shares and "invest" the proceeds in a managed bond. Capital gains tax may have been overlooked.

CAPITAL GAINS TAX LIABILITY AND PAYMENT

Preliminary Considerations

4–12 It may be helpful for the practitioner to ask the following questions:

1. Was the deceased a taxable person, i.e. ordinarily resident in the United Kingdom? If not there is no liability to capital gains tax. The executry "takes over" the deceased's residence for capital gains tax purposes.
2. Was it a valid chargeable disposal? This covers gifts. There is no comprehensive definition of "gift" but there may be a gift to a spouse, which is exempt.
3. When did the "disposal" occur? This is usually the date of the contract and not the date of performance. This is canvassed in the recent (English) case of *Underwood v HMRC* [2008] EWCA Civ 1423.
4. Was the asset chargeable for capital gains tax? Gains in Sterling and motor cars are not usually chargeable.
5. Do any transactions (which relate to the asset) and/or reliefs (which relate to the tax) apply? It is suggested that the executor applies the exemptions first. If it falls within an exemption the executor does not need to deal with the reliefs.

The Most Common Exemptions

4–13 The most common exemptions are as follows:

- National Savings Certificates, Premium Bonds and Savings Bonds (s.121).
- Assets with limited life expectancy, e.g. furniture (s.45).
- Gains on sale of personal foreign currency (s.269).
- Lottery/betting winnings (s.51(1)).
- First-hand qualifying life assurance policies (s.210).
- Only or main private dwelling houses together with gardens and grounds up to 0.5 hectares. Certain periods of the executor's absence from the house may be excluded, e.g. three years, a period during working abroad or up to four years when prevented by his working away from home. It should be noted that the last 36 months are excluded.
- Personal moveables worth under £6,000 (s.262). Watch the provisions regarding sets (s.262(4)) and disposals to connected persons).
- Motor cars and yachts (s.263).
- Works of art in certain circumstances (s.258).
- Gifts to housing associations (s.259).
- Interests under trusts except where second-hand or the trustees are non-resident (s.76).
- First-hand sales of medals for bravery (s.269).
- Gilt-edged securities and qualifying corporate bonds including options (s.115).

> **Attention!!**
>
> **It can be useful in a sale of heritage to allocate a portion of the price against these, provided of course the contract allows this.**

The basic computation that must be carried out for each disposal is as follows:

	£	£
Disposal proceeds		
Less: Incidental costs of disposal		
Less: Acquisition cost		
Incidental costs of acquisition		
Enhancement expenditure		
Unindexed gain		
Less: Indexation allowance		
Indexed gain		

As stated individuals, trustees and executors who dispose of assets after April 5, 1998 but before April 6, 2008 may be able to claim taper relief. For disposals post-April 5, 2008 neither taper relief nor indexation are applicable. Gains and losses after taper relief are then aggregated for each tax year, and finally an annual exemption is deducted.

Where allowable losses for a tax year exceed chargeable gains, the excess may be carried forward and used to offset chargeable gains in later tax years. In certain cases the losses may be set off against other income of the same and the preceding year to the extent that the losses relate to qualifying trading company shares; or carried back in certain circumstances.

RELIEFS

The annual exemption of £9,200 for 2007/2008 (£9,800 for 2008/2009) is **4–14** available to both husband and wife (s.3). Unused personal allowances cannot be set against capital gains tax.

From April 6, 1999 retirement relief was phased out over a five-year period.

Taper Relief

From April 6, 2008 taper relief and indexation allowance were abolished **4–15** for individuals, trustees and personal representatives. At the same time the flat rate of tax was introduced at 18 per cent and there was to be compulsory rebasing to the March 1982 value.

Taper relief only applies to gains before April 6, 2008. It was introduced by the Finance Act 1998. Chargeable gains are reduced by fixed percentages each year over a period of 10 years. The percentages are more generous for business assets. The following table shows the comparison of taper reliefs as applied to business and non-business assets.

Taper Relief and Business Assets

No. of whole years (after 5/4/98) for which asset held	% gain chargeable		Equivalent tax rates for higher rate/basic rate	
	Business assets	Non-business assets	Business assets	Non-business assets
0	100	100	40/23.00	40/23.00
1	92.5	100	37/21.27	40/23.00
2	85	100	34/19.55	40/23.00
3	77.5	95	31/17.82	38/21.85
4	70	90	28/16.10	36/20.70
5	62.5	85	25/14.37	34/19.55
6	55	80	22/12.65	32/18.40
7	47.5	75	19/10.92	30/17.25
8	40	70	16/9.20	28/16.10
9	32.5	65	13/7.47	26/14.95
10	25	60	10/5.25	24/13.80

DEFERMENTS

4–16 Deferments have the effect of deferring payment of the tax.

Gifts of business assets and certain others may qualify for a gain being "held over". If a transfer is made between spouses, the transaction is treated as a no gain/no loss. In effect the gain is held over. Joint elections to hold over the gain can be made: where business assets are gifted to a third party other than the spouse; or for transfers chargeable to inheritance tax (or would be but for exemption), e.g. a transfer into a discretionary trust. The advantage of holding over is that any tax will be paid by the donee in the future from money the value of which is reduced by inflation. However, the donor loses the benefit of his annual exemption. If the donee dies there is of course no gain because there is a free uplift at death. The replacement of a business asset within certain time limits may allow the gain to be "rolled-over" into a new asset. This also applies on the incorporation of a business and on reinvestment in unquoted shares. The effect is that the acquisition value of the asset is reduced by what would have been the gain with the result that the tax is deferred.

CALCULATION OF THE GAIN

4–17 The gain is calculated by deducting from the disposal value, the acquisition value, expenditure wholly and exclusively incurred by the deceased in establishing its value or title, e.g. legal fees, stamp duty, commission on sale, advertising, surveyors and valuation (not mortgage costs). Premiums paid under an insurance policy are excluded.

Only for the period up to April 5, 1998 and in respect of assets acquired before March 31, 1998, was a capital gain indexed by comparing the retail price index for the month in which the property was purchased (RI) with the index for the month in which the disposal (RD) took place. The Finance Act 1998 abolished the indexation allowance for assets acquired after March 31, 1998. However, for assets acquired after March 31, 1998 (and sold after April 5, 1998) indexation is allowed but only up to April 1998. Thereafter, and for assets acquired after March 31, 1998, taper relief was introduced. As mentioned taper relief reduces chargeable gains by fixed percentages over a period of 10 years, i.e. by 7.5 per cent per annum for business assets after one year and five per cent per annum for non-business assets after three years. If an asset was held by the deceased on March 17, 1998 it qualifies for an extra year's taper relief. Assuming indexation is applicable the fraction used is:

$$\frac{RD-RI}{RI}$$

This is expressed as a percentage to three decimal places and applied to the acquisition value/expenditure.

When it was available indexation could not (after April 5, 1995) be used to convert a gain into a loss or to increase a loss.

RELEVANT VALUES

The values will be based on either actual consideration (between non-connected persons) or market value. There is no gain/no loss between, e.g. spouses or charities. **4–18**

If the deceased made an election to March 31, 1982 values for all subsequent disposals, the relevant value is based on a rebasing to March 31, 1982. From April 6, 1988 no capital gains tax arose on gains before March 31, 1982. Assets acquired before that date are treated as having been disposed of on that date and reacquired at market value on the same day.

PART DISPOSALS

Capital gains tax can arise when there is only a part disposal, e.g. in the case of shares. The rules regarding sales of part of a holding of shares are fairly complex but basically, apart from same-day purchases and sales, and sales of shares purchased 30 days or less prior to sale (which are matched with each other), part sales of a holding are identified for CGT purposes after April 5, 1998 with shares or other securities of the same class in this order: **4–19**

- with other shares acquired after April 5, 1998 on a L(ast) I(n) F(irst) O(ut) basis;
- with shares acquired on or after April 6, 1982;
- with shares (deemed to form part of a 1982) holding acquired before March 31, 1982.

Special rules apply for Business Expansion Shares (BES) shares.

RATES AND PAYMENT OF CAPITAL GAINS TAX

4–20 Pre-April 6, 2008 the capital gain is taxed as if it were the deceased's top slice of income.

For disposals prior to April 6, 2008 capital gains were taxable at 10 per cent, 20 per cent or 40 per cent. They were *not* subject to the basic rate of income tax. When calculating the capital gains tax liability, gains were taxed as though they were the top slice of the individual's income for the tax year. The analogy of the cream on top of old fashioned milk bottles used to help students to visualise how it interacted with the taxpayer's other income. The rate of tax depends on the individual's taxable income.

Example

Mr Darcy made capital gains for 2007/2008 of £17,200, after taper relief of £4,050 but before the annual exemption. His taxable income for the year is £29,250.

	£
Net gains	*17,200*
Less: Annual exemption	*(9,200)*
Taxable gains	*8,000*

The rate bands are allocated between income and gains as follows:

	Income £	Gains £
Starting rate band: 2,230	*2,230*	
Lower/basic rate band: 2,230–34,600	*27,020*	*5,350*
Higher rate band		*2,650*
	29,250	*7,000*

The capital gains tax due is therefore calculated as follows:

	£
£5,350 @ 20%	*1,070*
£2,650 @ 40%	*1,460*
Total CGT	*2,530*

Attention!!

Although the tax payable is calculated at income tax rates, it is actually capital gains tax (s.6(3) TCGA 1992).

Where an individual's taxable income includes a taxable life policy gain the capital gains tax liability is calculated as though only the relevant portion of the chargeable event gain was taxable in that year. The relevant portion is the total chargeable event gain divided by the complete number of years the relevant policy was held.

Section 4 TCGA 1992

For disposals on or after April 6, 2008 a flat rate of 18 per cent is charged after allowing for losses and the annual exemption.

If the disposal above had been made on July 17, 2008 the calculation would have been as follows:

Net gains	21,800
Less: annual exemption	(9,800)
Taxable gains	12,000

The flat rate of 18 per cent is then applied to this resulting in an overall CGT liability of £2,160.

The tax is assessed on the gains made in the year of assessment. Under self-assessment CGT is due in accordance with the executor's self assessment or the Revenue's calculations thereof on his behalf either on January 31, i.e. 10 months after the end of the tax year or if later (provided the executor has notified HM Revenue & Customs of his chargeability within six months of the end of the tax year), three months from the issue of the notice requiring him to make a return. There is a surcharge for late payments and interest runs on over-payments and under-payments from the due dates.

AND FINALLY . . .

Write to the IR asking them to confirm that they have no claim against **4–21** the deceased's estate by way of CGT liability.

End Note

Capital gains tax was introduced 43 years ago. It is, and has been since **4–22** its introduction, chargeable on capital gains "accruing to a person on the disposal of assets".

One might have thought, therefore, that the nature of a disposal for capital gains tax would be absolutely clear. In fact there is no general definition of a "disposal" to be found in the legislation although particular provisions extend the meaning of the word to various trans-actions and other situations which would, or might, not be disposals within the general definition (TCGA 1992 ss.21–27). Nor is a coherent treatment to be found in case law. The nature of a disposal is discussed only obliquely in the decided cases. The recent decisions by the Special Commissioners, [2007] S.T.C. (S.C.D.) 659, and by Mr Justice Briggs in the High Court in *Underwood v HMRC* [2008] EWCA Civ 1423, bring the question of what exactly is a disposal for capital gains tax purposes sharply to the fore.

Chapter Five

INHERITANCE TAX ON DEATH

"Everything seems simple until you think about it."[1]

TAX FACTS

Inheritance Tax		
On death	From £0—£312,000 (after April 5, 2008)	nil
	£312,000—no upper limit	40%
Lifetime rates	From £0—£312,000	nil
	£312,000—no upper limit	20%

Inheritance Tax Facts

	Gross Transfers on death
Period	Nil-Rate Band
2007/08[2]	£300,000
2008/09[3]	£312,000
2009/10[4]	£325,000
2010/11[5]	£350,000

Principal Exemptions

During lifetime	
Annual Exemption	£3,000 (may be carried forward to succeeding year only to the extent unused).

---

[1] Audrey Niffenegger, *The Time Traveller's Wife* (London: Vintage Books, 2004).
[2] FA 2005 s.98.
[3] FA 2006 s.155.
[4] FA 2006 s.155.
[5] FA 2007 s.4.

During lifetime	
Small Gifts	£250 per donee. If the gift exceeds this, none of it is exempt.
Gifts out of income	If made out of income which has been taxed and donor left with sufficient to live on. Usually a pattern of expenditure is sought.
Gifts in consideration of marriage	From £1,000 to £5,000 depending on relationship to prospective bride or groom.
Disposition for maintenance under s.11 IHTA 1984	Exempt.

On Death as well	
Gifts to spouse	Exempt (provided she has UK domicile; if not restricted to £55,000).
Gifts to charities (UK)	Exempt.
Any portion of the nil-rate band which is not used at a taxpayer's death can be transferred to the executors of his/her surviving spouse or civil partner for the purposes of IHT charge on the death of the survivor on or after October 9, 2007.	

	Delivery dates
Chargeable lifetime transfers	Later of 12 months after transfer took place and three months after the date when the accountable party became liable.
PETs[6] which have become chargeable	12 months after the month in which the death took place.
Gifts with reservation which are chargeable on death	12 months after the month in which the death took place.
Transfers on death	Later of 12 months after the month in which the death took place.

---

[6] Potentially Exempt Transfers.

Penalties

If a late account is received and proceedings before the Special Commissioners to obtain it have not already been taken	A penalty of £100 is due.
If the account is more than six months late	The penalty is £200.
If the account is more than 12 months late	The penalty increases to a maximum of £3,000.
If the actual tax liability is less than these figures, the penalty cannot be more than the amount of the tax due.	

Please note that the Inheritance Tax (Delivery of Accounts) (Excepted Estates) Regulations 2002 (SI 2002/1733) came into effect on August 1, 2002 in respect of deaths occurring on or after April 6, 2002.

THE LEGISLATION

5–02 The legislation is contained in the Inheritance Tax Act 1984.

NEW IHT FORMS

5–03 HMRC have produced a new inheritance tax form, the form IHT400. This is in print and is to replace IHT200. Supplementary sheets D1—D20 are now also replaced by IHT401–423. The existing forms may be used until June 2009 at which point they will become obsolete when IHT400 comes into effect as the only appropriate forms to use. While it is still competent to proceed by way of the IHT200 and supplementary pages numbers D1 to D21, these can now be replaced with the new form, namely IHT400. This will replace IHT200 and the Schedules will now be IHT401 to IHT423. These forms can already be downloaded from HM Revenue & Customs website.

This form must be used from June 9, 2009 for deaths on or after March 18, 1986 where a full IHT form is required. From that date IHT200 forms will no longer be accepted by the HM Revenue & Customs.

IHT UPDATE

5–04 In an update, HM Revenue & Customs, in a recent edition of their of their IHT and trusts newsletter,[7] specifically referred to the following:

---

[7] Available at *http://www.hmrc.gov.uk/cto/newsletter-aug08.htm* [accessed April 23, 2009].

- **Transferable nil-rate band:** HMRC remind agents that they should provide the supporting details listed in the IHT216 claim form to support the claim for relief. So far in only 20 per cent of cases submitted by agents are all the requested documents provided. Without the requested documents, the claim cannot be processed causing delay to the issue of the D18/C1, increasing costs for HMRC and the estate unnecessarily. *This has now been amended for INHERITANCE TAX 400 forms.*
- **Excepted estates:** HMRC are piloting a new process where they compare the data provided on death with data the deceased provided to HMRC during their lifetime and information from other sources. They say that they will be focusing attention on estates where this information suggests that the estate does not meet the criteria to be an excepted estate.
- **Transfer of IHT banking:** HMRC have been using payslips for inheritance tax payments for a little while now and, since the end of June, they have been issuing a machine-readable payslip as a detachable slip on a printed document. This latest change is the next step along the way to transferring IHT banking to Shipley. The main impact for executors will be that HMRC will no longer issue a receipt for inheritance tax payments. It will still be possible to track payments through the entries on HMRC's calculations for tax already paid and money on account applied against tax and interest.
- **Too much information:** HMRC remind advisers that they *should not* apply for an IHT reference for an estate where there is no tax to pay. It is only necessary to apply for an IHT reference where the adviser is certain there is tax to pay.[8]
- **IHT email addresses:** HMRC's customer service email address is now ihtcustomerservice@btconnect.com and the forms orderline is hmrc.ihtorderline@btconnect.com.

INTRODUCTION

This section deals with the incidence of inheritance IHT on death. **5–05** Inheritance tax does not, of course, only occur on death and passing reference will be to its incidence during lifetime. At the basis of inheritance tax is the value placed on the diminution of the estate of the donor. Inheritance tax was actually introduced in 1986. It replaced capital transfer tax, which was the direct successor to estate duty. Broadly, it is due: on the assets (less debts and funeral expenses) of deceased persons which are transferred on death; on gifts made within seven years of death or made at any time when there is a reservation of benefit, which continues within seven years of death—such transfers become chargeable at the time of death; and transfers by executors to discretionary trusts or other relevant property trusts, or to companies— such transfers are immediately chargeable. Although it may not immediately concern us, for property in discretionary trusts, which should

---

[8] See *Inheritance Tax Manual* at IHTM 35184.

probably now be referred to as "relevant property trusts", there is a charge on the tenth anniversary of the creation of the trust and every subsequent tenth anniversary. Property leaving such trusts may also be subject to an inheritance tax charge. Assets are valued at the price, which they might reasonably be expected to receive if sold in the open market at the date of death. For gifts, the IHT value is the amount by which the gift reduces the donor's estate. If the gift is made *inter vivos* the donor bears the tax, if any, due on the gift, and the loss to the estate will include the tax. The values of some assets transferred on death may be reduced if they are sold for a lower amount within a specific period. Different time periods apply to listed securities and unit trusts units and to land and buildings. The government apply a flat rate of charge applied above a threshold (known as the "nil-rate band" (NRB)). Generally speaking the government increase this figure every year to reflect inflation. The amount of inheritance tax payable on a transfer depends on the total of transfers (excluding exempt transfers) in the previous seven years. This applies to transfers made on death as well as to lifetime transfers which are immediately chargeable or which become chargeable on death. No tax is payable on the part of the cumulative total below the threshold. Currently tax is charged at a single rate of 40 per cent on the amount above the threshold for transfers on death and within seven years before death, and at half the death rate for transfers which are immediately chargeable during lifetime. Inheritance tax on land and buildings, control holdings of shares, unlisted shares and securities, and businesses can be paid by instalments over 10 years.

Danger Warning!!

Watch out when transferring assets to (impecunious) beneficiaries, where inheritance tax on instalments is still due. If the beneficiary becomes insolvent HMRC will look to the other executors (who may be members of the firm of executors acting in the estate!) for IHT. This was the substance of the case of Executors of Howarth v Inland Revenue Commissioners [1997] S.T.I. 640 (Sp Comm.).

5–06   If, however, the asset is sold, and in some other circumstances, the tax outstanding becomes immediately payable. Not all transfers are subject to inheritance tax. The main exemptions include transfers between spouses and, of course, from December 5, 2005 civil partners (subject to some limitation if the transferee is domiciled abroad); transfers to charities; and an annual exemption for small lifetime gifts of £250 or less to each donee and the first £3,000 of lifetime gifts not otherwise exempt. Moreover, if the preceding fiscal year's annual exemption (of £3,000) has not been used, it or the balance remaining may still be used to exempt gifts in excess of £3,000.

Hence, if an individual has not made any gifts during this or the previous tax year, the first £6,000 of gifts made between now and the end of the tax year will be fully exempt. If particular conditions are observed, the value of agricultural property and business assets, including unlisted shares or securities, may be reduced by 100 per cent or 50 per cent. Where IHT is payable on the death of a person who had received assets within five years under a chargeable transfer, the tax payable on the second occasion is reduced. Similar relief also applies to a lifetime charge on the termination of a liferent.

Danger Warning!!

IHT may also be reduced by double taxation relief. If death duties or similar are paid in another country on property situated there, the foreign duties may be deducted from any United Kingdom IHT on the same property.

Please watch out for the rate of exchange. The rate of exchange for the value of the foreign assets will be the rate of exchange at date of death; the rate of exchange for foreign "death duties" will be rate at the date these are paid. Any expenses on fees to foreign solicitors should be at the rate of exchange when paid!

SUMMARY

Inheritance tax must be paid when there is a *chargeable transfer*. The **5–07** expression "chargeable transfer" is defined in the statute as:

> "[A]ny transfer of value which is made to an individual but is not an exempt transfer[9] . . . the transfer value [is defined] as a disposition made by a person the result of which the value of this estate immediately after the transfer is less than it would be but for the disposition."

This value in the diminution of the estate is at the heart of the inheritance tax liability.

While we think of inheritance tax as a tax due on death it can, and frequently does, occur during lifetime as a result of gifts.

Danger Warning!!

An undervalue can also be regarded as a gift as can failure to claim legal rights. Other matters involving alteration in corporate structure where value is transferred from one type of share to another can also constitute a gift but the scope of this is beyond this modest text.

TRANSFER OF VALUE

In a sense and as reinforced by s.4 of the IHTA 1984, a deceased person **5–08** is to be treated as if he had made a transfer of value immediately before his death. The value of this estate transferred is equal to the value of his

---

[9] IHT Act 1984 s.2 (1) and s.3(1).

whole estate immediately before death. The estate to which reference has been made is the summation of all property to which he was "beneficially entitled" immediately before his death apart from certain types of liferent.[10] Often, for various reasons, lifetime transfers are exempt or, to use the technical term, "potentially exempt" ("PETs") in that they become exempt if the person making the gift survives seven years. Gifts or transfers into certain types of trusts now known as relevant property trusts (formerly broadly known as discretionary trusts) are chargeable immediately. Actually these relevant property trusts will, from the Finance Act 2006, account for the bulk of trusts.

Half of the complexity of inheritance tax stems from its inception as a modification of capital transfer tax. Capital transfer tax was a tax on death estates and lifetime transfers. The Act which is now designed the Inheritance Tax Act 1984 was formerly the Capital Transfer Act 1984 and in its relatively unamended form continues to apply to transactions entered into since March 18, 1986.

TRANSFERS GIVING RISE TO INHERITANCE TAX LIABILITY

5–09 In summary there are in fact three instances where inheritance tax may take place as follows.

(1) A Potentially Exempt Transfer

5–10 This relates to a transfer made on or after March 18, 1986 by an individual (IHTA 1984 s.3A) to the extent that it constitutes a gift to another individual.

Potentially exempt transfers

3A.—(1) Any reference in this Act to a potentially exempt transfer is a reference to a transfer of value—

(a) which is made by an individual on or after 18th March 1986 but before 22nd March 2006; and

(b) which, apart from this section, would be a chargeable transfer (or to the extent to which, apart from this section, it would be such a transfer); and

(c) to the extent that it constitutes either a gift to another individual or a gift into an accumulation and maintenance trust or a disabled trust.

(1A) Any reference in this Act to a potentially exempt transfer is also a reference to a transfer of value—

(a) which is made by an individual on or after 22nd March 2006,

(b) which, apart from this section, would be a chargeable transfer (or to the extent to which, apart from this section, it would be such a transfer), and

(c) to the extent that it constitutes—

---

[10] IHT Act 1984 s.5.

  (i) a gift to another individual,
  (ii) a gift into a disabled trust, or
  (iii) a gift into a bereaved minor's trust on the coming to an end of an immediate post-death interest.

(1B) Subsections (1) and (1A) above have effect subject to any provision of this Act which provides that a disposition (or transfer of value) of a particular description is not a potentially exempt transfer.

 (2) Subject to subsection (6) below, a transfer of value falls within subsection (1)(c) or (1A)(c)(i) above, as a gift to another individual—

  (a) to the extent that the value transferred is attributable to property which, by virtue of the transfer, becomes comprised in the estate of that other individual; or
  (b) so far as that value is not attributable to property which becomes comprised in the estate of another person, to the extent that, by virtue of the transfer, the estate of that other individual is increased.

 (3) Subject to subsection (6) below, a transfer of value falls within subsection (1)(c) above, as a gift into an accumulation and maintenance trust or a disabled trust, to the extent that the value transferred is attributable to property which, by virtue of the transfer, becomes settled property to which section 71 or 89 of this Act applies.

(3A) Subject to subsection (6) below, a transfer of value falls within subsection (1A)(c)(ii) above to the extent that the value transferred is attributable to property which, by virtue of the transfer, becomes settled property to which section 89 below applies.

(3B) A transfer of value falls within subsection (1A)(c)(iii) above to the extent that the value transferred is attributable to settled property (whenever settled) that becomes property to which section 71A below applies in the following circumstances—

  (a) under the settlement, a person ("L") is beneficially entitled to an interest in possession in the settled property;
  (b) the interest in possession is an immediate post-death interest;
  (c) on or after 22nd March 2006, but during L's life, the interest in possession comes to an end;
  (d) L is beneficially entitled to the interest in possession immediately before it comes to an end; and
  (e) on the interest in possession coming to an end, the property—

    (i) continues to be held on the trusts of the settlement, and
    (ii) becomes property to which section 71A below applies.

 (4) A potentially exempt transfer which is made seven years or more before the death of the transferor is an exempt transfer

and any other potentially exempt transfer is a chargeable transfer.

(5) During the period beginning on the date of a potentially exempt transfer and ending immediately before—

(a) the seventh anniversary of that date, or
(b) if it is earlier, the death of the transferor,

it shall be assumed for the purposes of this Act that the transfer will prove to be an exempt transfer.

(6) Where, under any provision of this Act other than section 52 tax is in any circumstances to be charged as if a transfer of value had been made, that transfer shall be taken to be a transfer which is not a potentially exempt transfer.

(7) In the application of this section to an event on the happening of which tax is chargeable under section 52 below, the reference in subsection (1)(a) or (1A)(a) above to the individual by whom the transfer of value is made is a reference to the person who, by virtue of section 3(4) above, is treated as the transferor.

Danger Warning!!

A potentially exempt transfer can arise where a donor fails to exercise a right.

If the donor survives seven years after the gift the transfer becomes exempt. However, if he dies within the seven years it becomes chargeable at the rates in force at date of death. Where the amount of the gift(s), that is to say, the potentially exempt transactions, exceeds the nil-rate band in force at date of death, it or they may qualify for taper relief.

(2) A Chargeable Transfer Made During Lifetime

5–11   This will occur most frequently where the transfer is made to a relevant property trust and is immediately taxable but at only 50 per cent of the death rate. However, as again if the donor dies within seven years the transfer becomes taxable at the full rates in force.

Most transfers into trusts on or after March 22, 2006 will be chargeable with the possible exception of a transfer to a trust for a disabled person.

(3) Transfer on Death

5–12   This is the transfer with which this chapter will be principally concerned. As stated this covers all the estate to which the deceased was beneficially entitled.

The expression which is used, i.e. "beneficially entitled", requires some clarification. It broadly covers all assets which the deceased owns in the usual sense of the word and, in addition, all property over which he has a power to dispose of as he thinks fit; this is also included within the beneficial entitlement. It is important to recognise as regards joint bank accounts that, for most practical purposes, nominal title to a joint bank account in Scotland is irrelevant in determining who actually owns the amount. Generally speaking, the analogy is that bank accounts are loans to the bank and they remain the property of the person who made the loan, i.e. who contributed the funds irrespective of what destination was placed on the account. Many banks are under the impression that on the death of one of the joint owners the property vests in the survivor. This may be the case with foreign banks but it is not the case with Scottish banks.[11] In fact all that vests in the survivor is the right to operate the account which, for inheritance tax purposes, is clearly not the same as ownership. The situation may be different with English banks. In recent times where there have been cataclysmic problems with banks in Scotland and, indeed, elsewhere, great care must be taken in determining ownership. Sometimes practitioners south of the border and indeed Scottish commentators have difficulty in understanding that if a person in, say, England has an account with a Scottish bank, it will be governed by the Scottish rules.

Matters came to a head recently in the case of *Taylor v RCC*.[12] In this case a widow inherited inter alia her husband's estate's building society accounts. Apparently Mr Boland (the deceased) had indicated that he wished his sister in law and her husband and his nephews and nieces to inherit, i.e. Mr and Mrs Taylor and their children. Mrs Boland then arranged for the accounts to be placed in the joint names of Mr Taylor and her own name. Apparently only one signature was needed to uplift all or part of the amount at credit and on death under English Law and in practice the whole balance would pass to the survivor. *It should be noted that this is not the case in Scotland where a survivorship destination would not be implied.* However, when Mrs Boland died, HM Revenue & Customs determined that the late Mrs Boland was beneficially entitled to the whole amount of the accounts under s.5(2) of the Inheritance tax Act 1984. Section 5(2) provides:

> "A person who has a general power which enables him, or would if he were sui juris enable him, to dispose of any property other than settled property, or to charge money on any property other than settled property, shall be treated as beneficially entitled to the property or money; and for this purpose 'general power' means a power or authority enabling the person by whom it is exercisable to appoint or dispose of property as he thinks fit."

Although it turned on English law and practice, the case is interesting **5–13** because it also dealt with the proposition that a joint bank account could be regarded in certain cases as a gift with reservation. Say an elderly person has a bank account which she wishes her daughter to be able to operate for her, the understanding expressed in writing being that on her (the elderly person's) death, the proceeds or the balance of the account will be the daughter's. Meantime, the account is operated for the benefit of the mother. In Scotland there would really require to be some documentary evidence of the gift. In England, it may be assumed by the act of putting the account in joint names!

---

[11] If in fact there are any left!
[12] *Taylor v RCC* [2008] Sp C 704; [2008] STC (SCD)1159.

The legal profession in England and Wales has great difficulty with the Scottish concept of joint banking despite the fact that it is extremely logical. The problem is that there is a public perception which is shared by some of the legal, financial (and banking) and accountancy professions that a survivorship destination applies. HM Revenue & Customs in their manuals at IHTM15042 attempt to explain the position in England and Wales; at IHTM15051 they deal with joint bank and building society accounts in Scotland and at IHTM15054 they cover the position with joint bank accounts in Scotland and underline that special destinations do not apply.

The estate of the deceased also includes property liferented by him or in which he had (to use the unfortunate expression) "an interest in possession", provided that this interest was in existence on March 22, 2006 or the interest was an immediate post-death interest, a transitional serial interest or a disabled person's interest.

Excluded property is extra property situated outside the UK and owned by a person domiciled outside the UK. It might also include trust property outside the UK provided that the truster was domiciled outside the UK when the trust was set up.

Transfers not giving Rise to Inheritance Tax Liability

5–14 There are a number of transfers which do not give rise to inheritance tax liability. Some of these are not so well known and are well worth canvassing when dealing with lifetime gifts of the deceased.

Gifts Out of Normal Expenditure

5–15 These are types of gifts which are regular gifts or payments that are part of normal expenditure. These will be gifts which are made out of taxed income and do not require the donor to use capital. They are likely to be regular payments to someone, regular gifts for Christmas and birthdays or wedding/civil partnership anniversaries, or regular premiums on a life insurance policy—for someone else. They may also occur where, for example, a grandparent may make payment of school fees for a grandchild

Disposition for Maintenance (of Family)

5–16 This is also not so well known but exempt maintenance payments can be made to husband, wife or civil partner, ex-spouse or former civil partner, relatives who are dependent on the taxpayer because of old age or infirmity and children, including adopted children and step-children, who are under 18 years of age or in full-time education. It is not used as much as perhaps it should be. It is worth looking at the statutory provision s.11 of the Inheritance Tax Act 1984.

Dispositions for maintenance of family

> **11.**—(1) A disposition is not a transfer of value if it is made by one party to a marriage or civil partnership in favour of the other party or of a child of either party and is—
>
> (a) for the maintenance of the other party, or

(b) for the maintenance, education or training of the child for a period ending not later than the year in which he attains the age of eighteen or, after attaining that age, ceases to undergo full-time education or training.

(2) A disposition is not a transfer of value if it is made in favour of a child who is not in the care of a parent of his and is for his maintenance, education or training for a period ending not later than the year in which—

(a) he attains the age of eighteen, or
(b) after attaining that age he ceases to undergo full-time education or training;

but paragraph (b) above applies only if before attaining that age the child has for substantial periods been in the care of the person making the disposition.

(3) A disposition is not a transfer of value if it is made in favour of a dependent relative of the person making the disposition and is a reasonable provision for his care or maintenance.

(4) A disposition is not a transfer of value if it is made in favour of an illegitimate child of the person making the disposition and is for the maintenance, education or training of the child for a period ending not later than the year in which he attains the age of eighteen or, after attaining that age, ceases to undergo full-time education or training.

(5) Where a disposition satisfies the conditions of the preceding provisions of this section to a limited extent only, so much of it as satisfied them and so much of it as does not satisfy them shall be treated as separate dispositions.

(6) In this section—

"child" includes a step-child and an adopted child and "parent" shall be construed accordingly;
"civil partnership", in relation to a disposition made on the occasion of the dissolution or annulment of a civil partnership, and in relation to a disposition varying a disposition so made, includes a former civil partnership;
"dependent relative" means in relation to any person—

(a) a relative of his, or of his spouse or civil partner, who is incapacitated by old age or infirmity from maintaining himself, or
(b) his mother or father or his spouse's or civil partner's mother or father.

This can be used in unexpected ways. A recent example was the **5–17** *Phizackerley* case,[13] which has become famous for other reasons mainly to do with s.103 of the Inheritance Tax Act 1984. However the question of s.11 was adduced by counsel for the respondent, Mr James Kessler

---

[13] *Phizackerley v Revenue and Customs Commissioners* (2007) S.T.C. (S.C.D.) 328.

QC. Dr Phizackerley, a consultant biochemist, had lived in tied college accommodation until his retirement when he and his wife purchased a small house, title to which was put in their names as joint tenants. This form of tenure roughly equates to joint property with a survivorship destination in Scotland. A small mortgage was repaid two years later. It was agreed by parties that "Mrs Phizackerley did not work during her marriage, and the funds must have been provided by the Deceased." In 1996 Dr Phizackerley severed the joint tenancy (i.e. evacuated the survivorship destination) so that he and Mrs Phizackerley held the property they had purchased as tenants in common (without as joint proprietors without the survivorship destination). In the same week Mrs Phizackerley made a will which left the nil-rate sum on discretionary trusts and residue. Following the time honoured path and in the terms of the will, Mrs Phizackerley's half share in the house was "conveyed" to Dr Phizackerley, who promised to pay the trustees the nil-rate band sum £150,000 (index-linked). On Dr Phizackerley's death two years later his estate, ignoring the promise of payment to the trustees, was valued at just under £530,000.

The taxpayer was represented by James Kessler QC who argued that s.11 of IHTA 1984 should apply, under which a disposition is not a transfer of value if made by one party to a marriage in favour of another or of a child of either party and for the maintenance of the other party. The most basic requirement, he contended, of "maintenance" is a roof over one's head.

However, the Special Commissioner concluded that maintenance ordinarily "has a flavour of meeting recurring expenses" and that whilst it is wide enough to cover the transfer of an interest in a house that would apply "only if it relieves the recipient from income expenditure, for example on rent". In spite of Mr Kessler's "persuasive argument" the Special Commissioner rejected the maintenance argument and dismissed the appeal.

5–18   A more recent case where the attempt also failed was the case of *McKelvey v HM Revenue and Customs Commissioners* [2008] Sp C 694, which was directly concerned with the exemption under s.11 IHTA 1984. Here a daughter who cared for her widowed mother was diagnosed with a terminal illness; the daughter attempted to make provision for her mother's nursing care after her own death and transferred properties to her mother specifically so that they could be sold to pay for nursing costs. The daughter claimed that they were exempt transfers within s.11(3) IHTA 1984, which reads:

> "A disposition is not a transfer of value if it was made in favour of a dependent relative of the person making the disposition and is a reasonable provision for his care or maintenance."

HM Revenue & Customs accepted that gifts of this kind could be exempt, but on the particular facts of the case, principally since the mother refused to move into residential accommodation, the properties did not need to be sold for the purpose of paying for nursing care. Accordingly, HM Revenue & Customs claimed that no part of the value of the properties had been used for the mother's care and therefore the transfers could not have amounted to reasonable provision for that care; no provision was, in fact, required.

The Special Commissioner disagreed, taking the view that the meaning of "reasonable provision" was an objective standard and it was clear that at the time the gifts were made the mother would have needed paid care. The deceased's gift was reasonable—making the gifts for the purpose of providing funds for her mother's future care was reasonable. However, the Special Commissioner rejected this claim on the grounds that it was an over-provision, i.e. the value of the gifts was more than was needed. In effect it was not reasonable maintenance for the other party—it gave the other party security (as for the *Phizackerley* case above) and fell outside s.11 on those grounds.

It is disappointing that the Special Commissioner chose to be so precise when the grounds for such precision simply did not exist. What if the paid nursing care had been required for fewer years and the costs had gone up during that period? The figures would be completely different. However, having regard to the case of *Phizackerley*, the executors may have been happy with anything because, in that case, the Special Commissioner acknowledged that s.11 was wide enough!

Although in these two cases the taxpayer failed they are worth studying to see the possible expanding limits of s.11!

Funeral Expenses and Debts

The liabilities are taken into account in valuing the deceased's estate. **5–19** Reasonable funeral expenses can be deducted including a reasonable sum for mournings for family and servants and the cost of a gravestone or tombstone. In calculating these regard must be had to the taxpayer's lifestyle and origin. A mortgage and the security or charge is taken as reducing value of that property rather than reducing the estate generally. It is of the utmost importance for all appropriate debts and funeral expenses to be included.

Attention!!

In certain cases HM Revenue & Customs will allow, say, travelling expenses of the executor if these are necessary to arrange the funeral, etc.

Inheritance Tax (IHT)

The IHT standard threshold was set at £312,000 for 2008/2009. This is **5–20** commonly known as the IHT nil-rate band. In the October 2007 Pre-Budget Report, the Chancellor announced a new concession for married couples and civil partners. With effect for second deaths on or after October 9, 2007 the unused percentage of the nil-rate band from the first death estate can be carried forward and added to the nil-rate band available to the second. The second death must have occurred on or after October 9, 2007, when the change was first announced. The first death can be at any time. Indeed the charge on the first may even have been to estate duty (death duty), although it should be borne in mind that that estate duty did not initially give relief for bequests to the surviving spouse. Nevertheless the exempt threshold at that time can still be used, that is to say broadly treated as if it were the nil-rate band. As regards civil partners, logically, the first death must have occurred on or after December 5, 2005.[14] There is a further quirk in that civil partnerships entered into countries furth of Scotland, which are valid according to their law, also qualify. In these cases the first death must still be on or after December 5, 2005. Foreign marriages are also accepted provided they are valid according to the law of that country.

The combined threshold for couples is therefore a maximum of £624,000 for 2008/2009. This new arrangement applies no matter how long ago the first death occurred. For example:

On the first death, none of the original nil-rate band was used because the entire estate was left to a surviving spouse. Then if the nil-rate band when the surviving spouse dies is £350,000 that would be increased by 100 per cent to £700,000.

If on the first death, the chargeable estate was £107,500 when the nil-rate band was £215,000 (1997/1998), then 50 per cent of the original nil-rate band would be unused. If the nil-rate band when the surviving spouse dies is £350,000, then that would be increased by 50 per cent to £525,000.

HM Revenue & Customs have issued guidance, which will in due course be incorporated into the IHT manual, explaining how the new rules should be applied.[15] A pass at "Higher" level mathematics may be helpful in dealing with the algebraic formula.

Section 8A: Transfer of Unused Nil-Rate Band between Spouses and Civil Partners

Transfer of unused nil-rate band between spouses and civil partners

5–21   **8A.**—(1) This section applies where—

> (a) immediately before the death of a person (a "deceased person"), the deceased person had a spouse or civil partner ("the survivor"), and
>
> (b) the deceased person had unused nil-rate band on death.

> (2) A person has unused nil-rate band on death if—
> M > VT
> where—M is the maximum amount that could be transferred by a chargeable transfer made (under section 4 above) on the person's death if it were to be wholly chargeable to tax at the rate of nil per cent. (assuming, if necessary, that the value of the person's estate were sufficient but otherwise having regard to the circumstances of the person); and
> VT is the value actually transferred by the chargeable transfer so made (or nil if no chargeable transfer is so made).

> (3) Where a claim is made under this section, the nil-rate band maximum at the time of the survivor's death is to be treated for the purposes of the charge to tax on the death of the survivor as increased by the percentage specified in subsection (4) below (but subject to subsection (5) and section 8C below).

---

[14] When it was first possible to enter into a civil partnership in the UK.
[15] Useful guidance can be found at *http://www.hmrc.gov.uk/cto/iht/tnr-draftguidance.pdf* [accessed April 23, 2009].

(4) That percentage is—

$$\frac{E}{NRBMD} \times 100$$

where—E is the amount by which M is greater than VT in the case of the deceased person; and
NRBMD is the nil-rate band maximum at the time of the deceased person's death.

(5) If (apart from this subsection) the amount of the increase in the nil rate band maximum at the time of the survivor's death effected by this section would exceed the amount of that nil-rate band maximum, the amount of the increase is limited to the amount of that nil-rate band maximum.

(6) Subsection (5) above may apply either—

(a) because the percentage mentioned in subsection (4) above (as reduced under section 8C below where that section applies) is more than 100 because of the amount by which M is greater than VT in the case of one deceased person, or

(b) because this section applies in relation to the survivor by reference to the death of more than one person who had unused nil-rate band on death.

(7) In this Act "nil-rate band maximum" means the amount shown in the second column in the first row of the Table in Schedule 1 to this Act (upper limit of portion of value charged at rate of nil per cent.) and in the first column in the second row of that Table (lower limit of portion charged at next rate).

The relief is expressed[16] as a formula. In this case the formula is that relief is only available where M > VT. M is the maximum which could be charged on the death concerned without any IHT being due, and VT is the actual chargeable value of the transfer on death.

If that condition is met, then another formula determines the effect of the transfer. This is a percentage given by the formula E/NRBMD × 100%.

The NRBMD is the "nil rate band maximum on death"—in other words, for practical purposes, the nil-rate band as set for the year in question. E is found by the formula E = M − VT. All that this last formula means is that E is the unused amount of the nil-rate band on the first death.

Although this seems a complex way of setting out a simple idea, it is suggested that it copes with the potential situations arising in practice. **5–22**

One of the most complicated examples is shown below.

Mrs Pansy Lovage or Thistle survived her husband Peter Thistle, who died on October 4, 1996. Mr Thistle's executors provided the relevant information:

---

[16] In IHTA 1984 s.8A.

Net Estate	£200,000
Chargeable estate (legacies to Peter's children)	− £150,000
Residue to Pansy	£50,000
M > VT	
s.8A(4)	
E(M − VT) =	£50,000
Nil-rate band maximum on (first) death	£200,000
Percentage	$\dfrac{50,000 \times 100}{200,000} = 25\%$

With somewhat unseemly haste Pansy married her former school friend, John Burdock, who she met through a "friends reunited" website, on November 1, 2007. Unfortunately she passed away. On her death, her executors can transfer the nil-rate band on her first husband (Peter's) death as follows:

£300,000 + (£300,000 × 25%)	**= £375,000**

On Pansy's death (on January 1, 2009) the amount of the nil-rate band is calculated with the value for M being the actual rate of the nil-rate band available on the second death less any chargeable transfers. The value of the NRBMD (the nil-rate band maximum in force on Pansy's death) is as follows:

Pansy's estate	£400,000
deduct	
Legacies to her children	£105,000
Residue to second husband (John)	£295,000
s.8A(2) calculation	
M = **£375,000**	
VT = £105,000	= **£270,000**

Calculation in terms of s.8A(4)	
E(M − VT) = **£270,000**	
NRBMD = £300,000	
Therefore percentage = 90%	$\dfrac{270{,}000 \times 100}{300{,}000}$

The point to emphasise is that although Pansy left legacies to **5–23** "chargeable" beneficiaries, namely her children, of £105,000, which used up part of her single band of £300,000, nevertheless, the amount of the nil-rate band available for transfer on her death is 90 per cent because of the transfer from her first husband's death. This percentage can be used by John's executors on his death. If John dies (when the nil-rate band is say £400,000) his executors will have potentially £400,000 + (400,000 × 90%) = £780,000 to set against his estate.

It should be noted that however many husbands the deceased had, the maximum amount which can be transferred is limited to 100 per cent. The result on the above calculation may require to be reduced to 100 per cent.

Initially, where the death occurred many years ago, HMRC required the death certificate, the marriage or civil partnership certificate, a copy of the confirmation and a copy of any will and any deed of variation or similar executed on the estate, in order to make a claim. However, often to put it mildly where the first death occurred many years ago, HMRC accepted that detailed information may be hard to come by. Indeed in many cases it is impossible!

For more recent deaths, i.e. where the first death occurred after the **5–24** announcement on October 9, 2007, HM Revenue & Customs initially wanted: a copy of the IHT200, IHT205 (C5 in Scotland) or full written details of the assets in the estate and their values; a death certificate and marriage or civil partnership certificate for the couple; a copy of the confirmation and will, if there was one or a note of how the estate passed if there was no will; a copy of any deed of variation or other similar document if one was executed to change the people who inherited the estate; any valuation(s) of assets that pass under will or intestacy other than to the surviving spouse or civil partner; the value of any other assets that also passed on the death of the first spouse or civil partner, for example jointly owned assets, assets held in trust and gifts made in the seven years prior to death; and any evidence to support the availability of relief (such as agricultural or business relief) where the relievable assets pass to someone other than to the surviving spouse or civil partner. It goes without saying that trying to create this information several years, or even decades, later when the second death occurs will be extremely difficult; one of the end results of dealing with a death and confirmation should be the provision of all this information as a pack, which is to be kept with the will of the survivor.

Not only is it difficult to obtain this, it can also be extremely expensive. Perhaps because of this and the (unrealistic) nature of the request, HM Revenue & Customs only now require, initially, confirmation and a copy of the will and copy deed of variation to be submitted along with the new IHT402 form.

IHT 402 Form

 **HM Revenue & Customs**

Claim to transfer unused nil rate band

Schedule IHT402

When to use this form

Fill in this form if:
- the deceased died on or after 9 October 2007, and
- their spouse or civil partner died before them, and
- when the spouse or civil partner died their estate did not use up all of the nil rate band available to it, and
- you want to transfer the unused amount to the deceased's estate.

Filling in this form

You will need to find out who was the executor or administrator of the spouse or civil partner's estate as you will need information from them to complete this form.

Make full enquiries so that the figures you give and the statements you make are correct.

Information you will need

You will need to know:
- who benefited under the Will or intestacy of the spouse or civil partner and what the beneficiaries were entitled to receive
- whether any assets, such as jointly owned assets or assets in trust were part of the estate of the spouse or civil partner, and
- whether the spouse or civil partner had made any gifts or other transfers within seven years before the date of their death that were chargeable on their death *(see note 5 on page 4)*.

The executor or administrator of the spouse or civil partner should be able to help you find out this information.

You should obtain copies of the documents listed aside and use them alongside any records that exist about the spouse or civil partner's estate.

If there are no records, you should try and find out the information about the spouse or civil partner's estate from others who might know, for example, the solicitor who acted for the estate, the executors or administrators, other family members, close friends.

Name of deceased (person who has died now)

> Mrs Daisy Snowdrop

Date of death *DD MM YYYY*

> 0 1 | 0 1 | 2 0 0 9

IHT reference number (if known)

Documents to be sent with this form

You must send photocopies of the following documents with this form:
- copy of the grant of representation (Confirmation in Scotland) to the estate of the spouse or civil partner (if no grant has been taken out, please provide a copy of the death certificate – see the note on page 4 about obtaining copies of certificates)
- if the spouse or civil partner left a Will, a copy of it
- if a Deed of Variation or other similar document was executed to change the people who inherited the estate of the spouse or civil partner, a copy of it.

Deadline

You must send this form to us no later than 24 months after the end of the month in which the deceased died.
For example, if the spouse or civil partner died on 15 May 2006, and the deceased died on 10 October 2007, you would need to send this form to us by 31 October 2009.

Help

For more information or help:
- go to **www.hmrc.gov.uk/inheritancetax/**
- phone our Helpline on **0845 30 20 900**
  – if calling from outside the UK, phone **+44 115 974 3009**).

Spouse or civil partner's details

Fill in this section with details of the spouse or civil partner who died first.

1 Spouse or civil partner's name

Title – enter MR, MRS, MISS, MS or other title
> Mr

Surname or family name
> Snowdrop

First name(s)
> Garden George

2 Date of death *DD MM YYYY*
> 0 1 | 0 1 | 2 0 0 8

3 Last known permanent address
> Bluebell Glen Lodge
> Oban
>
> Postcode xxxxxx

4 Date of marriage or civil partnership *DD MM YYYY*
> 0 1 | 0 1 | 1 9 4 3

5 Place of marriage or civil partnership *(see note 6, page 4)*
> OBAN

Spouse or civil partner's **details** continued

6 Did the spouse or civil partner who died first leave a Will? Yes ☑ enclose a copy of the Will and any codicils, instruments of variation or disclaimers No ☐	8 Was a grant of representation (Confirmation in Scotland) obtained for the estate of the spouse or civil partner who died first? Yes ☑ enclose a copy of the grant No ☐ enclose a copy of the death certificate
7 What was the value of the spouse or civil partner's estate? (see note 1 on page 4) £ 200,000	

Spouse or civil partner's nil rate band

Fill in this section to work out the available nil rate band for the estate of the spouse or civil partner who died first.

9	Inheritance Tax, Capital Transfer Tax or Estate Duty nil rate band in force at the date of death (see note 2 on page 4)	£ 300,000
10	Total chargeable value of gifts and other transfers of value made in the seven years before the date of death (see notes 3 and 5 on page 4)	£
11	Nil rate band available against the estate of the spouse or civil partner who died first (box 9 minus box 10)	£ 300,000

Spouse or civil partner's estate

Fill in this section with details of the estate of the spouse or civil partner who died first. Enter the value of the assets at their date of death after deduction of exemptions or reliefs.

12 Legacies and assets passing under Will or intestacy of the spouse or civil partner who died first. Do not include legacies and assets that passed to the deceased who has died now (see note 3 on page 4)

Legacy/asset	Value £
Continue on a separate sheet if necessary	£

13	Share of assets jointly owned by the spouse or civil partner who died first, excluding assets that passed to the deceased who has died now (see note 3 on page 4)	£
14	Assets held in trust to which the spouse or civil partner who died first was entitled to benefit (see note 3 on page 4)	£
15	Gifts with reservation made by the spouse or civil partner who died first (see note 3 on page 4)	£
16	Total chargeable estate of the spouse or civil partner (box 12 + box 13 + box 14 + box 15)	£

Transferable nil rate band

17	Nil rate band available for transfer (box 11 *minus* box 16)	£ 300,000
18	Percentage by which to increase the nil rate band available on the deceased's death (box 17 *divided by* box 9 and *multiplied by* 100). Use four decimal places, **do not** round up	1 0 0 . 0 0 0 0 %
19	Nil rate band at the date of the deceased's death (the person who has died now) - see *IHT400 Rates and tables*	£ 312,000
20	Transferable nil rate band (box 19 *multiplied by* the box 18 percentage) *Round up to the nearest £*	£ 312,000

Example
- If the percentage in box 18 is 66.6666%, and
- the nil rate band in box 19 is £300,000
- then the figure to enter in box 20 would be £300,000 x 66.6666%

(or £300,000 x 66.6666 ÷ 100) = £200,000 rounded up to the nearest £

Exemptions and reliefs

21 List any exemptions or reliefs, other than spouse or civil partner exemption, taken into account in arriving at the values in boxes 10, 12, 13, 14 or 15 *(see note 4 on page 4)*

Box number	Exemptions or relief taken into account - *state amount and type* *(For example, box 14 Charity exemption £3,000)*

Pensions

Only answer question 22 where the spouse or civil partner who died first died on or after 6 April 2006.

22 Was the spouse or civil partner in receipt of a pension from:
- an Alternatively Secured Pension, or
- a pension scheme or annuity from which unauthorised payments were made after their death? No ✓   Yes ☐

If you have answered Yes, the calculation of the percentage to increase the deceased's nil rate band is complex. You may use the figure you worked out in box 20 provisionally. We will recalculate the percentage once you have sent us the form IHT400 for the deceased's estate.

If the spouse or civil partner was domiciled in Scotland at the date of death

Only answer question 23 where the spouse or civil partner who died first was domiciled in Scotland.

23 Was there anyone who was entitled to claim the legitim fund? No ☐   Yes ✓

If you have answered Yes, the calculation of the percentage to increase the deceased's nil rate band will depend on whether a claim for legitim is made. You may use the figure you worked out in box 20 provisionally. We will discuss the percentage once you have sent us the form IHT400 for the deceased's estate.

Notes

Your claim to transfer unused Inheritance Tax nil rate band
Where most or all of an estate passes to someone's surviving spouse or civil partner, those assets are generally exempt from Inheritance Tax. This means that most or all of the nil rate band available on the first death is not used.

The amount of the unused nil rate band can be transferred to the survivor of the marriage or civil partnership to increase the value of the nil rate band available on their death.

Since the transfer does not happen automatically, you must fill in this form and make a claim to transfer it. The claim must be made when the second spouse or civil partner dies.

These notes explain how the transfer works and where you can find information to help with filling in this form.

How the transfer works
On the deceased's death, the nil rate band that is available to their estate is increased by the percentage of the nil rate band that was unused when their spouse or civil partner died.

For example:

- A spouse or civil partner died and the nil rate band was £250,000.
- They left legacies totalling £125,000 to their children with the remainder to the surviving spouse or civil partner. The legacies to the children would use up one-half of the nil rate band, leaving the other half (50%) unused.
- In our example, on the deceased's death, the nil rate band is £300,000. So, their nil rate band would be increased by 50% to £450,000.
- If the deceased's estate did not exceed £450,000 there would be no Inheritance Tax to pay on their death. If it did, there would be Inheritance Tax to pay on the value above that figure.

Obtaining copies of grants of representation and Wills

- England and Wales:
  Phone **020 7947 7000**, or
  go to **www.hmcourts-service.gov.uk**

- Scotland:
  Phone **0131 247 2850**

- Northern Ireland:
  Phone **028 9023 5111**

Copies of death, marriage and or civil partnership certificates are available from the General Register Office

- in England and Wales:
  go to **www.gro.gov.uk**

- in Scotland:
  go to **www.gro-scotland.gov.uk**

- in Northern Ireland:
  go to **www.groni.gov.uk**

Spouse or civil partner's estate – notes to help you fill in this form

1 You can find the net value of the estate on the copy of the grant of representation (if one was taken out) or by adding together all the assets in the estate and deducting any liabilities.

2 For the IHT nil rate band in force at the date the spouse or civil partner died, please refer to form IHT400 Rates and tables. If it does not go back far enough, the rates for earlier years are available from:
- **www.hmrc.gov.uk/inheritancetax/** or
- the Probate and Inheritance Tax Helpline on **0845 30 20 900**.
  - If calling from outside the UK, phone **+44 115 974 3009**.

3 When filling in box 10 and boxes 12 to 15, you should include the value that was chargeable to tax. That is, the value after the deduction of exemptions and reliefs.

Spouse exemption where the first spouse died before 22 March 1972
Under Estate Duty there was no spouse exemption. All legacies, irrespective of the recipient and value should be included in box 12.

Spouse exemption where the first spouse died between 22 March 1972 and 12 November 1974 inclusive
During this period spouse exemption was limited to £15,000 so all legacies that passed to the deceased in excess of £15,000 should be included in box 12.

Spouse exemption after 12 November 1974
After that date there is no limit to spouse exemption unless the deceased was domiciled in the UK and the surviving spouse was not domiciled in the UK, when it is limited to £55,000. If that is the case, legacies that passed to the deceased in excess of £55,000 should be included in box 12.

4 List any exemptions or reliefs (other than spouse or civil partner exemption) you have taken into account in box 21. If you have been unable to find out whether or not any exemptions or relief applied when the spouse or civil partner died, leave this box blank.

For more information about the exemptions and reliefs that apply to Inheritance Tax, refer to IHT400 Notes.

If you are including assets which might qualify for an exemption or relief on this form, but are not sure whether the exemption or relief would have applied, tell us. We will discuss with you whether or not the exemption or relief might have applied.

5 For deaths between 27 July 1981 and 17 March 1986 you will need to know whether the spouse or civil partner had made any gifts or other transfers within ten years before the date of their death that were chargeable on their death.

6 Name of building, church or register office and locality.

5–25 However, it would be as well to start looking as soon as possible for these documents or securing copies to enable the questions on the new form to be completed! It may of course be that for a death many years ago where the spouse did not leave a will but assets were held jointly and passed by survivorship, and the residue was inherited by the surviving spouse on intestacy and as an excepted estate, the only documents which can be provided will be the death certificate and marriage certificate. Here, HM Revenue & Customs staff will take a view on the claim and may act sympathetically where it is clear that the documents cannot be produced. However, they are also warned that "they can accept the claim only 'provided the documents show the claim is valid and tax has been paid'".

Danger Warning!!

The executors have two years from the end of the month of the second death or three months from the first acting as such, whichever is the later. HMRC have no discretion to extend the time limits.

Danger Warning!!

Wills drafted before October 9, 2007 may now leave more than was originally intended, e.g. a legacy of "an amount equal to the largest amount which can pass without payment of inheritance tax" may pass double the amount of the full inheritance tax nil-rate band. Some concern has been expressed over the extent of the following type of wording in wills:

> "Discretionary FIVE In the event of my said spouse, surviving me for thirty days, I appoint my Trustees to be my Discretionary Trustees and I direct them to hold such sum or property (including the whole or part of my share of Twenty one Foxglove Close, Bearsden, or such property as shall be owned and occupied by me at my date of death whether jointly or otherwise) to such value as will exhaust the Nil Rate band of Inheritance Tax set out in Schedule 1 to the Inheritance Tax Act 1984 or any similar statutory successor, after taking into account
>
> (1) lifetime gifts made by me which are for Inheritance Tax purposes aggregable with or deemed to be part of my executry estate
> (2) legacies etc".

Attention!!

The concern centres over whether this clause or variations of it, which are lurking in (possibly tens of thousands of) wills in solicitor's offices in Scotland, also covers the increase in the transferred nil-rate band. Obviously, there is scope for ambiguity and certainly each clause must be considered on its merits. However, it is likely that the clause would carry the increased amount. It may be worth considering writing to testators along the following lines.

December 9, 2008
James Coltsfoot Esq
9 Cherryblossom Avenue
CAMBUSLANG

Dear James

I refer to our meeting a few months ago regarding your and your wife's Wills. You asked about tax saving Wills and I wondered if it would be helpful if I set out the position.

The thrust of the Will, which you have, is for use to be made of the Nil Rate Band (NRB), which is the exempt part of the estate for inheritance tax purposes, on the first death. This is presently standing at £312,000 though it is likely to go up. If estate is left to surviving spouses, it is exempt but the testator has not made use of his or her nil rate band.

*Thus if you were to "predecease" first leaving everything to Marion then while the estate would be exempt from inheritance tax purposes (as between spouses) when Marion passed away, the entire estate would be liable to inheritance tax, that is to say, both your individual estate and your joint estates which at this stage would **all be vested in Marion**.*

However if a legacy is made of the nil rate band (presently £312,000) then this amount is "taken out of the equation". The legacy would find its way into both Wills but would only operate on the first death. Until the 9th October 2007 this would have the effect of saving at current rates £124,800 on inheritance tax.

The method of dealing with this was merely to leave a legacy of the nil rate band. The legacy, if assets allow it and are sufficient, is for part of the estate to be passed on to the next generation. However, for most of us this sum cannot really be paid without undermining the surviving spouse's position. The other problem is that for many of us and I believe you hinted at this, the house is the main asset. The way we get round this is to set up in the will on death what is called a "mini discretionary trust". The discretionary trust is set up on the death and allows the half share in the house, which is then sold by the trustees to the widow. The widow does not pay for it but grants a standard security or bond so that when she comes to pass on, this is shown as a debt and diminishes her estate accordingly. This may seem slightly artificial but it does seem to work with the correct drafting. Discretionary Trusts are not without difficulties. In particular, there is a particularly penal aspect to say dividends on share holdings, which are in a discretionary trust. However many of these can be overcome with careful financial planning and in any event it is likely that the disadvantages of this will be more than outweighed by the benefits of the tax saving.

However, since October 9, 2007 it is possible for the executors of spouses who have inherited estate from a predeceasing husband to claim an uplift on the nil rate band so that their estate has potentially the benefit of up to a double nil rate band. This means that it may not be necessary to have a mini discretionary trust!

I am not suggesting that this clause be deleted. However, in your case, as you have been widowed twice and have inherited the entire estates of both your former wives, it may be that this clause will be applicable, that is to say, the legacy to the discretionary trust may now amount to two nil rate bands i.e. under current legislation to £624,000! You may wish to consider this and if so perhaps you might care to telephone to discuss it further.

With kind regards and best wishes

Yours sincerely,

Frederick G Clevercloggs

PS I know the fate of the Conservative Party is close to your heart and, of course, if they were returned to power it may be that they would alter matters perhaps to increasing the nil rate band even higher! Figures of a £1million as the nil rate band have been banded about. With the transferred nil rate band this could make the exempt amount of the second death a staggering £2million!

METHODOLOGY

5–26 Before grant of confirmation in Scotland can be obtained, it is necessary to satisfy the appropriate sheriff court that inheritance tax is not applicable or that it has been paid. This is accomplished by submitting to the appropriate sheriff court the necessary writs. The writs will consist of the will (if there is one) duly docquetted, and either a C5 generally if no inheritance tax is due, which is submitted along with the relevant C1. A cheque to cover the cost of confirmation dues and any certificates will also need to be tendered to the sheriff court. If there is no will, a bond of caution may be required.[17] If IHT is due the C1 must be stamped by HMRC signifying that IHT has been paid.

The completion of the C1 (confirmation) form will assist in determining whether or not a full inheritance tax set of forms IHT200 or their successor IHT400 are required. It hinges on the net qualifying value of the estate. The net qualifying value of the estate is the total of the estate less funeral expenses, debts and relief, but only, at this stage, as a result of benefits passing on the death to either the surviving spouse or civil partner or to a registered charity.

In order to estimate the amount of spouse, civil partner or charity exemption, it is necessary, where there are children or issue entitled to claim legitim, to calculate the amount of the legitim fund and then adjust the amount which would be payable to the spouse or civil partner or charity if the legitim fund were claimed in full after taking account of any legitim claimed or renounced before the application for confirmation is made.

5–27 There is sometimes confusion over what is an exempt estate and what is an excepted estate. The exempt estate is one which is below the inheritance tax level. Strictly speaking an exempt estate is a type of excepted estate. For deaths on or after September 1, 2006 an excepted

---

[17] The Scottish Law Commission have recommended the abolition of this in their recent report.

estate is an estate where no inheritance tax (IHT) is due and a full inheritance tax account is not required. From April 6, 2004 there are three types of excepted estate, i.e. low value estates , exempt estates and foreign domiciliaries.

Low value estates are estates where there can be no liability to IHT because the gross value of the estate does not exceed the IHT threshold and:

- the deceased died domiciled in the United Kingdom;
- the gross value of the estate does not exceed the excepted estate limit;
- if the estate includes any assets in trust, they are held in a single trust and the gross value does not exceed £150,000;
- if the estate includes foreign assets, their gross value does not exceed £100,000;
- if there are any specified transfers, their chargeable value does not exceed £150,000;
- the deceased had not made a gift with reservation of benefit; and
- the deceased did not have an alternatively secured pension fund, either as the original scheme member or as the dependant or relevant dependant of the original scheme member.

Exempt estates, as stated, are estates where there can be no liability to IHT because the gross value of the estate does not exceed £1,000,000 and there is no tax to pay because it qualifies for one or both of spouse/ civil partner exemption and/or charity exemption.

No other exemption or relief is applicable. Spouse or civil partner **5–28** exemption can only be deducted if both spouses or civil partners have always been domiciled in the United Kingdom (UK). Charity exemption can only be deducted if the gift is absolute and:

- the deceased died domiciled in the UK;
- the gross value of the estate does not exceed £1,000,000;
- the net chargeable value of the estate after deduction of liabilities and spouse or civil partner exemption and/or charity exemption only does not exceed the IHT threshold;
- if the estate includes any assets in trust, they are held in a single trust and the gross value does not exceed £150,000 (unless the settled property passes to a spouse or civil partner or to a charity when the limit is waived);
- if the estate includes foreign assets, their gross value does not exceed £100,000;
- if there are any specified transfers, their chargeable value does not exceed £150,000;
- the deceased had not made a gift with reservation of benefit; and
- the deceased did not have an alternatively secured pension fund, either as the original scheme member or as the dependant or relevant dependant of the original scheme member.

In Scotland, the spouse or civil partner exemption and/or charity exemption must be calculated on the hypothesis that any entitlement to legitim against the estate will be claimed in full. In other words, only the minimum amount of spouse or civil partner exemption and/or charity exemption available after accounting for legitim can be deducted to establish whether the IHT threshold is exceeded.

5–29   Foreign domiciliaries are estates where there can be no liability to IHT because the gross value of the estate in the UK does not exceed £150,000. The conditions for these estates are that:

- the deceased died domiciled outside the UK;
- the deceased was never domiciled in the UK or treated as domiciled in the UK for IHT purposes;
- the deceased's UK estate consisted only of cash or quoted shares and securities passing under a Will or intestacy or by survivorship;
- the gross value of the estate did not exceed £150,000; and
- the deceased did not have an alternatively secured pension fund, either as the original scheme member or as the dependant or relevant dependant of the original scheme member.

If dealing with an estate where the death was on or after September 1, 2006, there is a helpful algorithm to be found at the HMRC website: "Does this estate qualify as an excepted estate?", available at *http://www.hmrc.gov.uk/cto/customerguide/page3–59.htm* [accessed April 23, 2009].

An estate may be exempt and excepted in certain circumstances.

5–30   If the estate is not an excepted estate or an exempt estate it requires the submission of either the IHT200 series forms or the IHT400 series. To summarise, an exempt estate will be where the estate passes to the surviving spouse, civil partner or charity and the gross estate for inheritance tax does not exceed the taxable threshold. If, however, part of the estate passes to the spouse, civil partner or charity but the gross exceeds £1 million or part of the estate passes to the spouse, civil partner or charity and the value after deducting liabilities and the spouse, civil partner or charity exemption exceeds the taxable threshold, it is necessary to proceed with a Form IHT200 or its successor, an IHT400.

In the majority of cases where no inheritance tax is due this will be because the deceased's estate qualifies as an excepted estate or qualifies for small estates confirmation.[18] In such cases it is not necessary to complete form IHT200 or IHT400. A C5 can be completed instead. The possibility of the use of a C5 form should be investigated thoroughly since the alternative of completing the full range of IHT forms is a time-consuming and complicated (and often frustrating) procedure which inevitably will involve great expense for the estate.

The net qualifying value of the estate is found by ascertaining the gross value of the estate for inheritance tax. The gross value includes the estate which is included in the inventory for confirmation (plus any secured debt added back to the total), joint property with a survivorship

---

[18] Where the estate qualifies as a small estate the sheriff clerk will complete the inventory form C1 for a small estate if so requested by the executor.

destination, nominated property, trust property in which the deceased had a liferent, gifts within seven years (unless exempt) and any asset in which the deceased reserved an interest.

The net value for inheritance tax is the total of the gross less **5–31** deductions for debts, funeral expenses, etc. At this stage no deduction is made for exemptions and reliefs. The net qualifying value is the gross value of the estate after deduction of debts and funeral expenses and any relief such as to a surviving spouse or civil partner or to a charity only.

It should be noted that legitim will have to be taken into account and the amount adjusted which would have been payable to the spouse, civil partner or charity if the legitim fund were claimed in full. To be considered an excepted estate, the gross value must be below the excepted estates limit or less than £1 million, and that only where all or part of the estate passes to the spouse, civil partner or charity and after deduction of liabilities and those exemptions only, the estate is under the excepted estates figure. There are other restrictions such as specified transfers of cash, shares, property and heritable subjects which are under £100,000. In addition any foreign assets must be less than £75,000 and if there is an estate for inheritance tax purposes of a trust the total value is £100,000 also. The excepted limit will not apply if there was any question of reservation of benefit. The excepted estate limit is generally the same as the inheritance tax threshold, i.e. the nil-rate band. However, there is a particular quirk regarding this where the death occurred after April 5 and before August 6 and confirmation is applied for before the second of these dates. In this case the tax threshold for the previous year is relevant.

Whoever completes the inventory form C1 should indicate on page 4 that the estate falls within the excepted or small estate confirmation regimes. If it is a small estate which conforms to both descriptions both boxes on page 4 should be ticked "yes". Once form C1 is completed and the sheriff clerk or commissary clerk has all the other documentation required, confirmation will be issued provided all is in order. It may not be generally known but on granting confirmation the forms C1 are sent to HMRC, Inheritance Tax, Edinburgh, for retention. This is different from the corresponding procedure for excepted estates in the rest of the UK.

Attention!!

If the parties are not contacted by HMRC within 60 days of obtaining the grant the applicant has automatic clearance from IHT, so long as the estate did meet the excepted estate conditions.

There are estates where there can be no liability to IHT because the **5–32** gross value of the estate does not exceed £1 million and there is no tax to pay because either spouse or civil partner exemption and/or charity exemption only can be deducted against the assets. No other exemption or relief can be taken into account.

If any of the above conditions are not satisfied a form IHT200 or IHT400 must be delivered. Assuming IHT is payable this is accomplished by obtaining an IHT reference. Before paying inheritance tax it is necessary to apply either by post or online for an account reference and a payslip. The form is straightforward and the executor can expect to receive the payslip within three weeks. It is clearly imperative that if there is an urgency about the matter that this matter should be addressed quickly.

The other occasion where an IHT200 or IHT400 is needed is where there is a transfer nil-rate band allowance claimed. There are thus several occasions where it will be necessary to have the C1 stamped even when IHT is not due!

Post-June 2009

5–33   As explained at the beginning of this Chapter,[19] HMRC have promulgated new forms. These can be used for deaths from November 17, 2008. While it is still competent to proceed by way of the IHT200 and supplementary page numbers D1 to D21, these will be replaced with a new form, namely form IHT400. This is to replace IHT200; the Schedules, which do not as explained below entirely correspond with IHT200 Schedules, will now be IHT401 to IHT423. These forms can already be downloaded from H M Revenue & Customs website.

These new forms must be used from June 9, 2009 for deaths on or after March 18, 1986 where a full IHT form is required. From that date IHT200 forms will no longer be accepted.

---

[19] With impeccable timing to coincide with the final drafting of this text!

IHT400

 HM Revenue & Customs

Inheritance Tax account
IHT400

When to use this form

Fill in this form if:
- the deceased died on or after 18 March 1986, and
- there is Inheritance Tax to pay, or
- there is no Inheritance Tax to pay, but the estate does not qualify as an excepted estate.

The IHT400 letter, page 4, gives details about excepted estates.

Deadline

You must send this form to us within 12 months of the date of death. Interest will be payable after six months.

The Inheritance Tax (IHT) account

The account is made up of this form and separate Schedules. You will have to fill in some of the Schedules.

To help you get started
- Gather the deceased's papers and the information you have about the deceased's estate. Make a list of the deceased's assets, liabilities, investments and other financial interests and any gifts made.
- Fill in boxes 1 to 28 then work through pages 4 and 5 of this form to identify which Schedules you will need. If you do not have them all:
  – download them from www.hmrc.gov.uk/inheritancetax/ or
  – phone the Helpline to request them.
- Fill in the Schedules before moving on to complete this form.

IHT reference

If there is any tax to pay, you will need to apply for an IHT reference and payslip before you send this form to us. You can apply online at www.hmrc.gov.uk/inheritancetax/ or fill in form IHT422 and send it to us. Apply for a reference at least two weeks before you plan to send us this form.

Filling in this form
- Use the IHT400 Notes to help you fill in this form.
- Fill in the form in ink.
- Make full enquiries so you can show that the figures you give and the statements you make are correct.
- If an instrument of variation has been signed before applying for a grant, fill in the form to show the effect of the Will/intestacy and instrument together. *See IHT400 Notes.*

Answer all the questions and fill in the boxes to help us process your form.

Help

For more information or help or another copy of this form:
- go to www.hmrc.gov.uk/inheritancetax/
- phone our Helpline on **0845 30 20 900**
  – if calling from outside the UK, phone **+44 115 974 3009.**

Deceased's details

1 Deceased's name

Title - enter MR, MRS, MISS, MS or other title

> Mrs

Surname

> Snowdrop

First name(s)

> Daisy Crocus Primrose or

2 Date of death *DD MM YYYY*

> 0 1 | 0 1 | | |

3 Inheritance Tax reference number (if known)
See note at the top of this form

4 Was the deceased male or female?

Male [ ]   Female [✓]

5 Deceased's date of birth *DD MM YYYY*

> 0 1 | 0 1 | | |

6 Where was the deceased domiciled at the date of death?

- England & Wales [ ]
- Scotland [✓]
- Northern Ireland [ ]
- other country [ ] *specify country in box below.*

See IHT400 Notes for information about domicile.

If the deceased was not domiciled in the UK, fill in [IHT401] now, and then the rest of the form.

Please turn over

If the deceased was domiciled in Scotland at the date of death

7 Has the legitim fund been discharged in **full** *following the death? See IHT400 Notes*

Yes ☐ *Go to box 8*

No ☑ *Please provide a full explanation in the 'Additional information' boxes, pages 15 and 16*

Deceased's details

8 Was the deceased:

- married or in a civil partnership ☐
- single ☐
- widowed or a surviving civil partner ☑
- divorced or a former civil partner? ☐

9 If the deceased was married or in a civil partnership at the time of their death, on what date did the marriage or registration of the civil partnership take place?
DD MM YYYY

| 0 | 1 | 0 | 1 | 1 | 9 | 5 | 0 |

10 Who survived the deceased? *Tick all that apply*

- a spouse or civil partner ☑
- brothers or sisters ☑
- parents ☐
- children ☑ number | 0 | 7 |
- grandchildren ☑ number | 4 | 3 |

11 Deceased's last known permanent address

Postcode
| Z | 4 | 2 | | 2 | | | |

House number
| 2 | 2 | 2 | 2 |

Rest of address, including house name or flat number

| Damson House |
| Deanfield |
| Lanark |

12 Was the property in box 11 owned or part-owned by the deceased or did the deceased have a right to live in the property?

Yes ☐ *Go to box 13*

No ☑ *Give details below. For example, 'deceased lived with daughter' or 'address was a nursing home'*

| Patient Resident - Care Home |

13 Deceased's occupation, or former occupation if retired, for example, 'retired doctor'.

| retired Merchant Banker |

14 Deceased's National Insurance number (if known)

| Z | X | 1 | 2 | 3 | 4 | 5 | 6 | A |

15 Deceased's Income Tax or Unique Taxpayer Reference (if known)

| 4 | 3 | 3 | | | 5 | 4 | 3 | 2 | 1 |

16 Did anyone act under a power of attorney granted by the deceased during their lifetime? This may have been a general, enduring or lasting power of attorney.

No ☐

Yes ☑ *Please enclose a copy of the power of attorney*

IHT400   Page 2

Contact details of the person dealing with the estate

For example, a solicitor or executor.

17 Name and address of the firm or person dealing with the estate

Name

| Winter & Cress |

Postcode

| S | S | 0 | 0 | | 4 | 0 | | |

House or building number

| | 1 | 2 | 3 |

Rest of address, including house name or flat number

| Bluebell House |
| Buddlei Street |
| Glasgow |

18 Contact name *if different from box 17*

19 Phone number

| 0101 124567 |

20 DX number and town (if used)

| DX 00 GLASGOW |

21 Contact's reference

| Mr Clevercloggs |

22 Fax number

| 012345678 |

23 If we have to repay any overpaid Inheritance Tax, we need to know who to make the cheque out to.

Do you want any cheque we send to be made out to the firm or person shown at box 17?

Yes ✓ *Go to box 24*

No ☐ *Give the name(s) here, as you would like them to appear on the cheque.*

Deceased's Will

24 Did the deceased leave a Will?

No ☐ *Go to box 29*

Yes ✓ *Go to box 25. Please enclose a copy of the Will and any codicils when sending us your account. If an instrument of variation alters the amount of Inheritance Tax payable on this estate, please also send a copy.*

25 Is the address of the deceased as shown in the Will the same as the deceased's last known permanent address (at box 11)?

No ✓ *Go to box 26*

Yes ☐ *Go to box 27*

26 What happened to the property given as the deceased's residence in the Will?
If the deceased sold the property but used all the sale proceeds to buy another main residence for themselves and this happened more than once, there is no need to give details of all the events. Simply say that the 'residence was replaced by the current property'. In all other cases give details of exactly what happened to the property, and give the date of the event(s).

| Sold when deceased moved into care home and |
| proceeds invested for the said deceased |

Items referred to in the Will but not included in the estate

Only fill in boxes 27 and 28 if the deceased left a Will. If not go to box 29.

27	Are you including on this form all assets specifically referred to in the Will? (For example, land, buildings, personal possessions, works of art or shares.)

No ☑ Go to box 28

Yes ☐ Go to box 29

| 28 | Items referred to in the Will and not included on this form (any gifts should be shown on form IHT403) |

Items given away as gifts, sold or disposed of before the deceased's death	Who was the item given or sold to, or what happened to it?	Date of gift, sale or disposal	Value of the item at the date of gift, sale or disposal £	If the item was sold, what did the deceased do with the sale proceeds?

What makes up your Inheritance Tax account - Schedules

To make a complete account of the estate you may need to complete some separate Schedules.
Answer the following questions by ticking the No or Yes box.

29	Transfer of unused nil rate band

Do you want to transfer any unused nil rate band from the deceased's spouse or civil partner who died before them?

No ☐   Yes ☑   Use Schedule   **IHT402**

| 30 | Gifts and other transfers of value |

Did the deceased make any lifetime gifts or other transfers of value on or after 18 March 1986? *See IHT400 Notes*

No ☐   Yes ☑   Use Schedule   **IHT403**

| 31 | Jointly owned assets |

Did the deceased jointly own any assets (other than business or partnership assets) with any other person(s)?

No ☐   Yes ☑   Use Schedule   **IHT404**

| 32 | Houses, land, buildings and interests in land |

Did the deceased own any house, land or buildings or rights over land in the UK in their sole name?

No ☑   Yes ☐   Use Schedule   **IHT405**

| 33 | Bank and building society accounts |

Did the deceased hold any bank or building society accounts in their sole name, including National Savings and Premium Bonds?

No ☐   Yes ☑   Use Schedule   **IHT406**

| 34 | Household and personal goods |

Did the deceased own any household goods or personal possessions?

No ☐   Yes ☑   Use Schedule   **IHT407**

If the deceased did **not** own any household goods or personal possessions or they do not have any value, please explain the circumstances in the 'Additional information' boxes on pages 15 and 16.

| 35 | Household and personal goods donated to charity |

Do the people who inherit the deceased's household goods and personal possessions want to donate some or all of them to a UK registered charity and deduct charity exemption from the value of the estate?
For example, they may wish to donate the deceased's furniture to a charity shop.

No ☑   Yes ☐   Use Schedule   **IHT408**

The beleaguered practitioner is therefore faced with the possibility of **5–34** either using form IHT200 as aforementioned or going straight to the form IHT400. It is recommended that the new forms be used if only because HMRC are to remove full online support shortly!

A list of IHT400 Schedules and corresponding D Forms is reproduced below by authority of HM Revenue & Customs:

"List of IHT400 schedules and corresponding 'D' forms

Form number	Form title	Previous form
IHT400	Inheritance Tax Account IHT400	IHT200
IHT400 Calculation	Inheritance Tax Account IHT400 Calculation	IHT200(WS)
IHT401	Domicile outside the United Kingdom	D2
IHT402	Claim to transfer unused Inheritance Tax nil rate band	IHT216
IHT403	Gifts and other transfers of value	D3
IHT404	Jointly owned assets	D4
IHT405	Houses, land, buildings and interests in land	D12
IHT406	Bank and building society accounts	New form
IHT407	Household and personal goods	D10
IHT408	Household and personal goods given to charity	D10A
IHT409	Pensions	D6
IHT410	Life assurance and annuities	D9
IHT411	Listed stocks and shares	D7
IHT412	Unlisted stocks and shares and control holdings	New form
IHT413	Business or partnership interests and assets	D14
IHT414	Agricultural relief	D13
IHT415	Interest in another estate	D11
IHT416	Debts due to the deceased	D8
IHT417	Foreign assets	D15
IHT418	Assets held in trust	D5
IHT419	Debts owed by the deceased	D16
IHT420	National Heritage assets, conditional exemption and offers in lieu of tax	New
IHT421	Probate summary	D18
IHT422	Application for an Inheritance Tax reference	D21
IHT423	Direct payment scheme bank or building society account	D20
IHT400 Letter	Inheritance Tax forms Quick start guide	New—print only
IHT400 Rates & Tables	Inheritance Tax nil rate bands, limits and rates	IHT210A

Form number	Form title	Previous form
IHT400 Notes	Guide to completing the executor Inheritance Tax account	IHT210
IHT400 Help sheet	Inheritance Tax Account IHT400 Interest Help sheet	New
Deleted form	D1	
Deleted form	D17	
Deleted form	D3a"	

5–35 As can be seen, some of the IHT200 series have been omitted. D1 has been omitted. The questions are now on the main form. A form D17—additional information—has been replaced with a new Schedule IHT406 for listing bank and building society and National Savings Investments. One unfortunate change is that it will be necessary to actually include details of bank, building society accounts and National Savings/Premium Bonds in Schedule IHT406. Presumably, however, in Scotland practitioners will attempt to use the inventory section of the C1 or include these as a separate "inventory". Additional information space is now on pp.15 and 16 of the form IHT400. Alternatively, as stated, it might be worth attempting to avoid duplication by merely making a reference in D17 to the inventory form, e.g. items 3, 5 and 6 of the inventory and the totals carried forward. The final "subsection" is for D3a; gifts made as part of normal expenditure out of income are now to be shown on p.6 of Schedule IHT403 (gifts and other transfers of value).

Unfortunately it seems that HMRC do not keep a copy of the C1 account (including the inventory). It might be worthwhile sending an extra copy of the C1 including inventory (if separate) to HMRC when submitting the IHT400 and the C1 for stamping.

NEW SCHEDULES

5–36 Some new schedules have been introduced apart from IHT406 for bank/building society and National Savings. The IHT412 deals with unlisted stocks and shares, and control holdings, and the IHT420 covers National Heritage assets, conditional exemption and offers in lieu of tax. The IHT400 and schedule notes booklet contain all the notes which deal with the forms. In addition and "wherever possible", notes, examples and further explanations appear on the IHT400 and the Schedules. Where there are additional notes to some of the Schedules, these can be found in the booklet IHT400 notes on pp.18 to 42. Please note that there are therefore no separate notes for each of the Schedules. Notes for the IHT400 calculation apart from the interest calculations are contained in the form.[20]

There has been a fairly drastic re-writing of the forms and in addition to the changes in the forms there are also key changes in the way the forms work.

Thus for instalment and non-instalment option property, pp.6 to 10 of form IHT400 are divided into two columns, non-instalment option property and instalment option property. HMRC state that:

---

[20] IHT400 Helpsheet.

"This is so that the deceased's assets can be listed in a logical order with joint assets first, followed by the most common assets of house, bank accounts, cash, and so on."

The amount for each asset is inserted into one box.

The treatment of jointly-owned assets is specifically altered. These **5–37** should be listed on Schedule IHT404 whether they are held as joint property or joint with a survivorship destination. The corresponding English expressions are tenants in common or joint tenants. Assets which are either subject to instalment or non-instalment option property are to be shown in different columns.

The date of death value of the deceased's estate is not to include jointly owned assets passing by survivorship: box 11, form IHT404.

A substantial section is included to deal with the transfer of the unused nil-rate band and the number of items which are required has been drastically reduced. This is to be welcomed.

As was to be expected the matter of the transfer of unused nil-rate band was earmarked for special attention. Form IHT402 is now a Schedule to the IHT400 and the declaration on p.12 of the IHT400 has a clause relating to the claim, if one has been made. In addition the documents which must be submitted are now *photocopies* of the following:

- grant of confirmation to the estate of the first spouse or civil partner. If no grant was taken out, a copy of the death certificate;
- spouse or civil partner's will, if there was one; and
- deed of variation or similar document, if one was executed on the first estate.

Probably this last set of requirements (rather than the extended list **5–38** which HM Revenue & Customs imply will still be necessary with IHT200 series forms) would be sufficient inducement to start using the new forms as soon as possible!

The claim to transfer unused inheritance tax nil-rate band must be made by the executors within 24 months after the end of the month in which the second deceased died or, (if it ends later) the period of three months beginning with the date on which the executors first acted.

Example

If the civil partner died on October 10, 2008, the form would need to be received by October 31, 2010.

Attention!!

If no claim is made by the executors, any other person liable for tax may make a claim within such later period as an officer of Revenue & Customs may allow, IHTA84/S8B(1)(b).

Under the Inheritance Tax Act 1984 at s.8B(3)(b), HMRC has the discretion to accept a claim late if, for example, there was a dispute which must be settled before the executors can be identified. If the dispute means that a claim cannot be made within the two-year period and after the statutory extension of three months, the claim may still be admitted. It may be made if it is an intervention which is beyond the claimant's control, e.g. postal delay, records necessary to make the claim were lost through fire, flood or theft.

The household and personal goods form, which under the old system almost defied sense and coherence, has now been transmuted into form IHT400. Many practitioners took the view that attempting to complete the previous form would "lead to madness". Totals can now be allowed.

5–39   Thankfully the amount of detail which is required for most household and personal goods has been reduced on form IHT407. Probably the reason for this was that no one filled them in correctly anyway! The only household and personal goods to be listed individually are: (1) items of jewellery valued at over £500; (2) vehicles, boats and aircraft; and (3) antiques, works of art or collections. All other goods should be added up and the total inserted in box 4 of form IHT407.

There are now two Schedules for stocks and shares: (i) IHT411 for listed stocks and shares, including UK Government and municipal securities; and (ii) IHT412 for unlisted, traded unlisted and control holdings of stocks and shares.

On the face of it the new Schedules appear to ask more questions than the old 'D' forms. However, in many cases the questions and details of the information requested have merely been relocated!

METHODOLOGY

5–40   It is suggested that the following procedure be followed.

- Print off the IHT400 notes booklet.
- Deal with all questions on pp.1–4.
- Identify which Schedules the executor needs by answering the questions on pp.4 and 5.
- Complete the Schedules before the executor proceeds to p.6. These figures have to be transferred from the Schedules to the boxes.
- Complete instructions numbered 4 to 16 on the IHT400.

Information can be obtained from the HMRC website. There is a helpful checklist to guide the practitioner to remember what to include with the form and to identify any further actions necessary.

We can only speculate why at of all times, a new set of forms is being introduced at a time when other sections of HM Revenue & Customs staff will be re-allocated following the proposed closure of 20 HMRC offices in Scotland!

5–41   There are many problems associated with the new forms. Totals on the principal IHT400 can become corrupted and the only solution seems to be the heartbreaking way of starting a new form and re-entering the data! It is not completely clear why HM Revenue & Customs did not take the opportunity to make the forms composite, that is to say to carry the totals from the supplementary form on to the appropriate boxes on the principal IHT400. It is not clear why the name of the deceased and the date of death have to be manually entered into each supplementary form or indeed why, when the appropriate boxes are ticked, it is not possible for HM Revenue & Customs software to decide which supplementary forms are needed. In addition there does not appear to be any section where anything other than the total inheritance tax can be calculated. Thus it may be that tax is to be paid by the donee of a gift or on heritable property. This calculation will require to be made manually. Because of the cumbersome nature of the forms, there will always be a temptation to complete some of the supplementary forms by hand. There are other matters such as why HM Revenue & Customs need the most extraordinary amount of information, e.g. the Bond Number for premium bonds. Why is a copy of the deceased's power of attorney required? Most practitioners agree that the forms are more time consuming to complete! The section of IHT403 which requires details of gifts from normal expenditure has only seven columns. Presumably HM Revenue & Customs require the gifts to be allocated to tax years, i.e. for April 6 to April 5 in the following year. The form covers the situation if there are only gifts made in less than seven years before death or where the deceased passes away on April 5. All other dates of death potentially need eight columns to cover the seven calendar years before death. On some supplementary forms there is not enough space and on others such as the IHT411 it seems to need all the investments listed individually. It seemed to prefer to "want" share holdings and prices so that it could work out the totals. The temptation to download a form and fill in the totals by hand referring to "paper apart", i.e. the stockbroker's valuation, for these by hand is almost overwhelming!

Payment of the Tax

Because of difficulties over bank loans it may be that the direct payment **5–42** form IHT423 will and should be used more frequently. It seems that most banks etc. will be able to expedite these more quickly than formerly—perhaps a direct result of public investment in them!

Form IHT423

HM Revenue & Customs

Direct Payment Scheme
Bank or building society account
Schedule IHT423

When to use this form

Fill in this form if you want to pay the Inheritance Tax that is due, by transferring money from the deceased's bank or building society account(s).
Please fill in a separate form for each account.

Help

Please read the guidance notes on the Direct Payment Scheme in the IHT400 Notes before filling in this form.
For more information or help or another copy of this form:
• go to **www.hmrc.gov.uk/inheritancetax/**
• phone our Helpline on **0845 30 20 900**
  – if calling from outside the UK, phone **+44 115 974 3009.**

Where to send this form

The form should be sent to the bank or building society concerned and not to HM Revenue & Customs Inheritance Tax.

Name of deceased
Mrs Daisy Snowdrop

Date of death *DD MM YYYY*

0	1		0	1		2	0	0	9

IHT reference number

Transfer details

I/We have applied for a grant of representation or Confirmation for the estate of the deceased and request that the amount shown below is transferred from the deceased's account to HM Revenue & Customs to pay the Inheritance Tax due.

Deceased's account details

Name of bank or building society

Northern Rock

Sort code

1	1	–	1	1	–	1	1

Account number

1	2	3	4	5	6	7			

Building society account roll or reference number

Amount to be transferred

In words

Twenty three thousand one hundred and eleven

In figures

£	£23,111.00

Transfer to HM Revenue & Customs

Name of bank

Bank of England

Sort code

1	0	–	5	3	–	9	2

Account number

2	3	4	3	0	3	0	3

Please turn to page 2 to sign the Declaration. It is important that everyone who is applying for the grant of representation or Confirmation to the estate of the deceased signs this form.

Declaration

The amount shown on page 1 is required to pay all or part of the Inheritance Tax due. If HM Revenue & Customs needs to repay the tax paid before the grant or Confirmation is issued they are authorised to return the money to the account shown on page 1.

First representative	**Third representative**
Surname	Surname
Cheetham	
First name(s)	First name(s)
Charles	
Postcode	Postcode
G 1 1 2 X X	
Rest of address, including house number/flat number	Rest of address, including house number/flat number
Signature	Signature
Date *DD MM YYYY*	Date *DD MM YYYY*

Second representative	**Fourth representative**
Surname	Surname
First name(s)	First name(s)
Postcode	Postcode
Rest of address, including house number/flat number	Rest of address, including house number/flat number
Signature	Signature
Date *DD MM YYYY*	Date *DD MM YYYY*

Declaration

The amount shown on page 1 is required to pay all or part of the Inheritance Tax due. If HM Revenue & Customs needs to repay the tax paid before the grant or Confirmation is issued they are authorised to return the money to the account shown on page 1.

First representative

Surname

First name(s)

Postcode

Rest of address, including house number/flat number

Signature

Date *DD MM YYYY*

Second representative

Surname

First name(s)

Postcode

Rest of address, including house number/flat number

Signature

Date *DD MM YYYY*

Third representative

Surname

First name(s)

Postcode

Rest of address, including house number/flat number

Signature

Date *DD MM YYYY*

Fourth representative

Surname

First name(s)

Postcode

Rest of address, including house number/flat number

Signature

Date *DD MM YYYY*

Pre-June 2009

For the period up to June 2009 it will still be competent to complete the **5–43**
IHT200 form and any necessary supplementary forms. HMRC will wish
to have the new ones used as soon as possible and will begin to restrict
their online and other support for the IHT200 series from December
2008. However, they are still competent and are listed here for convenience along with a note of their relevance.

IHT 200

1. D1—the deceased's will   **5–44**
2. D2—Where the deceased had a domicile outwith the United
    Kingdom
3. D3—Gifts and transfers; and D3a—Gifts out of income
4. D4—Joint and nominated assets
5. D5—Assets held in trust
6. D6—Pensions
7. D7—Stocks and shares
8. D8—Debts due to the estate
9. D9—Life assurance and annuities
10. D10—Household and personal goods
11. D11—Interest in another estate
12. D12—Heritable Property
13. D13—Property subject to Agricultural relief
14. D14—Property subject to business relief
15. D15—Foreign Estate
16. D16—Debts owed by the estate
17. D17—Continuation Pages
18. D18—Probate Summary (This applies to England and Wales)
19. D19—Confirmation that no IHT is payable
20. D20—Application to transfer funds
21. D21—Application for IHT reference
22. Checklist

Copies of these forms can be ordered from HMRC. Alternatively, the
forms can be completed online and downloaded before sending off to
HMRC. It may have been worth investing in software to enable the
material to be saved and altered at a future date.

Before paying inheritance tax it is necessary to apply either by post or
online for an account reference and a payslip. The form is straightforward and the executor can expect to receive the payslip within three
weeks. It is clearly imperative that if there is an urgency about the matter
that this matter should be addressed quickly.

When the reference is obtained the IHT can be paid. It may only be
necessary to pay IHT on what is known as "non-instalment option
property". This will usually be anything other than heritable property
and certain shares in non public companies. Before describing the next
parts, it is helpful to consider gifts with reservation.

Gift with Reservation Rules

Gift with Reservation of Benefit

The HMRC website defines a gift with reservation as: **5–45**

"A gift which is not fully given away so that the person getting the gift does so with conditions attached or the person making the gift keeps back some benefit for themselves."

Perhaps the one which causes most difficulty is where, say, parents make over the house in which they live to their children and where the parents continue to live in the property. Their motives for this may be a misguided belief that this will avoid inheritance tax on the house when they die. Alternatively, they may hope to "save" the house from being utilised to pay care home fees when they are no longer able live on their own. The aim of both these motives is probably doomed to failure but the extent of this aspect of the matter is outwith the scope of this text.

The basis of HMRC's view on the subject is governed oddly by the terms of a letter to the (English) Law Society. This is printed in the Appendix.

Letter to Beneficiaries

Dear Mrs Cowslip,

The executor's late father's executry

As you know, we are acting for the executors of your late father.

We are presently investigating the estate and endeavouring to identify his assets and liabilities for inheritance tax purposes and to obtain confirmation of the executors from the Sheriff Court.

This, as you can imagine, will take some time and we will contact you to let you know the position.

We would take the opportunity of mentioning to you the question of deed of variation of the executor's father's will. It is competent under current legislation to "vary" the terms of a will, provided this is carried out in the proper form and provided that it is done within two years of death. It is frequently used by a beneficiary to pass on all or part of an inheritance for whatever reason. For example it may be used to redirect assets to the next generation. By a legal fiction, this is treated, for certain tax purposes, as a bequest by the testator.

Although it may seem some time off, we strongly suggest that beneficiaries consider this and take the appropriate advice from their legal, accountancy or financial advisors.

Please note that this firm only holds [details regarding the firm's financial certificate].

Yours sincerely

Chapter Six

PRE-OWNED ASSETS TAX

"The Revenue are fed up with locking the stable door after the horses have bolted and have now decided to shoot the horses."[1]

TAX FACTS

As for Income Tax

The election for having the charge treated as inheritance tax must be **6–01** made before January 31 in the year following the first year of assessment, e.g. If the taxpayer becomes liable to the income tax charge for 2006–2007, he has until January 31, 2008 to make the election.

If the deceased dies part way through the tax year, before they have made the election?	He is liable for income tax on the benefit derived from the pre-owned asset from April 6 in the first year of assessment up to date of death. The executors are not able to make an election after the date of death and the estate will be liable to pay the income tax due up to that date (provided it is not below the *de minimis* limit). This will be a debt on the estate for inheritance tax. The charge of course ends with the death of the taxpayer.
If the taxpayer dies before the start of the tax year when the charge to income tax on pre-owned assets comes into force?	As above the charge ends with death.

INTRODUCTION

The taxation of pre-owned assets was thrust into the spotlight in the pre- **6–02** Budget report of 2003. The charge hits those who, since March 17, 1986, had given away assets and were continuing to use them including those who had given their houses to their children but remained living there. It came into operation on April 6, 2005. The pre-owned assets tax (POT)[2] is an income tax charge, which operates alongside the inheritance tax gift with reservation of benefit rules.[3] Its raison d'être was to deter "con-

---

[1] Alan Barr at a lecture at Glasgow University.
[2] Sometimes known as "POAT".
[3] See Chapter 5 on Inheritance Tax.

trived and artificial" IHT saving strategies. Arguably it should be dealt with under the heading of income tax but because of its unique features and the fact that it straddles inheritance tax under the gifts with reservation and income tax it is dealt with under its own heading.

It is not thought that this will come up at the time of framing the executry tax returns but it may, and the consequences of it being omitted and later discovered by HMRC after the estate has been distributed are too horrendous to contemplate! A full treatment of what is undoubtedly a very complex tax are, of course, outwith the scope of this modest text but the following may provide an introduction and some help in determining if it is relevant and needs to be addressed.

The usual enquiries as to gifts within the seven years and earlier where chargeable transfers have been made should yield the information necessary to identify a possible charge to POT. The new IHT400 and the IHT403 have a specific section in the chargeable transfer sections. Despite the whole-scale panic with which it was received it has become something of a damp squib; most cases fall into the gift with reservation rules. It should be stressed that POT is a "freestanding" charge to income tax; it is and was not under any existing schedule and operated from 2005 to 2006 onwards. It is a "stand-alone" charge. The charge is the equivalent under the Income Tax (Trading and Other Income) Act 2005, which was to be in place for 2005/2006 of a Schedule D Case VI charge, and Schedule D Case VI losses can be set off against the chargeable amount. There is a *de minimis* restriction of £5,000 per annum.

6–03   The tax was first announced in the December 2003 pre-Budget report and found legislative form in s.84 and Sch.15 of the Finance Act 2004.

Charge to income tax by reference to enjoyment of property previously owned

84.—(1) Schedule 15 (which contains provisions imposing a charge to income tax by reference to benefits received in certain circumstances by a former owner of property) has effect.

(2) That Schedule has effect for the year 2005—06 and subsequent years of assessment.

Paragraph 3 of Sch.15 of the Finance Act 2004 is as follows:

(1) This paragraph applies where—

(a) an individual ("the chargeable person") occupies any land ("the relevant land"), whether alone or together with other persons, and

(b) the disposal condition or the contribution condition is met as respects the land.

(2) The disposal condition is that—

(a) at any time after 17th March 1986 the chargeable person owned an interest—

(i) in the relevant land, or

(ii) in other property the proceeds of the disposal of which were (directly or indirectly) applied by another person towards the acquisition of an interest in the relevant land, and

(b) the chargeable person has disposed of all, or part of, his interest in the relevant land or the other property, otherwise than by an excluded transaction.

(3) The contribution condition is that at any time after 17th March 1986 the chargeable person has directly or indirectly provided, otherwise than by an excluded transaction, any of the consideration given by another person for the acquisition of—

(a) an interest in the relevant land, or
(b) an interest in any other property the proceeds of the disposal of which were (directly or indirectly) applied by another person towards the acquisition of an interest in the relevant land.

(4) For the purposes of this paragraph a disposition which creates a new interest in land out of an existing interest in land is to be taken to be a disposal of part of the existing interest.

(5) Where this paragraph applies to a person in respect of the whole or part of a year of assessment, an amount equal to the chargeable amount determined under paragraph 4 is to be treated as income of his chargeable to income tax.

"The schedule provides for a charge to income tax on benefits received by a former owner of property. It applies to individuals (the chargeable person) who continue to receive benefits from certain types of property they once owned after 17 March 1986 but have since disposed of. The schedule has effect for the tax year 2005–06 and subsequent years."

If the deceased has either disposed of any property within these headings by way of gift or, in some circumstances, sold or contributed towards the purchase of the property in question and he continued to receive some benefit from the property he was potentially liable to the charge. The benefit may be occupation of the land, use of the corporeal moveable or the right to receive income from a trust holding incorporeal moveable property (intangible) property. Often the bare case will involve gift with reservation, not pre-owned assets tax.

To put it another way, the tax thus applies where a former owner of **6–04** land (and buildings) or corporeal moveables, which were disposed of after March 17, 1986, benefits in certain prescribed ways from the said land or corporeal moveable disposed of, or is a beneficiary of an "interested trust" created after the date. It might be observed that there would be a limited number and type of corporeal moveables which generate an annual value of over £5,000 per annum! Although it was targeted at abuses of the gift with reservation (GWR) for inheritance tax rules, the pre-owned assets tax rules have a potentially much wider ambit and are not restricted to gifts. Neither are all the statutory exemptions to the gift with reservation rules found in the pre-owned assets tax rules.

There is a *de minimis* restriction of £5,000 per annum.

There are three distinct POT charges in relation to land, corporeal moveables and incorporeal moveable (intangible) property. Incorporeal moveable (intangible) property is helpfully defined as any property other than corporeal moveables and interest in land; it covers such assets such as stocks and securities, insurance policies and bank and building society accounts.

6–05   A deceased can be liable to POT in relation to these assets in the following circumstances, where he occupied land, which either he used to own[4] or which was purchased using the proceeds of sale of land,[5] which he used to own or which was acquired using consideration provided by him (Finance Act 2004 Sch.15 para.3). As stated, it is unlikely that pre-owned assets tax would apply to the "classic" case where, for example, a father gifts his house to his children but continues to live in it "rent free" since this type of case will fall into the exemptions rule that the transaction is exempt from POT because it (the house) will be property which has been gifted with reservation and will still be aggregable for IHT purposes under the gift with reservation rules. Where he was in possession of or had the use of a corporeal moveable which either he used to own or which was purchased using the proceeds of sale of a corporeal moveable item which he used to own or which was acquired using consideration provided by him, this would also bring him into the pre-owned assets tax regime. Finally the taxpayer will be vulnerable, where incorporeal moveable (intangible) property is comprised in a trust in which he had an interest.

In relation to land and corporeal moveables, but not to incorporeal moveables (intangibles), a former owner will escape a pre-owned assets tax charge if the land or corporeal moveable was disposed of or if the consideration was provided by way an excluded transaction (FA 2004 Sch.15 para.6).

The legislation also has a number of exemptions, one of which is where the property that was potentially subject to the charge is otherwise contained within the former owner's estate or where that property is already property subject to a reservation for IHT purposes.

6–06   Where the charge applies, the former owner is charged to income tax on an amount calculated by reference to an assumed market rental of any interest in land or an assumed rate of interest in relation to the value of any corporeal moveables or incorporeal moveable (intangible) property.

The legislation also has rules which enable the former owner to avoid the tax by electing for the land, corporeal moveable or incorporeal moveable (intangible) property to be treated as property to be subject to a reservation for IHT purposes.

There are two particularly striking aspects of pre-owned assets tax for practitioners. First, there is its retrospective effect. Clients who had adopted IHT planning in the past which was then outside the gift with reservation rules would in many circumstances find themselves now facing a charge. The other striking aspect of the POT legislation is its width. It is as if the charge was to be made as wide as possible and then the exemptions and exclusions were listed.

---

[4] The Disposal element.
[5] The Contribution element.

DISPOSAL AND CONTRIBUTION REQUIREMENTS

In considering if there is a charge to pre-owned assets tax it is important **6–07** to focus on disposal and contribution elements. At its essence, therefore, the conditions required for the charge to apply are virtually identical where the property in question is land or corporeal moveables (chattels), but they differ slightly in respect of incorporeal moveable (intangible) property. Thus, the charge applies where the chargeable person occupies any land or uses or possesses any corporeal moveables and either the "disposal condition" or the "contribution condition" is applicable. The *disposal condition* applies if the chargeable person, at any time after March 17, 1986, owned land or corporeal moveables, or other property whose disposal proceeds were directly or indirectly applied by another person towards the acquisition of the relevant land or corporeal moveables, and then disposed of all or part of their interest in the relevant land or corporeal moveables (or other property). The *contribution condition* will apply if the chargeable person, at any time after March 17, 1986, provided any of the consideration given by another person for the acquisition of an interest in the land or corporeal moveable (chattel), or for the acquisition of any other property the proceeds of the disposal of which were directly or indirectly applied by another person towards an acquisition of an interest in the land or corporeal moveable (chattel).

INCORPOREAL MOVEABLE (INTANGIBLE) PROPERTY

In contrast to the provisions relating to land and corporeal moveables, **6–08** there is only one condition to be met for the charge to apply. The charge applies where the chargeable person conveys incorporeal moveable (intangible) property or adds incorporeal moveable (intangible) property to a trust after March 17, 1986 on terms that any income arising from the settled property would be treated as income arising under a trust where the truster retains an interest; this income is treated as income of the chargeable person as truster. The truster in this case is, of course, the chargeable person.

Example

In 2001 Mrs Candytuft conveyed £300,000 into a discretionary trust (for the benefit of her children). The trust purchased a small semi-detached villa for £250,000, which she occupied after April 5, 2005. Since she is enjoying the benefit of an asset, which was acquired with funds originally owned by her, the pre-owned assets rules will apply.

Please note that the provisions of this section do not apply to land and corporeal moveables included in a trust deed or will.

In many cases, it will be clear that a pre-owned assets tax exclusion or exemption applies and it will not be necessary to examine the matter in detail as to whether the disposal or contribution condition is met. It is important to note that unlike gifts with reservation provisions, for pre-owned assets tax liability there is no need for a gift to have actually been made. The legislation merely relates to disposals and dispositions. Pre-owned assets tax can apply to a sale as well as a gift.

6–09   It should also be noted that there does not need to be any direct correlation between the interest acquired as long as any consideration is provided for the acquisition of the interest.

If children buy property from their parents using cash previously gifted to them by their parents pre-owned assets tax problems will arise because the contribution has been breached. However, if the children buy from their own resources from the parents and subsequently the parents make cash gifts, then provided the children have sufficient cash in their own right not derived from the gifts, this would appear not to breach para.3(3).

As noted earlier it is not necessary for the individual to have owned the item he now uses. If it was purchased with the proceeds of sale of the item he used to own then the charge may apply. This is known as the "contribution condition". It may apply in the case where a person has never previously owned the land, the corporeal moveable, or the replaced property, but has after March 17, 1986 provided any of the consideration given by another person for the acquisition of an interest in the land or the corporeal moveable or an interest in any replaced property.

The Schedule provides for a charge to income tax on benefits received by a former owner of property. It applies to individuals (the chargeable person) who continue to receive benefits from certain types of property they once owned after March 17, 1986 but have since disposed of. The Schedule has effect for the tax year 2005–2006 and subsequent years.

EXCLUDED TRANSACTIONS

6–10   The concept of excluded transactions has no application to incorporeal moveable (intangible) property. It only applies to exclude from the income tax charge certain transactions relating to land and corporeal moveables. For the purposes of the disposal conditions relating to land and corporeal moveables, the disposal of any property is an excluded transaction in relation to the chargeable person if any of the following apply:

- It was a disposal of their whole interest in the property, except for any right expressly reserved by them over the property, either (a) by a transaction made at arm's length with a person not connected with them; (b) by a transaction such as might be expected to be made at arm's length between unconnected persons; or (c) the exclusion clearly only applies to sales of the entire interest in the property.
- **Transfers to spouses:** the transaction will be classed as excluded if the property was transferred to the owner's spouse. This extends to a former spouse where the transfer has been ordered by a court. This also applies if the disposal was by way of gift (or in accordance with a court order for the benefit of a former spouse) by virtue of which the property became the subject of a liferent.
- **Family maintenance:** if the disposal is a disposition falling within s.11 of the Inheritance Tax Act 1984 (disposition for maintenance of family) it will be classed as excluded.

- **Outright gift:** the disposal will be classed as excluded if it is an outright gift to an individual and is for the purposes of the Inheritance Tax Act 1984 a transfer of value that is wholly exempt by virtue of s.19 (annual exemption) or s.20 (small gifts).

Sales with Full Consideration

This is where there is no element of gift. These types of transactions **6–11** have never really been subject to the gift with reservation regulations. Any exclusion is of limited value. It must be a disposal of the owner's whole interest and the transaction must be made at arm's length with a person not connected with him or such as might be expected to be at arm's length between persons not connected with each other. A connected person is a spouse, uncle, aunt, nephew and niece or truster ("settlor" and "truster" have the same meanings as in IHTA 1984 (FA 2004 Sch.15 para.2)). Many of the privately arranged "Home Loan Schemes" may be struck at because they are to a connected person and are not "a transaction such as might be made at arm's length between persons not connected with each other". Obviously no one will sell his property to an unconnected person except for cash. If a discovery is made of these on examining the executry papers it would be as well to examine it closely to ensure that it did not fall within the pre-owned assets tax regime. If unsure it might be as well to report it in IHT403. It could be stated therein that the executors do not consider it to be liable to pre-owned assets tax. If this is accepted by HMRC then this will be an end to the matter.

If the arm's length requirement were not in place strange effects could result. Take the example of a person who owned a large detached mansion, who gifted it to children and who subsequently sold it; it was subsequently converted into a residential/care home. If the original owner went to live there he could have fallen foul of pre-owned assets tax if the arm's length requirement had not been in place!

Outright Transfers to Spouses

This includes transfers to former spouses; it also includes where it is **6–12** extended to former spouses but only where the transfer has been made by order of the court.

The scope of the rules are extremely wide; thus where an individual has incorporeal moveable (intangible) property by way of a liferent trust or discretionary trust of which he is a potential beneficiary, any income of the trust would be assessed on him under TA 1988 s.660A. However, in the first of these cases the property would be treated as part of his estate for IHT purposes and in both cases as property subject to a reservation for GWR purposes. In that event a POT exemption could apply.

The trusts which are therefore likely to be caught in relation to incorporeal moveables (intangibles), are those which have been outside the gift with reservation rules but caught by the rules relating to those trusts in which the truster retains a reversionary interest.

> **Danger Warning!!**
>
> *Many clients may have invested in packaged trust arrangements usually involving bonds or life policies. "Flexible Trusts", "Discounted Gift" and "Gift and Loan" schemes are popular examples. The position of these types is far from clear. While the Revenue have given certain informal assurances it, nevertheless, seems clear that the Revenue will look at these closely to see if there is any possible POT exposure.*

EXEMPTIONS FROM A PRE-OWNED ASSETS TAX CHARGE

6–13   The charging provisions relating to land, corporeal moveables and incorporeal moveable (intangible) property do not apply to a person at a time when their estate for the purposes of the Inheritance Tax Act 1984 includes the relevant property, or other property which derives its value from the relevant property, and whose value so far as attributable to the relevant property, is not substantially less than the value of the relevant property. The charging provisions also do not apply to a person at a time when, for IHT purposes, the relevant property or property deriving its value from relevant property falls within the gifts with reservation provisions set out in Finance Act 1986.

Some general examples may help to clarify the position.

Example 1

Mr Durward gave his house to his son in 1989 but continued to remain in it. In the year 2004 his son gave the property back to him.

The relevant property here is the house originally disposed of and because Mr Durward now occupies that property the first limb of the disposal condition applies. However, Mr Durward is now the beneficial owner of the relevant property, which is included in his estate and therefore a POT exemption.

Example 2

Mrs Redgauntlet gave her daughter £100,000 in 2000 which she (Miss Redgauntlet) used to buy a painting. In 2002 the daughter transferred the painting to a liferent trust for her mother and the trustees of the trust allowed Mrs Redgauntlet to hang the painting in the living room.

The consideration condition applies here because Mrs Redgauntlet provided consideration for the acquisition of the painting. The relevant property in a case falling within the consideration condition is the property now representing the consideration provided, which in this case is the painting itself. Mrs Redgauntlet has an interest in possession in the painting and it is therefore treated as part of her estate for IHT purposes. Therefore there is a POT exemption.

Example 3

In 1998 Mr Talisman transferred £200,000 to a liferent trust in which he was the liferentor! Shortly after that the trustees invested the funds in shares.

Mr Talisman is both the truster and the liferentor of the trust. Because the trust holds incorporeal moveable (intangible) property there is potential for a POT charge in these circumstances. However because the relevant property is the incorporeal moveable (intangible) property in which the truster now has an interest and Mr Talisman had an interest in that property, there will be a POT exemption.

It does not actually matter whether the property is subject to an IHT relief, e.g. business property relief; it will nevertheless form part of an individual's estate for the purposes of IHT.

Another aspect of this occurs where the replacement or derivative property is included in an individual's estate. Where the property which is now included in an individual's estate is not the relevant property but other property, which derives its value from the relevant property, the extent of the exemption can be limited depending upon the value of that other property as compared to the relevant property. It is difficult to give a definitive list of situations where this might occur because of the wide definition of "replacement or derivative property".

Example 4

Mr Kenilworth gave his home to his daughter in 1999 and his daughter subsequently sold the property and bought a new one with the proceeds of sale. In 2002 she gave the new property to her father.

He now occupies the property acquired out of the proceeds of the home he originally gave away and as such is caught by the second limb of the disposal condition.

For the purposes of the estate exemption the relevant property is the property Mr Kenilworth originally disposed of. This property is not included in his estate but property which derives its value from that property is included.

Example 5

In 2000, Mrs Lammermuir transferred £500,000 to a property investment company in which she was the 100 per cent shareholder. The company subsequently purchased a house in which Mrs Lammermuir now lives.

The contribution is satisfied because Mrs Lammermuir now occupies a house for which she provided the consideration.

For the purposes of the estate exemption the relevant property is the house as it is that which now represents the consideration provided. The house itself is not included in Mrs Lammermuir's estate but the shares in the company, which derive in part from their value, are included.

Example 6

Mr Antiquary transferred shares into a discretionary trust for his adult children in 2000. Under the terms of the trust the shares are to revert to Mr Antiquary in 2020.

He thus has a reversionary interest in the trust, which owns incorporeal moveable (intangible) property, and it will therefore be caught by the POT rules in relation to intangibles.

The relevant property in these circumstances is the incorporeal moveable (intangible) settled property, i.e. the shares and these are not included in Mr Antiquary's estate. However the reversionary interest, which derives its value from these shares, is included.

It should be noted that where replacement or derivative property is included in a person's estate the POT exemption may be limited.

If that part of the value of the replacement or derivative property is not substantially less than the value of the relevant property the POT exemption will apply in full.

Where a deceased's estate includes relevant property or replacement or derivative property then if any transaction by virtue of which the chargeable person's estate came to include the relevant property or by virtue of which the value of the replacement property came to be revived from relevant property then that liability is an excluded liability.

Example 7

Mr Ivanhoe gave his house to his daughter in 1988 but continued to occupy it. In 2003 his daughter wished to give it back to him but she could not afford to give the property back and Mr Ivanhoe was obliged to take out a mortgage to buy back the property.

Although the property would be included in the father's estate the father's debt to the lender would be an excluded liability because the creation of the liability and the purchase would be associated operations. In this situation the POT exemption is to be disallowed in whole or in part.

PROPERTY SUBJECT TO A RESERVATION FOR GWR PURPOSES

6–14 This is very much linked to the IHT rules. Where the property falls within one of the GWR exemptions no POT charge will apply. Where the property falls within the GWR exemption but it relates to replacement or derivative property, the extent of the exemption will be limited. The principal rule is that it relates to property subject to a reservation. This occurs where an individual has disposed of property by way of gift and he either has possession and enjoyment of the property not bona fide assumed by the donee or the property is not enjoyed to the entire exclusion or virtually to the entire exclusion of the donor and of any benefit to him.

The scope of the type of situations in which this occurs is fairly extensive but the more common ones would be:

- a gift of a family home where the donor continues to occupy the land;
- a gift of farmland where the donor continues to farm it;
- a gift of a painting or ornament, which remains in the donor's house following the gift;
- a gift of a motor vehicle, which the donor continues to drive; and
- a gift into a trust where the donor is a beneficiary or potential beneficiary.

There is other property, which would have been the property subject to a reservation for gift with reservation purposes. Pre-owned assets tax will not be due in those circumstances where the statutory exemption provides relief from an inheritance tax charge. In these circumstances there will also be no pre-owned assets tax charge.

As regards exempt transfers, these do not apply either for gift with **6–15** reservation rules or pre-owned assets tax. Here there are such things as gifts to spouses and small gifts. Gifts in consideration of marriage are not covered by exemption or exclusion in the pre-owned assets tax rules. There is a pre-owned assets tax exemption in relation to gifts to charities, to political parties, housing associations, for national purposes, for maintenance funds, for historic buildings and to employee trusts.

Consider the position where it is believed that the property is the subject of a gift with reservation but it transpires it is not. The Revenue will issue discovery notices for at least the preceding six years. The tax will be due and the rent plus interest will be due and, depending on the circumstances, there may also be penalties.

DE MINIMIS EXEMPTION

An exemption from charge under this Schedule applies where, in **6–16** relation to any person, the aggregate of the amounts specified below in respect of that year do not exceed £5,000. It should be noted, however, that where the amount exceeds £5,000 it is subject to the charge in full. The amount of £5,000 does not represent a nil-rate band.

POST-DEATH VARIATIONS

Post-death variations are changes in the distribution of a deceased's **6–17** estate after the date of death. Any disposition made by the chargeable person in relation to an interest in the estate of a deceased person is disregarded if under s.17 of the Inheritance Tax Act 1984 the disposition is not a transfer of value by the chargeable person for IHT purposes. For the purposes of this paragraph "estate" has the same meaning as it has for the purposes of the Inheritance Tax Act 1984.

A disposition made by an individual in relation to an interest in the estate is to be disregarded for the purposes of the POT rules if it is not treated as a transfer of land by the individual for the purposes of IHT. The most common instance of this is with a deed of variation, which may be made within two years of the date of death.

Example

Mr Robroy inherits a house on the death of his father. Within two years of his father's death he executes a deed of variation relative to his father's estate providing for the property to devolve jointly to his two adult children. Notwithstanding the variation it is Mr Robroy rather than the children who take up the occupation of the property.

Mr Robroy's disposition of the property falls within IHTA 1984 s.142(1) and is therefore to be disregarded for POT purposes. No POT charge therefore arises in relation to Mr Robroy's continuing occupation of the property.

CALCULATING THE CHARGE

How to Calculate the Benefit Subject to the Charge

6–18   Where the provisions of the regulations relating to land, corporeal moveables and/or incorporeal moveable (intangible) property apply to a person in respect of the whole or part of a year of assessment, an amount equal to the chargeable amount is treated as income of theirs chargeable to income tax.

Unless stated otherwise, the approach to valuing property for the purposes of Sch.15 follows the rule for inheritance tax. In other words, it is the price which the property might reasonably be expected to fetch if sold in the open market at that time, without any scope for a reduction on the ground that the whole property is to be placed on the market at one and the same time. The valuation date for property subject to the charge is April 6 in the relevant year of assessment or, if later, the first day of the taxable period. When valuing relevant land or a corporeal moveable it is not necessary to make an annual revaluation of the property. The property should rather be valued on a five-year cycle. Before the first five-year anniversary the valuation of the property will be that set at the first valuation date. Thereafter the valuation at the latest five-year anniversary will apply. The five-year anniversary is the fifth anniversary of April 6 in the first year of assessment in which the provisions of this Schedule relating to land or corporeal moveables apply to the chargeable person. The first valuation date is the date on which the provisions of this Schedule relating to land or corporeal moveables first applied to the chargeable person. If there is an interruption in the person's use or occupation of the property and the year of a five-year anniversary is not a taxable period, the year in which the date when the provisions of this Schedule applies again will be treated as the next five-year anniversary. As regards the charge in relation to land the chargeable amount is calculated as the appropriate rental value of the land less any payments made to the owner of land in respect of its occupation in pursuance of a legal obligation for the period during which the POT charge applies. Thus if the POT charge applies throughout the whole of the tax year the chargeable amount is calculated to the entire tax year, whereas if it only applies for one day of the week it will be reduced accordingly. Not surprisingly, therefore, calculating the appropriate rental value is a complex matter and comprises possibly five steps which are only summarised here:

1. The rental value is calculated for the taxable period ("R") and it is the rent which would have been payable during the taxable period if the property had been let to the individual for an annual rent equal to the annual value.

2. The value of the land at the valuation date is then calculated ("V") and is the price which the land might reasonably be expected to fetch if sold on the open market at the time.

3. Finally the value of the interest disposed of or acquired with the consideration provided is calculated ("DV").

4. This step is required where the disposal condition applies and the original disposal constituted a sale of the individual's whole interest and was not an excluded transaction.

5. Once RV and DV have been calculated the appropriate rental value is calculated by the following formula:

Appropriate rental value $= \dfrac{R \times DV}{V}$

As regards the charge in relation to corporeal moveables the following steps apply:

1. The value is calculated at the valuation date as the price which it might reasonably fetch if sold on the open market ("V").
2. The value of the interest disposed or acquired with the consideration provided is calculated ("DV").
3. As for 4. (above).
4. The appropriate amount is calculated as follows:

$$\dfrac{N \times DV}{V}$$

Where N is the deemed rate of interest to be prescribed by regulations.

As regards the charge in relation to intangibles this is slightly simpler and is represented by:

$$N - T$$

Where N is the amount of interest payable at the prescribed rate and T is the amount of tax which the executor has otherwise to pay in respect of that interest.

Avoidance of Double Charge to Income Tax

The Schedule contains provisions to avoid a double charge to income tax **6–19** arising if the provisions of this Schedule apply.

- If the chargeable person is subject to the charge *under more than one provision* of this Schedule, i.e. if they were chargeable in respect of land they occupied and also under incorporeal moveable (intangible property), or if the land was owned by a company whose shares had been owned by the taxpayer and had been conveyed to a trust of which he could be a potential beneficiary, the charge only applies to the tax provision producing the higher amount of tax. If this amount does not exceed the *de minimis* limit no tax will be payable, i.e. the lower amount is disregarded completely.
- If the chargeable person occupies land or possesses or uses a corporeal moveable and is chargeable to income tax under the provisions of this Schedule and under the benefits code of Part 3 of the Income Tax (Earnings and Pensions) Act 2003, the provisions of Part 3 have priority. Tax will only be chargeable under this Schedule on any amount that exceeds the amount treated as earnings under Part 3.

The Election into Inheritance Tax

The chargeable person has the option of electing that any relevant **6–20** property, otherwise subject to the charge, may be treated as subject to a gift with reservation for the purposes of Part 5 of the Finance Act 1986.

If an election is made the property will not be subject to the charge under this Schedule but will instead be subject to a charge to inheritance tax on death! The charge to inheritance tax will be due unless the occupation or use (of property otherwise within this Schedule) ceases permanently (and is not recommenced) at least seven years before their death. The election must be made on form IHT500. Guidance on how to complete the form, together with the form itself, can be found on the HMRC website.

Attention!!

The election must be made on or before "the relevant filing date". If the chargeable person was subject to income tax from the initial year of the charge the relevant filing date is January 31, 2007. If they become subject to the charge in a later year of assessment the relevant filing date is January 31 in the year of assessment immediately following, i.e. if they first became subject to the charge during the year 2007–2008, the election must be made by January 31, 2009. An extension may only be granted if the chargeable person can show a reasonable excuse for the failure to make the election by that date. The election takes effect for inheritance tax purposes from the initial year of the charge (2005–2006) or, if later, the date on which the chargeable person would have first become chargeable under this Schedule but for the election.

It may be possible to withdraw the election. If the election is withdrawn the property will be subject to the charge from the relevant tax year.

Chapter Seven

STAMP DUTY

"Stamp duty land tax is a modern self-assessed tax on land transactions involving any estate, interest, right or power in or over land in the United Kingdom."[1]

Tax facts

Stamp Duty Land Tax   **7–01**

Land dealings	From March 23, 2006	
Residential Property		
Non-disadvantaged areas	Up to £125,000	Nil
	£125,001–£250,000	1%
	£250,001–£500,000	3%
	£500,001 upwards	4%
Disadvantaged areas Stamp duty land tax is not charged on residential transactions in disadvantaged areas if the price of the property is less than £150,000.	Up to £150,000	Nil
	£150,001–£250,000	1%
	£250,001–£500,000	3%
	£500,001 upwards	4%
Non-residential properties (or mixed) disadvantaged and non-disadvantaged	Up to £150,000	Nil

[1] HMRC website: *http://www.hmrc.gov.uk* [accessed April 23, 2009].

Land dealings	From March 23, 2006	
	£150,001–£250,000	1%
	£250,001–£500,000	3%
	£500,001 upwards	4%
Danger Warning!!	After September 2, 2008 and up to December 31, 2009	
	Up to £175,000	Nil
Exemptions		
These do not require to be notified.	• No chargeable consideration • Transactions between spouses/civil partners on separation, divorce or annulment as a result of a court order, or by virtue of an agreement in the course of the annulment, separation or divorce • Conveyance of assets by executors to beneficiaries of a will or on intestacy unless for consideration • Variation of will within two years of the death providing not for consideration, other than the making of another variation in return	
From March 12, 2008 it is no longer necessary for the purchaser to self-certify that the transaction is exempt in order for the transaction to be registered.		
Submission of tax	Generally interest runs from 30 days after the expiry of 30 days after date of completion	
Penalties for failure to deliver stamp duty land tax return	• £100 if delivered within three months • Otherwise the discretionary trust rules will apply £200 • If not delivered within 12 months, penalty up to amount of tax chargeable	

Stamp Duty/Stamp Duty Reserve Tax on the Transfer of Shares and Securities

Rate	0.5%
Penalties	Generally penalty and interest runs from 30 days after the expiry of 30 days after date of completion
	If the document is less than one year late the maximum penalty will be an amount equivalent to the duty or £300, whichever is less
	If the executor's document is more than one year late the maximum penalty is an amount equivalent to the duty or £300, whichever is more

Arguably the oldest form of taxation in Scotland, stamp duty goes **7–02** back to 1694. The format did not materially change until it did so radically with the introduction in 2003 of what is virtually a new tax, stamp duty land tax ("SDLT"). This is leviable on transfers of heritable property in Scotland which have an effective date on or after December 1, 2003. Stamp taxes are payable on land, property and shares. The tax to be applied depends upon the nature of transaction involved. It will be either:

- stamp duty land tax (SDLT);
- stamp duty reserve tax (SDRT)[2]; or
- stamp duty (SD).

The legislation repealed stamp duty on all other property excluding stocks and shares. For deeds executed after November 30, 2003, stamp duty applies only to transfers of stock and marketable securities and to certain transfers of interest in partnerships. Particular rules apply to marketable security transactions. Thus, if heritable property is conveyed to the deceased, SDLT at rates of up to four per cent may be chargeable depending on whether the property is in a disadvantaged area, for business use or otherwise.

It is unlikely that the practitioner will be troubled with stamp duty land tax, stamp duty reserve tax or indeed stamp duty.

---

[2] Stamp Duty Reserve Tax (SDRT) was introduced in 1986 to deal with transactions in shares where no instrument of transfer was executed and which were therefore outside the scope of stamp duty. It is a transaction tax, charged on "agreements to transfer chargeable securities", unlike stamp duty which is charged upon documents. The main provisions are in the FA 1986 and the supporting Regulations at SI 1986/1711.

7–03   It may occur in the rare event where the deceased has purchased heritable property and has died prior to the submission of the return and/or paying the tax due. In the normal case, if the land transaction return and/or payment is not sent to HMRC within 30 days of the effective date of the transaction, penalties and interest might be payable.

If, acting on behalf of an executor where the deceased who has died since submitting a return for which HMRC have charged a penalty, the practitioner requires to advise HMRC immediately giving full details of the date of death and the deceased's own details. Likewise, in the even more unlikely instance if acting on behalf of an executor where the deceased who has died since submitting a return for which HMRC have charged a penalty, it is imperative to advise HMRC immediately giving full details of the date of death and the practitioner's own details.

SDLT office contact details can be found in the Appendix.

Chapter Eight

COUNCIL TAX

"Council tax is a system of local taxation collected by local authorities. It is a tax on domestic property. Some property is exempt from council tax. Some people do not have to pay council tax and some people get a discount."[1]

INTRODUCTION

Council tax replaced the community charge on April 1, 1993. It is based **8–01** on the relative value of each residence. Mainly speaking it is paid by the owner/occupier or the tenant of the house. There are eight broad valuation bands according to the estimated value as at April 1, 1991. The level of council tax is set by the local authority and there are of course discounts of 25 per cent for those living on their own. There is also be benefit available to assist those on low incomes but this assistance will not cover water and sewerage charges.

This is one of the areas where practitioners can "take their eye off the ball with dire results". As with most aspects of the work, it helps if the matter is dealt with correctly at the start! Local authority council tax officers are, like their HMRC counterparts, hard working and helpful. Similarly, they realise the difficulties under which they operate, e.g. time pressure, lack of manpower and seemingly inflexible computer systems. It helps if practitioners use the particular local authority's form and give as much information as quickly as possible to allow the records to be altered.

Where the house is owned by someone else it will generally be the owner/occupier or tenant who is liable. Empty houses such as holiday homes will be the responsibility of the owner.

Council tax is the tax levied by local authorities in Scotland to pay for **8–02** local services such as policing and rubbish collection. It applies to all domestic residential property, including houses, bungalows, flats, mobile homes and houseboats, whether the house is owned or rented.

All properties were valued and put into a "valuation band". The local authority assessor is responsible for valuing houses and placing them in one of eight valuation bands, for example for Fife the valuation bands are as follows:

---

[1] From Citizens Advice Bureau website, available at: *http://www.adviceguide.org.uk/index/ life/tax/council_tax.htm* [accessed April 23, 2009].

Range of values

    A: Up to £27,000
    B: Over £27,000 and up to £35,000
    C: Over £35,000 and up to £45,000
    D: Over £45,000 and up to £58,000
    E: Over £58,000 and up to £80,000
    F: Over £80,000 and up to £106,000
    G: Over £106,000 and up to £212,000
    H: Over £212,000

The valuation band in which the property has been placed is shown on the front of the deceased's demand notice. The practitioner should specifically request this document or, if it is not available, any piece of correspondence which has the unique reference on it. It greatly helps the local authority if this can be quoted. It also helps to identify the local authority concerned! The valuation band is based on the amount which it would have reasonably been expected to realise had it been sold on the open market on April 1, 1991 based upon the following criteria:

- the sale was with vacant possession;
- the property was in a reasonable state of repair; and
- the size and the extent of the property and the physical state of the locality were the same as at the time when the valuation was made.

8–03 The amount of council tax to be paid is based on the property band, e.g. a person in a band H property will actually pay three times as much as a person in a band A property ignoring rebates, discounts, etc.

Danger Warning!!

The council tax must be paid even if an appeal has been lodged if the taxpayer disagrees with the property band. Once the appeal has been settled a revised bill is issued if necessary.

As stated, the valuation band determines how much council tax is paid. It is necessary on death to intimate the death to the local authority. They may not need a death certificate. They should be asked if there is any council tax outstanding and for the relevant form to claim relief. Local authorities have their own forms. The form should be completed and sent off as soon as possible along with any documents requested.

In terms of Sch.11 of the Local Government Finance Act 1992, and the Council Tax (Exempt Dwellings) Scotland Order 1992 (as amended), a dwelling house may be exempt from council tax (including the water charge). Where the property which has become unoccupied as a result of the death of a single resident and council tax liability is due solely by the estate of a deceased person and a grant of confirmation has not been made, exemption for an unlimited period will be granted. Once a grant of confirmation has been made, exemption for a maximum of six months will be granted from the date of award, and a 50 per cent council tax discount will be granted thereafter until ownership of the property changes. If the house has not been the home of one person, the death should still be intimated since the surviving spouse may be entitled to a 25 per cent discount (Single Person Discount Form). In addition to this certain categories of people are not "counted" when establishing how many adults are resident. These categories include full-time students, apprentices, severely mentally impaired persons, carers, recent school leavers and people in hospital or care homes.

Furnished second or holiday homes in Scotland will be liable for council tax but will have a 10–50 per cent discount because no one lives there on a permanent basis.

Water and Sewerage Charges

The local authority is obliged collect water and sewerage charges for the **8–04** water authority.

Local authorities operate various rebate schemes. It is important to check that the deceased was receiving all benefits to which he or she was entitled.

Disablement Relief

If a permanently disabled person lived in a house which has been altered **8–05** to meet the needs of that person, a reduction in the amount of council tax payable may be applied. In such cases the valuation band used to calculate the council tax payable, i.e. the disabled band will be one band lower than the actual property band.

DISCOUNTS

Discounts may be granted as claimed under the following circumstances: **8–06**

- 10 per cent reduction for a second home;
- 25 per cent reduction where only one adult lives in a house;
- 50 per cent reduction where no one lives in a house (maximum period of six months); and
- 50 per cent reduction for tied accommodation.

(For this purpose, an adult is a person who is aged 18 or over.)

The calculations are based on the number of persons (i.e. persons aged over 18) living in a house, although there are exemptions, namely prisoners serving sentences, persons who are severely mentally impaired, children aged 18 or over who are still at school, students including youth training trainees, long-term hospital patients, persons in residential care and care workers.

EXEMPTIONS

Certain unoccupied properties are exempt, i.e. no council tax is due, in **8–07** certain circumstances. The most common circumstances are:

- properties that are unoccupied AND unfurnished (maximum period of six months);

- properties last occupied by a person now in residential care;
- properties last occupied by a person now providing care, e.g. to an elderly relative;
- properties that are the responsibility of a deceased's estate;
- properties undergoing renovation (maximum period of 12 months from date last occupied—effective from April 1, 2000); and
- properties that are wholly occupied by students, persons who are severely mentally impaired or persons under 18 will be treated as exempt and no council tax will be payable.

REBATES

8–08 Council tax rebates may be awarded to those on low income.

JOINT AND SEVERAL LIABILITY

8–09 The legislation allows local authorities to treat couples who are married or living together as husband and wife to be held jointly and severally liable for the full amount payable. Joint owners or tenants, whether or not they are named on the demand notice, are also be jointly and severally liable.

PAYMENT

8–10 Council tax is normally payable by 10 instalments on or before the 15th of each month from April to January inclusive. Direct debits are payable on either the 1st or the 15th of each month. The position should be checked to ascertain the position since if, at any time, a monthly instalment is not paid timeously the right to pay by instalments will be lost and the full year's charge will be payable within a further seven days.

Danger Warning!!

Any unpaid arrears are recoverable by summary warrant proceedings with the addition of a 10 per cent statutory penalty.

CHANGES IN CIRCUMSTANCES

8–11 It is important to advise the local authority of relevant changes in circumstances. Details of any change of address or circumstances which might affect the amount which the taxpayer is liable to pay should be notified in writing to the Benefits and Council Tax Team. Failure to alert the council of any changes which might affect discounts or exemptions may result in a £50 fine.

PART 2

ADMINISTRATION PERIOD

Chapter Nine

INCOME TAX DURING ADMINISTRATION

"As there is no statutory definition of 'income', over the years, lawyers have attempted to define the nebulous concept of 'income' which is subject to tax. In the case of London county council v Attorney Gen. (1901), Lord MacNaughton said, 'income tax, if I may be pardoned for saying so, is a tax income.' As a definition this is of little assistance."[1]

TAX FACTS

		2008	2009
Dividend rate	10%		
Upper Dividend rate	32.5%		
Savings Rate	10%	£0 to	
New savings rate	10%		Up to £2,320[2]
Starting Rate 10%	10%	£0–£2,230 (on all income)	£2,320 (only applies where taxable non-savings is under £2,320)
Basic Rate on earned and property income	22%		
Basic rate on savings income	20%		

> **Attention!!**
>
> *As mentioned earlier, the tax law re-write programme is underway. This has not proved an unqualified success and this can be seen, to a certain extent, in the ongoing programme of repeal of large sections of the ICTA 1988. The code, such as it is, is contained in Ch.6 of the ITTOIA 2005. For a while the two sets of sections in the two acts continued. However, at the time of going to press, it may be that most of the relevant sections of the ICTA will be repealed but some not necessarily re-enacted in the ITTOIA. Where possible, the reference to the section in the ICTA has been preferred as current at the time of writing but practitioners may wish to check.*

---

[1] Quoted in J.S. Barlow et al, *Wills, Administration and Taxation Law and Practice*, 9th edn (London: Thomson Sweet & Maxwell, 2008).

[2] If the savings income is above this the 10 per cent savings rate will not be applicable!

9–02 This section deals with income tax arising during the administration of the executry. There are particular rules for income arising during the period of administration. The period of administration starts from the date of death (or more correctly with the following day) and ends on the date when it can be said that the residue is ascertained. As stated earlier Scots law is fortunate in having a definition of the "end of the administration period". Section 702 TA[3] 1988 provides that:

Application to Scotland

702. For the purpose of the application of this Part to Scotland—

(a) any reference to the completion of the administration of an estate shall be construed as a reference to the date at which, after discharge of, or provision for, liabilities falling to be met out of the deceased's estate (including, without prejudice to the generality of the foregoing, debts, legacies immediately payable, prior rights of surviving spouse or civil partner on intestacy and legal rights of surviving spouse or civil partner or children), the free balance held in trust for behoof of the residuary legatees has been ascertained;

(b) For paragraph (b) of section 697(1) the following paragraph shall be substituted—

"(b) the amount of any of the aggregate income of the estate for that year to which a person has become entitled by virtue of a specific disposition";

(c) "real estate" means heritable estate, and

(d) "charge on residue" shall include, in addition to the liabilities specified in section 701(6), any sums required to meet claims in respect of prior rights by surviving spouse or civil partner or in respect of legal rights by surviving spouse or civil partner or children.

But see also ITTOIA 2005 s.653:

Meaning of "the administration period" and "the final tax year"

653.—(1)In this Chapter "the administration period", in relation to the estate of a deceased person, means the period beginning with the deceased's death and ending with the completion of the administration of the estate.

(2) In the application of subsection (1) to Scotland, the reference to the completion of the administration is to be taken as a

---

[3] Repealed by the Corporation Tax Act 2009, Sch.3(1), para.1 (effective April 1, 2009 and has effect for corporation tax purposes for accounting periods ending on or after that day, and for income tax and capital gains tax purposes, for the tax year 2009—10 and subsequent tax years).

reference to the date at which, after discharge of, or provision for, liabilities falling to be met out of the deceased's estate, the free balance held in trust for the residuary legatees or for the persons with the right to the intestate estate has been ascertained.

(3) In this Chapter "the final tax year" means the tax year in which the administration period ends.

PRELIMINARY

Executors are taxed as a body, not as individuals. There are no personal **9–03** allowances, even the deceased's unused allowances. There is no liability to higher rate tax at 40 per cent or entitlement to the lower rate tax bands of 10 per cent or 20 per cent. There is no upper rate dividend rate. However, in the administration period of the executry, all UK income from savings or investments ("savings income") whether interest on UK fixed interest stocks, interest on gilts or bank and building society interest, is taxed at 20 per cent. From April 6, 1999 changes were made to the treatment of tax credits on equity income and equity-based income. This is now known as dividend income and will be deemed to be taxed at 10 per cent. Other income such as rental income is taxed at 20 per cent and is referred to as non-savings income taxed at basic rate. This last type of income, i.e. non-savings income, used to be taxed at 22 per cent but this was reduced to 20 per cent from April 5, 2008.

RETURNS

The tax return for executors is the SA900 which extends (currently) to 12 **9–04** pages. There is a new SA900 for the year ending April 5, 2009. There are supplementary pages for self-assessment by an executor as a sole trader, partnership income, income from land and property in the UK, foreign income and gains and tax credit relief, CGT, non-residence, details of executors, capital transactions, deductions, discretionary payments, computation of tax pool and charges and reliefs. The supplementary pages must be completed first and the return requires details of the total income less reliefs, double taxation relief, CGT, income from UK banks and building societies, dividends from UK companies, calculation of tax, overpayments and repayment claims and details of the executors. A tax return guide and tax calculation guide will be available to assist the completion of the return and there are notes to cover the various supplementary pages.

CLASSIFICATION OF RESIDUARY BENEFICIARIES

HMRC used to send a letter to executors on form 920 asking for details **9–05** of the executors and residuary beneficiaries in an estate. The executors are asked to state whether the beneficiaries' interest in the residue is absolute, limited or discretionary. A beneficiary who is entitled to at least some of the capital of the residue has an absolute interest. A beneficiary who is entitled to income only from the residue has a "limited" interest. A liferentor is the most common example of a beneficiary with a limited interest in the residue. Under self assessment the position is different. The forms are still useful in categorising income of the executry.

A discretionary or relevant property interest is defined on form 922 as one where the beneficiary does not become entitled to any income until the trustees exercise their discretion in favour of the beneficiary. The discretionary interest may not arise until the trust commences at the end of the administration of the executry, but if the discretion is exercised during the administration of the executry, the beneficiary is treated by TA 1988 s.698(3) as re-enacted in s.650 of the ITTOIA 2005 as having a limited interest in the residue. Any income paid to the discretionary beneficiary during the administration of the executry will therefore not be subject to the income tax rate payable by (discretionary) trusts.

ALLOCATION OF EXECUTRY INCOME

9–06 The amount of the residuary income due to the absolute beneficiaries is ascertained by deducting from the aggregate income:

1. the amount of any annual interest, annuity or payment which is a charge on residue and this includes the prior and legal rights of spouses and children;
2. any administration expenses paid out by the executors of the income during the year; and
3. the amount of the income to which a person has become entitled by virtue of a specific legacy. Most wills exclude interest on pecuniary legacies, but specific legacies may have income derived from the asset (e.g. rent from heritage or dividends from shares).

If the deductions from the aggregate income exceed the amount of the aggregate income, the excess is carried forward and treated as a deduction for the following year.

INCOME OF LIMITED INTERESTS IN RESIDUE

9–07 A distinction is made between income received from United Kingdom estates and income from foreign estates. The distinction depends on the executors' tax liability and not on the location of the asset from which the income is received.

An executry is a United Kingdom estate if UK IT has been deducted from all its income or if the executors are directly assessable to UK IT on all its income. All other executries are foreign estates. Most executries are United Kingdom estates.

Please note that the executors may not have paid the income to the beneficiary in the same year as they received it. In that event, the rates of tax paid by the executors and payable by the beneficiary may not be the same. The net income is grossed up at the rates in force at the time of payment.

If a beneficiary is prejudiced by payment being postponed to a subsequent year, he may claim against the executors for his loss. Thus, executors holding income received in 1995/1996 should have considered paying it to the beneficiaries before April 5, 1996 in view of the proposed reductions in the rates of tax announced in the Budget for 1996/1997, particularly the reduction of the IT on bank and building society interest from 25 per cent to 20 per cent. This applied to a limited extent for the lowering of the BRI tax rate from 24 per cent in the year 1996/1997 to 23 per cent in 1997/1998. A similar situation occurred when the basic tax rate was reduced in 2000/2001 to 22 per cent (from 23 per cent in 1999/2000). Indeed it also occurred in 2008/2009 when the rate for non-savings income was reduced from 22 per cent to 20 per cent. Higher rate executors will have to pay more IT if the interest is paid in the following year if the rates reduce. Those entitled to a repayment of IT will receive less, as follows.

BRI Received in 1999/2000 and Paid in 2000/2001

9–08

	Gross	Tax	Net
1999/2003 (23%)	£100.00	£ 23.00	£77.00
2000/2001 (22%)	£ 98.72	£ 21.72	£77.00

The net amount is multiplied by 100/78 for grossing up in 2000/2001.
The higher rate IT was £18 (instead of £17).
The IT repayment was £21.72 (instead of £23).
This may occur with rental and trading income where the rate was 22 per cent during the year to April 5, 2008 and 20 per cent thereafter.

INCOME OF ABSOLUTE INTERESTS IN RESIDUE

The arrangements for the taxation of the income received by absolute **9–09** beneficiaries is based on the proposition that the income paid is deemed to be the income of the beneficiary in the year in which it is paid to him. If the income comes from a United Kingdom estate, it is deemed to be a net payment which is grossed up at the applicable rate in force at the time of payment. Any sum paid to an absolute (residuary) beneficiary is deemed to be net income up to the total of the income due to him for that year and any previous years. This was known as the aggregated income entitlement ("AIE") (now referred to as "assumed income entitlement"). The balance over the AIE is treated as being a capital sum. TA 1988 s.696(3) refers to "any sum paid" but s.701(12) defines "sums paid" as including assets transferred to a beneficiary and debts set off or released. These provisions have now been enacted in the "horribly" named Income Tax (Trading and Other Income) Act 2005 (ITTOIA 2005) s.665.

Assumed income entitlement

> **665.**—(1) Whether a person has an assumed income entitlement for a tax year in respect of an absolute interest in the whole or part of the residue of an estate depends on the results of the following steps:
> Step 1
> Find the amount of the person's share of the residuary income of the estate that is attributable to that interest for that tax year

and each previous tax year during which the person had that interest (see sections 666 to 669).

Step 2

If the estate is a UK estate in relation to any tax year for which an amount has been found under step 1, deduct from that amount income tax on that amount at the applicable rate for that year (see section 670).

Step 3

Add together the amounts found under step 1 after making any deductions necessary under step 2.

Step 4

Add together the basic amounts relating to the person's absolute interest in respect of which the person was liable for income tax for all previous tax years (or would have been so liable if the person had been a person liable for income tax for those years).

(2) For the purposes of this Chapter the person has an assumed income entitlement for the tax year if the amount resulting from step 3 exceeds the amount resulting from step 4.

(3) The assumed income entitlement is equal to the excess.

(4) This section is subject to—

section 671 (successive absolute interests), and section 672 (successive interests: assumed income entitlement of holder of absolute interest following limited interest).

Executors making general payments to account to absolute beneficiaries should be aware that they are paying income (even although the payment is described as being of capital) and should issue tax deduction (R185 (Estate Income)) certificates to the beneficiaries so that they may include the income in their own tax returns or repayment claims.

DEDUCTIONS FROM INCOME

9–10 If executors receive rents or income from a business, they may deduct the expenses incurred in the assessment of their IT liability in the usual way. In addition, relief is allowed for up to one year's interest on a loan applied by the executors in paying the IHT due by them on the deceased's moveable estate before they obtain confirmation. No relief is given on a loan to pay any interest due on the IHT. The relief is given in the year in which the interest is paid, but it may be carried forward or back if there is insufficient income in that year.

The relief may be applied to reduce an assessment of IT due on untaxed income received by the executors or it may generate a repayment on other taxed income.

A deduction is allowed from the aggregate income of an estate of the administration expenses which are properly chargeable against income (e.g. the 5 per cent commission plus posts and VAT, i.e. 7 per cent allowed on the collection of revenue under the General Table of Fees). This deduction reduces the beneficiaries' income and therefore their higher rate IT liability or their entitlement to a repayment of IT. The deduction does not generate any IT relief and therefore does not affect the executors' IT liability.

Executors are allowed to deduct from executry income interest on a loan[4] which has been obtained to pay inheritance tax but only on that section of the loan which relates to non-instalment property and only for one year after death.

TESSAs, ISAs and PEPs are only exempt during the lifetime of the **9–11** executor. Although the income may be received after death, it is important to check that no tax has been deducted in respect of that proportion of income which accrued during the period to death.[5] Prior to April 6, 2008 only business and rental income were taxed at 22 per cent. Now they are taxed at 20 per cent. The underlying theory of executry income certification is that when income is certified to a beneficiary it must be identified with the source from which it came. As regards tax credits paid after April 5, 1999 the 10 per cent will meet the full liability for the executry for that source. Basic-rate taxed beneficiaries will not pay any more. Non-taxpaying beneficiaries will not be able to recover any of that income and higher-rate executors will require to pay tax thereon at 32.5 per cent, i.e. a further 12.5 per cent.

To summarise, the rates of income tax for which executors are liable is based on the type of income received:

- interest—this is paid at the rate of 20 per cent;
- dividend income—only Tax at 10 per cent is paid on any dividend received. This is not repayable;
- everything else—this depends on the executor's liability to tax on the particular type of income. However this has been reduced to 20 per cent. It is likely that the only types of income will arise where the deceased was:

  — carrying on a business, in which event the executors may require to continue it until selling it or handing it over to the beneficiaries; they will be liable for the profits as trading income under ITTOIA 2005 Pt 2; and
  — rental income, in which event it is likely that some rent may be due during the administration before the asset is realised or transferred to the residuary beneficiary.

Danger Warning!!

Watch out for the case where the deceased bequeathed a specific legacy to a beneficiary of, e.g. a house. That income is technically the beneficiary's.

Apportionment of Income between the Executors and the Deceased

This has already been dealt with in Chapter 3. **9–12**

Most of the income is already taxed at source before the executors receive it. They are responsible for making a return of the untaxed income to the Inland Revenue. Under self assessment an executor must

---

[4] Not an overdraft.
[5] It seems to be beyond the systems of some (of our great) financial organisations to do this or to clearly demonstrate that this has been done!

submit his tax return by September 30 following the end of the fiscal year if he wishes to do so by using a paper return. It formerly was necessary to have the self-assessment in by the end of September following the end of the tax year to have HMRC to calculate the tax liability. Now HMRC do this whatever time it is submitted. Otherwise the return must be submitted by January 31, following the end of the tax year online with any balance of tax due; with the executries the executor should aim to have the return submitted to the HMRC as soon as possible after April 5. A self-assessment tax return is deemed to be final (except in cases of fraud) if the HMRC do not raise any enquiries within 12 months. For the avoidance of doubt, it might be better to ask HMRC to calculate the tax so that they have to look at the return sooner, thus avoiding questions on it after the estate has been wound up. If the practitioner waits until the estate is wound up he may be too late and receive a claim for interest and penalties, which the executors will not wish to pay out of the estate; the executor will also prejudice the beneficiary's relationship with the local tax office. It may be questionable if in fact the penalty can be paid from executry funds since it could be argued that penalties are personal to the executor!

9–13 The executor should again check the inventory for assets, which generate untaxed income, and make a diary note to return the income as soon as possible after April 5, particularly for those which generate accrued income such as government and fixed interest stocks. These main assets which generate taxable untaxed interest were listed earlier but the most common are:

- interest paid gross on National Savings products, including NS bank accounts;
- other bank/building society interests where an election to have interest paid gross has been made by the deceased;
- income bonds and government stocks on the National Savings Register and, as regards newly purchased government stock, where election to have interest net has not been made or, in respect of existing government stocks, where election to pay interest gross has been made;
- the interest paid on National Savings Certificates is not taxable;
- rent of heritable property;
- trading income: if the deceased's business is not terminated at death, the executors will receive some trading income, which they must include in the self-assessment form. The other sources will continue to produce income in the executry until the assets are realised or transferred. The income will have to be assessed in the executry tax return, i.e. the SA900 or by letter to the executor's firm's or the deceased's tax district;
- interest paid on TESSAs, PEPs and ISAs after death. The interest accrued to death is tax-free and the payer may and should deduct tax from the proportion due after death. If the post-death interest is paid gross (incorrectly) it must be included in the executor's return;
- interest paid gross on a few government stocks, e.g. 3.5 per cent war loan;
- certain types of income from abroad; and

- interest received from the Capital Taxes Office on over-payments of IHT is not taxable; similarly no relief is due on any interest due on IHT paid late.

It is important to remember that if the executors receive any residuary executry income gross, they must account for it and pay tax at the appropriate rates, either 10 per cent or 20 per cent thereon so that income which is passed on to the beneficiaries has tax deducted from it at the appropriate rate of tax (TA 1988 s.698A). This is grossed up for the beneficiary's own tax return at the appropriate rate or rates in force when payment to the beneficiary is made.

Scrip Dividends

It may be that there is in operation a mandate to reinvest dividends in **9–14** stock. These can be a nightmare for the practitioner. Over the years the deceased executor may have accumulated literally scores of share certificates, which must be listed. Almost invariably one or more will be missing! Most large companies operate an ordinary dividend stock option alternative scheme.

Because of possible delay in notifying the company of the death, the mandate may still operate and a stock or scrip dividend may be (and frequently is!) received during the period of administration. This will have suffered tax at the notional rate of 10 per cent. Although this must be shown as income of the executry, the tax will not be recoverable by the beneficiaries. The gross amount cannot be used to cover charges such as interest on a loan to pay IHT. However, expenses of administration in certification should be deducted first from this. If it is evident from the scrip supplied to the executor with the executry papers that the deceased was operating a stock dividend mandate, the executor should write to the registrar cancelling the mandate to receive stock dividends. As if matters were not complicated enough, it is likely that the company will only operate the scheme so that it gives rise to a full number of shares. There may often be a trivial cash dividend on the balance of shares upon which the stock dividend mandate does not operate. The Revenue may regard it as an enhanced scrip dividend if the value of the stock exceeds the net cash dividend by 15 per cent at the start of the next day's trading.

Danger Warning!!

The executors should notify the Inland Revenue that they are liable to tax within six months of the end of the year they became liable, complete a self assessment return and pay any tax due on the estate income and gains.

Forms R185

The R185 (Trust Income) and R185 (Estate Income) forms, which **9–15** trustees and executors respectively use to provide beneficiaries with details of income from a trust or deceased estate, have been amended to reflect the changes to the SA107 Trusts, etc. supplementary pages to the main return.

Who is the Return Made to?

9–16   The deceased individual's tax office will be responsible for dealing with any tax liability for the administration period except where the deceased was a Lloyds underwriter, or where a trust has been created under the terms of the deceased person's will. However, if the tax liability is over £10,000 or the case is regarded as complex HMRC Trusts Edinburgh will become involved.

Responsible office unknown

9–17   Occasionally the responsible office is unknown, but it may be obvious that liability will arise. If so, the office dealing with the address of the first-named executor will deal with the tax arising during the administration period liability, unless as above, the case is one where HMRC Trusts Edinburgh has responsibility.

In many cases, tax on estates is either already covered by tax deducted from the income, or is so small that it is impractical to deal with under normal self-assessment procedures. To minimise costs and administrative burdens for executors and agents, the HMRC generally allow tax liabilities for estates under about £400,000 to be settled by a one-off payment; it is likely that this facility will be extended for other estates except complex ones. They will supply the executors with a payslip, but where it is complex HMRC will still require self-assessment returns. It seems to be more complex where repayment of tax is claimed or made, say for example where the interest on the loan to pay inheritance tax generates a repayment.

HMRC say this can be made by letter. However in practice it will be necessary to produce a self-assessment form SA900.

Statements of Residuary Income (Forms 922)

9–18   HMRC Trusts Edinburgh currently issues forms 922 (statement of residuary income) annually for a large number of estates. This form is used to calculate and allocate estate income to the beneficiaries of the estate.

Apparently HMRC are reviewing the need for these forms, and expect to issue fewer of them in future. They are also looking at whether the detailed information which they currently request can be summarised.

Once the period of administration ends, it cannot be stressed enough to report of any untaxed income arising or disposals of a capital nature by way of letter so that the beneficiary's return can be checked and a reference pay slip issued for the executor to make settlement of any tax liability. It should be noted that where a trust has been created the relevant trust office will also deal with any administration period. In other cases where the above conditions are not met HMRC Trust Office Edinburgh will take over responsibility for tax matters from the date of death.

9–19   Returns in most executries are made by letter requesting assessment of the tax accompanied by a statement of income. In larger estates, HMRC will contact the executor asking for information about the estate. If appropriate, they will issue a self assessment tax return form for the trustees and executors for completion. Subsequently the executor may receive form 922. The executors are asked on form 922a to provide details of residuary income. In the event that there are any untaxed and/ or capital gains they may be asked to complete the self assessment tax return. If the HMRC issue a return form, the executors should prepare their own statement of income promptly after April 5.

If the executors are not approached by the HMRC and have received untaxed income or have made capital gains, they are obliged to notify the IR **no later than six months after the end of the tax year.** If they fail to do this they will incur a penalty. The IR will send a self-assessment form and (on request) the appropriate schedules, which make up the executor's tax return.

The executor will have to consider to which tax office the executor must make the return. Pre-self assessment the returns were made to the solicitor's local tax office. Under self assessment the return is supposed to be made to the deceased's tax office. In practice the solicitor's tax district will encourage the solicitor to submit returns to them. As stated the request for the completion of a tax return in larger estates may come from HMRC in Edinburgh.

Returns

The tax return for executors is the SA900 which extends (currently) to 12 pages. There are supplementary pages for self-assessment by an executor as a sole trader, partnership income, income from land and property in the UK, foreign income and gains and tax credit relief, capital gains tax, non-residence, details of executors, capital transactions, deductions, discretionary payments, computation of tax pool and charges and reliefs. The supplementary pages must be completed first and the return requires details of the total income less reliefs, double taxation relief, CGT, income from UK banks and building societies, dividends from UK companies, calculation of tax, overpayments and repayment claims and details of the executors. A 26–page tax return guide and an 11–page tax calculation guide will be available to assist the completion of the return and there are notes to cover the various supplementary pages.

9–20

Online returns

Returns may be made online. However, there have been difficulties with this recently. In a helpful article in *Taxation*[6] Allison Plager outlined the difficulties which have arisen with HMRC software and commercial software having also had to cope with the new forms:

9–21

"The new tax year saw tax advisers having to cope not only with major legislative changes—for example the new capital gains tax and domicile and residence regimes—but they have also had to familiarise themselves with the new deadline for filing paper self assessment returns and the new style return itself."

Income from Limited Interests

Under the old rules, as the liferentor was not entitled to a share of the capital the actual amounts paid to him were treated as net income and certified as such so that he could apply for repayment or report the

9–22

[6] Allison Plager, "Computer says 'no'", *Taxation* (September 11, 2008).

liability for higher rate tax assessment. Now there are no apportionments on a daily basis. The liferentor/beneficiary is taxed on the grossed up equivalent of payments to which he is entitled during that year.

TA 1988 s.695 makes a distinction between income received from United Kingdom estates and from foreign estates as defined in s.701(9) and (10). The distinction depends on the executors' tax liability and not on the location of the asset from which the income is received.

As mentioned, an executry is a United Kingdom estate if UK IT has been deducted from all of its income or if the executors are directly assessable to UK IT on all its income. All other executries are foreign estates. Most executries are United Kingdom Estates.

Income from Discretionary Interests

9–23 A "discretionary interest" is defined on form 922 as one where the beneficiary is not entitled to any income until the trustees exercise their discretion in favour of the beneficiary. The discretionary interest may not arise until the trust commences at the end of the administration of the executry, but if the discretion is exercised during the administration of the executry, the beneficiary is treated as having a limited interest in the residue. Any income paid to the discretionary beneficiary during the administration of the executry may therefore not be subject to any additional rate income tax which is payable by the discretionary trustees. If the income is paid by the executors to the trustees at the end of the administration of the executry the trustees will be liable for tax at the additional rate of income tax on it. We have to be clear when the executry ends. The rule of thumb is when the executry account is prepared. Thereafter, if the will provides that the residue must be "transferred" to an accumulation and maintenance trust then the rate will be at the trust rate of 40 per cent or dividend trust rate of 32.5 per cent.

Income from Absolute Interests

9–24 The amount of the residuary income due to the absolute beneficiaries is ascertained by deducting from the aggregate income. The amount of any annual interest, annuity or payment which is a charge on residue and this extends to include the interest on prior and legal rights of spouses and children. Any administration expenses may be paid by the executors out of the income during the year and the amount of the income to which a person has become entitled by virtue of a specific legacy. Most wills exclude interest on pecuniary legacies, but specific legacies may have income derived from the asset, e.g. rent from heritage or dividends from shares. If the deductions from the aggregate income exceed the amount of the aggregate income, the excess is carried forward and treated as a deduction for the following year.

ALLOCATION OF EXECUTRY INCOME PART II

9–25 It is important to identify the types of income with which the executors are concerned. For convenience they will be considered under the following heads:

- legatee's income;

- interest on prior and legal rights; and
- residuary beneficiaries' income.

Legatee's Income

Most legacies are bequeathed without an entitlement to interest on them **9–26** but there may be a specific legacy of an asset which generates its own income, e.g. shares or heritable property which is let. In the case of shares the income goes to the beneficiary and not to the residuary beneficiaries. Tax at 10 per cent, non-recoverable after April 5, 1999, on shares will generally have already been deducted on the dividends during the administration. It may be that the legacy produces untaxed income. If, for example, rent is received on a legacy of a house, before transfer to the beneficiary, subject to a furnished let the executors will pay the rent to the legatee gross. This income is excluded from executry income. The legatee must include this income in his own return whether or not he has received it (unless of course he renounces it). He may be liable to tax at the higher rate. The executor should therefore ensure that the income is paid to him promptly. It is suggested that the executor advise him to include it in his tax return. Collection expenses may be deducted, if appropriate.

Interest on Prior and Legal Rights

Interest attaches to the legal rights of *jus relicti, jus relictae* and legitim at **9–27** the estate rate. Interest, currently at seven per cent, is payable (gross) on the prior monetary rights from the date of death until payment. If the claim is made late, the interest may be substantial. This may exceed the residuary income and allow a deficit to be carried forward.

Residuary Beneficiaries' Income

Income from absolute interests

The criterion here is that the beneficiary is entitled to receive a share of **9–28** the capital at the end of the administration period. If he is only entitled to receive the income, his interest is limited.

From April 6, 1995 sweeping changes were made by FA 1995 to payments made to beneficiaries during the course of the administration and at the end. The FA 1995 Sch.18 (Deceased's Persons' Estates) made alterations to the code set out in TA 1988 Pt XVI, still in force despite the repeal and re-enactment of much of the ICTA (as part of the tax re-write programme). Now any payment made to a beneficiary is income unless it exceeds the assumed income entitlement (AIE) of the beneficiary during the administration to date, i.e. the income of the current year and any undistributed income from the previous year. In effect a pure receipts basis is introduced for income. The arrangements are similar for both absolute and limited interests categories. In both cases the actual income received by a beneficiary is certified and is used for his own tax return. As regards the absolute interest any undistributed income is carried forward to the beneficiary's AIE for the following year.

The relevant section of the Income and Corporation Taxes Act 1988, namely s.701, although repealed and largely re-enacted, is helpful in that it contains much of the relevant information in one section. For ease of reference, it is reproduced and should be studied carefully by all engaged in executry tax work.

Interpretation

701.—(1) The following provisions of this section shall have effect for the purpose of the interpretation of sections 695 to 700.

(2) A person shall be deemed to have an absolute interest in the residue of the estate of a deceased person, or in a part of such residue, if and so long as the capital of the residue or of that part would, if the residue had been ascertained, be properly payable to him, or to another in his right, for his benefit, or is properly so payable, whether directly by the personal representatives or indirectly through a trustee or other person.

(3) A person shall be deemed to have a limited interest in the residue of the estate of a deceased person, or in a part of such residue, during any period, being a period during which he has not an absolute interest in the residue or in that part, where the income of the residue or of that part for that period would, if the residue had been ascertained at the commencement of that period, be properly payable to him, or to another in his right, for his benefit, whether directly by the personal representatives or indirectly through a trustee or other person.

(3A) "Applicable rate", in relation to any amount which a person is deemed by virtue of this Part to receive or to have a right to receive, means the basic rate or the dividend ordinary rate according as the income of the residue of the estate out of which that amount is or would be paid bears tax at the basic rate or the dividend ordinary rate; and in determining for the purposes of this Part whether or how much of any payment is or would be deemed to be made out of income that bears tax at one rate rather than another—

(a) such apportionments of the amounts bearing tax at different rates shall be made between different persons with interests in the residue of the estate as are just and reasonable in relation to their different interests; and

(b) subject to paragraph (a) above, it shall be assumed:

(i) that payments are to be made out of income bearing tax at the basic rate before they are made out of income bearing tax the dividend ordinary rate.

(4) "Personal representatives" means, in relation to the estate of a deceased person, his personal representatives as defined in relation to England and Wales by section 55 of the Administration of Estates Act 1925, and persons having in relation to the deceased under the law of another country any functions corresponding to the functions for administration purposes under the law of England and Wales of personal representatives as so defined; and references to "personal representatives as such" shall be construed as references to personal representatives in their capacity as having such functions.

(5) "Specific disposition" means a specific devise or bequest made by a testator, and includes the disposition of personal chattels made by section 46 of the Administration of Estates Act 1925 and any disposition having, whether by virtue of any enactment or otherwise, under the law of another country an effect similar to that of a specific devise or bequest under the law of England and Wales.

Real estate included (either by a specific or general description) in a residuary gift made by the will of a testator shall be deemed to be a part of the residue of his estate and not to be the subject of a specific disposition.

(6) Subject to subsection (7) below, "charges on residue" means, in relation to the estate of a deceased person, the following liabilities, properly payable there out and interest payable in respect of those liabilities, that is to say—

(a) funeral, testamentary and administration expenses and debts, and

(b) general legacies, demonstrative legacies, annuities and any sum payable out of residue to which a person is entitled under the law of intestacy of any part of the United Kingdom or any other country, and

(c) any other liabilities of his personal representatives as such.

(7) Where, as between persons interested under a specific disposition or in a general or demonstrative legacy or in an annuity and persons interested in the residue of the estate, any such liabilities as are mentioned in subsection (6) above fall exclusively or primarily upon the property that is the subject of the specific disposition or upon the legacy or annuity, only such part (if any) of those liabilities as falls ultimately upon the residue shall be treated as charges on residue.

(8) References to the aggregate income of the estate of a deceased person for any year of assessment shall be construed as references to the aggregate income from all sources for that year of the personal representatives of the deceased as such, treated as consisting of—

(a) any such income which is chargeable to United Kingdom income tax by deduction or otherwise, such income being computed at the amount on which that tax falls to be borne for that year;

(b) any such income which would have been so chargeable if it had arisen in the United Kingdom to a person resident and ordinarily resident there, such income being computed at the full amount thereof actually arising during that year, less such deductions as would have been allowable if it had been charged to United Kingdom income tax;

(c) any amount of income treated as arising to the personal representatives under section 410(4) of ITTOIA 2005 (stock dividends) that would be charged to income tax under Chapter 5 of Part 4 of that Act if income arising to personal representatives were so charged (see section 413 of that Act);

(d) in a case where section 419(2) of that Act applies (release of loans to participator in close company: debts due from personal representatives), the amount that would be charged to income tax under Chapter 6 of Part 4 apart from that section; and

(e) any amount that would have been treated as income of the personal representatives as such under section 466 of that Act if the condition in section 466(2) had been met (gains from contracts for life insurance);

This subsection has effect subject to sections 249(5), 421(2) and 547(1)(c).

(9) "United Kingdom estate" means, as regards any year of assessment or accounting period, an estate the income of which comprises only income which either—

(a) has borne United Kingdom income tax by deduction, or

(b) in respect of which the personal representatives are directly assessable to United Kingdom income tax, not being an estate any part of the income of which is income in respect of which the personal representatives are entitled to claim exemption from United Kingdom income tax by reference to the fact that they are not resident, or not ordinarily resident, in the United Kingdom.

(10) "Foreign estate" means, as regards any year of assessment or accounting period, an estate which is not a United Kingdom estate.

(10A) Amounts to which section 699A(1)(a) and (b) applies shall be disregarded in determining whether an estate is a United Kingdom estate or a foreign estate, except that any estate the aggregate income of which comprises only such amounts shall be a United Kingdom estate.

(11) In a case in which different parts of the estate of a deceased person are the subjects respectively of different residuary dispositions, this Part shall have effect in relation to each of those parts with the substitution—

(a) for references to the estate of references to that part of the estate; and

(b) for references to the personal representatives of the deceased as such of references to his personal representatives in their capacity as having the functions referred to in subsection (4) above in relation to that part of the estate.

(12) In this Part—

(a) references to sums paid include references to assets that are transferred or that are appropriated by a personal representative to himself, and to debts that are set off or released;

(b) references to sums payable include references to assets as to which an obligation to transfer or a right of a personal representative to appropriate to himself is subsisting on the completion of the administration and to debts as to which an obligation to release or set off, or a right of a personal representative so to do in his own favour, is then subsisting; and

(c) references to amount shall be construed, in relation to such assets as are referred to in paragraph (a) or (b) above, as references to their value at the date on which they were transferred or appropriated, or at the completion of the administration, as the case may require, and, in relation to such debts as are so referred to, as references to the amount thereof.

(13) In this Part references to the administration period shall be construed in accordance with section 695(1).

Danger Warning!!

It is important to note that in terms of s.701(12)(a), "[r]eference to sums paid include references to assets that are transferred . . . and to debts that these are set off or released". This subsection is and can be extremely important.

EXPENSES

Expenses are of two kinds, those deductible for income tax and those deductible for certification.   **9–29**

Expenses Deductible for Income Tax

In addition to income received on a revenue producing specific legacy **9–30** and claims for interest on prior and legal rights claims, the following may be deducted from income for income tax purposes (and may lead to a repayment of income tax.

- Interest on a Bank Loan (but not on an overdraft) for payment of IHT on moveable property (not on confirmation dues or funeral account), restricted to one year's interest.
- Interest paid since death on any qualifying loan.
- Usual deductions from rent of heritable property, which is let (e.g. 10 per cent deduction in furnished lettings for wear and tear of the furniture). Losses on income from lettings cannot be set off against other income but may be carried forward to be set against future profits from letting. As regards income from furnished lets that has been assessed, included in the deductions would be legal expenses in collection.
- If the executors are carrying on a trade (as distinct from winding-up the deceased's business) they will be entitled to the usual deductions from their trading profit and may set a trading loss against other executry income.

Expenses Deductible for Certification Only

Administration expenses payable out of income

9–31 This deduction may only be made against a beneficiary's share of the executry income for the calculation of any liability he may have; **it may not be deducted in the assessment of any untaxed executry income** or give rise to a repayment of tax on the executry income. Where the income consists of different rates of tax it is recommended that the expenses are set off against the lower. This produces the result that the beneficiary is perceived to be receiving income taxed at the executry's highest rate!

Administration Expenses

9–32 It may be time consuming to actually work out what the estate rate of expenses actually is. The general business section of the Law Society's Table of Fees lays down the scale of charges, e.g. commission at five per cent plus posts and incidents, if appropriate, plus VAT, say seven per cent, is normally allowed on the amounts of the interest and dividends which are actually received, i.e. whether net or gross.

Expenses charged against revenue are deducted from the income in the certificate and may reduce the beneficiary's higher rate liability. Conversely if the executors know that the beneficiary is able to reclaim all the tax it may be possible to ignore expenses, e.g. in the case of charities, to enable the beneficiary to claim the maximum amount of tax or to allocate them against capital but only if the deed allows this.

It is competent to carry forward any surplus of deductions against income to income of a future year.

IHT PAID ON INCOME ACCRUED TO DATE OF DEATH

9–33 Relief IHT paid on income which accrued to date of death applied only in the calculation of any liability of a beneficiary to pay income tax at the higher rate (TA 1988 s.699). It was not a competent deduction in calculating the executors' income tax liability. The section was repealed by the Income Tax (Trading and Other Income) Act 2005 (c.5) Sch.1(1) para.289 and re-enacted in ITTAOIA 2005 (s.669) as follows:

Reduction in residuary income: inheritance tax on accrued income

    669.—(1) This section applies if on the death of a person ("D") income which accrued before D's death ("pre-death income") is taken into account both—

        (a) in determining the value of D's estate for the purposes of inheritance tax charged on D's death, and

        (b) in calculating the residuary income of D's estate for a tax year.

    (2) A reduction is made in the residuary income of D's estate for that tax year in ascertaining the extra liability, if any, of a person with an absolute interest in the whole or part of the residue of D's estate or any other estate to which that residuary income is relevant.

(3) A person's extra liability is the amount by which the person's liability to income tax exceeds the amount it would be if—

    (a) income charged at the higher rate were charged—

        (i) in the case of savings income of an amount not exceeding the starting rate limit for savings, at the starting rate for savings and

        (ii) in any other case, at the basic rate, and

    (b) income charged at the dividend upper rate were charged at the dividend ordinary rate.

(4) The amount of the reduction under subsection (2) is calculated as follows:

Step 1

Calculate the net pre-death income by subtracting from the pre-death income any liabilities which have been taken account both—

    (a) in determining the value of D's estate for the purposes of inheritance tax, and

    (b) in calculating the residuary income of D's estate for the tax year.

Step 2

Calculate the inheritance tax attributable to net pre-death income by multiplying the inheritance tax to be charged by—

$$\frac{NPDI}{VE}$$

where—NPDI is the net pre-death income, and
VE is the value of D's estate.

Step 3

Gross up the inheritance tax attributable to net pre-death income by reference to the basic rate for the tax year.

(5) The amount of pre-death income taken into account in determining the value of D's estate is taken to be the actual amount of income accruing before D's death, less income tax at the basic rate for the tax year in which D died.

(6) Subsection (5) applies even if the income so accruing was not valued separately or its amount was not known at the date of D's death.

(7) For the purposes of this section, the amounts agreed between the persons liable for inheritance tax and an officer of Revenue and Customs, or determined in proceedings between them, as the value of the estate and the amount of inheritance tax to be charged are conclusive.

(8) Evidence of those amounts and of any facts relevant to their calculation may be given by the production of a document that appears to be a certificate from an officer of Revenue and Customs.

THE ACCRUED INCOME SCHEME

The scheme, originally conceived to strike at the practice of "bond **9–34** washing", applies to bearer bonds, UK and foreign securities, and securities whether secured or unsecured by government companies, local authorities and other institutions. The exclusions are also numerous and include ordinary or preference shares and national savings certificates. We are concerned most frequently with gilts.

The scheme only applies where the nominal value of the gilts and fixed interest exceeds £5,000. The price at which a gilt or loan stocks is sold will generally reflect an adjustment for accrued interest. For example, if a gilt pays interest every six months, a person who sells at the end of month four will receive a payment, which reflects four months' accrued interest. A person who sells at the end of month five would normally sell on an ex-interest basis and the purchase would take a deduction of one month's interest (as the seller would receive this).

Section 148 FA 1996 made important changes to the treatment of accrued income in respect of deaths on or after April 6, 1996. There had been indications that the accrued income scheme would be altered and s.14 provides that the accrued income scheme shall not apply to the vesting of securities on executors on death or on the transfer of securities by executors to beneficiaries before the first interest date after the date of death. This, it is suggested, will be quite rare. It still applies where an executor sells (but does not transfer to a beneficiary as above) and/or transfers after the first interest payment, a gilt or fixed interest loan stock. If the will sets up a trust, there is a transfer when the executors allocate a fixed interest stock to the trustees' satisfaction of the legacy or share of residue, even if the trustees are the same persons as the executors. Executors should, if possible, transfer fixed interest stocks to the beneficiaries on or near an interest date when the amount of the accrued interest is small. The executor may sell it either cum-interest (buyer received next interest payment) or ex-interest (the seller receives the next interest payment even though it is paid after he has sold the gilt or loan stock). In practice, gilts are quoted on an ex-interest basis from six weeks or so before interest is due for payment. The Bank of England has now reduced this to 10 days.

Example: taxation of accrued income on fixed interest stocks sold in an executry

Jackson Pollock died on February 1, 2008. The accrued income provisions apply in full and in particular to sales during administration. He held £10,000 nine per cent Treasury Stock 2020 for which the interest is payable on March 15 and September 15 and £5,000 12.5 per cent Exchequer Stock 2022 for which the interest is payable on February 22 and August 22. His executors sold both holdings for settlement on July 23, 2008 to provide cash for legacies. The contract note received from the stockbrokers showed that the price of the 12.5 per cent Exchequer Stock was ex-interest and that 30 days gross interest (£51.37) was deducted from the price for the period from July 23 to August 22. The contract note for the sale of the nine per cent Treasury Stock showed that the sale was cum interest and that 130 days gross interest (£320.55) was added to the price for the period from March 15 to July 23. In due course the executors received the half-year's interest due on August 22 and the purchaser received the half-year's interest due on September 15. The executors have to make a return of the accrued interest for the year to April 5, 2009 as follows:

£10,000 9% Treasury Stock 2020
Gross Interest accrued from 15/3/08 to sale on   £320.55
23/7/08 (130 days)
Less £5,000 12.5% Exchequer Stock 2022
Gross Interest accrued from sale on 23/7/08 to   £ 51.37
22/8/08 (30 days)

£269.18

Tax on £269 at 20% = £53.80

As regards estates of persons who died before April 6, 1996 apportionment of accrued income may arise:

- at death (but is rarely applied);
- on sales during the administration. It still applies after April 5, 1996;
- on transfer to a beneficiary. It still applies after April 5, 1996 if after (including transfer to a trust) the first interest date after death is past.

It is necessary to consider the impact at each of these occurrences. It follows that it is best to avoid transferring a gilt to a beneficiary when it is full of interest. The Revenue may raise an assessment on the executors in respect of this possibility at a time when the funds have been distributed.

END OF EXECUTRY

The end of an executry, which continues into a trust, may not be obvious **9–35** and it is important for tax, e.g. the start of the rate applicable to trusts or the change in the CGT exemption of executors and trustees. This period of the executry is referred to as the administration period. The end of the administration period occurs when the free balance available to the beneficiaries is ascertained. This will be when the account of charge and discharge is completed and approved.

The HMRC computer dealing with self assessment tax returns crashed on January 31, 2008, the day on which most tax returns were due.[7] At the time of the first computer "outage", there was very little information available to assist the advisor trying to lodge a return before the deadline. However, later that afternoon, an announcement was posted on the HMRC website giving inter alia executors (and their advisors) an extra 24 hours to file their returns, without penalty. The incentive to meet the filing deadline is to avoid an automatic £100 penalty. Legally the penalty can be "capped" at nil, simply by paying all the tax by the due date. If, however, the tax is subsequently increased, e.g. after an enquiry, the penalty increases (up to the limit of £100.)

---

[7] Keith Gordon, "Penalties for late tax returns", *Accounting Web* (February 28, 2008) *www.accountingweb.co.uk* (accessed June 17, 2009).

> **Attention!!**
>
> *A late return means that HM Revenue & Customs have an extra period to open an enquiry into the tax return. Thus a 2007/2008 return (due on January 31, 2009) delivered on February 20, 2009 can be the subject of an enquiry at any time before May 1, 2010. BUT every executor is entitled to have a self assessment penalty waived if he has a reasonable excuse, objectively construed, for being late (Taxes Management Act 1970 s.93(8)).*

PLANNING: PRACTICE

Introduction

9–36   There is scope for a certain amount of planning. In the "Picasso" case study[8] disaster can ensue with a substantial executry lasting perhaps several years where only one payment is made at the end to a beneficiary who may be near the limit of higher rate tax. It is easy for an executry to go on for two years if there is inheritance tax, and longer than that if there are any complications, e.g. if there is a business. Three to four years can easily elapse.

There are two main options, pay now or later—or something in between!

The solution here is to know the beneficiaries and for some prediction to be attempted as to their tax rate in advance to the end of the fiscal year. A sustained attempt should be made to ascertain the beneficiaries' personal circumstances, either directly if they are existing clients (or at least not someone else's clients) or indirectly through their own solicitors or other professional advisors. A suggested questionnaire letter is printed in the Appendix.

Charities and the super-rich are the least difficult groups with which to deal. Charities will obtain repayment of all the tax. However, with the super-rich there may be some advantage in making a payment to account just after the end of the fiscal year so that they will have at least earned some interest during the period before they have to pay the higher tax rate assessment. With people in between these two groups, and particularly the elderly and children, it may be appropriate to spread the income so that most use is made of the allowances and entitlements to lower tax rates. It is helpful to obtain a note of the marginal tax rate.

9–37   On the subject of the super-rich remember a high earner may be about to retire and may prefer a payment to be delayed until during the year in which this takes place, especially if he will then not be paying tax at the higher rate.

At the root of planning lies the truism that executors do not have allowances. Individuals do. It is necessary to make payments in the manner and at the time which allows the beneficiary to claim maximum tax allowances and utilise payment of tax at lower rates.

Great care is needed in dealing with the type of beneficiary with income on the margin between basic and higher rate taxes and older

---

[8] See the Appendix.

beneficiaries who have taxable income around the margin (after allowances). Of course, "Murphy's Law" will generally operate to ensure that there are two beneficiaries, one on income support, the other a high-flying merchant banker earning over £150,000 a year. However, all is not lost. Under the new rules each beneficiary is treated as having an interest in the corresponding share of residue and this share can be dealt with separately. Each beneficiary would have their own assumed income entitlement (AIE) and their respective shares of income can be paid out at different times. It would be best to have their approval to avoid having to make compensatory payments. Please note that it is not possible to specifically allocate one type of taxed income to a charity and other types of income to another beneficiary. These different types of income must be allocated in a "just and reasonable" manner among all residuary beneficiaries.

Allocation of an Asset Beneficiary

It was formerly thought that specifically allocating an asset, e.g. transfer- **9–38** ring a holding of shares, to a beneficiary did not operate as a cash distribution although the contrary view had been expressed by the Revenue! The question turned on the interpretation of the former TA 1988 s.701(12) which provides that references to sums paid (to beneficiaries) "include assets that are transferred or that are appropriated by a personal representative to himself, and to debts that are set off or released". It is suggested that any asset transferred to a beneficiary is equivalent to a sum paid. Please note that this should not be confused with a specific legacy of a revenue-producing asset. It is the beneficiary's income from the date of death. It is not appropriate for the executors to return it for income tax, although they may be able to deduct a fee from the revenue collected. If the asset is revenue producing and the revenue is paid gross, e.g. rent, this should be accounted to the beneficiary gross. If the revenue is received net, e.g. a dividend, it should be accounted net. In the case of a residuary beneficiary it is important to note that a transfer of, say, furniture plenishings and personal effects to the surviving spouse could operate as a "sum paid". It is recommended that the position be clarified to see if it is appropriate at that point in the executry (which may be quite early on) for a transfer to be made. Possibly this could be exploited by different constructions being argued as to when the transfer of these items takes place! The provision could be useful if a beneficiary requires an early "payment" since higher income usually takes place in the early years of an executry.

Timing the Payment

As mentioned above the payment of income can be made to different **9–39** beneficiaries at different times. If a beneficiary pays no tax, e.g. a charity, its whole AIE should be paid as soon as possible, certainly before April 5 of the year in which the income occurs. Unless the executor knows that there is to be an increase in tax rates there is nothing to be gained by delay. It is rare for a charity to ask for a legacy to be delayed! All beneficiaries should agree if compensatory interest is not to be paid. It is also important to remember that with beneficiaries paying no tax, delay in payment may mean that the benefit of personal allowance is lost forever. This was particularly important before April 6, 2000 for the common case of beneficiary, namely a widow who may have underage children, with additional personal allowance and bereavement allowance both of which cannot be carried forward if not used. This benefit was largely eroded by FA 2000 which abolished additional personal allowance and severely restricted widows' bereavement allowance. The possibility of variation or disclaimer can be considered if all is left to the widow.

The effect of the beneficiary's age may be taken into account. The age allowance can make a real difference, e.g. a beneficiary or a beneficiary's spouse may be about to turn 75 during the course of the administration.

The personal allowances are set out at the start of this text and elsewhere. Care should be taken with older beneficiaries whose income may be near the margin, i.e. where their income (limit for age related allowances is reduced by 50 per cent where one spouse was born before April 6, 1935) is around, e.g. £21,800 for the year ending on April 5, 2009.

Danger Warning!!

The income falling within the margin can be taxed effectively at up to 33 per cent!

Beneficiaries Not of Full Capacity

9–40   Watch out for beneficiaries under the age of 16. It is difficult to imagine anything more catastrophic than if the opportunity to pay money to or for behoof of a child is lost and with it the chance to recover all the tax paid, given that the child may have no other income. Most wills provide a formula for payments to a parent or guardian of the child. But even if not, the executor should fully explore the possibility of paying the amount to a parent (under indemnity if necessary). It would be disastrous if succeeding years' personal allowances were to be lost. At current rates and, not including any lower rate tax band, up to £107.00 could be lost each year. If the payment is applied for the child, the tax may be recovered under the child's personal allowance, but it is important to make the payment in time to allow this all to work.

Capital Gains Tax

9–41   It used to be necessary to watch out also for the possibility of a beneficiary's capital gains tax liability as the payment of income might have forced the capital gains tax into the higher rate band. This is no longer applicable as the capital gains tax is taxed at the flat rate of 18 per cent.

Administration Expenses Chargeable against Revenue

9–42   It may be a time-consuming exercise to actually work out what the estate rate of expenses actually is. The general business section of the Law Society's Table of Fees lays down the scale of charges, e.g. commission at five per cent plus posts plus VAT, say seven per cent, is normally allowed on interest and dividends on what is actually received, whether net or gross.

Expenses charged against revenue are deducted from the income in the certificate and may reduce the beneficiary's higher rate liability. Conversely if it is known that the beneficiary is definitely able to reclaim all the tax, try to ignore administrative expenses, e.g. in the case of charities, to enable the beneficiary to reclaim the maximum amount of tax.

Changes in Rates

With the changes in the Budget announced earlier it is sometimes **9–43** possible to predict the effect of tax rates for the ensuing fiscal year. However, with the present arrangements this facility is strictly curtailed. Legislation provides that income paid to a beneficiary shall be deemed to be paid under deduction of tax at the rate in force when it is paid to the beneficiary. What do the executors do if they are unable to obtain information from the beneficiaries? In this case on balance it is suggested that the executors make a payment before April 5.

A common sense approach is necessary where the amounts involved are so small that any benefit is used up in additional legal and accountancy fees.

Financial Health Warning?

In future executors will require to pay much more attention to the **9–44** distribution of estates and its impact upon the beneficiaries' tax position. Failure to have regard to this could give rise to a negligence claim by the beneficiaries. Information must be made available to the beneficiaries as soon after the end of the tax year as possible so that they can comply with the new time limits regarding self-assessment and avoid surcharges, interest and penalties. The beneficiary has a statutory right to receive a statement of income.

Discharges and/or Variations

This matter will be dealt with in more detail later but it may be helpful **9–45** to have a brief reminder of the position at this stage. Consideration by the executor and/or the executors of variations and/or discharges (disclaimers) under s.142 IHTA will be standard practice. Until April 6, 1995 there were no statutory provisions which made variations or discharges (disclaimers) retrospective for IT purposes. This could be compared with TCGA 1992 s.62 for capital gains. Obviously a discharge is only available where no income or interest has been accepted by the beneficiary. When the bequest is a pecuniary legacy which has interest and it is disclaimed the beneficiary will not be liable to IT on the interest. In the case of a variation of residue or a share thereof the original beneficiary was liable to IT for the period from the date of death until the date of variation or disclaimer, although the executor was assessed initially. The new beneficiary was assessed thereafter. It might have been appropriate in the deed of variation to allow the disclaiming beneficiary some interest, if only to pay the tax levied. Clearly if there is to be a variation then it is best to make it as soon as possible. If not a situation could arise where a higher earning beneficiary who does not vary timeously could be assessed on tax at the higher rate on income he has not received. Any income actually paid to the beneficiary before the variation will, of course, be his for IT purposes.

If a parent wishes to benefit a child, it is suggested that this be done by disclaimer if this is practical under the will, to avoid HM Revenue & Customs treating it as a "settlement". Clearly we cannot over-emphasise the importance of addressing these matters at the earliest opportunity in appropriate cases and bringing the matter to the attention of beneficiaries, perhaps even by including a paragraph in the letter at the start of the executry.

Legal Rights[9]

9–46 "Interest" attaches to the legal rights of *jus relicti, jus relictae* and legitim at the estate rate. Interest is payable on the prior monetary rights from the date of death till payment. If the claim is made late, the interest may be substantial. This may exceed the executry income and allow a deficit to be carried forward.

CASE STUDY

9–47 Harry Beaton died on March 1, 2008, leaving a legacy of his cottage, Brigadoon, Whitecraigs (which at date of death was leased to a tenant on a Short Assured Tenancy), to his friend, Charles Dalrymple; and the residue of his estate: one-sixth to his father, Archie; one-sixth to his cousin, Mrs Fiona Campbell or Albright; one-sixth to Charles and one-half to Fiona's son Jeffrey.

His executry is likely to "go on" for some years and involve substantial inheritance tax liability. His estate includes substantial investments in bank and building society, stocks and shares and heritable property.

Dramatis Personae

9–48 Harry (date of death: March 1, 2008) died unmarried and without issue, and was a prosperous mining engineer, living and working in America on a short-term contract, where he died. He had rented out his cottage, Brigadoon, on December 31, 2007.

Charles (date of birth: January 1, 1943) divorced many years ago with grown-up children, and is an Aberdeen solicitor earning in excess of £250,000 per annum. In addition he has substantial investment income. He is planning to retire on December 31, 2008 to become a Wesleyan Itinerant Minister of the most zealous kind.

Archie (date of birth: April 7, 1935) is retired. His only income is his state retirement pension of £69 per week. He is married to Jean who is a few months older.

Fiona (date of birth: January 1, 1952) has been recently widowed. Her older bankrupt husband (aged 65) died on April 6, 2006 leaving her

---

[9] By the time of publication it is likely that the Scottish Law Commission will have reported on this.

penniless. She supplements her widow's pension with part-time income which gives her a total income of about £4,500 per annum for the year to April 5, 2008 and £5,500 per annum for the following year from all sources. For sentimental reasons she would like to have Harry's antique desk worth about £600 as a part of her share of the residue.

Jeffrey (date of birth: March 2, 1991) is a schoolboy with no income.

Executry Income

During the period from date of death to April 5, 2008 only bank interest **9–49** is received of £3,000 (tax: £750).

Harry's executors receive the following income during the year to April 5, 2009:

Rental Income on Brigadoon (gross)		£ 3,000
Other Rental Income (net of expenses)		£37,500
Interest	(Tax £3,000)	£12,000
Taxed Dividends Net	(Tax Credit £544)	£ 4,901

No monies were paid to the beneficiaries before April 5, 2008. "Know the beneficiary" letters were sent out and certain information was obtained from the beneficiaries. How should Harry's executors deal with the executry taxation implications for 2008/2009 and beyond 2009/2010?

HMRC may expect expenses to be deducted and since there is non-repayable dividend income there is a clear advantage to all parties in deducting this from non-repayable income.

The summary of residuary income is as shown below.

Summary of Residuary Income

For the period from March 1, 2008 (date of death) to April 5, 2008 (and **9–50** from April 6, 2008 to April 5, 2009):

	£Net 07/08	(08/09)	£Tax 07/08	(08/09)	£Gross 07/08	(08/09)
Rental Income (2008/09) Tax thereon @ 20%	nil	(30,000)		(7,500)	nil	(37,500)
Savings Income Taxed Interest @ 20%	3,000	(12,000)	750	(3,000)	3,750	(15,000)
Total	3,000	(42,000)	750	(10,500)	3,750	(52,500)
NRSF (non-repayable dividend income)						
UK Dividends		(£4,901)				
Less Expenses		(£4,901)				
Totals	**3,000**	**(42,000)**	**750**	**(10,500)**	**3,750**	**(52,500)**

Allocation

	£Net 07/08	(08/09)	£Tax 07/08	(08/09)	£Gross 07/08	(08/09)
Archie one-sixth	500	(7,000)	125	(1,750)	625	(8,750)
Fiona one-sixth	500	(7,000)	125	(1,750)	625	(8,750)
Charles one-sixth	500	(7,000)	125	(1,750)	625	(8,750)
Jeffrey one-half	1,500	(21,000)	375	(5,250)	1,875	(26,250)
Total	3,000	(42,000)	750	(10,500)	3,750	(52,500)

SOLUTIONS

Charles

9–51 The rental income from the specific legacy of the cottage is fairly straightforward. The rental income is regarded as the income of the beneficiary and the executors do not require to return it to HM Revenue & Customs. As Charles is a higher rate executor, it may be appropriate to deduct expenses when it is understood he would only pay tax at 10 per cent, 20 per cent (non savings) or 20 per cent (savings).

His assumed income entitlement (AIE) at April 5, 2009 is £7,500.00 as shown in the table below.

Solution

Assumed income entitlement—Charles

	Basic Rate Income	Non Dividend Savings Income	Dividend Income	Total
Net income 2007/08		£500		£500
Distributed		Nil		
Net Income 2008/09	£5,000	£2,000		£7,000
Total	£5,000	£2,500		£7,500
The figure of £7,500 is grossed up at 2008/09 rates[10]				
Gross	£6,250	£3,125		£9,375
Tax	£1,250	£625		£1,875
Net	£5,000	£2,500		£7,500

In effect Charles will receive £9,375 gross at 2008/2009 rates. However, because he is a higher taxpayer he will pay an extra £1,875, i.e. 20 per cent of £10,000. Had this been deferred until after April 5, 2009 he would have saved £1,875 in tax and this sum could have been devoted to good works!

Archie

9–52 His taxable income is £3,588 up to April 5, 2009. Although he is only 74 years old at April 5, 2009 he is entitled to Age Allowance of £9,030. This rises to £9,490 in 2009/2010 when he becomes 75. He also has married couples allowance (MCA) which, because his wife is over 75, will be 10 per cent of £6,625 for 2008/2009 and 10 per cent of £6,965 for 2009/2010. His AIE at April 5, 2009 is £7,500 (as for Charles) as shown in the table below.

---

[10] This is much simpler since the basic rate and the non-dividend savings rate are the same, i.e. 20 per cent.

Solution

Assumed income entitlement—Archie

	Basic Rate Income	Non Dividend Savings Income	Dividend Income	Total
Net income 2007/08		£500		£500
Distributed		nil		
Net Income 2008/09	£5,000	£2,000		£7,000
Total	£5,000	£2,500		£7,500
The figure of £7,500 is grossed up at 2008/09 rates[11]				
Gross	£6,250	£3,125		£9,375
Tax	£1,250	£625		£1,875
Net	£5,000	£2,500		£7,500

If the whole amount of £7,500 (equivalent to £9,375 at 2008/2009 rates) is paid over to Archie before April 5, 2009 the repayment will be as below.

		Gross	Tax	Non repayable
Basic Rate Income				
National income retirement pension		£3,588		
Executry Income		£9,375	£1,875	
Total		£12,963		
Deduct				
Age Allowance		£9,030		
		£3,933		
Tax Due				
At 10%				
At 20%		£786.60		
Deduct: MCA	@ 10% of	£662.50	(−£124.10)	
	Repayment due		£1,750.90	

---

[11] This is much simpler since the basic rate and the non-dividend savings rate are the same, i.e. 20 per cent.

Fiona

9–53 The executors agreed to her request for the desk and delivered this to her on March 30, 2008. In terms of the former TA 1988 s.701(12)(a), "[r]eference to sums paid include references to assets that are transferred . . . and to debts that these are set off or released".

This will relate to the year 2007/2008 for which her AIE is £500 after allowing for tax of £125. The first £500 of the value of the desk is allocated to net income. The balance of £100 is a capital payment to account. Strictly speaking, administrative (management) expenses should deducted but the *de minimis* rule could be argued.

Solution

Assumed income entitlement—Fiona

	Basic Rate Income	Non Dividend Savings Income	Dividend Income	Total
Net income 2007/08		£500		£500
The figure of £500 is grossed up at 2007/08 rates[12]				
Gross	£625		£625	
Tax	£125		£125	
Net	£500		£500	

		Gross	Tax	Non repayable
Basic Rate Income				
Part time		£4,000		
Executry Income		£625	£125	
Total		£4,625		
Deduct				
Personal Allowance		£6,035		
		(−£1,410)		
Tax Due		nil		
	Repayment due		£125	

---

[12] This is much simpler since the basic rate and the non-dividend savings rate are the same, i.e. 20 per cent.

Fiona's assumed income entitlement for 2008/2009 is as follows:

	Basic Rate Income	Non Dividend Savings Income	Dividend Income	Total
Net income 2007/08		£500		£500
Distributed		£500		£500
Net Income 2008/09	£5,000	£2,000		£7,000
Total	£5,000	£2,000		£7,000
The figure of £7,500 is grossed up at 2008/09 rates[13]				
Gross	£6,250	£2,500		£8,750
Tax	£1,250	£500		£1,720
Net	£5,000	£2,000		£7,500

Fiona's repayment for the year to April 5, 2009 is as follows.

	Gross	Tax	Non repayable
Basic Rate Income			
Part-time Income	£5,500		
Executry Income	£8,750	£1,720	
Total	£14,250		
Deduct			
Personal Allowance	£6,035		
	£8,215		
Tax Due			
At 20%	£1,643	£1,643	
		(-£77)	

Jeffrey

He has no income to set against his annual personal allowances which **9–54** will be lost forever if not utilised. The personal allowance for 2007/2008 of £5,225 is lost, as is the lower rate entitlement for that year. However, he has £6,035 for the current year (2008/2009). There is, of course, no lower rate entitlement. The "starting rate band", which might have been

---

[13] This is much simpler since the basic rate and the non-dividend savings rate are the same, i.e. 20 per cent.

available has also been lost (see Note*). It is imperative that a substantial payment is made to him before April 5, 2009. The executors estimate that his AIE at April 5, 2009 will be £22,500 as shown below.

	Basic Rate Income	Non Dividend Savings Income	Dividend Income	Total
Net income 2007/08		£1,500		£1,500
Distributed		Nil		
Net Income 2008/09	£15,000	£6,000		£21000
Total	£15,000	£7,500		£22,500
The figure of £22,500 is grossed up at 2008/09 rates[14]				
Gross	£18,750	£9,375		£28,125
Tax	£3,750	£1,875		£5,625
Net	£15,000	£7,500		£22,500

Jeffrey's Potential Tax Repayment claim of year to April 5, 2009:

		Gross	Tax	Non repayable
Executry Income		28,125	£5,625	
Deduct				
Personal Allowance		£6,035		
	£22,890	£22,890		
Tax Due				
At 10%	Nil (see Note*)	£		
At 20%	£22,890	£4,578	£4,578	
		£		
	Repayment due		£1,047	

*Note

Jeffrey has non savings income of £18,750 and savings income of £9,375. His personal allowance is £6,035 because he is (obviously) under 65. His taxable income is £22,890. The calculation below shows how this is worked out. After taking the personal allowance off his earnings, the amount of taxable earnings is more than £2,320 (£18,750 − £ 6,035 = £12,715) so none of savings income is taxed at 10 per cent. All of his income is taxed at 20 per cent!

---

[14] This is much simpler since the basic rate and the non-dividend savings rate are the same, i.e. 20 per cent.

If no income is paid before April 5, 2009 a chance of a good repayment will be lost for that year. The opportunity to reclaim £375 (net £1,500; gross £1,875) of tax for the previous year has already been lost. Of course, it is only necessary to pay £8,355 of income in 2008/2009 to secure maximum benefit. This should be addressed as soon as possible. If not and it is carried over to next year the position is worse because he will also have lost the benefit of the PA and the lower rate band for 2008/2009. In addition if the scale of income stays the same his income is likely to be "pushed" into the higher rate tax band for 2009/2010.

EXECUTRIES BECOMING TRUSTS

In the recent pre-Budget statement[15] the Chancellor announced the increase in tax rates on relevant property trusts to 40 per cent from April 5, 2012 and on dividends to 32.5 per cent. It will become increasingly important to decide when the administration period finishes and when the trust commences! **9–55**

---

[15] October 2008.

Chapter Ten

CAPITAL GAINS TAX DURING ADMINISTRATION

"The deceased and executor are treated as entirely separate and therefore any losses of the deceased unused at death cannot be carried forward to offset against gains realised by the executor.[1] Likewise, any losses realised by the executor cannot be carried back to offset against gains prior to death."[2]

TABLE OF FACTS

10–01

The Annual Exempt Amount (AEA)	£9,200 for executries (first 3 years)	£9,600 for executries (first 3 years)
CGT Tax Rates		
Individuals	40%	18%
Trusts and estates	40%	18%
Date return to be made		
Date payment to be made	To be paid (along with any balance of income tax due) on January 31 following the end of the tax year	
Penalty for late payment and time limits for submission		
Broadly speaking as for income tax		

---

[1] But losses up to death may be carried back.
[2] Penny Bates, "Don't fear the reaper", *Taxation* (December 3, 2007).

REVALUATION AT DEATH OF GAINS AND LOSSES AT DEATH

TCGA 1992 s.62

The changes in value occurring at death may be described as a "free **10–02** uplift" or revaluation for capital gains tax. There is no deemed disposal by the deceased at his death. Any increase in values at death is therefore not chargeable and any loss at death is now relieved. Death can be truly said to impose an impenetrable barrier for CGT. No transfer of unused allowances or reliefs is allowed between the deceased and his executors. It should also be noted, although it is not entirely relevant at this stage, that assets which form part of a liferent trust are also subject to the free uplift at the liferentor's date of death. This still applies to immediate post-death interests (IPDIs) created after March 22, 2006 but not where the relevant property regime is now applied; in that case, where a gain was held over relief is applicable, and the gain will be chargeable on the death of the liferentor.

As already noted, losses incurred *before* the year of death can be carried back and set off against gains in the last three fiscal years before the fiscal year in which death occurred.

Example—charge on hold over gain

James Willowherb set up a liferent trust for his daughter Rona in 1999. He conveyed into the trust inter alia a semi-detached bungalow in Bearsden, which was not his normal residence and which had a held-over gain of £40,000. The original cost of the house was £150,000 and its value at Rona's death was £250,000. On Rona's death the held-over gain of £40,000 becomes chargeable.

The tax-free uplift only applies to the balance of the gain which is £60,000 (£250,000—£150,000—£40,000); this balance of gain amount is cancelled for CGT purposes.

As stated, the deceased's executors will be liable for tax on any capital gains realised by the deceased executor, during the period to the date of death. This is reported under the normal self-assessment rules, but the time limit for assessment is restricted to three years after January 31 following the year of assessment in which death occurred (TMA 1970 s.40(1)).

Preliminary

Executors' acquisition costs: TCGA 1992 s.62(1)(b)

The executors are deemed to have acquired the deceased's assets for a **10–03** consideration equal to their market value at date of death, i.e. the confirmation value.

BASIS OF VALUATION OF ASSETS

TCGA 1992 s.272 defines the "market value" as the price which the **10–04** assets might reasonably be expected to fetch on a sale in the open market (with no reduction for flooding the market).

If inheritance tax is chargeable on an estate, the value of an asset ascertained for IHT is its market value at death for CGT (TCGA 1992 s.274).

VALUATION OF QUOTED INVESTMENTS: TCGA 1992 s.272

10–05 The market value of shares and securities quoted in the Stock Exchange Official List is (except in exceptional circumstances) the lower of:

(a) one-quarter of the difference between the lower and higher closing prices quoted in the List added to the lower price; or
(b) halfway between the highest and lowest prices at which bargains were recorded for the relevant date.

The normal "quarter up" valuation is (a), based on the London exchange prices and is used when no bargains were recorded.

If the exchange was closed on the date of death, the market value is the lower of the valuations on the previous and subsequent trading days.

VALUATION OF UNIT TRUSTS: TCGA 1992 s.272

10–06 Units are valued at the managers' selling/bid (lower) price on the date of death or on the latest date before death if no prices were quoted then. There is no provision for using the "quarter up" basis or the price on the next trading day after death. Open-ended investment companies (OEICs) have one price quoted on a particular day for their retail investment shares.

VALUATION OF OPEN-ENDED INVESTMENT COMPANIES (OEICs)

10–07 Open-ended investment companies (OEICs) are stock market-quoted collective investment schemes. They are similar to investment trusts and unit trusts in that they invest in a variety of assets to generate a return for investors. They are bought and sold at a single quoted price.

VALUATION OF UNQUOTED INVESTMENTS: TCGA 1992 s.273

10–08 The investments are valued on the open market basis noted above, on the presumption that there is available to the theoretical purchaser all the information which a prudent purchaser might reasonably require if he was buying the asset from a willing seller at arm's length. The value will reflect the degree of voting control (if any) or influence exercisable by the deceased (e.g. the right to enforce or prevent the passing of a special resolution). The adjustment of the value may require prolonged negotiations with HMRC's Shares Valuation Department. If the shares qualify for business property relief at 100 per cent, there will be no valuation for IHT (and CGT) until the disposal of the shares.

BENEFICIARIES' ACQUISITION COSTS: TCGA 1992 SS.62 AND 64

All beneficiaries acquiring assets under a will or on intestacy are defined **10–09** in s.64 as "legatees", including beneficiaries who take assets in satisfaction of pecuniary legacies and trustees for beneficiaries. The definition is not restricted to beneficiaries who receive legacies from the estate.

A legatee takes over an asset from the executors at their acquisition cost irrespective of the date of transfer to him and the value of the asset at that date. His entitlement to taper relief (when this was appropriate), for example, therefore started at death. There is no disposal on the transfer by the executors to the legatee.

The date of the legatee's acquisition is the same as the executors' (date of death or subsequent purchase) for calculation of the taper relief but business assets will not qualify for business taper relief unless the executors *and* the beneficiary qualify for relief. The executors may be unable to satisfy the qualifying conditions which apply to the beneficiary. If the executors do not qualify for relief at the business rate but the beneficiary does qualify, the beneficiary will only be entitled to taper relief at the non-business rate during the executors' administration. They should therefore transfer the business asset to the beneficiary as soon as possible so that his taper relief at the business rate may commence.

ALLOWABLE EXPENDITURE: TCGA 1992 SS.38 AND 64

TCGA 1992 s.38 contains the general provisions which apply to all **10–10** disposals. Section 64 deals with the expenses in executries and trusts.

The allowable deductions from the consideration in the calculation of a gain are as follows.

- Acquisition cost: the market value at death is the executors' acquisition cost. Executors do not normally make investments, but they may receive scrip or bonus issues at no cost on shares acquired at death or they may take up rights issues to protect their investment. The price paid for the rights is added to the death value to form the new acquisition cost.
- Enhancement expenditure: the expenditure must be incurred "wholly and exclusively" for the enhancement and includes expenditure incurred in establishing a title to an asset. In an executry the expenditure might consist of essential repairs to a neglected property or the restoration of fire damage before the property is sold.

A scale has been agreed with HM Revenue & Customs under TCGA 1992 s.38(1)(b), for the executors' expenses of obtaining confirmation and is contained in SP2/04,[3] HMRC will accept either this scale or the actual expenses in calculating executors' gains and losses on the sale of assets contained in a deceased's estate. The revised scale is based on the total value of the estate as follows:

---

[3] Replacing SP/8/94.

GROSS VALUE OF ESTATE	Expenditure allowed
£50,000 or less	1.8% of the confirmation value of the asset sold by the executor.
£50,000 to but not more than £90,000	A fixed amount of £900, to be split proportionally among all the assets of the estate.
Over £90,000 but not exceeding £400,000	1% of confirmation value.
Over £400,000 but not more than £500,000	A fixed amount of £4,000 to be divided as for £50k to £90k above.
Over £500,000 but not more than £1million	0.8% of confirmation value.
Over £1million but not more than £5million	A fixed amount of £8,000.
Over £5million	0.16% subject to a maximum of £10,000.

10–11   The revised scale takes effect where the death in question occurred on or after April 6, 2004.

The advantage of this is scale is that HM Revenue & Customs will not question it. It is particularly important that if the calculation is being carried out that the practitioner checks that this has been allowed for since it does not appear that some software systems automatically factor it in!

Example

Administration Expenses
Estate £100,000   Asset £16,000
Allowance 1% × £16,000 = £160

Estate £420,000   Asset £16,000
Allowance 16/420 × £4,000 = £153

Estate £550,000   Asset £16,000
Allowance 0.8 × £16,000 = £128

Disposal costs

These may include professional fees and outlays of the sale. The Table of Fees for General Business allows commission of up to 1.5 per cent plus VAT on the price for sales of stocks and shares (see Chapter 7).

CAPITAL GAINS TAX

10–12 As stated, in October 2007 the Chancellor announced massive changes to capital gains tax which apply to all sales made on or after April 6, 2008. Trusts and executries will now be much less complicated and probably cheaper. **The changes consist of a flat 18 per cent tax rate and the abolition of taper relief and indexation relief.**

In January 2008 the Chancellor proposed a new entrepreneur's relief for people selling a business. However it is unlikely that this will affect trusts or executries.

The annual exemption for 2008/2009 for executries will be £9,600 per annum. The exemption at the rate to be fixed will be available for the first three tax years of the executry; for trusts the exemption is half that amount, i.e. £4,800. Whatever gain is over and above this will be taxed at 18 per cent.

Example: sale by executors

Peter Dale's Executors held 10,000 ordinary shares in Barsetshire **10–13** Properties Plc, purchased at 20p each (£2,000) on March 1, 2005 which the executors sold in May 2008. The gross estate was £305,000.

Taper and Indexation Allowance are not applicable. The calculation of the CGT payable is:

Net proceeds of sale		£25,900.00	
Less acquisition value		£2,000.00	
Confirmation cost 1% of £2,000		£20.00	
Legal Expenses of sale (£25,900 @ 1.75%)		£453.25	£2,473.75
Net capital gain			£23,426.75
Less Annual exemption			£9,600.00
Chargeable gain			£13,826.75
CGT thereon at 18% =		£2,488.82	

THE POSITION BEFORE THE BUDGET 2008

Indexation Allowance: TCGA 1992 ss.53–57

Before April 5, 1998

This allowance, which intended to compensate for the effect of inflation **10–14** in the calculation of capital gains, was restricted by the FA 1994. The allowance was not available after April 6, 1995: (1) to turn a gain into a loss—the indexation will be restricted to the sum required to reduce the gain to zero, so that there is neither a gain nor a loss; nor (2) to increase a loss—no indexation was allowed if there was a capital loss.

The indexation allowance compared the Retail Price Index (RPI) for the month in which the death (acquisition) occurred with the RPI for the month in which the disposal occurred as in the following calculation:

$$\frac{RD - RI}{RI}$$

Where RD is the RPI for the month of disposal and RI is the RPI for the month of acquisition (death). The calculation is made to three decimal places and is called the "indexation factor", which is then multiplied by the acquisition cost (death value).

The current Retail Price Index commenced in January 1987. The index at September 1997 stood at 159.3.

After April 5, 1998

The Finance Act 1998 abolished the indexation allowance on assets **10–15** acquired after March 31, 1998. The indexation of assets acquired before then was fixed at April 1998. Taper relief reduces the gain by fixed percentages over a period of 10 years.

TAPER RELIEF (TR)

10–16 This relief reduced chargeable gains by a fixed percentage which increases over a period of 10 years. This is compared with the indexation allowance which was calculated on the acquisition cost. A modest cost would only generate a modest amount of indexation even if the asset was held for many years. TR is not linked to inflation and gives an arbitrary fixed reduction to chargeable gains. The maximum percentage reduction becomes fixed after 10 years although the actual reduction will increase if the gain continues to increase after 10 years. The TR percentage never reduces a gain to zero. Different percentages are allowed for business and non-business assets as shown:

No. of years	Non-Business	Business
0	0	0
1	0	50%
2	0	75%
3	5%	75%
4	10%	75%
5	15%	75%
6	20%	75%
7	25%	75%
8	30%	75%
9	35%	75%
10	40%	75%

The qualifying periods are measured incomplete years after April 5, 1998. No extra relief is due for ownership before April 6, 1998. The qualifying periods for executry assets held on April 5, 1998 will be fiscal years. If a non-business asset is held on Budget Day (March 17, 1998) it is deemed to have earned an additional year's TR. For assets acquired after April 5, 1998 the periods will be calculated in complete years—364 days will not be enough!

CAPITAL LOSSES IN EXECUTRIES

10–17 If executors incur a capital loss, they may carry it forward to set it against gains in the subsequent fiscal years during the Administration Period, but they may not transfer the loss to the beneficiaries.

As stated capital losses can normally only be set against gains arising in the same year of assessment or, if in excess of any such gains, carried forward. However, TCGA 1992 s.62(2) provides that CGT losses arising from disposals by the deceased in the year of death may be "carried back"; these losses may be set off against gains arising in the deceased's lifetime, but only during the previous three years of assessment. The losses are to be set off against more recent years before earlier years.

REVALUATION OF QUOTED INVESTMENTS SOLD AT A LOSS

10–18 If quoted investments are sold at a loss within 12 months after the death, the executors may elect to substitute the gross proceeds of sale (without any deduction for the expenses of sale) for the date of death values (IHTA 1984 s.179). All the investments sold must be revalued and any gains on the sales are deducted from the losses in the adjustment of the IHT. Any purchases by the executors within two months after the last sale are also taken into account.

If a sale is likely to be at a price above date of death value, the executors should consider transferring the investment to the beneficiary so that he may sell it. Such an arrangement would increase the loss on other sales and give a larger saving of IHT. The saving would have been lost if the beneficiary had to pay CGT at the same rate (40 per cent).

The adjusted values for IHT become the executors' acquisition costs for CGT. In theory the executors make small losses on the sales representing the administration and sale expenses (which are disallowed for IHT), but in practice such losses are ignored.

ANNUAL EXEMPTION AND RATE OF TAX

The executors have the same exemption as an individual (£9,600 for **10–19** 2008/2009) for the year of death and the next two fiscal years. They have no exemption thereafter. It may be that if, after three years without sale, transfer or other disposal of shares after three years, the executors are probably experiencing other problems of which the loss of annual exemption is the least of their worries! The trust exemption (generally one-half the lifetime rate) only applies if there is a continuing trust after the completion of the executry administration.

The executors are liable for CGT at 18 per cent for 2008/2009.

Example: sale by beneficiaries

Assume that it was appropriate, since the residue had been ascertained and **10–20** *the asset could be transferred to the late Mr Dale's two daughters who each had their personal annual allowances available. The calculation would be as follows:*

Lily Dale takes over half the shares at date of death value. The calculation of the CGT payable is:

Net proceeds of sale		£12,950
Less Date of Death value	£1,000.00	
Cost of Confirmation (say not applicable)		
Legal Expenses of sale not applicable		
	£1,000.00	
Net capital gain		£11,950.00
Less Annual exemption		£9,600.00
Chargeable gain		£2,350.00
CGT thereon at 18% =	£423.00	

Since the executry is time barred as regards its annual exemption or has used its annual exemption, there is a saving in effect of £1,728 (£9,600 at 18 per cent).

The same gain and liability is obtained for the other daughter Belle Dale, resulting in a potential saving of twice that amount. Practitioner's clients may be impressed if the executor has saved them this amount. Conversely, if he has not they may be considering other options!

> ***Danger Warning!!***
>
> *In an exercise of the above kind, it may be necessary to ensure that all financial service requirements have been complied with, e.g. client identification, know the executor's client, etc. either by the executor's selves or by the brokers.*

> ***Danger Warning!!***
>
> *It may be important to ensure that wherever possible in the executry if an executry asset is sold at profit that the profit is assessed to capital gains tax rather than inheritance tax. This was probably the case prior to Budget 2008 with dutiable estates since expenses of sale could be allowed, but these were not applicable if the asset was assessed to additional IHT. However the position is now much more acute since the rate of IHT is at 40 per cent whereas CGT is now at 18 per cent. If the estate is not dutiable it is important to investigate the possibility of revising the value of the asset. This may be quite in order since if the sale is fairly recent as regards the date of death it may be possible to argue that it was an under-estimate. The problem is that if the estate is not likely to be dutiable HMRC are not likely to be concerned as regards IHT.*

It may occur that the executry carries on into a new tax year and the executors wish to have matters finalised without waiting till after April 5 the following year! In these and in other cases HMRC will give a Post-transaction valuation check for capital gains tax.

SPEEDWELL CASE STUDY

10–21 Mrs Augustine Toadflax or Speedwell died intestate on October 1, 2003. She left estate which included a heritable property known as Orchid House in Greater Stichwort, Renfrewshire, which was valued by surveyors at £110,000 for IHT purposes. (When asked to look at it again the surveyors increased this to £120,000.) Mrs Speedwell's relatives were many and various but eventually her elder (and elderly) sister, Mrs Fennella Toadflax or Nightshade was appointed executrix. Confirmation was, in due course, obtained and Mrs Nightshade proceeded to ingather the estate. It should be explained that Mrs Speedwell had made a will prior to her death, in which she instructed her solicitors to destroy, which they duly did; this will had left a substantial bequest to Rudyard Willowherb. On February 15, 2002, Willowherb raised two actions in the Court of Session, the thrust of which was to reinstate the will and the bequest. He also obtained interdict and interim interdict against Mrs Nightshade intromitting further with the estate. More importantly he obtained legal aid and was able to run the actions for several years until October 10, 2006 when the executor, who was becoming alarmed at own spiralling legal expenses, made an offer and the actions were dismissed. No expenses were awarded since the pursuer had received legal aid.

Mrs Nightshade proceeded to sell the house and was successful in receiving an offer for £212,750. Although her solicitors had advised of the capital gains tax implications she concluded missives.

On the fact of it, the capital gains tax position looked like:

- Sale price (£212,750.00) less acquisition value;
- Confirmation dues, sale expenses and taper relief of £120,000.00, £1,400.00, £9,397.01 and £4,097 respectively
- Bringing out a tapered gain of £77,855.99, upon which CGT would be a staggering £31,142.40.

However, after much research (and soul searching) the solicitors suggest that the expenses of the court action be taken into account as deductions under s.38(1)(b):

Acquisition and disposal costs etc.

38.—(1)Except as otherwise expressly provided, the sums allowable as a deduction from the consideration in the computation of the gain accruing to a person on the disposal of an asset shall be restricted to—

(a) the amount or value of the consideration, in money or money's worth, given by him or on his behalf wholly and exclusively for the acquisition of the asset, together with the incidental costs to him of the acquisition or, if the asset was not acquired by him, any expenditure wholly and exclusively incurred by him in providing the asset,

(b) the amount of any expenditure wholly and exclusively incurred on the asset by him or on his behalf for the purpose of enhancing the value of the asset, being expenditure reflected in the state or nature of the asset at the time of the disposal, *and any expenditure wholly and exclusively incurred by him in establishing, preserving or defending his title to, or to a right over, the asset,*

(c) the incidental costs to him of making the disposal.

(2) For the purposes of this section and for the purposes of all other provisions of this Act, the incidental costs to the person making the disposal of the acquisition of the asset or of its disposal shall consist of expenditure wholly and exclusively incurred by him for the purposes of the acquisition or, as the case may be, the disposal, being fees, commission or remuneration paid for the professional services of any surveyor or valuer, or auctioneer, or accountant, or agent or legal adviser and costs of transfer or conveyance (including stamp duty[or stamp duty land tax]) together—

(a) in the case of the acquisition of an asset, with costs of advertising to find a seller, and

(b) in the case of a disposal, with costs of advertising to find a buyer and costs reasonably incurred in making any valuation or apportionment required for the purposes of the computation of the gain, including in particular expenses reasonably incurred in ascertaining market value where required by this Act.

(3) Except as provided by section 40, no payment of interest shall be allowable under this section.

(4) Any provision in this Act introducing the assumption that assets are sold and immediately reacquired shall not imply that any expenditure is incurred as incidental to the sale or reacquisition.

HM Revenue & Customs agree and the gain is recalculated as follows:

Sale price as at May 16, 2007		£212,750.00
1. Acquisition Value at date of death		
October 1, 2003	£120,000.00	
2. Confirmation/Executry Dues	£1,400.00	
3. Legal Expenses re Court Action	£50,786.53	
4. Expenses of Sale	£9,397.01	£201,583.54
5. Indexation	nil	
Untapered Gain		£11,166.46
6. Gain with taper Relief, i.e. 95%		£10,608.14
Capital Gains Tax at 40%		£4,243.25

NOTES

1. Revised Acquisition Value at date of death
   October 20, 2003

2. Confirmation/Executry Dues		
PER SCALE SP2/04		£1,400.00
3. Legal Expenses re court action		
Sheriff Officer's fees	£242.28	
Client (Defender's) legal fees and outlays	£13,846.74	
Precognitions	£288.00	
Faculty Services	£3,407.51	
Settlement	£10,000.00	
Defender's legal expenses (SLAB)	£23,000.00	
	£50,786.53	
4. Expenses of Sale		
Searchers		
F10	£28.00	
F10	£30.00	
Quick copies of writs	£30.00	
Saffron & Co		
Valuation fee	Not deductible	
GSPC		
Advertising fees	£294.00	
Commission on sale	£1,975.00	
Coal Mining Report	£24.00	
Beneficiary's expenses		
Fee re sale of house	£5,000.00	
Cheetham & Co		
Conveyancing fees	£2,016.01	
	£9,397.01	

As stated the executors are now liable to pay capital gains tax at 18 per **10–22** cent on gains made on sales of assets after (as of April 5, 2008) the date of death. It may be that relief is available to exempt cases in many instances. In these cases no capital gains tax will be payable.

If the executors transfer assets into the names of the beneficiaries, that is to say the residuary beneficiaries, as to account of their shares, the beneficiaries acquire the assets at the date of death value in the confirmation. Obviously when they dispose of these assets they will be charged on any gains realised and of course they will be entitled to the "benefit" of any losses.

However, before proceeding to deal with the sales of assets the executors should "take a step back" and reflect on their available options. In many cases of course they will have no option but to sell shares to realise enough liquid capital to pay off, for example, a bank loan which has been taken out to pay inheritance tax. They should, of course, take advice from stockbrokers or other qualified persons before taking matters further. In this connection agents and solicitors must be careful to ensure their own position. Do they have a full certificate or merely an incidental financial certificate? However over and apart from these considerations they may wish to take certain matters into account as follows.

The Wishes of the Beneficiaries

It is necessary for the executors to consult the beneficiaries to obtain **10–23** their views. Beneficiaries of course should not be given advice directly by the solicitors but should be encouraged to take their own advice and air their own views. A beneficiary may want to ensure that the value of their inheritance is kept up so he may be in favour of selling an asset which is depreciating and retaining ones which are going up in value. On the other hand a beneficiary with capital gains tax liability from his personal holdings might be "happy" to receive an asset which is going down in value to enable him to realise a loss which can be set against his gains.

On the other hand a beneficiary with losses on his personal account may wish an asset which is going up in value transferred to him. The residuary beneficiary can then sell the asset at a gain.

This is fairly academic in the current situation at the time of writing (February 2009) when the stockmarket appears at times to be in "freefall" or certainly to be facing a substantial downturn.

Charities

Where the residuary beneficiary is a charity it is more than likely that the **10–24** charity will want the asset to be transferred to it and sold on its behalf as a bare trustee.

It would probably be considered professional negligence for a solicitor to advise executors to sell assets which were appreciating in the executry and where a capital gain was likely and tax payable when, if the asset was transferred to the charity instead, the charitable beneficiary could sell it free of capital gains tax. It should be noted that similar considerations would apply to a foreign beneficiary who would not be liable for capital gains tax.

When dealing with a residuary beneficiary who is a charity it might be appropriate to raise the position with the charity at the outset. The charity may well have a policy on this.[4]

10–25 It is appreciated that all this procedure may take some considerable time while the market of course is variable. Clearly the executors' duty is to realise the estate and this should not be lost sight of.

It used to be regarded as a truism that if the asset was sold as quickly as possible then the executors' duty will be fulfilled. However, if delay took place and the asset went down through delay in the executor not selling it as soon as possible then this would clearly be a matter for concern and possible claim.

Notwithstanding this it might be as well to have regard to taking the wishes of the charity at the outset. Obviously where the share shows a downturn then it might be as well to sell as most charities will wish cash rather than shares. However this should be checked with the charity itself, possibly before confirmation is obtained.

An Asset Varying in Value

10–26 Clearly having an asset which increases in value will show profit. However, the executors and possibly the beneficiaries may not receive the benefit of a valuable asset.

One of the assets which is being sold may give rise to a loss which may lead to a saving in tax. However, as stated above, the executors should not delay unnecessarily before selling. If there is a strong possibility of the asset increasing it would be unwise to sell it. However, few of us are blessed with the prescience to predict this type of thing.

Dealing With a Loss

10–27 A loss on the sale can be "set off" against any gains in the same tax year. However, if the loss exceeds the gains it can be carried forward and "set off" against future gains in future years. If it is not necessary to sell the asset the executors may consider transferring a loss-making asset to a beneficiary.

Finally, it is important to ascertain if a gain is likely to arise. The executors should have the question of the annual exemption in the tax year at date of death and the two following years in mind. If it is at all possible then it may be possible to spread the sales over two tax years. Strictly speaking this would only be advisable if it became impossible to sell the shares just before and after April 5.

Above all it is important for the executors to monitor the share price so that no time is lost in making the decision to sell or transfer.

TAXATION OF CHARGEABLE GAINS: USE OF FORM CG34

HM Revenue & Customs Post-Transaction Valuation Service

10–28 HM Revenue & Customs offer a free valuation-checking service to assist the completion of the details of the executor's capital gains on the executry tax return. HM Revenue & Customs can be asked to check

---

[4] The Institute of Legacy Managers website: *http://www.ilmnet.org* [accessed April 25, 2009] has details.

valuations after a disposal has been made of a chargeable asset but before the return is made. This is not generally known about but can be extremely useful particularly where the sale has been made early in the tax year and the executors (and the beneficiaries) want to move matters on, for example, to have a payment to account made. This is assessed is completing and submitting completing form CG34.

Attention!!

The post-transaction valuation service may not be used for an asset that is the subject of a negligible value claim. Form CG34 cannot precede the negligible value claim for an asset.

Form CG34

Application for post transaction valuation check

Please complete all relevant items and send the application to your HMRC Office (**not** to any of the Valuation Offices)

Taxpayer details

Name __The Executors of the late Augustine Speedwell__

Address __c/o Cheetham & Steele__

_____ Postcode _____

Reference | National Insurance number *(where appropriate)*

S/AS

Agent's name __Cheetham & Steele__ Reference _____

Address _____

_____ Postcode _____

Details of disposal

Date of disposal 16 / 05 / 2007

Name and address of purchaser

Name __Mr and Mrs G Bargain__

Address __1 Southland Drive__

__Lewis__ Postcode _____

Reason for valuation

√ *as appropriate*

☐ Rebasing to 31 March 1982

☐ Market value disposal (disposal to a connected person or a bargain not at arm's length)

☐ Negligible value claim

☒ Other - *please specify* __The Executors wish to pay beneficiaries prior__
__to 5th April 2008__

Valuation required

Description of asset to be valued	Valuation date	Valuation offered
Greater Stichwort, Renfrewshire	1/10/2003	£120,000

Shares - The description should include the name of the company, the registration number (if known), the class and the number of shares to be valued. Enter in the table your valuation **per share** and not the total value of your holding.

Goodwill - The description should provide sufficient information to identify the asset. If an incorporation is involved the details provided should identify the name and nature of the business from which the transfer has been made and also, the name and company registration number of the recipient company together with the registered office address.

Land - The description should provide sufficient information to identify the property, with details of your interest in the property and details of any tenancies existing at the valuation date. The term 'land' includes both land and buildings.

Other - The description should provide sufficient information to identify the asset.

Please turn over
HMRC 06/06

You should also provide

√ to show items enclosed

☐ A capital gains computation for the disposal with an estimate of your capital gains tax liability for the tax year in which you made the disposal, or for companies the corporation tax liability on chargeable gains, or for partnership disposals, estimates of the liabilities of the individual partners

☐ Details of any reliefs due or to be claimed in respect of the disposal

☐ A copy of any valuation report obtained

☐ If available, the cost and date of acquisition of the asset and details of any improvements made

☐ For **share** valuations - full accounts for the three years up to the valuation date

☐ For **goodwill** valuations - full accounts for the three years up to the valuation date

☐ For **land** valuations -

• if you held a leasehold interest, a copy of the lease applying at the valuation date

• if the land was let at the valuation date, a copy of any tenancy agreement applying at that date

• a plan showing the location of the land if the valuation is of undeveloped land

☐ Any other papers you feel may be relevant

Use this space to provide any other information that you consider is relevant to your valuation

PER ATTACHED SCHEDULE

10–29   Where an asset has become of negligible value the executor may claim it to be treated as though it had been sold and immediately reacquired for the amount specified in the claim (s.24(2) of the Taxation of Chargeable Gains Act 1992) and thus to qualify for an allowable capital loss.

VALUATION IN DEEDS OF VARIATION: TCGA 1992 s.62

10–30   Deeds of variation made within two years after death under IHTA 1984 s.142 may also contain an election for CGT under TCGA 1992 s.62. The election is voluntary and should only be included in the deed if appropriate. No election should be inserted in the deed if the variation only refers to assets that are not subject to CGT, e.g. cash, government securities or NS products.

If the variation refers to quoted investments (or other assets subject to CGT), the consequences of an election should be considered so as to decide whether it is appropriate to include an election.

If there is no election, the original beneficiary, who acquired the investment at its date of death value (provided it has been transferred to him) will make a disposal for CGT at the date of the deed of variation and the new beneficiary will acquire the investment at its value on the same date.

10–31   If there is an election under s.62, the new beneficiary will take over the investment at its date of death value and there will be no disposal by the original beneficiary. The new beneficiary's taper relief will run from the date of death if there is an election or from the date of the deed of variation if there is no election.

The decision whether to elect will therefore depend on the respective values at death and variation. The values are likely to be more important than the commencing dates of the taper relief, if that is relevant. There may be a conflict of interest between the beneficiaries, but that should not be a problem because they are usually related. A higher acquisition value will help the new beneficiary for future capital gains tax.

If the higher value is at the date of variation, an election should not be made, provided (1) the asset has been transferred to the beneficiary and (2) the gain on the disposal by the original beneficiary is within his exemption. The beneficiary has no acquisition cost until the asset has been transferred to him. If the death value is the higher, an election should be made so that the new beneficiary will take over the investment at death.

Notice of the election has to be given to the Revenue within six months after the date of the deed. The notice is given to the tax district dealing with the executry income.

MAIN RESIDENCE RELIEF: TCGA 1992 ss.222 AND 225

10–32   The entitlement to the main residence relief under s.222 requires occupation by the owner, which does not apply in executries because the executors own the house but do not occupy it as executors and if it is occupied, the occupier is not the owner. Section 225 allows the relief in trusts where the dwelling house has been the main residence of a person who is entitled to occupy it in terms of the trust deed. The relief under s.225 is extended to executries where the house has been used as a main residence before and after the death by one or more individuals, who under the will or intestacy are entitled to the whole or most of the proceeds of the sale by the executors absolutely or for life. The individuals or the group of individuals (although not necessarily all of them) must have a "relevant entitlement" which is an entitlement as legatee to the whole or any part of the net proceeds of disposal, or to an interest in possession in the net proceeds of disposal. Executors must make the claim to only or main residence relief. The relevant entitlement or, where more than one, all the relevant entitlements amount to at least 75 per cent of the "net proceeds of disposal", i.e. the consideration received less sale costs.

Attention!!

In applying the 75 per cent rule, none of the proceeds are needed to meet the liabilities (including inheritance tax) of the estate.

In theory a capital gains tax liability should seldom arise on heritage in an executry, because the district valuer will take the sale price as the date of death value, if the sale takes place within a reasonable time after death. The concession could be useful for a delayed sale at the end of the executry especially if the annual exemption has expired.

If there is no main residence relief and if a sale is delayed, it may be **10–33** possible to negotiate a date of death value which is lower than the sale price, leaving a capital gain which is within the executors' exemption.

If a residuary beneficiary in an estate subject to IHT is inheriting a house, which is his main residence, it may be beneficial to postpone any sale of the house until after the administration of the executry.

The adjustment of the value of the house with the district valuer will be a matter of professional judgement and it may be possible to agree a low value which saves IHT. If the house is sold during the executry, the sale price will be the value.

If the sale is postponed, the beneficiary will take over the house as legatee at the agreed value. The house will then be owned and occupied by the beneficiary as his main residence and any gain on the subsequent sale will be relieved.

EXECUTRIES BECOMING CONTINUING TRUSTS

A Trust set up under a will does not start until the executors have made **10–34** over the trust fund (e.g. a legacy) to the trustees, who will probably be themselves acting in a different capacity.

If the trust fund is part of the residue of the estate, the trust will not start until the residue is established at the end of the Administration Period. If the trust is discretionary (e.g. an accumulation and maintenance trust) the IT liability at the trust rates will not start until the trust starts.

The trustees' CGT exemption is half the executors' rate. The change of exemption applies from the start of the trust. The executors may have the full exemption in the same year as the trustees' half exemption starts.

Both exemptions may be used to minimise the CGT. Executors and trustees are all liable for CGT at18 per cent.

10–35 There is no legal objection to cash being provided by a beneficiary to meet the executors' requirements so that the executors may transfer an asset to him.

The executors may also arrange for an investment to be sold on behalf of a beneficiary to provide such cash, without transferring the investment to him, but such an arrangement is dangerous and may be treated by the Revenue as a sale by the executors unless there is clear evidence of the investment being allocated to the beneficiary and the sale being by him. If the sale is not urgent, it is safer to transfer the asset to the beneficiary before the sale. The cost of the transfer is usually modest, e.g. a stock transfer or a confirmation docket, and is deductible in the calculation of the gain.

If the investment has not been transferred or formally allocated to the beneficiary (e.g. in an interim division) the Revenue may argue that the beneficiary has disposed of a right to the investment only (not the investment itself) and that his acquisition cost was therefore nil.

10–36 The evidence of a beneficiary's sale might consist of:

1. an allocation of the investment to the beneficiary by the executors in an interim division;
2. correspondence with the beneficiary, recording his instructions to sell the investment on his behalf;
3. a contract note in the name of the beneficiary;
4. a tax return of the gain by the beneficiary; and
5. no tax return by the executors.

In the calculation of his capital gain in these circumstances, it may be possible for a beneficiary to deduct the administration and transfer expenses incurred by the executors in terms of TCGA 1992 s.64 or at least the costs allowed to him in SP 8/94 as noted above.

Expenses in administration of estates and trusts

64.—(1) In the case of a gain accruing to a person on the disposal of, or of a right or interest in or over, an asset held by another person as trustee, or as a personal representative of a deceased person, to which he became absolutely entitled as legatee or as against the trustee—

(a) any expenditure within section 38(2) incurred by him in relation to the transfer of the asset to him by the personal representative or trustee, and

(b) any such expenditure incurred in relation to the transfer of the asset by the personal representative or trustee,

shall be allowable as a deduction in the computation of the gain accruing to that person on the disposal.

(2) In this Act, unless the context otherwise requires, "legatee" includes any person taking under a testamentary disposition or

on an intestacy or partial intestacy, whether he takes beneficially or as trustee, and a person taking under a donatio mortis causa shall be treated (except for the purposes of section 62) as a legatee and his acquisition as made at the time of the donor's death.

(3) For the purposes of the definition of "legatee" above, and of any reference in this Act to a person acquiring an asset "as legatee", property taken under a testamentary disposition or on an intestacy or partial intestacy includes any asset appropriated by the personal representatives in or towards satisfaction of a pecuniary legacy or any other interest or share in the property devolving under the disposition or intestacy.

A sale by a beneficiary may be useful if the executors have used their CGT annual exemption or if they have no exemption because the administration has run over the third tax year after death. It used to be necessary to have regard to the beneficiary's CGT rate when the rate of capital gains tax was affected by the beneficiary's income. He may have been liable at 20 per cent if his IT lower rate band had not been used, or he may have been liable at 40 per cent compared with the executors' 34 per cent. Now this is academic since the capital gains tax rate for executries (and trusts) is the same as for individuals.

Capital Losses in Executries

If executors incur a capital loss, they may carry it forward to set it against **10–37** gains in the subsequent fiscal years during the Administration Period, but they may not transfer the loss to the beneficiaries.

Revaluation of Quoted Investments Sold at a Loss

If quoted investments are sold at a loss within 12 months after the death, **10–38** the executors may elect to substitute the gross proceeds of sale (without any deduction for the expenses of sale) for the date of death values (IHTA 1984 s.179). All the investments sold must be re-valued and any gains on the sales are deducted from the losses in the adjustment of the IHT. Any purchases by the executors within two months after the last sale are also taken into account.

If a sale is likely to be at a price above date of death value, the executors should consider transferring the investment to a beneficiary so that he may sell it. Such an arrangement would increase the loss on the other sales and give a larger saving of IHT.

The adjusted values for IHT become the executors' acquisition costs for CGT. In theory the executors make small losses on the sales representing the administration and sale expenses (which are disallowed for IHT), but in practice such losses are ignored for CGT.

Chapter Eleven

INHERITANCE TAX DURING ADMINISTRATION

"Why was there no General Election in 2007? Almost certainly the answer can be summarised in two words: inheritance tax."[1]

TAX FACTS

11–01

	Rates	
Gross Transfers on death	40%	
Chargeable Lifetime Transfers	20%	
	Gross Transfers on death	
Period	Nil Rate Band	
2007/08[2]	£300,000	
2008/09[3]	£312,000	
2009/10[4]	£325,000	
2010/11[5]	£350,000	
Any portion of the nil rate band which is not used at a executor's death can be transferred to the executors of their surviving spouse or civil partner for the purposes of IHT charge on the death of the survivor on or after October 9, 2007		
	Delivery dates	
Chargeable lifetime transfers	Later of 12 months after transfer took place and three months after the date when the accountable party became liable	
PETs[6] which have become chargeable	12 months after the month in which the death took place	

---

[1] Fabian Society Pamphlet, Fabian Ideas no.623, "How to Defend Inheritance Tax".
[2] FA 2005 s.98.
[3] FA 2006 s.155.
[4] FA 2006 s.155.
[5] FA 2007 s.4.
[6] Potentially Exempt Transfers.

	Delivery dates
Gifts with reservation which are chargeable on death	12 months after the month in which the death took place
Transfers on death	Later of 12 months after the month in which the death and took place

The focus of inheritance tax during administration will be mainly concerned with revising and finalising inheritance tax liability and reporting as soon as possible any additional inheritance tax which may be due, and of course reporting any matters which would lead to a reduction or repayment of inheritance tax.

At the outset it should be stressed that any matter which generates additional inheritance tax should be reported to HMRC as soon as it becomes known and the amount of additional inheritance tax tendered as soon as it is possible to do so. It is strongly advised that the practitioner should not wait "until all the information" is available. Report it and pay the tax at the outset. This may mean reclaiming tax at a later stage but this is a small inconvenience when faced with a penalty notice and the ignominy of having to explain the executor's folly to a client! The case of *Robertson* mentioned later illustrates the difficulties which may ensue.

Losses on Realisation of Assets

In the current climate it is important to track the value of shares and **11–02** other assets which might give rise to a loss.

It may transpire that due to a downturn in the market or for whatever reason the shares or other assets of the estate must be sold at a price less than that at date of death. In this situation it is important to take a view. Needless to say, HM Revenue & Customs have been inundated with these claims and have issued guidance in a recent HMRC IHT & Trust Newsletter.

IHTA 1984 ss.178–198 details the situations where relief is available where certain assets are sold for less than their market value at date of death. If the investments are sold within 12 months of the death at less than their market value *the sale price* is taken instead of the market value at date of death. In many cases this will lead to a repayment of inheritance tax. The types of assets sold are stocks and shares and unit trusts. It should be noted that this also applies to investments which are contained in a trust of which the deceased was a liferentor.

Please note that the brokerage commission and stamp duty should be excluded from the calculation. In effect these cannot be utilised to in effect increase any loss.

Example

James Buttercup's executors find on their investigations that he had made **11–03** *gifts and charitable transfers up to the limit of his nil rate band. His estate at date of death was £600,000 which included shares in a publicly quoted company, Imperial Pixie Industries Plc. The shares were worth at date of death for inheritance tax purposes £60,000 and inheritance tax was paid on the estate. Unfortunately his executors were unable to transfer the asset but* *required to sell it to pay off the loan for inheritance tax purposes for £59,000 within 12 months and claimed relief using form IHT35 receiving a refund of tax paid on the £1,000 reduction in value, i.e. £400.*

It is vitally important to identify the one-year anniversary after date of death for various reasons. However we are here concerned only with the question of the time limit for realisation. It is important then to check and to insert the anniversary date in the practitioner's diary or "bring forward system" or otherwise to ensure that this anniversary does not go by. In most cases if shares are to be sold this will be done shortly after confirmation has been obtained and exhibited to the companies concerned.

Sometimes and in recent times this is more relevant. It may occur that after the expiry of a year from death the company may have called in the receivers or filed for liquidation.

11–04   It may be that the value of the shares at this stage is nil. Obviously the executors are not in a position to sell the shares and no relief is available. However, the Finance Act 1983 s.199 inserted a new s.186B into IHTA 1984 which provided that the shares can be treated as sold immediately before the end of the one-year period.

Sometimes, for various reasons, the year anniversary goes by without the executors being in a position to sell the assets. There may be legal disputes over the will and obtaining of confirmation is delayed.

If the period goes by and the shares are sold at a spectacular loss then this clearly is a matter for concern.

11–05   It may be possible however to partially mitigate the situation by deed of variation. If a deed of variation is produced which leaves that particular shareholding to a charity then it may be possible to at least reclaim the inheritance tax which was paid. This would need the co-operation of the charity. This matter is treated later in the text under Post Death Variations. It may be a comfort, however small, for the beneficiaries to know that at least the inheritance tax has not been paid on an asset which has vanished or diminished in value!

It should be noted that if the executors utilise the inheritance tax relief provisions the new sale price becomes the acquisition value for capital gains tax.

Capital

11–06   Where the deceased held shares in two separate companies, if each holding is worth £2,000 and they are both sold within the 12 months for £1,000 and £3,000 respectively they must aggregate the share prices to calculate the overall loss. It is not competent merely to select the loss-making sale. There are provisions for reinvestment of a share but these rarely occur.

It should be noted that when sales take place the executors may also acquire an allowable loss for capital gains tax purposes. However, if the election is made for relief it is in fact that price which becomes the executors' acquisition value for capital gains tax as well. They will not therefore be able to claim a capital gains tax loss in these circumstances. Of course this may not be a problem with loss; it may be a problem in connection with a gain since inheritance tax is presently charged at 40 per cent on the estate (over the nil rate band, etc.). Capital gains tax is only now payable at 18 per cent of the chargeable gain. It will always be important therefore to attempt to have the gain treated as a capital gain (rather than under inheritance tax) wherever possible.

Heritable Property

The other asset which may be relevant under this heading is a house or **11–07** interest in land. This may be sold for less than the market value at date of death and indeed under current conditions this may well be likely. The claim can be made for relief but in this case the sale must take place within four years of the date of death. The question is the date of conclusion of the missives. This can also lead to a refund of inheritance tax.

HMRC are of course given the power to substitute what they would consider a correct value at date of death. It almost goes without saying that every effort should be made to have HM Revenue & Customs commit themselves to a date of death value as soon as possible.

Please watch out where the deceased was a joint owner of the house. Discount which may be available on jointly-owned land may be lost if a claim is made.

Pansy owns half of Pixie Cottage. This is valued at £400,000 at her date of death and the value of her one-half share is discounted by 10 per cent to £180,000. Within four years of her death the whole property is sold for £360,000. The sale value of the property for these purposes is a half share of the gross proceeds, say £190,000. It would therefore be inappropriate to claim as it may be that additional inheritance tax would be payable.

What Happens if a Share which has been Transferred to a Beneficiary Goes Down in Value?

In fulfilling their prime duty to realise assets to pay debts expenses, tax **11–08** including IHT and legacies it may transpire that a, say, volatile share has gone down in value.

Example

Mr Gerald Bee Orchid, the residuary beneficiary under the estate of his late father, asked for and received a transfer to him from the executors of a holding of 100,000 Hairy Holdings Plc shares of 25p each. Hairy Holdings Plc was a publicly quoted company, whose business involved mining for gold in Iceland. At the date of death it was worth £20 per share or £2 million. After a few months the share which was always very volatile started to slide. It had actually gone up in value shortly after death to £25 and Gerald, thinking that Christmas had come a little early, sold 5,000 shares. However, shortly after it had started to slide. Approximately 11 months after the date of death it went down to £5 per share . Gerald's nerve broke and he sold the remainder of the holding. He was the sole residuary beneficiary.

The position therefore was as follows:

No. of		Share price at	Value at date	IHT at 40%	Proceeds
shares		date of death	of death		before
					brokerage
100,000	Hairy Holdings Plc	£20.00	£2,000,000.00	£800,000.00	
5,000	Sold	£25.00			£125,000.00
95,000	Sold	£5.00			£475,000.00
					£600,000.00
	total loss				
	loss on sale	£1,400,000.00			
	Add IHT	£ 800,000.00			

The above make fairly dismal reading to say the least of it. However, Gerald's solicitor, the redoubtable Mr Clevercloggs, suggests that it may be possible to mitigate the loss.

Is there any way whereby Gerald can secure inheritance tax relief?

11–09 Section 179 IHTA 1984 is reproduced below:

> **179.**—(1) On a claim being made in that behalf by the appropriate person there shall be determined for the purposes of this Chapter the amount (if any) by which—
>
> > (a) the aggregate of the values which, apart from this Chapter, would be the values for the purposes of tax of all the qualifying investments comprised in a person's estate immediately before his death which are sold by the appropriate person within the period of twelve months immediately following the date of the death exceeds
> >
> > (b) the aggregate of the values of those investments at the time they were so sold, taking the value of any particular investments for this purpose as the price for which they were so sold or, if it is greater, the best consideration which could reasonably have been obtained for them at the time of the sale.
>
> (2) Subject to the following provisions of this Chapter, in determining the tax chargeable on the death in question, the value of the investments to which the claim relates shall be treated as reduced by an amount equal to the loss on sale.
>
> (3) A claim made by the appropriate person under this Chapter shall specify the capacity in which he makes the claim, and the reference in subsection (1) above to qualifying investments which are sold by him is a reference to investments which, immediately before their sale, were held by him in the capacity in which he makes the claim.

11–10 Gerald's solicitors have been told that the Hairy Holdings Plc shares are a "qualifying investment". The difficulty is that the tax had been paid by the estate and the shares transferred to Gerald as an individual; the result of this is that there could not now be a claim for relief on the sale of any of the shares.

Relief under s.179 cannot be given where, for example, an executor accounts for tax on shares and transfers them to a beneficiary who sells at a loss. The beneficiary cannot claim because he is not the appropriate person, and the trustee cannot claim because he has not sold the shares.

The appropriate person is the person *responsible for paying the inheritance tax*, which will generally be the executors: the person liable for inheritance tax attributable to the value of those investments, or, if there is more than one such person, and one of them is in fact paying the tax, that person. In addition, s.179(3) IHTA 1984 refers to the appropriate person specifying "the capacity in which he makes the claim".

The complication in this case is that the sole beneficiary is also a **11–11** trustee and an executor of the estate. The difficulty is that he has a dual capacity as both an executor and sole beneficiary. It could be argued that because Gerald is executor and sole beneficiary, it was somewhat artificial to maintain that he is not "in fact" paying. One difficulty here is that the sole beneficiary already has a liability to pay tax on property transferred, albeit the principal liability is with the executors (s.200 IHTA 1984). The provisions identify the appropriate person as the person responsible for paying the IHT. It can be argued that the executors were liable to pay the tax and did in fact do so. This makes them the "appropriate person".

The shares could be transferred back to the executors but it is difficult to see what this would achieve, if anything. After some consideration Gerald's solicitors suggest a deed of variation to provide for a specific legacy of the shares to the sole beneficiary with a specific liability to pay the tax in the following terms:

DEED OF VARIATION

> relative to the estate of the **late GREGORY BEE ORCHID** residing at Number Thirty five Pixie Crescent, Newton Mearns, Glasgow ("the said deceased")
>
> by
>
> **(FIRST) GERALD BEE ORCHID,** residing at Number Ten Halfling Drive, Newton Mearns, Glasgow, ("Mr Bee Orchid")
>
> and
>
> **(SECOND)** The said Gerald Bee Orchid and **GANDALF BAY CLEVERCLOGGS,** Solicitor, Number One Thousand Chives Street, Glasgow, the Executors of the said deceased, ("the Executors")

WHEREAS

(Primo)   The parties to this deed are as designed above. The said deceased died at Glasgow on Twelfth December Two thousand and seven leaving Settlement dated 27th July 2000 and registered in the Sheriff Court Books of the Commissariot of North Strathclyde at Paisley on 25th March 2008.

(Secundo)   The Executors were appointed in terms of the said deceased's Settlement, conform to Confirmation granted by the Sheriff of North Strathclyde at Paisley dated 25th March 2008.

(Tertio)   The said deceased was survived by his son, the said Gerald Bee Orchid, who is the son and only child of the said deceased and is the person who has legal rights against the estate of the said deceased; he is also the residuary beneficiary.

(Quarto)   Mr Gerald Bee Orchid, being of full legal capacity and the only persons whose rights are, in terms of the said Settlement, being varied, having read the said Settlement of the said deceased and being of age and sound mind and having been advised that he is entitled to seek independent legal advice and has elected not to do so and now wishes to vary the distribution of the estate laid down by the said Settlement by Deed of Variation under Section 142(2) of the Inheritance Act 1984 and Section 62 (7) Taxation of Chargeable Gains Act 1992 as follows:

NOW THEREFORE THE PARTIES AGREE:

FIRST   the said Settlement of the said deceased is hereby varied by the insertion of the following clause:

"I direct my Executors to make over as soon as convenient to them after my death (*Primo*) to my son, **GERALD BEE ORCHID,** residing at Number Ten Halfling Drive, Newton Mearns, Glasgow G00 5OO, my entire holding of Hairy Holdings plc and that subject to payment by him of all inheritance tax and any other government duties exigible on my death thereon, that is to say, this legacy is to bear its rateable proportion of any government duties in respect of death and (*Secundo*) to **CANCER RESEARCH UK,** Sixty one Lincoln's Inn Fields, London, WC2A 3PX the sum of **ONE HUNDRED POUNDS (£100.00) STERLING.**"

SECOND   None of the expenses of these presents shall be paid from the deceased's estate.

THIRD   The Executors consent to and concur the provisions hereto which are hereby declared irrevocable.

FOURTH   The parties hereto elect and give written notice to the Board of Her Majesty's Revenue & Customs in terms of Section 142 (2) of the said Inheritance Tax Act 1984 that Section 142 (1) shall retrospectively apply to these presents and the parties hereto do hereby give notice to the Board of Her Majesty's Revenue & Customs of their intention to have the foregoing Variation treated as if it had been effected by the deceased. The parties hereto also give notice in terms of Section 62 (7) of the Taxation of Chargeable Gains Act 1992 that Section 62 (6) of the said last mentioned Act shall apply to these presents to the said Settlement of the said deceased.

FIFTH   (This clause can now be omitted) *(The parties hereto certify that transfer in respect of which this transaction is made is one, which falls within category L or category M of the Schedule to the Stamp Duty (Exempt Instruments) Regulation 1987)*: IN WITNESS WHEREOF these presents, consisting of this and the preceding page are subscribed by the . . .

As can be seen the deed includes a charitable legacy. The purpose of this is to back up the deed's *bona fides*! The deed is submitted to HM Revenue & Customs. They are obliged to accept this and to act on it. It is unlikely that they will require the executors and Gerald to "unpick" and resubmit fresh IHT forms, but will repay the inheritance tax back to the persons nominated to receive the repayment, e.g. Mr Cleverclogs' firm.

Form IHT35

Page 1

<table>
<tr><td colspan="2">Inland Revenue Capital Taxes</td><td colspan="2">Claim for relief
Loss on sale of SHARES</td></tr>
</table>

Name of deceased	Date of death	IR CT reference
GREGORY BEE-ORCHID	01/06/2008	ST 123456

Name and full postal address of the person IR CT should contact.

	Your reference (if any)
GB CLEVERCLOGGS ESQ SOLICITOR 1000 CHIVE STREET GLASGOW	GBO

Your telephone number

0141 1234 5678

When you have completed this form, please send it to IR Capital Taxes office with which you have been corresponding. If you have not yet been in correspondence about this estate, please send it to: IR Capital Taxes, Ferrers House, PO Box 38, Castle Meadow Road, Nottingham NG2 1BB. If using the DX postal system, send it to DX 701201 Nottingham 4.

Notes

1. This form is for claiming relief when you sell **'qualifying investments'** which were part of the deceased's estate **within 12 months of the date of death.** Include all qualifying investments sold, not just those sold at a loss. Generally, 'qualifying investments' are:
   - shares or securities quoted or listed on a recognised stock exchange at the date of death
   - holdings in authorised unit trusts.
   They **do not** include any holdings in *unquoted* private companies.
   Shareholdings in AIM companies are regarded as "unquoted" for (and only for) the purposes of *business relief, loss on sale relief* and *instalments*.

2. A **sale** includes an appropriation made by the personal representatives in satisfaction of a pecuniary legacy, with the consent of the legatee, and where there is no power of appropriation without that consent.

3. You may only make the claim if you are the **'appropriate person(s)'**. The 'appropriate person(s)' are those liable for the inheritance tax on the value of the investments (for example, the executors, the administrators, the trustees or donees). If there is more than one group of people liable for the tax, the 'appropriate persons' are those who are actually paying the tax. You must state on page 4 of this form in what capacity you claim the relief (eg executor, administrator, trustee or donee). If you are a beneficiary you are unlikely to be an 'appropriate person'. *All appropriate persons must sign this form. We cannot accept a claim signed by agents.*

4. You may claim provisional relief within 12 months of the date of death. *If we give provisional relief, we may review it later.*

5. The date of sale or purchase is the contract date unless either was made as a result of an option. If so, state the date the option was granted.

6. The relief is based on the gross sale price but restricted by the net cost of any purchase. So you must exclude the expenses of the sales and any purchase you make (eg commission, fees).

7. The value of qualifying investments at the date of death, sale or purchase must:
   - take into account interest on Government Stocks (gilts), loan and debenture stocks;
   - exclude dividends due but unpaid.

8. A 'capital payment' includes:
   - money or money's worth which is not income for income tax purposes;
   - the proceeds of any sale of 'rights'.

9. A change in a holding (eg as a result of a bonus or rights issue) is one which gives rise to a 'new holding' as defined by s126 Taxation of Chargeable Gains Act 1992.

10. The market value of any investment for capital gains tax purposes is the value at the date of death **after** adjustment for this relief.

If you need help completing this form, please telephone IHT helpline on 0845 3020 900

Claim for relief

1. Please give details of the qualifying investments *(see note 1)* to which your claim for relief relates. Attach a separate sheet if you need more space.

Full description of holding (including the number of shares or amount of stock held)	Date of death		Sales		
	Price	Value £	Date *(see note 4)*	Price	Gross proceeds *(see note 5)* £
HAIRY HOLDINGS plc					
5,000 SHARES SOLD	20.00	100,000.00	01/11/2008	25.00	125,000.00
95,000 SHARES SOLD	20.00	1,900,000.00	01/03/2009	5.00	475,000.00
Total A		£2,000,000.0		Total B	£600,000.00
				Net Loss (Total A minus total B) = C	£1,400,000.00

2

2. Have there been any purchases of 'qualifying investments' *(see note 1 on page 1)* by the claimant(s) in the same capacity between the date of death and two months after the latest sale shown in part 1 above?

Yes ☐ No ☑

If 'Yes', complete the table below. If 'No' go straight to part 3 overleaf. *If you need more space, please attach a separate sheet clearly marked as referring to part 2.*

Description of holding	Purchases		Restriction of relief
	Date	Sum paid (excluding expenses)	
		0.00	
		0.00	If there have been any purchases , the relief is restricted
			To calculate the restriction (E), show
		0.00	$\dfrac{D \text{ (purchases)}}{B \text{ (proceeds)}} \times C \text{ (net loss)} = E$
		0.00	Total E $\quad$ £0.00
			Net loss (C) - restriction (E) = Allowable loss
		0.00	
	Total D $\quad$ £0.00		Allowable loss $\quad$ £1,400,000.00

3. Please answer the following questions about the 12 month period following the date of death:

a) Have any qualifying investments *(see note 1 on page 1)* been exchanged (with or without payment)?   Yes ☐ No ☑

b) Have any capital payments *(see note 8 on page 1)* been received for any **sold** qualifying investments?   Yes ☐ No ☑

c) Have any 'calls' been paid on any of the **sold** qualifying investments?   Yes ☐ No ☑

d) Have there been any changes in the holding *(see note 9 on page 1)* of any of the **sold** qualifying investments?   Yes ☐ No ☑

e) Has any option to buy or sell qualifying investments been acquired or exercised (whenever the option was acquired)?   Yes ☐ No ☑

If you answer 'Yes' to any question, you must give details. If you need more space, attach a separate sheet.

Repayment

Since the Cheques Act 1992, all cheques are 'not negotiable'. This means that they can only be paid into an account in the name(s) of the person(s) in whose favour a cheque is drawn. Please state here the name of the person(s) to whom any repayment cheque should be made payable.

> GRABIT & RUNE
> 1000 CHIVE STREET
> GLASGOW

This claim will not be dealt with unless one of the boxes below has been ticked.

Declaration by the appropriate person(s) (see note 3 on page 1)

To the best of my knowledge and belief, the details given on this form and attached schedule(s) are true and complete.

1. ☑ I undertake not to sell or exchange further qualifying investments in the 12 months after the date of death in my capacity as the appropriate person and/or I undertake not to make purchases of any qualifying investments in the two months after the date of the last sale included in this claim in my capacity as the appropriate person.

   or

2. ☐ If further sales, exchanges or purchases are intended, I understand that the relief granted will be **provisional** and I undertake to provide details of any further sales or exchanges and any purchases made to the IR Capital Taxes. I understand that a clearance certificate cannot be issued until the relief is final.

GERALD BEE-ORCHID *Sawker* LEGATEE 25/12/2008	Name Signature Capacity *(see note 3)* Date	
	Name Signature Capacity *(see note 3)* Date	

Gains on Realisation of Assets

11–12   There is a clear danger in underestimating the value of property, particularly heritable property. Apart from the fact that it is illegal and unethical, HM Revenue & Customs may utilise their powers. Valuations should as a rule be obtained for heritable properties. HM Revenue & Customs are probably much more vigilant given the lowering of the capital gains tax rate to 18 per cent as opposed to 40 per cent inheritance tax. As stated, HM Revenue & Customs should be encouraged to agree a date of death valuation as soon as possible so that if the property is sold it comes under capital gains tax rather than inheritance tax. The expression is "ascertain". Of course if it is sold at a loss within the two-year period this value is subject to other considerations before mentioned such as other assets not being realised at a "profit" which exceeds the gain on the sale of the heritable property.

Clearance Certificate

11–13   It is strongly recommended that a clearance certificate be obtained from HMRC before finalising the account of charge and discharge. This will give some (but not complete) assurance that there is no more inheritance tax to pay.

    As long as HMRC are satisfied that the executor has the necessary account and details have been supplied and all the inheritance tax and interest due settled, they will provide a clearance certificate if it is applied for. The issue of the clearance certificate means that no further tax is due. Obviously it is based on a true and complete statement of the facts. Again obviously if there has been fraud or a failure to disclose material facts or further property is later shown which should have been included in the transfer or if further tax becomes payable as a result of a deed of variation, then clearance will not apply. The clearance certificate is the executry equivalent of a contract *uberimmae fidei*.

    If tax is being paid on instalment property by instalments, it is not necessary to wait until the executor has paid all the instalments to apply for a clearance certificate. If all the tax has been paid on the assets that do not have the instalment option, HMRC may issue a clearance certificate *and that excuses the executor from further tax on those assets*.

    Form IHT30 should be completed when it is considered that all the inheritance tax has been paid and the form should be sent in duplicate to the inheritance tax office which has been dealing with the executry.

    When satisfied that all the tax has been paid, HMRC will affix their official stamp on one copy of the form and return. This constitutes the clearance certificate.

Form IHT30

 **HM Revenue & Customs**

Application for a clearance certificate

Inheritance Tax Act 1984 s239(2) or Finance Act 1975 sch.4 para.25(2) or Finance Act 1894 s11(2)

Name and address of the person to whom HMRC Capital Taxes should send the certificate.	IHT reference *(if known)*
G B CLEVERCLOGGS ESQ SOLICITOR 1000 CHIVE STREET GLASGOW	ST 123456
	Your reference
	GBO
	Telephone number
	0141 1234 4567

- Send this form to us only when you believe that all the inheritance tax due has been paid.
- Fill in **one section only** of sections A, B, C or D.
- Section B is for a liability arising on death in respect of a lifetime transfer. Section A is for any other liability arising on death, most commonly in respect of the deceased's own estate or the coming to an end on death of an interest in possession in settled property.
- Fill in section E by entering the relevant date(s) **and** tick either the 'Yes' or 'No' box as appropriate.

Probate and IHT Helpline Tel: 0845 30 20 900

HMRC Capital Taxes, P.O. Box 38, Ferrers House, Castle Meadow Road, Nottingham, NG2 1BB. (DX 701201 Nottingham 4)

HMRC Capital Taxes, Meldrum House, 15 Drumsheugh Gardens, Edinburgh EH3 7UG. (DX ED 542001 Edinburgh 14)

HMRC Capital Taxes, Level 3, Dorchester House, 52-58 Great Victoria Street, Belfast, BT2 7QL. (DX 2001 NR Belfast 2)

Please send the completed form in duplicate to HMRC Capital Taxes office dealing with the estate

Section A   Liability arising on a death

Full name of the person who has died	GREGORY BEE-ORCHID
Date of death	01/06/2008
Title under which the property is taxable (e.g. 'Will of the deceased' or 'Settlement dated...')	

Section B   Liability in respect of a lifetime transfer

Full name of the person who **made** the transfer	
Date of death	
Please give details of the transfer, including the date on which it was made	

Section C   Liability in respect of a settlement without an interest in possession

Full title and date of the settlement	
Please give brief details, including the date of the chargeable event	

Section D   Liability in respect of funds in an alternatively secured or unsecured pension

Full name of the person who has died	
Date of death	
Name of pension scheme	
Name of pension provider	

Section E   Application in respect of property or transfers of value included in:

Original account(s) or inventory(ies) dated	01/08/2008
Corrective account(s) or inventory(ies) dated	15/09/2008
Calculation(s) of tax from HMRC Capital Taxes dated	

Have there been changes to the value since the above?
If you have answered 'Yes', please give details on a separate sheet.   Yes ☐   No ☑

IHT30   HMRC 08/06

Section F   Repayment

A repayment cheque can only be paid into the account of the person(s) to whom the cheque is made payable. If you believe that a repayment of tax may be due, please state the name(s) of the person(s) to whom any repayment cheque should be made payable. This information is only required if a repayment of tax is claimed.

> GRABIT & RUNE
> 1000 CHIVE STREET
> GLASGOW

Section G   Declaration by the appropriate person(s)

To the best of my/our knowledge and belief, the information given above is correct. I am/We are not aware of any other information which I/we should disclose. I/We apply for a statutory certificate of discharge.

GANDALF BAY CLEVERCLOGGS	Name	
Gandalf B Clevercloggs	Signature	
EXECUTOR	Capacity*	
01/03/2009	Date	

GORDON BEE-ORCHID	Name	
S Bee-orchid	Signature	
EXECUTOR	Capacity*	
01/03/2009	Date	

* Capacity i.e. Executor, Administrator, Transferee, Trustee. Professional agents must not sign this form on behalf of the appropriate person(s).

Section H   Certificate (for official use only)

The Commissioners of HM Revenue & Customs discharge the above named applicant(s) from any (further) claim for tax or duty on the value attributable to the property at section E, on the occasion specified at section A, B, C or D **except for any tax which is being paid by instalments.**

The certificate is not valid unless HMRC stamp this box

Signed by	
	(name stamp or block capitals)
Signature	
	for and on behalf of the Commissioners
Date	

This certificate does not itself constitute a determination of values of individual items for any other HM Revenue & Customs purpose. In particular, the issue of the certificate does not necessarily mean that values have been "ascertained" or that values may be taken as market values for capital gains tax within the provisions of section 274 and paragraph 9, schedule 11, Taxation of Chargeable Gains Act 1992. This certificate is not valid in certain circumstances, such as in the case of fraud or failure to disclose material facts or if further tax becomes payable as a result of an instrument of variation - see section 239 (4) Inheritance Tax Act 1984.

Chapter Twelve

STAMP DUTY

Tax facts as for Chapter 7.

It is likely that the executor may not be troubled with or will only rarely **12–01** encounter stamp duty land tax (SDLT) or stamp duty (SD) during the administration period. He is unlikely to encounter stamp duty reserve tax (SDRT)[1] at all.

As regards heritable subjects, the stamp duty land tax regime applies. It will be rare for executors to purchase heritable property during the executry. However, it may be that a house is to be transferred to a beneficiary. Where before Budget day 2008 this could be registered or recorded, the Keeper of the Registers would require an SDLT60 "certification that no land transaction return is required for a land transaction" form is used for this (the first box, i.e. transfer or conveyance of freehold interest in land (in Scotland, ownership) for no chargeable consideration, is "ticked"). However, the SDLT60 form was abolished for transactions with an effective date after Budget day 2008, i.e. March 12, 2008.

Accordingly, it is now no longer necessary to complete or submit with the deed for registration, either a land transaction return (form SDLT1) or self-certificate (form SDLT60) if the transaction is below the new notification threshold. From March 12, 2008, this will apply to land transactions (including linked land transactions) where the chargeable consideration is less than £40,000.

Please note that at present the HMRC form prescribed by regulations does not permit solicitors to sign the certificate that no SDLT is due on behalf of their clients (form SDLT60). The person making the transaction can only sign the form. However, HMRC have indicated that they intend to amend that form by regulations in 2008 so that agents will be able to sign the declaration in the certificate on behalf of their clients.

It will be much more common for executors to be involved in **12–02** transferring shares. If shares were being transferred to a beneficiary before March 13, 2008, it was necessary for a certificate to be completed for the stock transfer under the Deed, Stamp Duty (Exempt Instruments) Regulations 1987, Schedule Category M or Category L.

---

[1] Leaflet SD7, available at *http://www.hmrc.gov.uk/leaflets/sd7.pdf* [accessed April 27, 2009] has the details. A copy of the rates of interest is also available at *http://www.hmrc.gov.uk/rates/interest.htm* [accessed April 27, 2009]. Stamp duty reserve tax (SDRT) was introduced in 1986 to deal with transactions in shares where no instrument of transfer was executed and which were therefore outside the scope of stamp duty. It is a transaction tax, charged on "agreements to transfer chargeable securities", unlike stamp duty which is charged upon documents. The main provisions are in the FA 1986 and the supporting Regulations at SI 1986/1711.

However, in his 2008 Budget Report, the Chancellor of the Exchequer announced inter alia changes to legislation that would remove from the charge or self certification of certain instruments, principally stock transfers dealing with transfers on death and deeds of variation. This affected deeds executed on or after March 13, 2008. The stock transfers can be sent direct to company registrars. Apparently the Treasury calculated that this will remove 230,000 deeds from the "stamping process". This found legislative form in The Finance Act 2008.

Abolition of fixed stamp duty on certain instruments

99.—(1) Schedule 32 contains provision abolishing fixed stamp duty on certain instruments.

(2) The amendments and saving made by that Schedule have effect in relation to instruments executed on or after 13 March 2008 and not stamped before 19 March 2008.

(3) For the purposes of section 14(4) of the Stamp Act 1891 (instruments not to be given in evidence etc unless stamped in accordance with the law in force at the time of first execution), the law in force at the time of execution of an instrument—

(a) executed on or after 13 March 2008 but before 19 March 2008, and

(b) not stamped before 19 March 2008,

shall be deemed to be the law as varied in accordance with Schedule 32.

Otherwise *ad valorem* stamp duty will be payable.

SDLT office contact details can be found in the Appendix.

Chapter Thirteen

COUNCIL TAX

Tax Facts Nil

It would be helpful to write that the executor is unlikely to be involved in **13–01** council tax during the administration period. However, problems with council tax seem to be common.

It is not clear why this should be. Probably it is due to executors and solicitors failing to keep their local council tax authorities fully informed. It may be that local authorities do not register the changes. Many councils issue *pro forma* letters for executors to notify changes.

An example of these is as shown:

> *Mrssrs Grabit & Rune*
> *1000 Chive Street*
> *Glasgow*
>
> *Dear Sirs,*
>
> *COUNCIL TAX 2008/09*
> *REFERENCE NUMBER 12345678*
> *SUBJECT: Executors of the late Gregory Bee-Orchid*
>
> *I have now ended Council Tax exemption with effect from now which is 6 months after confirmation was obtained.*
>
> *An amended notice will be issued shortly confirming the balance due. However, if the property remains unoccupied a 50% discount may be applicable and I enclose a form for you to complete and return. Alternatively, if the property is unoccupied, **and completely unfurnished**, further exemption may be considered under the "New or Existing" category. I also enclose a form for this.*
>
> *I trust this is helpful.*
>
> *Yours faithfully*

Another problem may be that the council's computer systems for **13–02** issuing council tax notices are somewhat inflexible. It may be that when the time comes for the notices to be issued for the next council tax year generally shortly before April, the computer systems are not robust enough to cope with the change and issue, for the ensuing year. It would seem to automatically issue council tax notices for the full amount.

Often it may seem that councils prefer to deal with matters on the telephone. However, the agent requires that there is something on the file and it is probably cheaper for it to be a carbon of a letter rather than the charge for several telephone calls and a file entry.

Sometimes, and in the present climate where the property market is quite slow, some time will elapse from date of death until the sale of properties.

13–03   Under the legislation council tax exemption under statute only applies for six months from date of death or obtaining confirmation.

After that, if the property remains occupied a 50 per cent discount may be applicable under Sch.11 of the Local Government Finance Act 1992 and the Council Tax (Exempt Dwellings) Scotland Order 1992 (as amended). If the property is unoccupied and completely unfurnished, the local authority may consider the property for further exemption under the "new or existing" category. Separate forms are applicable for both of these situations. However, for the latter this may only apply for another six months.

PART 3

POST ADMINISTRATION

Chapter Fourteen

INTRODUCTION

"Don't query our position!
Don't criticise our wealth!
Don't mention those exploited
By politics and stealth!"[1]

The third period of the administration of executries is the time when it is **14–01** most necessary to consider whether the will of the deceased or the effect of the rules of intestacy should be varied. This time will most likely occur when the account of charge and discharge is in draft. At this time, it is likely that beneficiaries, prompted by their advisors, have been considering it and it might be that beneficiaries who had been considering it but rejected it, may now wish to change their minds. It should not of course have been the first time the matter has been suggested to them! A former practitioner used to boast that most variations in which he had been involved took place pre-confirmation. The C1, will and deed of variation were submitted to the sheriff court when applying for confirmation!

It may be that some of the estate has already been transferred to the beneficiary. However, it is at this stage, i.e. when the beneficiaries have the account of charge and discharge in front of them, that they have the full picture. It can be argued that it is then and only then that they can make an informed decision. In addition, it is necessary to again consider the time restrictions. Thus, it may be that the two-year limit is now that much closer. It cannot be stressed enough that practitioners should finally explain the options for variation, perhaps along with the account of charge and discharge.

A suggested letter follows. **14–02**

Dear Mr Dandelion,

Your late mother's executry.

I refer to our previous correspondence and now enclose my firm's account of charge and discharge for your information/approval. The executors have approved this and the Auditor of Court has taxed our fees. The balance due to you is as shown on page 7 of the account.

I also enclose a receipt/discharge for you to sign and return to us. When we receive these from all beneficiaries, we shall uplift the deposits and pay the sums brought out and additional interest to you and the other residuary beneficiaries.

---

[1] CH4 Hymn 253.

We would again refer you to our earlier letter and to subsequent correspon-
dence and to conversations regarding altering the terms of your mother's
will by deed of variation. We do not propose to rehearse the arguments for
and against this but merely point out that, the two-year limit for this will
expire in approximately two months' time on the [insert date]. If you wish
to avail yourself of this option it is essential that the you let us know by the
end of this month; if we do not hear from you we shall assume you do not
wish to take any further steps.

With kind regards and best wishes

Yours sincerely

VARIATIONS OR DISCHARGES

14–03 This matter will be considered later. However, for the sake of avoiding duplication it is proposed to deal with all common methods of variation under the second section of this part, namely post administration with variation.

It is considered most helpful if the post-administration section is considered under two heads:

- Without variation; and
- With variation.

PART 3: SECTION 1

POST ADMINISTRATION WITHOUT DISCHARGE

Chapter Fifteen

INCOME TAX

Tax facts as for Chapter 3.

CERTIFICATION OF EXECUTRY INCOME

At the end of the administration when the residuary beneficiaries are **15–01** paid out, it is necessary to issue certificates of deduction of tax. It may have been necessary to issue these certificates if payments to account or assets were transferred to account. The form of certificate is the R185 (Estate Income) and this is shown below.

Form R185 (Estate Income)

 **HM Revenue & Customs**   **Statement of income from estates**

Personal representatives (who can be **either** executors or administrators) should use this form to advise beneficiaries about income from the residue of the estate of a deceased person:

- for each year during the administration of the estate if a 'sum' is paid to the beneficiary in that year, and
- for the year in which the administration of the estate is completed.

The beneficiary's estate income for the year ended 5 April `2 0 0 9` is the deemed income shown on page 2 of this form.

The beneficiary	The deceased person
Full name of beneficiary	**Full name of deceased person**
Miss Gardenia Lane	Mrs Rose Street or Lane
Address	**Date of death** *DD MM YYYY*
4 Carl Street	`0 4` `0 5` `2 0 0 8`
Glasgow	
Postcode G11 2AA	

Notes for personal representatives

Personal representatives should complete the relevant boxes on page 2 and give the form to the beneficiary. There is information on page 2 to help you do this.

For the purpose of this form, a 'sum' includes cash, assets transferred or appropriated, and debts set off or released.

If the administration period has been ongoing for more than a year, the following example shows how to work out the income which each beneficiary should show in their Tax Return/repayment form.

Step 1
Add the net amount of the beneficiary's share of the residuary income for the tax year to any net amount brought forward.

Step 2
Compare the figure in Step 1 with the sum paid to the beneficiary in the tax year.
- If the sum paid is greater than or equal to the result of Step 1, the beneficiary's share of residuary income for the tax year is the amount at Step 1.
- If the sum paid is less than the result of Step 1, the beneficiary's share is the sum actually paid in the tax year. The balance of the beneficiary's entitlement is carried forward to the next tax year, and will then be their income entitlement in the next year if no distributions are made.

For the final tax year of the administration period, the beneficiary's share of residuary income will be treated as having been fully paid.

Notes for beneficiaries

Keep this form and refer to it if making a Tax Return or claiming a tax repayment.

If you need to complete a Tax Return the box numbers on page 2 match those on the *Trusts etc.* pages (SA107) of the Tax Return. Transfer the amounts of income after tax taken off from those boxes to the corresponding boxes on the SA107.

If you need to claim a tax repayment transfer the figures at boxes 15 to 17 to the boxes in section 4 of the R40 *Tax Repayment Form*, as follows:
- income and tax paid or tax credit at box 15 – to boxes 4.3 and 4.4 on the R40
- income and tax paid or tax credit at box 16 – to boxes 4.5 and 4.6 on the R40
- income and tax paid or tax credit at box 17 – to boxes 4.7 and 4.8 on the R40.

Please note that the tax described as 'non-repayable' or 'non-payable' cannot be repaid.

R185(Estate Income)   Page 1   HMRC 05/08

Income from the estates of deceased persons

Income from UK estates

If the beneficiary was in receipt of income from a UK estate only, enter the net income and tax paid or tax credit in boxes 15 to 20.

15 Income taxed at basic rate – after tax taken off.
This includes rental income and profits from a trade.

£ ☐☐☐☐☐☐☐☐ . ☐☐

Tax paid or tax credit on box 15 income

£ ☐☐☐☐☐☐☐☐ . ☐☐

16 Income taxed at savings rate – after tax taken off.
This includes savings income such as interest from a bank or building society account.

£ ☐☐☐☐☐☐ 9 6 . 3 2

Tax paid or tax credit on box 16 income

£ ☐☐☐☐☐☐ 2 4 . 0 8

17 Income taxed at dividend rate – after tax taken off.
This includes dividend income from foreign companies.

£ ☐☐☐☐☐☐☐☐ . ☐☐

Tax paid or tax credit on box 17 income

£ ☐☐☐☐☐☐☐☐ . ☐☐

18 Income taxed at non-repayable basic rate – after tax taken off. *This includes gains realised on certain life insurance policies.*

£ ☐☐☐☐☐☐☐☐ . ☐☐

Tax paid or tax credit on box 18 income

£ ☐☐☐☐☐☐☐☐ . ☐☐

19 Income taxed at non-repayable savings rate – after tax taken off. *This includes gains realised on certain life insurance policies and any undistributed estate income carried forward from 1998-99 or earlier years.*

£ ☐☐☐☐☐☐☐☐ . ☐☐

Tax paid or tax credit on box 19 income

£ ☐☐☐☐☐☐☐☐ . ☐☐

20 Income taxed at non-payable dividend rate – after tax taken off. *This includes dividends from UK companies.*

£ ☐☐☐☐☐ 1 4 1 . 0 9

Tax paid or tax credit on box 20 income

£ ☐☐☐☐☐☐ 1 5 . 6 8

Income from foreign estates

If the beneficiary was in receipt of income from a foreign estate, do not complete boxes 15 to 20. Instead, enter the income in box 21 and any relief for UK tax already accounted for in box 22.

21 Foreign estate income

£ ☐☐☐☐☐☐☐☐ . ☐☐

22 Relief for UK tax already accounted for

£ ☐☐☐☐☐☐☐☐ . ☐☐

Foreign tax paid on estate income

Complete box 23 if any **foreign tax credit relief** is claimable in respect of foreign income arising to a UK estate **or** a foreign estate.

23 Foreign tax for which foreign tax credit relief has not been claimed

£ ☐☐☐☐☐☐☐ . ☐☐

Signature and date

I confirm that the information given on this form is correct.

Signature of executor or administrator

☐

Date *DD MM YYYY*

1 5 0 2 2 0 0 9

Page 2

MRS ROSE LANE DECEASED

Income for the Period May 4, 2008 to February 2, 2009

Summary

	Net	Tax	Gross
Income Bearing Non Repayable Tax Credits	£352.72	£39.19	£391.91
Income Bearing Lower Rate Repayable Tax	£240.80	£60.21	£301.01

Divisible thus:

Miss Gardenia Lane 40%			
Income Bearing Non Repayable Tax Credits (UK Dividends)	£141.09	£15.68	£156.77
Income Bearing Lower Rate Repayable Tax (Interest)	£96.32	£24.08	£120.40
Mrs Poppy Smith 60%			
Income Bearing Non Repayable Tax Credits	£211.63	£23.51	£235.14
Income Bearing Lower Rate Repayable Tax	£144.48	£36.13	£180.61

Income for the Period May 4, 2008 to February 2, 2009

			Dividend	Tax Credit
HBOS Plc				
1,092 Ordinary Shares of 25p	12.05.08		£ 352.72	£ 39.19

		Net	Tax	Gross
Lloyds TSB Bank Plc				
Account Number 0000000	03.07.08	£ 1.86	£ 0.47	£ 2.33
Account Number 0000000	03.07.08	52.34	13.09	65.43
Nationwide Building Society				
Account Number 000000	18.08.08	121.26	30.32	151.58
Account Number 000000	18.08.08	26.41	6.60	33.01
Royal Bank of Scotland Plc				
Funds held on Temporary Deposit		38.93	9.73	48.66
		£ 240.80	£ 60.21	£ 301.01

15–02   As previously stated, HMRC recognise that executry income does not come in regularly and that beneficiaries should not be asked to pay income tax at higher rates on income which they have not yet received. Until the administration of the estate is completed, no beneficiary has any right to the property of the estate or the income of it. It follows that no beneficiary is liable to income tax on the income of the estate. The executors are responsible for the tax. The completion of the administration is a question of fact depending whether the residue has been ascertained.

Smaller executries exempt from IHT are usually completed within about 9–12 months. Beneficiaries who pay tax at the higher rate are liable to be charged interest and penalties if they return their share of the executry income late. It is important, therefore, to issue the tax certificates to them as soon as possible after April 5. If the executry runs over two or more years and payments to account are made the executors are required to issue tax certificates for each year in which a payment to a beneficiary is made. The certificate is the R185 (Estate Income).

Prior to April 5, 1995 amended tax certificates were issued to the beneficiaries after the end of the administration period. They would return the amended amounts in their tax returns to the subsequent April 5 and pay any higher rate tax.

This will not arise now, as the beneficiaries will only return the income **15–03** as they receive it as shown in the example. Particular care should be taken in the month or so prior to April 5 when information on the beneficiary's circumstances along with the information as to executry income is available to enable the executor to decide if a payment to account should be made then, or delayed until after April 5.

Take the case of Lily Dale. It is known that she pays tax at the higher rate and will continue to do so in the near future. Any payment to account made to her after April 5, 2009 does not have to be declared by her until after April 5, 2010 and the tax at the higher rate will not require to be paid until (not later than) January 31, 2011.

Income for the Period May 4, 2008 to February 2, 2009

DETAILS FOR R185 (Estate Income)
for year ending April 5, 2008

		LILY DALE	
BENEFICIARY		PHILIP DALE	
DECEASED		JANUARY 1, 2007	
DATE OF DEATH		APRIL 5, 2008	
YEAR ENDING		J. Dale	
SIGNED BY		c/o	
ADDRESS		Cheetham & Steele	
		Broken Chambers	
		Glasgow	

	BRI	LRI	TOTAL
	£	£	£
GROSS	NIL	2,743.75	2,743.75
TAX	NIL	548.75	548.75
NET	NIL	2,195.00	2,195.00

Sometimes there will be a delay in the period between the account of **15–04** charge and discharge being prepared and being returned approved to the agents. During this period, additional interest may have accrued on deposit on client account. Strictly speaking, this balance, i.e. the sum due to the residuary beneficiary or beneficiaries, is held by the executors on bare trust. A bare trust in this context is one in which the beneficiary has an immediate and absolute right to both capital and income. The balance due is held in the name of the executor as trustee but as trustee he has no discretion over what income to pay the beneficiary. The executor has the duty to pay over the amount when the account is approved. In effect, the executor/trustee is a nominee in whose name the balance is held. Conversely, the beneficiaries of a bare trust have the right to take actual possession of their share of property.

The income thus arising should be returned by each residuary beneficiary separately; however, no objection will be taken if the executors include this in the R185 (Estate Income).

Inevitably, there will be an interval of time between completing the account of charge and discharge, having it approved by the executors and finally settling with the beneficiaries. Strictly speaking, the income during this period should not be included in the R185 (Estate Income) but notified to the beneficiary as his income to be included in his tax return. The executors are in the position of "bare trustees" for this period since the residue has been ascertained.

Attention!!

Right to Information

Under TA 1988 s.700(5) a beneficiary who requires to complete a tax return has the right, if he so requests in writing, to be supplied by the executors with a note of the amount (if any) of any income paid to him and a note of the tax deducted therefrom broken down into different rates. It is suggested that this may be obtempered by the production of a R185 (Estate Income).

Chapter Sixteen

CAPITAL GAINS TAX

CAPITAL GAINS TAX FACTS FOR THE YEARS ENDING APRIL 5

	2008	2009
The Annual Exempt Amount (AEA)	£9,200 for individuals executries (first 3 years) and £4,600 for some trustees	£9,600 for individuals executries (first 3 years) and £4,800 for some trustees
CGT Tax Rates		
Individuals	10%, 20% or 40%	18%
Trusts and estates	40%	18%
Exemptions		
Individuals and estates***	£9,200	£9,600
Trusts	£4,600	£4,800
Chattels (proceeds) 5/3 of excess gain chargeable	£6,000	£6,000
Date Return to be made		
Date payment to be made	To be paid (along with any balance of income tax due) on January 31 following the end of the tax year	
Penalty for late payment and time limits for submission		
Broadly speaking as for income tax		

16–01

In exceptional cases, it may be that it is necessary to realise further assets but it is to be hoped that any assets which required to be realised will already have been sold. If not, similar considerations as to those contained in the Capital Gains section of Part Two, Chapter 10 will also be relevant here. The question of loss of relief on sale may have been lost and some thought may be given to investigating if it is desirable to transfer the holdings to the beneficiaries for them to sell.

> *Attention!!*
>
> *If selling on the instructions of beneficiaries' it is likely that client identification/money laundering regulations will be required to be complied with.*

Chapter Seventeen

INHERITANCE TAX

Tax facts as for Ch.5.

If all necessary information is on the inheritance tax forms and all the **17–01** tax and interest due has been paid, HMRC will send a letter confirming that no more inheritance tax is due. It is probably best practice to obtain a clearance certificate.

If not already obtained certificates of clearance should be obtained from HM Revenue & Customs in the appropriate cases.

The executors should apply for a clearance certificate using form IHT30 once they have supplied the necessary account and paid all the inheritance tax and interest due. When the clearance certificate has been obtained no further tax is due on the transfers described in the certificate, unless:

- there has been fraud or a failure to disclose material facts;
- further property is later shown to have been included in the transfer; or
- further tax becomes payable because of an instrument of variation.

If tax is being paid by instalments, it is not necessary to wait until the **17–02** executor has paid all the instalments to get a clearance certificate. If you all the tax on the assets that do not have the instalment option have been paid, the executor may be given a clearance certificate that clears the executor from further tax on those assets.

The executor should complete form IHT30 when the executor believes that all the inheritance tax has been paid and send the form in duplicate to the inheritance tax office that has been dealing with the deceased's case.

When HMRC are satisfied that the executor has paid all the tax, they stamp one copy of the form and return it to the executor. This is the executor's clearance certificate.

Attention!!

It should be noted that the format of this form has not altered following on the introduction of the IHT400 series.

HMRC remind us that copies of all records should be kept regarding **17–03** inheritance tax paid. This may be necessary to prove to HMRC that everything required has been carried out "if HM Revenue & Customs (HMRC) asks to see how you arrived at your figures". The records to be kept should certainly include: a copy of the will and all signed inheritance tax forms; all the records and papers used to complete the forms; the necessary paperwork from the death of a first spouse or civil partner in case it is necessary later to transfer their unused inheritance tax threshold (or "nil rate band") to the second partner upon their death; valuations for houses and land, including farmland or woodland, stocks and shares, personal belongings, jewellery, antiques, pensions and trusts. HMRC recommend keeping all documents for at least 12 years after confirmation—and longer if there may eventually be cause to transfer an unused inheritance tax threshold!

Chapter Eighteen

PRE-OWNED ASSETS TAX, STAMP DUTY AND COUNCIL TAX

There is unlikely to be anything arising under this head. It is likely that **18–01** all assets of the executry will have been transferred during the course of the administration period. Similar considerations will apply as for those set out in the corresponding sections under Part Two.

As regards council tax, if a change in ownership takes place in heritable property, i.e. by being transferred to a beneficiary or sold, then the position is as stated in Part Two. The only other matter which may arise after the administration period may be the annoying one of receiving a council tax notice for payment some time after the house has been sold or transferred. The practitioner will have intimated this to the local authority but for reasons which are not altogether clear the local authority's records may not have been altered. This must be addressed quickly by contacting the local authority in writing and advising them of the position. It may also be appropriate to advise the beneficiary who has received the legacy of the house. They should be asked if they have received a council tax notice from the local authority. It may be that the house is not in joint names and may not be sold; it is important to identify when the exemption period is to expire and if a 50 per cent discount may be applicable.

PART 3: SECTION 2

POST ADMINISTRATION WITH VARIATION

The order of dealing with the different taxes has been altered to reflect the impact of variations which is greater for IHT.

Chapter Nineteen

INHERITANCE TAX

Tax facts as for Ch.5.

POST-DEATH VARIATIONS

"THE ... CASE, in which everybody began at the winning post, the magistrate having to pull them backwards till they reached the starter's line, demonstrated a tendency which had long interested and puzzled me."[1]

Introduction

19–01 The pre-Budget announcement by the Chancellor of the Exchequer on October 10, 2007 had an indirect but staggering impact on post-death variations. Henceforth it would be possible for, say, the executors of a widow, whose predeceasing husband had died leaving everything to her and who had not used his annual nil-rate band, to, in effect, claim an additional nil-rate band, based on the deceased husband's estate. In effect the first nil-rate band could be "carried forward" to the second death.

There was, until the pre-Budget statement, a window of opportunity after death for making sometimes quite spectacular savings in tax. In England and Wales, claims against practitioners for failure to exploit and/or advise on this were common. With the nil-rate band then at £300,000[2] a claim could amount to £120,000.[3]

A deed of variation could thus present a major tax planning opportunity. It was and still should be considered in virtually all cases. In pre-Budget statement times, for example, a surviving spouse might wish to redirect part of his or her inheritance to his or her children in order to take advantage of the nil-rate band of IHT for the estate. Alternatively, a beneficiary may wish to set up a discretionary trust arrangement from

---

[1] Austin Coates, *Myself a Mandarin* (Oxford in Asia Paperbacks, 1988).
[2] 2007/2008.
[3] £300,000 at 40 per cent.

which he or she could be eligible to benefit but which should escape IHT on his or her eventual death. The impact of other taxes needed to be considered carefully.

The popular notion that it is possible to rewrite/vary the will itself (or **19–02** the law of intestacy or the doctrine of survivorship) is a misconception since the will itself cannot be varied after the testator has died. It is, however, possible for an original beneficiary to sign a deed of variation in order to make some sort of bequest and to redirect all or part of an inheritance. By means of a statutory fiction, HMRC would and will, if required, treat this bequest as having been made by the deceased person and not by the original beneficiary for inheritance tax purposes and/or for most capital gains tax purposes but *not* for any other purpose apart from a limited one for income tax.

Arguably one of the most popular tax saving provisions of all time, s.142 of the Inheritance Tax Act 1984 (and s.62 of the Taxation of Chargeable Gains Act 1992) expanded in a most spectacular manner and, somewhat surprisingly, had survived successive Labour Governments. Broadly stated it allowed a two-year period after death in which to "rewrite" a deceased's will or to alter the destination of property on intestacy.

At the risk of repetition *ad nauseam* it is and should be one of the first matters addressed by executry practitioners after death. Traditionally, as mentioned above, it was utilised when a spouse died leaving everything to the surviving spouse, "whom failing" to their children, by directing part or all of the estate to children. The benefit of the nil-rate band was saved and at the then current rates of IHT the saving, on the second death, could be as much as staggering £120,000[4] in IHT in even relatively modest estates.

It can be an extremely valuable source of income for executry **19–03** practitioners. The other side of the coin is that if the practitioner fails to advise on it and indicate the possibility, it is likely to be a source of (and rightly so), at the least, a complaint to the new Scottish Legal Complaints Commission and, at worst, a claim for professional negligence.

Its utility is not restricted to IHT saving. Its "sister" provision s.62(6) of the Taxation of Chargeable Gains Act 1992 for capital gains tax must also be considered. The effect of income tax and other taxes such as stamp duty should also be considered. Each of these will be dealt with separately. Consideration in this section of the text will thereafter be given to the interaction of these taxes. It will cover the current IHT, CGT and stamp duty provisions and in particular how these three taxes interact. Finally some possible future trends will be identified.

Incidentally these writs are sometimes called deeds of family arrangement but this is a technical English law term. They used to be referred to as deeds of election and discharge. Generally they will be referred to as "deeds of variation".[5]

---

[4] 40 per cent of £253,000.
[5] HMRC refer to "Instruments of Variation"—IOV.

> **Danger Warning!!**
>
> *Consideration by the executor and/or the executors of variations and/or discharges (disclaimers) under s.142 IHTA will be standard practice. Executors and their advisors will be required to pay much more attention to the possible savings to be made. Failure to have regard to this could give rise to a negligence claim by the beneficiaries. The executors and beneficiaries should be advised of the potential saving at the first available opportunity. It should be mentioned at every opportunity. At the earliest opportunity these should be conveyed to them in writing; they should be encouraged to pass the information on to their professional advisors. It is not necessary to reiterate that this advice should be fully minuted and signed by them if possible.*

METHODS OF VARIATION

19–04 Although deeds of variation have been given some considerable prominence in the last decade or so they have of course always been competent. In pre-capital transfer tax and pre-inheritance tax days, it was generally the case that the beneficiary wishing to alter the estate would do so by deed of election and discharge. This of course could be done by reference to legal rights. The deed of election and discharge method or route was preferred by practitioners since they felt that it was only when the beneficiary was in a position to see all the estate by reference to the account of charge and discharge or similar that he or she was able to make an informed election and discharge. Now more commonly these are referred to as disclaimers. It is possible to use the disclaimer method of "varying" the terms of the will or intestacy.

There are further methods of "post-mortem" alteration over and above deeds of variation and disclaimers, namely the two-year discretionary trust or what is known as a "precatory trust". The last of these is not used with much frequency north of the border and testators and others have shown some resistance to the use of what is otherwise an excellent idea in many cases, namely the two-year discretionary trust. Both of these will be considered but the main thrust of the text will be directed towards deeds of variation if only because they do not suffer from the disadvantages attaching to disclaimers.

Leaving the question of executry tax to one side for the moment, beneficiaries entitled under will or intestacy may not require or indeed need legacies left to them. Generally speaking, they may resolve to alter the legacy or the destination of the legacy. If this is carried out in a certain manner, which will be discussed in more detail, this may result in a saving of inheritance tax. The variation route consists of an instruction from a beneficiary to the executors to redirect the inheritance to someone other than himself or herself. Taking this by itself, it amounts to an *inter vivos* gift, that is to say, the original beneficiary is *gifting* the asset of the inheritance to another party. Clearly, this requires to be in writing since executors need firm written instruction to effect this. A disclaimer consists in a beneficiary refusing to take a legacy or benefit under will or intestacy. If the beneficiary refuses to accept, the inheritance passes as if the legacy to him had never existed. What happens to the legacy is determined by the terms of the will or the laws of intestate succession. The will may provide for a destination over to A, whom failing to B. In these circumstances if A disclaims then it may well be that B would be entitled to the legacy without further consideration.

Danger Warning!!

It is not competent to disclaim a gift if a benefit from it has been accepted and received by the beneficiary. This could be an acceptance in part but the effect of this will be to negate the option of disclaimer. It may be, of course, that a beneficiary is entitled to several legacies under a will. In these circumstances he may disclaim one and accept the other.

If he disclaims a legacy, for example, and there is no destination then it will likely pass into residue. If the residue gift is disclaimed then in the absence of a destination the section will pass into intestacy and be dealt with as set out in Chapter 2. If the bequest is made jointly between A and B and A disclaims then B will take instead.

Please note that if a disclaimer takes place, it may still be competent **19–05** for the beneficiary to receive under the rules of testacy, for example if a testator leaves everything to his spouse and if she disclaims then the law of intestacy would apply. It may be, in certain circumstances, that it would be more favourable or beneficial for her to benefit under the rules of intestacy than under testacy since the latter may give rise to a more effective legal rights claim by children. As can be seen, there is a certain amount of uncertainty in disclaiming. If a beneficiary disclaims the result will not necessarily be within his or her control. This is probably the main reason why most people will elect for a deed of variation, which, as stated, transfers the asset to the new beneficiary actually nominated by the person varying. There are certain other advantages of variation over disclaimer. It is possible to vary *even though the original beneficiary has received entitlement*, whether by income or having property transferred to him. It is possible and is frequently carried out that variation takes place once the administration of the estate is complete. If the tax advantages are to be secured, however, it is necessary to observe the time limits. In addition, the original beneficiary can make a partial variation of the bequest. This is not possible in the case of a disclaimer unless of course the will makes a specific provision for this. This is fairly unusual. Of course, if a beneficiary has accepted the legacy, then the option of disclaiming will, except in very restricted circumstances, be denied to him!

As stated the main advantage of variation is that the beneficiary can control who ultimately receives the asset.

Example

Take the case of Agatha Cowslip who inherits under the will of her late husband his entire estate. Shortly after her husband's death she receives a substantial win from a small holding of premium bonds. She has a child, a son, who is an extremely prosperous merchant banker and two grand-children. She decides that it would be appropriate to vary the will to leave the residue directly to the grandchildren. The variation makes this possible. Clearly if she was to disclaim, the chances are that the estate would go to her child. She could of course have made a lifetime gift, which could form a potentially exempt transfer, but as she is in poor health she feels that the chances of her surviving the seven years necessary are unlikely. The deed of variation completely circumvents this and makes the transfer as if it had been made directly to the grandchildren.

Danger Warning!!

It may be of course that the effect of this variation may rule out the possibility of the surviving spouse exemption and bring the estate into inheritance tax. If the estate is above the nil-rate band then careful consideration must be given to her decision to vary but otherwise or if it is below the nil-rate band then the potential for saving of inheritance tax is considerable.

19–06   While clients are normally advised not to let the "tax dog" wag the variation tail this may well be the type of exception since in these circumstances variations are usually made with a view to saving, either directly or potentially, tax whether inheritance, capital gains or otherwise.

INHERITANCE TAX

19–07 The rules are contained in the statutory provisions which are reproduced here for reference. Section 142 of the Inheritance Tax Act 1984 (Alteration of dispositions taking effect on death) provides:

> **142.**—(1) Where within the period of two years after a person's death—
>
> > (a) any of the dispositions (whether effected by will, under the law relating to intestacy or otherwise) of the property comprised in his estate immediately before his death are varied, or
> >
> > (b) the benefit conferred by any of those dispositions is disclaimed, by an instrument in writing made by the persons or any of the persons who benefit or would benefit under the dispositions, this Act shall apply as if the variation had been effected by the deceased or, as the case may be, the disclaimed benefit had never been conferred.
>
> (2) Subsection (1) above shall not apply to a variation unless the instrument contains a statement, made by all the relevant persons, to the effect that they intend the subsection to apply to the variation.
>
> (2A) For the purposes of subsection (2) above the relevant persons are—
>
> > (a) the person or persons making the instrument, and

(b) where the variation results in additional tax being payable, the personal representatives.

Personal representatives may decline to make a statement under subsection (2) above only if no, or no sufficient, assets are held by them in that capacity for discharging the additional tax.

(3) Subsection (1) above shall not apply to a variation or disclaimer made for any consideration in money or money's worth other than consideration consisting of the making; in respect of another of the dispositions, of a variation or disclaimer to which that subsection applies.

(4) Where a variation to which subsection (1) above applies results in property being held in trust for a person for a period which ends not more than two years after the death, this Act shall apply as if the disposition of the property that takes effect at the end of the period had had effect from the beginning of the period; but this subsection shall not affect the application of this Act in relation to any distribution or application of property occurring before that disposition takes effect.

(5) For the purposes of subsection (1) above the property comprised in a person's estate includes any excluded property but not any property to which he is treated as entitled by virtue of section 49(1) above or section 102 of the Finance Act 1986.

(6) Subsection (1) above applies whether or not the administration of the estate is complete or the property concerned has been distributed in accordance with the original dispositions.

(7) In the application of subsection (4) above to Scotland, property which is subject to a proper liferent shall be deemed to be held in trust for the liferentor.

The rules can be summarised as follows. **19–08**

- The document must be signed within two years of death.
- It extends to both intestate testate and estates.
- All property of the deceased can be the subject of the document.
- It also extends to "excluded property".[6] It does not obviously extend to the subject of a liferent by the deceased (s.142(5)), nor property gifted by the deceased but subject to a reservation in his favour at date of death which still exists at the death. Section 102(3) FA 1986 provides that the deceased is deemed to be beneficially entitled to the property.
- The deed must be in writing.
- The deed must be made and subscribed by persons who inherit or might inherit.
- All deeds executed after July 31, 2002 must be intimated in writing to the then Inland Revenue, now Her Majesty's Customs & Excise, within six months from the date of execution.[7]

---

[6] Such as reversionary interest.
[7] Section 142(2)(f).

The *IHT Newsletter* (April/May 2002) announced that, following the Finance Act 2002, from August 1, 2002 a deed should include an election as to whether the deed is to be treated as a disposal by the deceased for IHT and capital gains tax. These elections should be separate. The election may be made for one but not the other or neither. It may be applied to one tax or both or neither. *The election must specify the statutory provisions.* If the deed alters, i.e. by increasing or decreasing, the IHT payable, the deed or document containing the election must be sent to the Inland Revenue, now Her Majesty's Customs & Excise, within six months of its date. Some agents send all deeds to HMRC for intimation. However, if IHT is not affected HMRC will send it back with a checklist (IOV2).

- There must be no external financial consideration[8] other than another variation of another interest under the will or estate.
- If the result is increased IHT the executors require to be parties to the IR Notice (s.142(2)), but apart from that there are the general common law principles of intimation to the executors in the deed itself which may be necessary to create a *jus quaesitum tertio*.

Danger Warning!!

Please ensure that the deed indicates that the expenses of it are not being met from the estate (but by the person varying).

THE MAIN AREAS OF USE

19–09 If a beneficiary gifts property this will form a "transfer of value" for inheritance tax purposes, what is usually referred to as a "potentially exempt transfer" ("PET"). The usual rule is that if the donor dies within seven years of the transfer, then inheritance tax may be payable. This transfer will be aggregated with the rest of his estate. As we can see above, s.142 introduces a fiction that for IHT purposes and provided the rules are complied with, this will be treated as a bequest from the deceased.

1. Beneficiaries of a deceased's estate (whether testate or intestate) can agree to vary the will or intestate provisions for any number of reasons. Since the 1970s this has been possible for tax reasons but can and often is also entered into for non-tax reasons. It gives the beneficiaries the benefit of hindsight.
2. A deceased may not have kept his will up to date or may not have made a will at all and the beneficiaries can agree among themselves to vary matters to suit themselves.
3. This variation can minimise aggregation of the deceased's estate with that of a surviving spouse and thus utilise all or at

---

[8] Section 142(3)(g).

least part of the nil-rate band tax threshold. It must first of all be ascertained whether the deceased had made potentially exempt transfers (PETs) in his lifetime and whether there are any agricultural or business assets or other assets in the estate which could attract full or partial exemption from IHT. In the most straightforward situation it would be envisaged that the deceased's will leaves everything to the surviving spouse. The surviving spouse assesses that he/she is well enough off and that he/she can pass a substantial part (usually up to the nil-rate IHT threshold, currently £312,000) to members of the family. Matters are not always as clear-cut as this. It may be that it is uncertain as to whether the widow(er) will have enough to live on and a discretionary trust may be considered or that the main value of the estate is tied up in the family home, in which case consideration might be given to transferring the deceased's half of the home to the family. In addition it should be considered whether this will have the effect of losing the transferred nil-rate band exemption.

Attention!!

In considering the question of, for example, the transferred nil-rate band relief, it is often perhaps overlooked that this is only available to spouses or civil partners and overlooks the many beneficiaries who receive legacies, etc from persons other than spouses or civil partners!

---

4. It may be possible to earmark items of estate which qualify for relief, either whole or at 50 per cent, and if the widow(er) does not need these then to pass these assets to the family; thus the business/agricultural relief is used, as it may be that in the future this will be lost either by different tax rules or changing use of the property and the spouse not qualifying for the relief, such as with an active business or farm which the surviving spouse may not operate. This approach can be used either on its own or in conjunction with a nil-rate band legacy to maximise the tax advantage.
5. A son or daughter of a deceased who stands to inherit estate from his/her parent may not require the legacy and may prefer to direct it to his own family or to a trust, such as an "18–25 trust" or discretionary trust to his/her own family as a means of reducing the eventual IHT in his/her own estate. This will usually have no impact on the IHT (if any) on the deceased parents' estate which may in any event be below the threshold for IHT. There may be no point in an already wealthy person inheriting, say, £100,000 from his own parent when that will just increase his or her own eventual IHT and the opportunity may be used to direct it elsewhere. This may be accomplished by way of disclaimer or assignation by the wealthy son or daughter. Depending on the terms of the original will either of these documents may be used to redirect this portion of the estate

without necessarily involving other beneficiaries, not so well off, who may wish to accept their portion of the estate.

6. A legacy can be made to a person or charity who the beneficiaries think may have been omitted from the will.

7. A dependant or a faithful employee or relative can be given a liferent or right of occupancy of the deceased's house to protect the position of the dependant relative for the future.

8. The various assets of the estate can be arranged amongst various beneficiaries to suit themselves. Some of these effects may be completed in other ways outside of a deed of variation, e.g. simply by disposition, gift or exchange between the parties but it may frequently be seen as convenient and discreet to deal with them by way of deed of variation.

9. The variation can resolve any uncertainty or defect in the will. A deed of variation may be cheaper than going to court!

10. It is not always possible to vary the dispositions effected by a will. A deed of variation normally requires the consent of all beneficiaries who are interested in the property which is to be redirected. Problems are likely to arise if some beneficiaries are under 18 years old or any greater age specified in the will. In England and Wales it may be possible to give the executors the power to "agree" to a variation on behalf of persons not of full legal capacity but this is not competent in Scotland at present.

11. It is not competent to use the deed of variation to alter the powers of, say, executors or trustees. However, it may be competent to achieve this if, say, a legacy is "given" under the deed of variation. It may be appropriate to use this to have one or more powers included to the executors or trustees.

12. Although it is usual to have one deed of variation, it is competent to have several deeds of variation but only insofar as they relate to different assets. It is not generally competent to have two deeds of variation for the same asset, that is to say "two bites of the cherry". In "Post-Death Planning: Variations and Disclaimers", Ralph Ray[9] offers an ingenious solution with a view to avoiding the problems created by *Russell v Commissioners of Inland Revenue* [1988] STC 195, i.e. preventing a variation for s.142 purposes to the effect of giving a share of a particular property which *had already been the subject matter of a deed of variation*. Ray's idea is to overcome this problem by using both a s.142 variation and a s.144 discretionary trust. Within two years of death the relevant assets are transferred under a deed of variation into a s.144 two-year discretionary trust. The assets can then be redirected out of the discretionary trust without further inheritance tax within the two-year period (or up to 10 years if the assets are within the nil-rate band). This has the added benefit of avoiding problems in excluding or reducing the interest of an underage beneficiary since he is only a potential beneficiary.

---

[9] Ralph Ray, "Post-Death Planning: Variations and Disclaimers", *Tolley's Tax Digests*, Issue 19, May 2004.

Example
Maxim dies leaving inter alia Manderley to his daughter, Victoria, who promptly varies her father's will whereby Manderley is left to a s.144 discretionary trust, which has an extremely wide range of beneficiaries'[10] income.

13. Posthumous increases: it is competent to transfer, free of inheritance tax, the benefit of certain posthumous increases in the value of an estate within the two-year period.[11]
14. Variations by executors/beneficiaries of a deceased beneficiary can "create" posthumous equalisation, using the nil-rate bands and mitigating the bunching effect of assets of two estates being assessed in one estate.

Example
Tam dies leaving £300,000 to his "common law wife" Sharon. She dies later leaving her estate to her son, Neil. Her estate is £400,000. Since neither Tam nor Sharon made any lifetime chargeable transfers, unless there is a variation (or disclaimer) on Sharon's death, the inheritance tax on £700,000 is £155,200. After taking advice Neil asks Sharon's executors to vary Tam's will, so that Neil inherits Tam's £300,000 directly from Tam and the £400,000 direct from Sharon's estate. They agree and as a result of this variation inheritance tax on Tam's death is nil and on Sharon's death is £35,000. A considerable saving of £120,200 is made. HM Revenue & Customs may try to challenge the validity of the variation, on the basis that Neil is not varying the aggregate inheritances from his parents except by reduction of inheritance tax. Some thought may be given for a trust to be set up under the deed of variation. Generally the benefit of these types of situation must be viewed in the light of the impact of the transferred nil-rate band allowance. The main use will be where the parents are not married or where the nil-rate band has already been used up, say in lifetime transfers within the seven years of death.

Danger Warning!!

It should be noted that it is not possible to increase the estate of someone who has pre-deceased; see Re Corbishley's Trust [1880] 14 Ch 3 846. However, this restriction does not apply if the person whose estate is increased has survived the other, but also dies in the two-year period, i.e. in succession.
HM Revenue & Customs may try to argue that the variation is invalid in that the son has not varied the amount of the aggregate inheritances, rather he is attempting to pay less inheritance tax.

---

[10] Ray suggests in the above article dealing with an example on which Manderley is based that there could be a power to add beneficiaries. The clever is part is that it will not be necessary for inheritance tax purposes for Victoria to be excluded as a beneficiary, because for inheritance tax she is not the truster. For capital gains tax purposes, she will be the truster (following the decision in *Marshall v Kerr* [1994] S.T.C. 638). She will also be the truster for income tax purposes; in particular, where income paid to or for the benefit of her minor children is treated as hers.
[11] Ralph Ray, fn.10 above, art.5.5.

15. There are some side benefits of the legislation. It will, in addition to the original making a gift to another party via a deed of variation and avoiding PET rules, also enable a gift to made and overcome the gift with reservation provisions, i.e. the original beneficiary *may retain an interest* and not fall foul of the gift with reservation rules; under Sch.15 to the FA 2004 which prevents the gift being vulnerable to the pre-owned asset tax regime:

Changes in distribution of deceased's estate

16. Any disposition made by a person ("the chargeable person") in relation to an interest in the estate of a deceased person is to be disregarded for the purposes of this Schedule if by virtue of section 17 of IHTA 1984 (changes in distribution of deceased's estate, etc.) the disposition is not treated for the purposes of inheritance tax as a transfer of value by the chargeable person.

16. The other problem can arise when, for whatever reason, the executors have transferred a share which has plummeted in value. Reference was made to the situation in which the unfortunate Mr Bee Orchid found himself in earlier and how a deed of variation alleviated the position.

Miscellaneous

19–10 Note it will not always be advisable to make the election under s.142. For example if the beneficiary is the spouse or civil partner, the beneficiary may decide not to elect and to retain the surviving spouse exemption. A gift may then be made to the children in the hope that the donor will survive seven years.

Danger Warning!!

HMRC may look askance at variations whereby beneficiaries who are liable to IHT give up their entitlement to a beneficiary who is not, e.g. a spouse of the deceased. Their hope may be that the spouse may then gift the subject of the asset to the person who originally varied the bequest.

Obviously HMRC will be, and rightly so, suspicious of such an arrangement and may enquire if there had been any discussions between parties before the variation took place as to how it may be redirected back to the original person varying it and indeed whether there has been in fact any subsequent variation. If there has been any such "collusion" at the least the benefit will be struck at. At worst penalties may be levied.

Attention!!

Beneficiaries sometimes form the view that a variation can be made, e.g. to leave estate to a wife instead of to children, the children believing that their mother will make a gift after the estate is wound up to adjust the position to what it was under the will. The children should be robustly advised that HMRC are not stupid and this type of arrangement will easily be picked up by HMRC, certainly on the death of the mother!

Under this heading there may also be a problem if a liferent is created **19–11**
under the variation which is terminable at the instance of the trustees.
As stated above s.142(4) stipulates that:

> "Sub-section 4 provides that where the variation results in property
> being held in trust for a person for a period which ends not more
> than two years after the death, this Act shall apply as if the
> Disposition on the property that takes effect at the end of the
> period had effect from the beginning of the period."

This would mean that if a liferent trust was set up and terminated within,
say, 18 months of death the variation would be treated as if it had been
made at death. Obviously this type of arrangement would be struck at
and any inheritance tax saving lost. If on the other hand the spouse had
not survived the two-year period clearly it would have been the death of
the liferentrix and not the variation which had caused the liferent to
terminate. Sub-section 4 would not apply in these circumstances.

Après Budget Statement

The Budget statement by the Right Honourable Alistair Darling on **19–12**
October 10, 2007, which has been referred to, had a quite startling effect
on the need for deeds of variation. This is now enshrined in s.8A of the
Inheritance Tax Act 1984. Many deeds of variation which were framed
with the sole purpose of "capturing" the nil-rate band on the death of
the first spouse or civil partner are now no longer necessary. Please note
that this only relates to married couples or couples who have entered
into a civil partnership. For those many thousands of couples who die
unmarried with children the deed of variation may still be a viable
option.

Disclaimers—Discharges and/or Variations

What is a Disclaimer?

A disclaimer is a refusal to accept property under a will or intestacy. To **19–13**
be valid, a *disclaimer must be made before accepting any income or other
benefit from the property*. The law relating to disclaimers is technical and
obscure and it is normally preferable to have a deed of variation instead.
When a disclaimer is effected, the asset disclaimed passes according to
the will if there is a substitute beneficiary, e.g. into residue or according
to the laws of intestacy. It is not always practical or indeed possible to
disclaim in favour of a particular person. Hence, if a specific bequest is
disclaimed the property falls into the residue under the will; if it is the
residue itself which is disclaimed, the property will pass perhaps to a co-
residuary legatee or under the law relating to intestacy. Property can also
be disclaimed on intestacy. A disclaimer is, therefore, an all-or-nothing
event; it is not generally possible to retain part and disclaim the rest of a
single gift.

If a parent wishes to benefit a child, it is suggested that this be done by
disclaimer if this is practical under the will, to avoid the IR treating the
deed of variation as a "settlement". Clearly the importance of addressing

these matters at the earliest opportunity in appropriate cases and bringing the matter to the attention of beneficiaries cannot be over-emphasised.

Partial Disclaimers

19–14 The law of England does not allow partial disclaimers. However, they may be available in the (extremely unlikely) event that the will authorises them. If the will does not authorise them there is the possibility of including the power (to vary) by deed of variation. As explained some other element would require to be included, e.g. a legacy to Cancer Research UK. In his excellent publication "Post-Death Tax Planning: Variations and Disclaimers" Ralph Ray[12] suggests that it may be possible to arrange matters that:

> "On a disclaimer, the assets involved might fall into an appropriate receptacle, e.g. a flexible life interest or discretionary trust, rather than merely passing to the person entitled under the will in default of the person making the disclaimer."

However, this may actually involve a deed of variation anyway This can be arranged by way of a variation. In Scotland the position is not so rigid and partial disclaimers will be accepted by HM Revenue & Customs.

However, an interest cannot be disclaimed once the beneficiary has received a benefit under the will or intestacy, e.g. rents from property or dividends from shares.

Form of Deeds

19–15 There is no statutory style or form. The deed must identify the deceased's estate which is being varied and must actually vary it. It is imperative that the deed makes reference to the relevant sections of the Inheritance Tax Act 1984 and the Taxation of Chargeable Gains Act 1992.

There can be:

    (a) an assignation by one or more persons of their rights to another (including in Scotland a partial assignation);
    (b) a disclaimer where rights are given up or renounced by a beneficiary (including in Scotland a partial disclaimer);
    (c) a variation where there are several people involved; or
    (d) a variation by the Court of Session under the Trust (Scotland) Act 1961.

In intestate cases, it may not be possible to achieve the desired result by a single person disclaiming and it may be preferable to avoid doubt by *having a variation by all concerned to ensure that the estate reaches the right person* (on a strict interpretation of s.2 of the Succession (Scotland) Act 1964).

---

[12] Ralph Ray, "Post-Death Planning: Variations and Disclaimers", *Tolley's Tax Digests*, Issue 19, May 2004.

More than One Deed?

In their press release (May 1985) The Inland Revenue (as HM Revenue **19–16** & Customs were then known) took the view that the one deed was to be regarded as irrevocable and amending deeds would not usually be accepted (*Russell v IRC* [1988] S.T.C. 195). Of course it may be the case that one beneficiary may wish to vary at a later time than the beneficiary, e.g. Jane Thursday, who is entitled to one-third of the residue of the estate of her late father, Sir Roger Sunday Bart, wishes to vary the will to allow her share to be redirected to her daughter, Tuesday Thursday. This is carried out but then her sister, Horatia Sunday, decides that her share should be directed to Cancer Research UK. It is quite in order for a second deed of variation to be made, *provided it is not over the same item of residue*; it would also be competent for a third deed of variation by her brother, the new Sir Roger, to vary his one-third share but he declines to do so!

Notice to the Inland Revenue

As indicated above, in appropriate cases, i.e. where there is an immedi- **19–17** ate effect on tax, notice requires to be given within six months from the date of the deed effecting the deed of variation.

The other main relevant statutory reference is to s.143 of the IHTA 1984—precatory bequest. An example of this might be, "[a]ll my furniture and personal effects to my sister to distribute amongst my friends and relatives as she thinks fit". This is deemed to be transferred by the deceased's will.

Section 144 of the IHTA 1984, which sets up the two-year discretion-ary trust will, has already been referred to. Where the deceased leaves property by will which creates a discretionary trust *and* the executors or trustees are given power to select beneficiaries or decide on the amount of share they are to receive, then, if such discretionary powers are exercised within two years of the testator's death, there will be no further inheritance tax on the exercise of the executors' or trustees' discretion and conveyance of the funds. There is, however, no similar provision for capital gains tax so when the discretion is exercised there *will be a deemed disposal* by the trustees and a potential capital gains tax charge (subject to possible holdover). There will also be income tax during the two-year discretionary trust period at the trust rate (40 per cent). Where under a will or otherwise survivorship for up to a six-month period is a condition of receiving the bequest, then that period is ignored and it is assessed at the beginning of the period in question.

A disclaimer of an interest, such as a reversionary interest in a trust, will *not* be a transfer of value for inheritance tax. This does not extend to a variation. There is no actual time limit in s.93 of the Inheritance Tax Act 1984. However, apart from s.93, the variation provisions of s.142 *do not apply* to trust property even if the deceased had power of appoint-ment or a liferent.

Alimentary Liferents

It is understood that the law provides that if an alimentary liferent is **19–18** accepted it cannot be renounced or varied but *if it has not been accepted* then any benefit can be disclaimed (*Douglas v Hamilton*, 1961 S.C. 205).

It is important to ensure therefore that no benefit is conferred if there is any prospect of variation to have a court petition under the 1961 Act.

LEGAL RIGHTS

19–19 It is worth noting that in the context of post-death arrangements the view of HM Revenue & Customs is that legal rights may be deemed claimed unless positively disclaimed within two years of the death.

> ***Danger Warning!!***
>
> *Attention is drawn to s.3(3) of the IHTA 1984 in terms of which a deliberate omission to assert legal rights may be treated as a transfer of value if gratuitous and made outwith two years of the death.*

The other matter is related to legitim for children not of full legal capacity. Where a testator leaves his whole estate to the surviving spouse but there are children under the age of 18 entitled to legitim then the executors have a choice under s.147. They may either (a) elect to pay inheritance tax at the testator's death as if the children had claimed their legal rights or (b) (the high risk strategy nowadays!) choose to ignore the question of legal rights and make over the whole estate to the widow. If the executors choose to administer as if the children had claimed their legal rights and the child later renounces these *within two years after attaining majority* so that the legitim share is cancelled and goes to the mother, that renunciation is not a transfer of value for inheritance tax under s.147. In the alternative situation, if the child chooses in the two years after age 16 to claim legal fights, that means any inheritance tax which would have been payable on the death of the testator is payable *with interest* from then.

POST-BUDGET STATEMENT

19–20 Many of the uses of variation pre-Budget will still be relevant post-Budget statement, such as updating a will, earmarking assets which qualify for relief, redirection of a legacy, posthumous increases, charitable legacies, etc. It is in the area of minimising aggregation of the deceased's estate with that of a surviving spouse, thus utilising all or at least part of the nil-rate band tax threshold, where care is required.

As previously stated the ability to transfer the unused element of the inheritance tax nil-rate band came into effect on October 9, 2007 in respect of the death of a surviving spouse or civil partner on or after that date. It does not matter when the first spouse (or civil partner) died: it could have been in the era of inheritance tax, capital transfer tax or even estate duty. However, it should be noted that in the era of estate duty surviving spouse exemption was not available. However, the exempt threshold applicable at that time can be utilised in the same manner as for the nil-rate band. It is unlikely that there will be many cases where estate duty provisions will be successful, given the low rate of the threshold!

The effect of the three new sections of the Inheritance Tax Act 1984 **19–21** can be summarised as follows:

- Section 8A deals with the "transfer of unused nil-rate band between spouses and civil partners" and explains the operation of formulae used to calculate the transferable amount.
- Section 8B deals with "claims under s.8A" and explains who should make the claim to the unused nil-rate band and the related time limits.
- Section 8C concerns itself with "s.8A and subsequent charges" and explains the operation of the formulae where, after the death of the first spouse or civil partner, there is a charge under IHTA 1984.

These sections are reproduced in full below.

Transfer of unused nil-rate band between spouses and civil partners

8A.—(1) This section applies where—

    (a) immediately before the death of a person (a "deceased person"), the deceased person had a spouse or civil partner ("the survivor"), and

    (b) the deceased person had unused nil-rate band on death.

(2) A person has unused nil-rate band on death if—

$$M > VT$$

where—M is the maximum amount that could be transferred by a chargeable transfer made (under section 4 above) on the person's death if it were to be wholly chargeable to tax at the rate of nil per cent. (assuming, if necessary, that the value of the person's estate were sufficient but otherwise having regard to the circumstances of the person); and

VT is the value actually transferred by the chargeable transfer so made (or nil if no chargeable transfer is so made).

(3) Where a claim is made under this section, the nil-rate band maximum at the time of the survivor's death is to be treated for the purposes of the charge to tax on the death of the survivor as increased by the percentage specified in subsection (4) below (but subject to subsection (5) and section 8C below).

(4) That percentage is—

$$\frac{E}{NRBMD} \times 100$$

Where—

E is the amount by which M is greater than VT in the case of the deceased person; and

NRBMD is the nil-rate band maximum at the time of the deceased person's death.

(5) If (apart from this subsection) the amount of the increase in the nil rate band maximum at the time of the survivor's death effected by this section would exceed the amount of that nil-

rate band maximum, the amount of the increase is limited to the amount of that nil-rate band maximum.

(6) Subsection (5) above may apply either—

    (a) because the percentage mentioned in subsection (4) above (as reduced under section 8C below where that section applies) is more than 100 because of the amount by which M is greater than VT in the case of one deceased person, or

    (b) because this section applies in relation to the survivor by reference to the death of more than one person who had unused nil-rate band on death.

(7) In this Act "nil-rate band maximum" means the amount shown in the second column in the first row of the Table in Schedule 1 to this Act (upper limit of portion of value charged at rate of nil per cent.) and in the first column in the second row of that Table (lower limit of portion charged at next rate).

Claims under section 8A

8B.—(1) A claim under section 8A above may be made—

    (a) by the personal representatives of the survivor within the permitted period, or

    (b) (if no claim is so made) by any other person liable to the tax chargeable on the survivor's death within such later period as an officer of Revenue and Customs may in the particular case allow.

(2) If no claim under section 8A above has been made in relation to a person (P) by reference to whose death that section applies in relation to the survivor, the claim under that section in relation to the survivor may include a claim under that section in relation to P if that does not affect the tax chargeable on the value transferred by the chargeable transfer of value made on P's death.

(3) In subsection (1)(a) above "the permitted period" means—

    (a) the period of two years from the end of the month in which the survivor dies or (if it ends later) the period of three months beginning with the date on which the personal representatives first act as such, or

    (b) such longer period as an officer of Revenue and Customs may in the particular case allow.

(4) A claim made within either of the periods mentioned in subsection (3)(a) above may be withdrawn no later than one month after the end of the period concerned.

Section 8A and subsequent charges

8C.—(1) This section applies where—

    (a) the conditions in subsection (1)(a) and (b) of section 8A above are met, and

(b) after the death of the deceased person, tax is charged on an amount under any of sections 32, 32A and 126 below by reference to the rate or rates that would have been applicable to the amount if it were included in the value transferred by the chargeable transfer made (under section 4 above) on the deceased person's death.

(2) If the tax is charged before the death of the survivor, the percentage referred to in subsection (3) of section 8A above is (instead of that specified in subsection (4) of that section)—

$$\left(\frac{E}{NRBMD} - \frac{TA}{NRBME} \right) \times 100$$

where—
E and NRBMD have the same meaning as in subsection (4) of that section;
TA is the amount on which tax is charged; and
NRBME is the nil-rate band maximum at the time of the event occasioning the charge.

(3) If this section has applied by reason of a previous event or events, the reference in subsection (2) to the fraction

$$\frac{TA}{NRBME}$$

is to the aggregate of that fraction in respect of the current event and the previous event (or each of the previous events).

(4) If the tax is charged after the death of the survivor, it is charged as if the personal nil-rate band maximum of the deceased person were appropriately reduced.

(5) In subsection (4) above—
"the personal nil-rate band maximum of the deceased person" is the nil rate band maximum which is treated by Schedule 2 to this Act as applying in relation to the deceased person's death, increased in accordance with section 8A above where that section effected an increase in that nil-rate band maximum in the case of the deceased person (as survivor of another deceased person), and
"appropriately reduced" means reduced by the amount (if any) by which the amount on which tax was charged at the rate of nil per cent. on the death of the survivor was increased by reason of the operation of section 8A above by virtue of the position of the deceased person.

Please note that this new rule, introduced by FA 2008 Sch.4, which inserts new sections 8A, 8B and 8C into IHTA 1984, affects only spouses and civil partners. At the risk of repetition, it does not assist co-habitants.

Example

Patricia ("Pat") Snowdrop tragically dies on October 11, 2007, predeceased **19–22** *by her lifelong (civil) partner, Lily Valley, who died on October 8, 2007. Pat's estate (including an estimate of the estate she is to receive from Lily,* *who left everything to Pat) is likely to be £2 million. If Lily did not use her NRB before death, Pat's executors are able to claim a transferred nil-rate band allowance of 100 per cent, i.e. the first £600,000[13] of the estate will be exempt. IHT will therefore be £560,000 instead of £680,000.*

If Lily had made a chargeable transfer of half of her estate on October 7, 2007, she would have used up 50 per cent of her NRB and Pat's executors could only claim a transferred nil-rate band allowance of a 50 per cent uplift, i.e. only the first £450,000 of Pat's estate will be exempt. The IHT would be £620,000 in that case. It is interesting and important to note that even if Lily had no assets at her date of death or indeed was not domiciled in the UK or actually owned assets in the UK, Pat's executors would still be entitled to the 100 per cent uplift!

Example

Redford ("Red") Clover dies on March 15, 2007 with an estate of £500,000, leaving £240,000 to his daughter Y and the residue to his widow, the fickle and impecunious Poppy. The nil-rate band when Red dies is £300,000. Accordingly 360,000/500,000 or 72 per cent of his NRB is available for transfer. Poppy shortly after marries Fox who dies on May 14, 2008 and also leaves 60 per cent of his nil-rate band unused. Poppy herself dies on June 14, 2010 with an estate of £800,000 when the individual nil-rate band is £350,000. Poppy's nil-rate band is increased to reflect the transfer from Red and Fox. However, although her executors are theoretically entitled to an increase of over 100 per cent, nevertheless, the increase is restricted to 100 per cent of the nil-rate band in force at the time. Therefore, Poppy's executors' nil-rate band is £700,000, leaving £100,000 chargeable to IHT on Poppy's death.

There are one or two important matters to consider following from the proposition that the transferred nil-rate band can only be set against "the charge to tax on the death of the survivor". Obviously, this will, therefore, include inheritance tax charged on the survivor's free estate, on any gift with reservation of benefit property and on the value of trust property in which a liferent has been enjoyed. What is not immediately obvious is that *it can also be allocated against tax on a failed potentially exempt transfer (which is tax arising on the death of the donor) and additional tax due on an immediately chargeable lifetime transfer.* These take priority over the IHTA 1984 s.4 charge on death.

Example

19–23 *Gardenia died before her husband Laban and left him her entire estate. He then married Genevieve but Laban himself died on November 1, 2007. Laban's executors can claim Gardenia's inheritance tax nil-rate band, which was not used. Paradoxically, if he bequeaths his total estate to Genevieve, this nil-rate band (stemming from Gardenia) will be wasted since, obviously, Genevieve can only inherit one nil-rate band. The solution is to set up a discretionary trust for Genevieve and Laban's issue in Laban's will and leave the residue to Genevieve. Alternatively, instead of setting up a*

---

[13] *The nil-rate band was £300,000 at that time.*

trust in his will he could he could make a lifetime chargeable transfer of the nil-rate band into a discretionary trust. This could be for the benefit of Genevieve and Laban's issue.

Note: no inheritance tax will be due on the death of Laban and on Genevieve's death her executors can still claim an additional nil-rate band under s.8B(2) of the Inheritance Tax Act 1984.

What Steps should be Taken when a Testator has Died and his Will Contains an Inheritance Tax Nil-Rate Band Discretionary Trust with Residue to Spouse?

Within two years of death

The executors should, in consultation with the beneficiaries and their **19–24** professional advisors, review the position in due course but should the testator die with a will which creates a trust, the provisions of s.144 IHTA 1984 clearly allow the trust to be liquidated within two years of death with no inheritance tax consequences. In other words, the trust assets can be conveyed to the surviving spouse and the nil-rate band will be restored (providing full spouse exemption is available) as though the assets had passed directly to the surviving spouse.

The trust can thus be deconstructed. The trustees can resolve to convey the assets of the trust to the spouse. *This must be done within two years of death* and this allows it be "read back" as a result of IHTA 1984. Gloriously, the net effect will be under s.144 that the deceased has not used up any part of his inheritance tax nil-rate band which is available on the death of the surviving spouse (or civil partner).

Attention!!

If carrying this out it would be as well to wait more than three months from the date of death before doing it in order to avoid the "Frankland trap".[1] This is because s.144(1) provides for reading back where there is an event on which tax would otherwise be chargeable. Tax is not chargeable on an exit from a discretionary trust within three months of creation.

Attention!!

If the trustees decide to create an immediate post-death interest trust for the spouse, it is not necessary to wait three months. Section 144 was amended in FA 2006 (s.144(3) to (6)) to provide expressly for reading back where appointments created IPDI trusts.

Where the death occurred more than two years ago

Unfortunately in the case of deaths occurring more than two years ago **19–25** involving the creation of a nil-rate band discretionary trust, *nothing can be done to obtain a transferred nil-rate band for the surviving spouse.* Transfers of trust assets to the spouse will actually result in extra capital being included in the surviving spouse's estate; there will be no increased nil-rate band. The only matter may be for the trustees to investigate giving the spouse, after two years, a liferent. There would be no inheritance tax consequences and there may be income tax benefits.

In a helpful article in a recent issue of *Taxation*,[14] Chris Whitehouse indicates:

> "Care will be required when administering estates where wills contain a nil rate band legacy. Wills that were drafted before 9 October 2007 may now pass more than was originally intended. For example, a cash gift of 'an amount equal to the largest amount that can pass without payment of inheritance tax' has the potential to pass double the amount of the full inheritance tax nil rate band. Hence, in a case where a surviving widow wanted a nil rate band legacy to pass to relatives and the residue to charity, pay particular attention to the wording used in the will. A reference to 'an amount equal to the nil rate band in force at my death' would be construed as limited to a single nil rate band."

Post Death Variations Styles

19–26 *DEED OF VARIATION where it is wished to provide for a legacy to one grandchild (discretionary trust) who requires help for a nervous complaint and one who does not (he received an outright legacy). Inheritance tax has been paid on the estate.*

> **DEED OF VARIATION** relative to the estate of the late **MRS GRETA PARSLEY or RASPBERRY** late of 5, Marjoram Court, Glasgow, ("the said deceased")
> by
> (FIRST) **MRS MARGARET RASPBERRY or ANISEED** residing at 11 Rosemary Street, Helensburgh, ("Mrs Aniseed")
> and(SECOND) **GORDON CORIANDER** , Chartered Accountant, residing at 22 Bay Court, Glasgow, **WILLIAM GREEN**, residing at 7 Blue Street, Milngavie, Glasgow, and **MISS FAWN SCARLETT**, Solicitor, Glasgow, the Executors of the said deceased ("the executors").

WHEREAS

(PRIMO) The parties to this deed are as designed above. The said deceased died at Foxglove on the Seventh day of June 2008, leaving a Trust Disposition and Settlement dated 1st May 1998 and registered in the Sheriff Court Books of the Commissariot of Tayside Central and Fife in Scotland on 4th September 2008.

(SECUNDO) The executors were appointed in terms of the deceased's Trust Disposition and Settlement conform to Confirmation granted by the Sheriff of Tayside, Central and Fife on 4th September 2008.

---

[14] C. Whitehouse, "A bigger band", *Taxation* (September 24, 2008).

(TERTIO) The said deceased was survived by Mrs Aniseed and by Mrs ANISEED's children, who are **GILBERT ANISEED** and **GEORGE ANISEED**, both residing at 11 Rosemary Street, aforesaid. Mrs Aniseed is the only daughter and only child of the said deceased and is the only person who has legal rights against the Estate of the said deceased; she is the Residuary Beneficiary.

(QUARTO) Mrs Aniseed being of full legal capacity and the only person whose rights are, in terms of the said Trust Disposition and Settlement, being varied, hereby having read the said Trust Disposition and Settlement of the said deceased and being of age and sound mind and having been advised that she is entitled to seek independent legal advice and has elected not to do so and wishes to vary the distribution of the estate laid down by the said Trust Disposition and Settlement by Deed of variation under Section 142 of the IHT Act 1984 and Section 62(7) of the Taxation of Chargeable Gains Act 1992 as follows: **NOW THEREFORE THE PARTIES AGREE:**

(FIRST) The said Trust Disposition and Settlement of the said deceased is hereby varied by the addition of the following clauses—

I direct my Trustees and Executors to pay over as soon as convenient to them after my death, free of IHT and any other Government Duties exigible on my death and without interest a legacy of **TWO HUNDRED THOUSAND POUNDS (£200,000) STERLING** to my grandson the said **CAIN ANISEED** (otherwise designed as "Cain")

AND

I direct my Trustees and Executors to pay and assign to my daughter, the said Mrs Margaret Aniseed, residing at Eleven Grey Street, Helensburgh, the said David Beige, Chartered Accountant residing at 22 Indigo Drive, Glasgow and **MISS SKYE BLUE**, Solicitor, Dumbarton, and to such other person or persons, body or bodies, as may hereafter be appointed or assumed and to the survivors and survivor of them as my Trustees for the purposes aftermentioned (the major number from time to time resident in the United Kingdom being a *quorum* and the power to act of any Trustee who is an individual being suspended during absence from the United Kingdom) and to the assignees of my Trustees (all hereinafter referred to as "my trustees") the sum of **TWO HUNDRED THOUSAND POUNDS (£200,000) STERLING** (or property to such value) (which sum or property is referred to as the "Discretionary Fund") for the personal support, maintenance and education or otherwise or for the benefit of the Family Beneficiaries defined below or such one or more of them to the exclusion of the others or other in such manner and, if more than one, in such shares as my trustees from time to time in their absolute discretion think fit.

"Family Beneficiaries" means my children, grandchildren and remoter issue, my nieces and nephews and the spouses, widows or widowers of any such persons.

My trustees shall have the fullest powers of and in regard to retention, realisation, investment, appropriation, transfer of property without realisation and management of my estate as if they were absolute beneficial owners; and shall have power to do everything they may consider necessary or expedient for administration of the trust; And in particular and without prejudice to these general powers my trustees shall have power to:

(ONE)

(a) to the extent that they deem it appropriate to do so, meet from the Discretionary Fund the funeral expenses (including the cost of a Memorial) of any of the Family Beneficiaries.

(b) invest the whole or any part thereof in the purchase or improvement of any dwelling-house or flat to permit the same to be used as a residence for any of the Family Beneficiaries whether alone or jointly with any other person or persons without being required to insist upon the payment by any person whether or not a joint occupier thereof but my Trustees shall have an absolute discretion as to the terms on which they permit the flat or dwelling-house to be occupied.

(c) exercise the powers of investment without seeking to balance the interest of Family Beneficiaries entitled to capital and income respectively.

(d) invest in corporeal moveables notwithstanding that the value of the Discretionary Fund may become depleted and to permit any one or more of the Family Beneficiaries to have the use and enjoyment of any corporeal moveable in such manner and subject to such conditions as my trustees may consider reasonable without being liable to account for any consequential loss.

(e) to raise capital out of the Discretionary Fund and to lend it on such terms as to interest, security and repayment and otherwise as they think fit to any person to whom or charitable or other body to which they consider that it would be in the interests of the Family Beneficiaries to make a loan without being liable for any consequent loss of capital.

(f) to apply any part or parts of the capital of the Discretionary Fund or towards meeting the cost of:

- altering or adapting any residence or accommodation in the ownership of any person or body for the more convenient occupation thereof as a whole.
- purchasing any domestic appliances or procuring domestic assistance for any of the Family Beneficiaries or persons with whom they reside from time to time.
- purchasing caravans or motor cars appropriate to the needs of any Family Beneficiaries and the person or persons with whom they from time to time reside.
- holidays for any of the Family Beneficiaries or the expenses incurred by any person or persons to enable them to accompany any beneficiary on holiday or the provision of holidays unaccompanied by them for any person who bears the daily burden of caring for them.
- to accepting the receipt of any person caring or having financial responsibility for any of the Family Beneficiaries as a full and sufficient Discharge for any money intended to be paid to them;

AND

(TWO)

Retention, etc. (1)	to retain, sell, purchase, lease or hire the Discretionary Fund or any part thereof;
Investment (2)	to invest the whole or any part of the Discretionary Fund in heritable and leasehold property, investments, securities, insurance policies, deposits and other assets of whatever description, whether producing income or not, whether or not falling within the class of investments authorised for trust funds, whether or not payable to bearer and wherever situated;
Insurance (3)	to effect, maintain and acquire policies of insurance of whatever description; and to insure any property on whatever terms they think fit including on a first loss basis;
Management of heritage (4)	to administer and manage any heritable or real property forming part of the Discretionary Fund; to repair, maintain, renew and improve the same and to erect additional buildings and structures to grant, vary and terminate leases and rights of tenancy or occupancy; to plant, thin and cut down timber; to work or let minerals; all as my trustees may think proper and as if they were absolute owners of the Discretionary Fund;
Borrow and lend (5)	to borrow or lend with or without security; and to grant continue any guarantee or indemnity for the benefit of any of the Family Beneficiaries actual or prospective;
Occupation by beneficiaries (6)	to lend or allow to be used the whole or any part of the Discretionary Fund at such rate of interest or rent as they may consider appropriate, or free of interest or rent, to or by any person who is for the time being entitled to payment of a share of the income of the Discretionary Fund or to whom or for whose benefit the income may be paid or applied in the exercise of a discretion then available to my trustees;
Nominees (7)	to allow the Discretionary Fund or any part thereof to be registered in the names of or held or the documents of title to be held by any person, firm, corporation or other body as nominee of my trustees;

Delegation of investment management (8)	revocably to delegate any power or powers of making, managing, realising or otherwise dealing with any investment or deposit comprised in the Discretionary Fund to any person or persons upon such terms as to remuneration or otherwise as my trustees may think fit and no trustee shall be responsible for the default of any such agent if the trustee in question employed him in good faith;
Additions (9)	to accept as an addition to the Discretionary Fund any other property which may be made over to them;
Appropriation (10)	to set apart and appropriate specific property of any description to represent the whole or part of the share, prospective or otherwise, of any beneficiary at such valuation as my trustees shall determine, so that thereafter the particular share or part shall have the full benefit of the appropriated investments or assets;
Settlement (11)	to settle with any beneficiary entitled to any part of the Discretionary Fund by conveying to him or her in satisfaction thereof either specific property or money, or partly one and partly the other, as to my trustees shall seem proper and at such valuation as they shall determine and to compel acceptance accordingly;
Conflict of Interest (12)	to enter into any transaction or do any act otherwise authorised by law or by this deed notwithstanding that my trustee is or might be acting *auctor in rem suam* or with a conflict of interest between such trustee and himself as an individual or as trustee of any other trust or any partnership of which a trustee is a partner or any company of which a trustee is a shareholder or director or in relation to any combination of these capacities provided that the trustee or trustees with whom there is or may be any such conflict is or are not sole trustee or trustees;
Participation in discretion (13)	to participate in the exercise of any discretion granted to my trustees notwithstanding that a trustee is or may be a or the sole beneficiary in whose favour the discretion is then exercised provided that there is at least one trustee not so favoured;
Resignation (14)	to resign office notwithstanding any benefit hereunder;

Agents (15)	to appoint one or more of their own number to act as solicitor or agent or any other capacity and to allow him or them the same remuneration to which he or they would have been entitled if not a trustee or trustees;
Non-resident Trustees (16)	to appoint any one or more trustees resident out of the United Kingdom and themselves to resign office;
Administration Abroad (17)	to carry on the administration of the trust hereby created in some place out of the United Kingdom;
Renunciation (18)	to renounce for themselves and their successors in office the power to exercise any of the foregoing powers in this purpose as if the same were vested in them beneficially and not as trustees;
Immunities (19)	my trustees shall not be liable for depreciation in value of the property in my estate, nor for omissions or errors in judgement, or for neglect in management, nor for insolvency of debtors, nor for the acts, omissions, neglects or defaults of each other or of any agent employed by them.
No Apportionment (20)	there shall be no apportionment as between capital or income on any occasion.

(SECOND)   Mrs Aniseed hereby renounces all legal rights competent to her in respect of legitim or otherwise and accepts the terms set out in the said Trust Disposition and Settlement and in this Deed of Variation.

(THIRD)   None of the expenses of these presents shall be paid from the said deceased's estate.

(FOURTH)   The Executors consent to and concur in the provisions hereto which are hereby declared irrevocable.

(FIFTH)   The parties hereto elect and give written notice to the HMRC in terms of Section 142(2) of the said IHT Act 1984 that Section 142 (1) shall retrospectively apply to these presents and the parties hereto do hereby give notice to the HMRC of their intention to have the foregoing variation treated as if it had been effected by the said deceased. The parties also give notice in terms of Section 62(7) of the Taxation of Chargeable Gains Act 1992 that Section 62(6) of the said last-mentioned Act shall retrospectively apply to these presents to said Trust Disposition and Settlement of the said deceased.

(SIXTH)   The parties hereto certify that the transfer in respect of which this transaction is made is one which falls within Category L or Category M of the Schedule to the Stamp Duty (Exempt Instruments) Regulations 1987; IN WITNESS WHEREOF these presents are, together with the copy Trust Disposition and Settlement annexed hereto, subscribed as follows: by the said [. . .].

> *Danger Warning!!*
>
> *It is imperative to include the magic words to the effect that the person varying is invoking s.142(2) of the said IHT Act 1984 that s.142(1) (and if appropriate the provisions of the capital gains tax legislation) and it is to retrospectively apply. If this is omitted it may be treated at the least as a PET! The recent case of* **Wills v Gibb**[15] *deals with this. In this case the English Courts allowed rectification of the deed to include it.*

> *Attention!!*
>
> *In Scotland it may be that the useful s.8 of The Law Reform (Miscellaneous Provisions) (Scotland) Act 1985 (printed below) could be used.*

Rectification of defectively expressed documents

8.—(1) Subject to section 9 of this Act, where the court is satisfied, on an application made to it, that—

(a) a document intended to express or to give effect to an agreement fails to express accurately the common intention of the parties to the agreement at the date when it was made; or

(b) a document intended to create, transfer, vary or renounce a right, not being a document falling within paragraph (a) above, fails to express accurately the intention of the grantor of the document at the date when it was executed,

it may order the document to be rectified in any manner that it may specify in order to give effect to that intention.

(2) For the purposes of subsection (1) above, the court shall be entitled to have regard to all relevant evidence, whether written or oral.

(3) Subject to section 9 of this Act, in ordering the rectification of a document under subsection (1) above (in this subsection referred to as "the original document"), the court may, at its own instance or on an application made to it, order the rectification of any other document intended for any of the purposes mentioned in paragraph (a) or (b) of subsection (1) above which is defectively expressed by reason of the defect in the original document.

(4) Subject to section 9(4) of this Act, a document ordered to be rectified under this section shall have effect as if it had always been so rectified.

(5) Subject to section 9(5) of this Act, where a document recorded in the Register of Sasines is ordered to be rectified under this

---

[15] *Wills v Gibb* [2007] EWCH 3361 (Ch); [2008] S.T.C. 786; [2007] S.T.I. 1970, Ch D.

section and the order is likewise recorded, the document shall be treated as having been always so recorded as rectified.

(6) Nothing in this section shall apply to a document of a testamentary nature.

(7) It shall be competent to register in the Register of Inhibitions and Adjudications a notice of an application under this section for the rectification of a deed relating to land, being an application in respect of which authority for service or citation has been granted; and the land to which the application relates shall be rendered litigious as from the date of registration of such a notice.

(8) A notice under subsection (7) above shall specify the names and designations of the parties to the application and the date when authority for service or citation was granted and contain a description of the land to which the application relates.

(9) In this section and section 9 of this Act "the court" means the Court of Session or the sheriff.

Minute of Meeting Where it is Wished to "Cancel" the Nil-Rate Band Trust

MINUTE OF FIRST MEETING of the **19–27** *Trustees*
appointed by and acting under Will of the late
GODFREY GORMAN MONKSHOOD, 10
Primrose Drive, Inchinnan, Glasgow G3 3AB
(who died on 1st November 2008) dated 1st
January 2004 held within the Chambers of
Messrs Cheatham & Steele, Solicitors,
Glasgow at 134 James Street, Glasgow on
Friday 13th March 2009.

Present: Mrs Greta Gael Coriander or Monkshood, Miss Gladys Monkshood, Donald Cheatham, Solicitor and Frederick Steele, Solicitor, Trustees.

In Attendance: Miss Adele Cheadle, Solicitor and Mr James Bond, Stockbroker, Glasgow

Apology

An apology was intimated from Miss Gladys Monkshood, one of the Trustees, nominated under the Will, who was unable to attend owing to ill health. The best wishes of those present were expressed and the hope that she would soon be restored to full health.

Acceptance of Trustees

The Will incorporating the trust deed having been read over and submitted, the Trustees present, Mrs Greta Gael Coriander or Monkshood, Donald Cheatham, Solicitor and Frederick Steele, Solicitor, all trustees, accepted the office of Trustee conferred on them as is evidenced by their signatures endorsed on the deed and hereto.

Appointment of Factors

The Trustees appointed Messrs Cheatham & Steele, Solicitors, Glasgow to be the Law Agents and Factors to the Trust.

Factors Report

The Factors reported that the funds and the share certificates, stock transfers and dividend mandates, which had been prepared in advance were to hand. The total amounted to £320,000 which was the amount of the nil rate band at date of death.

The Law Agents were instructed as follows:

> 1. *to register the stock transfers, lodge the dividend mandates and which were duly signed.*
> 2. *To have the Deed of Trust registered in the Books of Council and Session and to obtain an Extract.*
> 3. *To pay the expenses of creating the Trust and investments.*
> 4. *To lodge the form 41G (Trust) with HMRC.*

The Trustees fully discussed the question of investing the capital of the Trust and instructed the Factors to arrange for the purchase of the following additional stocks and shares.

Miss Cheadle reported on the terms of the trust deed; this had been prepared some years ago and inter alia provided for the allocation of a sum equal to the nil rate band to setting up of the trust. However, with the change in the law which allowed the executors to claim an additional nil rate band on the death of Mrs Monkshood and given the amount of the estate, it might be that the trustees would wish to consider making all the assets over to the spouse and residuary beneficiary, Mrs Monkshood. She further explained that if this was done within two years of death, HMRC would treat this as having made directly to Mrs Monkshood and enable her executors on her death to claim an additional nil rate band exemption. Although it was not necessary in terms of the trust provisions the trustees having absolute discretion, the other potential beneficiaries namely the issue of the said deceased (including Miss Monkshood) had been advised that such a motion might be considered by the trustees and that they might wish to take advice.

After discussion the trustees, with the exception of Mrs Monkshood who declared an interest and took no part in the discussion and decision, the trustees resolved to make over the entire assets of the trust to Mrs Monkshood and the trustees were instructed to transfer the trust assets accordingly

The Revenue of the Trust

The Factors were instructed to collect the revenue (if any) from any investments and to this to the credit of Mrs Monkshood.

Date of next Meeting

Resolved that it should be left to the Factors to arrange a suitable time for all parties if it was considered a meeting was necessary as and when Miss Brown had fully recovered.

Chapter Twenty

CAPITAL GAINS TAX

Tax facts as for Ch.10.

CAPITAL GAINS TAX

The statutory provisions are as follows. **20–01**
Section 62 of the Taxation of Chargeable Gains Act 1992—general provisions:

Death: general provisions

62.—(1) For the purposes of this Act the assets of which a deceased person was competent to dispose—

    (a) shall be deemed to be acquired on his death by the personal representatives or other person on whom they devolve for a consideration equal to their market value at the date of the death, but

    (b) shall not be deemed to be disposed of by him on his death (whether or not they were the subject of a testamentary disposition).

  (2) Allowable losses sustained by an individual in the year of assessment in which he dies may, so far as they cannot be deducted from chargeable gains accruing in that year, be deducted from chargeable gains accruing to the deceased in the 3 years of assessment preceding the year of assessment in which the death occurs, taking chargeable gains accruing in a later year before those accruing in an earlier year.

 (2A) Amounts deductible from chargeable gains for any year in accordance with subsection (2) above shall not be so deductible from any such gains so far as they are gains that are treated as accruing by virtue of section 87 or 89(2) (read, where appropriate, with section 10A).

  (3) In relation to property forming part of the estate of a deceased person the personal representatives shall for the purposes of this Act be treated as being a single and continuing body of persons (distinct from the persons who may from time to time be the personal representatives), and that body shall be treated as having the deceased's residence, ordinary residence, and domicile at the date of death.

  (4) On a person acquiring any asset as legatee (as defined in section 64)—

    (a) no chargeable gain shall accrue to the personal representatives, and

    (b) the legatee shall be treated as if the personal representatives' acquisition of the asset had been his acquisition of it.

(5) Notwithstanding section 17(1) no chargeable gain shall accrue to any person on his making a disposal by way of donatio mortis causa.

(6) Subject to subsections (7) and (8) below, where within the period of 2 years after a person's death any of the dispositions (whether effected by will, under the law relating to intestacy or otherwise) of the property of which he was competent to dispose are varied, or the benefit conferred by any of those dispositions is disclaimed, by an instrument in writing made by the persons or any of the persons who benefit or would benefit under the dispositions—

(a) the variation or disclaimer shall not constitute a disposal for the purposes of this Act, and

(b) this section shall apply as if the variation had been effected by the deceased or, as the case may be, the disclaimed benefit had never been conferred.

(7) Subsection (6) above does not apply to a variation unless the instrument contains a statement by the persons making the instrument to the effect that they intend the subsection to apply to the variation.

(8) Subsection (6) above does not apply to a variation or disclaimer made for any consideration in money or money's worth other than consideration consisting of the making of a variation or disclaimer in respect of another of the dispositions.

(9) Subsection (6) above applies whether or not the administration of the estate is complete or the property has been distributed in accordance with the original dispositions.

(10) In this section references to assets of which a deceased person was competent to dispose are references to assets of the deceased which (otherwise than in right of a power of appointment or of the testamentary power conferred by statute to dispose of entailed interests) he could, if of full age and capacity, have disposed of by his will, assuming that all the assets were situated in England and, if he was not domiciled in the United Kingdom, that he was domiciled in England, and include references to his severable share in any assets to which, immediately before his death, he was beneficially entitled as a joint tenant.

20–02 The rules, which parallel those for inheritance tax, can be summarised as follows:

1. The document must be signed within two years of death.
2. It extends to both intestate testate and estates.
3. All property of the deceased can be the subject of the document.
4. The deed must be in writing.
5. The deed must be made and subscribed by persons who inherit or might inherit.
6. All deeds executed after July 31, 2002 must be intimated in written form to HMRC within six months from the date of

execution.[1] The IHT Newsletter dated April/May 2002 announced that, following the Finance Act 2002, from August 1, 2002 a deed should include an election as to whether the deed is to be treated as a disposal by the deceased for IHT and capital gains tax. These elections should be separate. The election may be made for one but not the other or neither. It may be applied to one tax or both or neither. The election must specify the statutory provisions. If the deed alters, i.e. by increasing or decreasing, the IHT payable the deed/document containing the election must be sent to HMRC within six months of its date.

7. There must be no external financial consideration[2] other than another variation of another interest under the will or estate.

The main areas of use

In the common type of situation where the variation was to effect, in the case of a widow receiving all her husband's estate by his will, an additional bequest superimposed on the will that their son should receive certain shares, there is no capital gains tax on the variation but the son is deemed to acquire at date of death value (if they elect for s.62(6)(a) to apply). Otherwise there would be a disposal by the widow as grantor of the variation and capital gains tax on her gift of shares to the son based on the rise in value from death to variation.

20–03

Danger Warning!!

Capital gains tax—to elect or not

Sometimes it may be appropriate to elect that s.142 exemption for IHT applies to variation but not for capital gains tax purposes, for example where the variation applies to specific assets which then show a loss compared with their value at the date of death, or where the executors' annual exemption is available to utilise and cover the gain; or where the whole estate is in cash and there will not be a liability to capital gains tax. In theory it is possible to elect for CGT but not IHT, but that is rare in practice.

No election should be inserted in the Deed if the Variation if it only refers to assets which are not subject to CGT, e.g. cash or government securities or NS products.

Please note that all beneficiaries acquiring assets under a will or on intestacy are defined in s.64 as "legatees", including beneficiaries who take assets in satisfaction of pecuniary legacies and trustees for beneficiaries. The definition is not restricted to beneficiaries who receive legacies from the estate.

A legatee takes over an asset from the executors at their acquisition cost irrespective of the date of transfer to him and the value of the asset at that date. There is no disposal on the transfer by the executors to the legatee.

---

[1] IHTA 1984, s.142(2)(f).
[2] IHTA 1984, s.142(3)(g).

20–04   If there is no election, the original beneficiary, who acquired the investment at its date of death value (provided it has been transferred to him) will make a disposal for CGT at the date of the deed of variation and the new beneficiary will acquire the investment at its value on the same date.

If there is an election under s.62, the new beneficiary will take over the investment at its date of death value and there will be no disposal by the original beneficiary.

The decision whether to elect will therefore depend on the respective values at death and variation. The values are likely to be more important than the commencing dates of the taper relief. There may be a conflict of interest between the beneficiaries, but that should not be a problem, because they are usually related. A higher acquisition value may help the new beneficiary for future capital gains tax.

20–05   If the higher value is at the date of variation, an election should *not* be made, provided (1) the asset has been transferred to the beneficiary and (2) the gain on the disposal by the original beneficiary is within his (the original beneficiary's) exemption. The beneficiary has no acquisition cost until the asset has been transferred to him. If the death value is the higher, an election should be made so that the new beneficiary will take over the investment at the higher value at date of death.

Notice of the election has to be given to HM Revenue & Customs within six months after the date of the deed. The notice is given to the tax district dealing with the executry income.

EXAMPLES OF CGT CALCULATIONS

Andrew Norman Other's Executry

Example 1: Sale by the executors 2008/2009

20–06   *Andrew Norman Other died on January 9, 2008, leaving a legacy to his son Noel Oscar Other and the residue of his estate to his widow Mary (aged 66). The value of the estate for confirmation was £250,000.*

The estate included 10,000 ordinary shares in Widgets Plc valued at death at 20p each (£2,000). In June 2008 the executors sold the shares for £2 each. The executors are deemed to have acquired the deceased's assets for a consideration equal to their market value at date of death.

The executors then calculated the amount of their capital gain on the sale of the Widgets shares. To reduce their tax liability they sold their holding of 5,000 Tamson Industries ordinary shares in July 2008 at a net loss of £7,730.00 after expenses without indexation.

The calculation of the CGT payable is:

Net proceeds of sale		£20,000.00
Less Date of death value	£2,000.00	
Cost of Confirmation		
(£2,000 × 1%)	£20.00	
Legal expenses of sale		
(£10,000 × 1.75%)	£350.00	£ 2,370.00
Net gain		£17,630.00
Less loss on sale of Tamson Industries	£7,730.00	
(no Indexation allowed)		
Annual Exemption	£7,900.00	£15,630.00
Chargeable gain		£ 360.00
CGT thereon at 18% = £680.00		

Example 2: Deeds of variation with and without CGT elections

The facts are as in Example 1, but with no sale of the Widgets shares. In **20–07** *March 2008 the executors transferred the shares to Mrs Other when they were worth 50p each.*

Mrs Other, who was not in good health, was worried about the IHT payable on her death. After consulting the solicitors, she signed a deed of variation on June 4, 2008 transferring the shares, which were then worth £1 each, to her son Noel Other.

Mrs Other told the solicitors that she did not expect to make any CGT disposals in 2008/2009. It is not now necessary to have regard to Mrs Other's other income in 2008/2009 since the Finance Act 2008 reduced the rate to 18 per cent.

With CGT election. *The transfer of the Widgets shares by Mrs Other to her son in the deed of variation is not a CGT disposal by her because the election under TCGA 1992 s.62 has been made. The son takes over the Widgets shares as "legatee" at the date of death at a cost of £2,000 and Mrs Other has no CGT liability.*

The Widgets dividends received by the executors between the dates of death and the variation will be allocated to the beneficiary to whom the executors pay the dividends.

If they pay the dividends to Mrs Other, she will not have to pay any more income tax on them because her total income is within the lower rate band.

No CGT election. *The deed of variation was a disposal by Mrs Other for CGT in June 2008. Mrs Other acquired the Widgets shares as "legatee" under her husband's will at the date of death value.*

Her CGT liability is as follows:
The calculation of the CGT payable is:

Open market value of shares in June 2008		£20,000.00
Less Mrs Other's acquisition cost	£2,000.00	
Executors' cost of Confirmation (1%)	£20.00	
Legal expenses of transfer		
(£2000 × 2%)	£40.00	£2,060.00
Net capital gain		£17,940.00
Less Annual Exemption		£9,600.00
Chargeable gain		£8,340.00
CGT on £8340 @ 18% = £1,501.20		

    The open market value of the shares (one-quarter up) is taken as the consideration, because Mrs Other and her son are connected persons (TCGA 1992 s.18). Mr Other acquires the shares at this value on the date of the deed for his capital gains tax acquisition value. The CGT is at 18 per cent irrespective of Mrs Other's gross income. The CGT is payable on January 31, 2009, which was the last date for the lodging of Mrs Other's self assessment tax return. A penalty of £100 is payable if the return is lodged late and interest is charged on the unpaid tax.

    If there had been a gift of the Widgets shares without a deed of variation, Mrs Other's IHT Annual Allowances of £3,000 for 2007/2008 and 2008/2009 would have reduced the value of the gift which would have been a potentially exempt transfer for the next seven years. The variation exempts the transfer with immediate effect and leaves her annual exemptions available for other gifts.

Example 3: Sale by beneficiary

20–08   *The facts are as in Example 2. The 10,000 Widgets shares were acquired by the beneficiary Noel Other by the deed of variation dated June 4, 2008. He sold the shares on December 20, 2008 for £30,820 net of expenses. He was then carrying forward £500 of CGT losses. The shares do not qualify for business assets taper relief.*

    The calculation of the CGT payable is:

ACQUISITION COSTS AND TAPER

DATES	NUMBER	COST	INDEXATION	TOTAL
NO CGT ELECTION				
4.6.2008	10,000	£20,000	N/A	£20,000
WITH CGT ELECTION				
9.1.2008	10,000	£ 2,000	N/A	£ 2,000
TAPER YEARS—NOT APPLICABLE				
TAPER RELIEF—NOT APPLICABLE				

CGT COMPUTATION	NO ELECTION	WITH ELECTION
PROCEEDS	£30,820	£30,820
COST	£20,000	£2,000
GAIN	£10,820	£28,820
LOSS CARRIED FORWARD	£500	£500
CHARGEABLE GAIN	£10,320	£28,320
EXEMPTION (SAY)	£9,600	£9,600
	£720	£18,760
CGT AT 18%	£129.60	£3,369.60

Chapter Twenty One

INCOME TAX

"Though I know some things are indispensible, like a buck or two."[1]

Tax facts as for Ch.9.

Income Tax

Strictly speaking there are no income tax provisions which correspond to **21–01** s.142. However, there are still income tax consequences of making a deed of variation or disclaimer. Section 698 of the Income and Corporation Taxes Act 1988 should be studied closely. Section 698 is reproduced below. Although re-enacted in the ITTOIA 2005, it may be easier to follow in the form in which it appeared in the ICTA 1988:

Special provisions as to certain interests in residue

698.—(1)Where the personal representatives of a deceased person have as such a right in relation to the estate of another deceased person such that, if that right were vested in them for their own benefit, they would have an absolute or limited interest in the residue of that estate or in a part of that residue, they shall be deemed to have that interest notwithstanding that that right is not vested in them for their own benefit, and any amount deemed to be paid to them as income by virtue of this Part shall be treated as part of the aggregate income of the estate of the person whose personal representatives they are.

(1A) Subsection (1B) below applies where—

    (a) successively during the administration period there are different persons with interests in the residue of the estate of a deceased person or in parts of such a residue;

    (b) the later interest or, as the case may be, each of the later interests arises or is created on the cessation otherwise than by death of the interest that precedes it; and

    (c) the earlier or, as the case may be, earliest interest is a limited interest.

(1B) Where this subsection applies, this Part shall have effect in relation to any payment made in respect of any of the interests referred to in subsection (1A) above—

    (a) as if all those interests were the same interest so that none of them is to be treated as having ceased on being succeeded by any of the others;

---

[1] From the film *Calamity Jane* (1953) (Sammy Fain/Paul Francis Webster).

(b) as if (subject to paragraph (c) below) the interest which is deemed to exist by virtue of paragraph (a) above ('the deemed single interest') were an interest of—

  (i) except in a case to which sub-paragraph (ii) below applies, the person in respect of whose interest or previous interest the payment is made;
  (ii) in a case where the person entitled to receive the payment is any other person who has or has had an interest which is deemed to be comprised in the deemed single interest, that other person;

and

(c) in so far as any of the later interests is an absolute interest as if, for the purposes of section 696(3A) to (5)—

  (i) the earlier interest or interests had never existed and the absolute interest had always existed;
  (ii) the sums (if any) which were deemed in relation to the earlier interest or interests to have been paid as income for any year of assessment to any of the persons entitled thereto were sums previously paid during the administration period in respect of the absolute interest; and
  (iii) those sums were sums falling to be treated as sums paid as income to the person entitled to the absolute interest.

(2) Where successively during the administration period there are different persons with absolute interests in the residue of the estate of a deceased person or in parts of such a residue, the aggregate payments and assumed income entitlement referred to in subsections (3A) and (3B) of section 696 shall be computed for the purposes of that section in relation to an absolute interest subsisting at any time ('the subsequent interest')—

(a) as if the subsequent interest and any previous absolute interest corresponding to the subsequent interest, or relating to any part of the residue to which the subsequent interest relates, were the same interest; and

(b) as if the residuary income for any year of the person entitled to the previous interest were residuary income of the person entitled to the subsequent interest and any amount deemed to be paid as income to the person entitled to the previous interest were an amount deemed to have been paid to the person entitled to the subsequent interest.

(3) Where, upon the exercise of a discretion, any of the income of the residue of the estate of a deceased person for any period (being the administration period or a part of the administration period) would, if the residue had been ascertained at the commencement of that period, be properly payable to any

person, or to another in his right, for his benefit, whether directly by the personal representatives or indirectly through a trustee or other person—

(a) the amount of any sum paid pursuant to an exercise of the discretion in favour of that person shall be deemed for all tax purposes to have been paid to that person as income for the year of assessment in which it was paid; and

(b) sections 695(4) to (6) shall have effect in relation to an amount which is deemed to have been paid as income by virtue of paragraph (a) above.

What does this mean in practice?

Notwithstanding that for IHT and CGT purposes a deed of variation **21–02** may be retrospective to the date of death, it is not retrospective to the date of death for income tax purposes and is only effective from the date of its execution. However, an element of retrospection for income tax purposes has been introduced by the back door because of new rules which were introduced for payments made on or after April 6, 1995. This arose because of, and in preparation for, self-assessment for personal representatives and beneficiaries of estates. The practical effect of these rules is that deeds of variation can now have some retrospective effect for income tax purposes if the deed of variation relates to the residue of an estate *which is still in the course of administration when the variation is made*. The retrospective effect is simply the effect of the rules, including statutory provisions for successive interests in residue. If, for instance, payments had been made to the original beneficiary before the execution of the deed of variation, HMRC would *not* accept that the deed retrospectively changed any income tax liabilities based on such payments. Under self-assessment a beneficiary with an absolute interest in residue is liable to income tax on payments made to him or her during the administration period in respect of his or her absolute interest. Any such payments are treated as income for the year of payment. It should, however, be noted that any such payments will only be treated as income to the extent that they do not exceed the assumed income entitlement of the beneficiary at the time the payment is made. The assumed income entitlement is the cumulative share of the estate income, for all years up to and including the year of payment, to which the beneficiary is entitled whether or not that share has actually been paid out. For example, if a testator dies on June 1, 2007 and if his widow signs a deed of variation on December 1, 2007 redirecting the whole of the residuary estate to her adult son, no part of the income will be assessed on the widow unless the executors have previously paid any sum to her in respect of her absolute interest.

Danger Warning!!

Consideration by the executor and/or the executors of variations and/or discharges (disclaimers) under s.142 IHTA will be standard practice. Until April 6, 1995 there were no statutory provisions which made

> *variations or discharges (disclaimers) retrospective for IT purposes. This could be compared with TCGA 1992 s.62 for capital gains. Obviously a discharge is only available where no income or interest has been accepted by the beneficiary. When the bequest is a pecuniary legacy which has interest and it is disclaimed, the beneficiary will not be liable to income tax on the interest. In the case of a variation of residue or a share thereof the original beneficiary was liable to income tax for the period from the date of death until the date of variation or disclaimer, although the executor was assessed initially. The new beneficiary was assessed thereafter. It might have been appropriate in the deed of variation to allow the disclaiming beneficiary some interest, if only to pay the tax levied. Clearly if there is to be a variation then it is best to be made as soon as possible. If not a situation could arise where a higher earning beneficiary who does not vary timeously could be assessed on tax at the higher rate on income he has not received.*

In future executors will require to pay much more attention to the distribution of estates and its impact upon the beneficiaries' tax position. *Failure to have regard to this could give rise to a negligence claim by the beneficiaries.* Information must be made available to the beneficiaries as soon after the end of the tax year as possible so that they can comply with the new time-limits regarding self-assessment and avoid surcharges, interest and penalties. The beneficiary has a statutory right to receive a statement of income.

Executries becoming Continuing Trusts

21–03 Practitioners should also consider certain other matters. Any income due to and received by an original beneficiary up to the date of execution of the deed of variation is strictly speaking that person's income. If income or property is paid over to the original beneficiary then this is chargeable as income of his. This does not of course preclude him from carrying out a deed of variation later which redirects inter alia the asset which he has received. However, there is no retrospective provision in these circumstances.

The other matter is where a deed of variation is made in favour of a charity. If at all possible this should be executed as soon as possible after death to enable the charity, unlike the original beneficiary, to claim exemption from income tax (TA 1988 s.505).

The view is sometimes taken that the original beneficiary who makes a deed of variation which creates a trust is actually the truster for income tax purposes.

21–04 A further possibility is if the trust set up is such that the original beneficiary retains a possibility of benefit, the income of the trust property will be taxed on that person. Please also note that if the trust is in favour of underage children, payment to or for the benefit of the underage children may be taxed as the income of the truster.

Consideration of relief under gift aid provisions is theoretically possible although this is fraught with difficulty. Where the beneficiary has been left a legacy in a will, if the deed of variation route is used to redirect this legacy to a charity within the two-year period, it could and should have the effect of the deceased's estate qualifying for the benefit of the charity exemption under the Inheritance Tax Act 1984 s.23. Another aspect is, as stated above, that deeds of variation do not generally operate for income tax purposes retrospectively. It might be that the beneficiary could receive income tax gift aid benefit. In "Post-Death Tax Planning: Variations and Disclaimers" the author, Ralph Ray,[2] guessed that this is likely to fail for two reasons.

> "First because The Finance Act 1990 Section 25 requires the gift aid to be by way of an outright cash payment, whereas the variation is made pursuant to the Section 142 Instrument and deeming arrangements. Secondly, following the decision of *St Dunstans v Major* [1997] STC SCD 212 by obtaining the IHT reduction, the donor of the purported gift aid payment received a benefit within the Finance Act 1990 Section 25 (2) (e) thereby disqualifying the payment."

He suggests that gifts of shares charity may be a possibility. It may be that a beneficiary varying a will may provide for shares to be made over to the charity and the Deed of Variation is executed to reflect this. It would be important to make the relevant inheritance tax and capital gains tax statement. There may well be an inheritance tax saving of, and an income tax saving assuming, the person varying has a tax rate of 40 per cent and he has sufficient taxable income to utilise the relief. This is obviously a matter which would require careful consideration on the individual circumstances.

Danger Warning!!

EXECUTRIES BECOMING CONTINUING TRUSTS

A trust set up under a will does not start until the executors have made over the trust fund (e.g. a legacy) to the trustees, who will probably be themselves acting in a different capacity.

If the trust fund is part of the residue of the estate, the Trust will not start until the residue is established at the end of the administration period. If the trust is discretionary (e.g. an accumulation and maintenance trust) the income tax liability at the trust rates will not start until the trust commences.

If the executors pay income into the discretionary trust from the executry the trustees will have to pay additional income tax at the trust rates on the income they receive from the executry at 40 per cent (32.4 per cent on non-tax recoverable tax dividends). If the executors pay the income direct to the trust beneficiaries during the executry administration, there is no liability for the additional income tax.

---

[2] Ralph Ray, "Post-Death Planning: Variations and Disclaimers", *Tolley's Tax Digests*, Issue 19, May 2004.

The trustees' CGT exemption is half the executors' rate. The change of exemption applies from the start of the trust. The executors may have the full exemption in the same year as the trustees' half exemption starts. Both exemptions may be used to minimise the CGT. Executors and trustees are all liable for CGT at the trust rate of 18 per cent.

Chapter Twenty Two

MISCELLANEOUS ITEMS: STAMP DUTY, ETC.

As regards non-heritable subjects all deeds executed after May 1, 1987 **22–01** are exempt subject to the appropriate certificate appearing on the Deed (Stamp Duty (Exempt Instruments) Regulations 1987, Schedule Category M or Category L. It is no longer necessary to include the certificate in the relevant documents.

As regards heritable subjects the stamp duty land tax regime applies. It is now no longer necessary to submit an SDLT60 "certification that no land transaction return is required for a land transaction".

Pre-Owned Assets Tax

Changes in the Distribution of a Deceased's Estate

Schedule 15, para.16 of the Finance Act 2004 provides that any **22–02** disposition made by the chargeable person in relation to an interest in the estate of a deceased person is disregarded for the purposes of this Schedule if under s.17 of the Inheritance Tax Act 1984 the disposition is not a transfer of value by the chargeable person for IHT purposes. For the purposes of this paragraph "estate" has the same meaning as it has for the purposes of the Inheritance Tax Act 1984.

A disposition made by an individual in relation to an interest in estate is to be disregarded for the purposes of the POT rules if it is not treated as a transfer of land by the individual for the purposes of IHT. The most common instance of this is with a deed of variation which may be made within two years of the date of death.

Example

Mr Robroy inherits a house on the death of his father. Within two years of **22–03** *his father's death he executes a deed of variation relative to his father's estate providing for the property to devolve jointly to his two adult children. Notwithstanding the variation it is Mr Robroy rather than the children who take up the occupation of the property.*

Mr Robroy's disposition of the property falls within IHT 1984 s.142(1) and is therefore to be disregarded for POT purposes. No POT charge therefore arises in relation to Mr Robroy's continuing occupation of the property.

Chapter Twenty Three

HOW TO AVOID PROFESSIONAL NEGLIGENCE CLAIMS IN EXECUTRY TAX

"The term 'professional' stems from the fact that professionals used to profess an oath."[1]

Imagine

23–01   Imagine, if you will, before reading this text, the last letter you signed, the last form you completed or the last deed you drafted. Try to visualise the care (or even the lack of care) which you employed in framing it, reading it over and, if appropriate, signing it.

Now imagine, say, six months or a year or two years from now, that you are in court being examined (or cross-examined) by counsel or agent for a disappointed beneficiary or executor client on the terms of that letter, form or writ. You are asked to explain why you framed the letter, form or writ, which is now the subject of the claim or complaint, in this way. The appropriate reply, "I had to get it out quickly to avoid . . .", will not be sufficient.

For many reasons, negligence claims of course are rare and the chances of you being in this position are probably less than 0.01 per cent; however, if instead of appearing in court you find yourself the subject of a complaint to the newly constituted Scottish Complaints Commission (if the work complained of postdates October 1, 2008), to the Law Society of Scotland (if the work predates October 1, 2008) or to the firm's professional indemnity insurer, the odds lengthen exponentially.

23–02   The purpose of this chapter is to deal with avoiding claims which may be made in connection with executry tax matters. The factors relevant to avoiding claims and/or complaints are similar.

Before dealing with the avoidance it is appropriate to provide a brief framework of the legal aspects of professional negligence as it applies to solicitors and to provide a framework for what follows. It is not meant to be a sustained and comprehensive treatment of the law. For this, reference may be made to Professor Rennie's excellent book, *Solicitor's Negligence* and/or to one of the many English law texts such as *Jackson and Powell on Professional Negligence*.[2]

Before considering the professional negligence aspect, it is worthwhile having in mind a clear picture of what a "professional" is. Generally speaking, it is characterised by the nature of the work being highly specialised, mental rather than manual and requiring a considerable period of theoretical and practical training. In addition, there is the

---

[1] Robert Rennie, *Solicitor's Negligence* (Lexis Nexis, UK, 1997).
[2] John Powell, Roger Stewart and Rupert Jackson, *Jackson and Powell on Professional Negligence*, 5th edn (Sweet and Maxwell, UK, 2002).

moral aspect whereby practitioners or professionals are usually perceived to be committed to professional ethics, that is to say certain moral standards, which go beyond the general level. They also, generally speaking, belong to a society or a professional association, which seeks to regulate training and uphold the standards of the profession. Finally, they are generally of a high status, social or otherwise, and are vested in certain privileges, which are granted by Parliament. The legal profession in Scotland embodies all these four characteristics.

It is also perhaps worth stating at the outset that professionals by their **23–03** very nature operate in situations where success cannot always be achieved, thus in litigation it could be argued that one person is successful and the other is not. However, high degrees of skill may have been utilised by the agents or solicitors acting for both parties.

Sometimes also, success is beyond a professional person's control. Even when the critical factors are within his control, he still cannot guarantee success. In matters of tight judgment on aspects of great complexity, no human being can be right every time.

Consideration of ethics can often provide a guide to the practitioner. For this reason the formation of The Scottish Forum for Professional Ethics is to be welcomed. They are:

"A voluntary association of professional bodies and interested individuals in Scotland whose aim is to sustain inter-professional dialogue and exchange on the ethical basis and dilemmas of professional life."

Their objects are stated to be:

"To support professional bodies in Scotland and their members, as well as interested individuals, in serving the public interest through the highest standards of ethical practice. To nurture inter-professional dialogue, exchange, and collaboration between professional bodies, their members, and interested individuals. To maintain a network of professional bodies and their members and of interested individuals in Scotland to promote the sharing of perspectives on the ethical dilemmas which are encountered in professional practice. To contribute to the public and professional debate on the role of professional bodies in a changing society."

The basic problem therefore for professional negligence is to define what **23–04** standards the law will require of a professional person and which standards provide protection for the consumer. Generally, professional persons who possess a certain minimum degree of competence should exercise reasonable care in the discharge of their profession. See the old English case of *Lanphier v Phipos*,[3] in particular Lord Chief Justice Tindals' remarks:

"Every person who enters into a learned profession undertakes to bring to the exercise of it a reasonable degree of care of skill. He

---

[3] *Lanphier v Phipos* (1838) 173 E.R. 581.

does not undertake, if he is an attorney, that at all events you shall gain the executor's case, nor does a surgeon undertake that he will perform a cure; nor does he undertake to use the highest possible degree of skill."

An extremely useful definition, which is often referred to, is by Lord President Clyde in *Hunter v Hanley*[4] at 205:

"To establish liability . . . where deviation from normal practice, three facts require to be established. First of all it must be proved that there is a usual and normal practice; secondly it must be proved that the defender has not adopted that practice; thirdly it must be established the course . . . adopted is one which no professional person of ordinary skill would have taken if they had been acting with ordinary care. This is clearly a heavy onus on a pursuer to establish these three facts, and without all three, his case will fail. If this is the test, then it matters nothing how far or how little he or she deviates from the ordinary practice. For the extent of deviation is not the test. The deviation must be of a kind which satisfies the third requirement."

Although the title of this Chapter relates to negligence claims it should be pointed out that these claims may arise out of contractual liability as well as delictual liability.

23–05   Thus, where there is a contract between the professional person and the client whereby services are to be provided in return for a fee or alternatively a reasonable fee, it is generally implied that the professional person will exercise a reasonable degree of skill and care. This is as opposed to the question of delict where the professional owed and/or breached a duty of care to the claimant who has suffered damage or loss as a result.

It should be borne in mind of course that the test for the person to whom the professional (solicitor) owes a duty of care is fairly circumscribed.

Examples of failure could include, in the context of tax, the failure to actually prepare a tax return at all, the failure to follow the instructions given by the executor, the failure to take reasonable steps to ascertain the wishes as regards the tax liability, to see that the return is signed and that all time limits have been observed. It may well be that proper advice has not been given on claiming reliefs or foreign law aspects or overseas transactions.

The damages of course will be mitigated or restricted by the usual rules for damages as to remoteness, etc.

PENALTIES

Incorrect Returns

23–06   The HM Customs and Excise and the Inland Revenue each had their own penalties for incorrect documents. These old penalties are to be replaced by the Finance Acts 2007 and 2008. Schedule 24 of the Finance

---

[4] *Hunter v Hanley*, 1955 S.C. 200.

Act 2007 introduced a new single-penalty structure for incorrect returns covering inter alia income tax and capital gains tax. These penalties became effective for return periods beginning after March 31, 2008 where the return is filed on or after April 1, 2009.

Attention!!

Schedule 40 of the Finance Act 2008 now extends this to other taxes and duties administered by HMRC, including inheritance tax and stamp duties. It is likely that this will become operational from April 2010. Also, a third party becomes liable to a penalty where the third party is the cause of an error in a return by deliberately supplying false information or deliberately withholding information from the person responsible for the return.

THE NEW RULES

This is mentioned earlier but the penalty will be determined by the **23–07** amount of tax understated, the nature of the behaviour giving rise to the understatement and the extent of disclosure by the executor. The use of suspended penalties will be extended. For incorrect returns, the measure is expected to be in force for return periods commencing on or after April 1, 2009 where the return is due to be filed on or after April 1, 2010.

New penalties for failure to notify are expected to have effect for failure to meet notification obligations which arise on or after April 1, 2009. The new provisions for incorrect returns will provide for penalties in line with Sch.24. There will be no penalty where an executor simply makes a mistake but there will be a penalty of up to:

- 30 per cent for failure to take reasonable care;
- 70 per cent for a deliberate understatement; and
- 100 per cent for a deliberate understatement with concealment.

Each penalty is to be substantially reduced where the executor makes a disclosure and actively tries to correct the return. It will also reflect in his favour if this is unprompted. For an unprompted disclosure of a failure to take reasonable care, the penalty could be reduced to nil. Where an executor discloses fully when prompted by a challenge from HMRC each penalty could be reduced by up to a half. Of particular importance to practitioners will be the provisions regarding third parties such as solicitors, accountants, tax advisors and the like.

Where a return is incorrect because, say, a solicitor has deliberately **23–08** provided false information or deliberately withheld information from the executor, with the intention of causing an understatement of tax due, there will be a new provision allowing a penalty to be charged on the third party.

In summary, the existing provisions are to be replaced by a single regime, which will cover inaccurate returns, claims, accounts and other documents for each of the taxes. The old, somewhat incriminatory references to fraud and negligence are replaced by clearer language in "deliberate inaccuracy" and "failure to take reasonable care". Of course, neglect is already established in case law to include a failure to take reasonable care. The levels of penalty are to be the amount of tax understated (the potential lost revenue) and the seriousness of the error, with a reduction for the extent of disclosure including cooperation in allowing HMRC access to records. It is likely that notwithstanding all this there will be considerable scope for negotiation.

As if matters were not bad enough for the beleaguered practitioner, a further nail has been hammered in with the announcement that HMRC are to deal with the investigation by HMRC of fraud in tax matters. As Jonathan Levy states in a splendid article in *Taxation Magazine*, "Not a civil affair"[5]:

> "Advisors who act dishonestly may be prosecuted by Revenue and Customs Prosecution Office. The civil investigation of fraud has evolved over the last few years. It is fair to say that HMRC are more aggressive, equipped with more powers, and more proactive in this area than used to be the case. HMRC are also increasingly blurring the distinction between civil and criminal."

Fraud/dishonesty differentiates tax evasion from tax avoidance.

The procedure regarding these investigations follows a specific pattern. After an initial interview HMRC ask for a detailed and complete "follow-up report".

It may be speculated that these changes stem from the former "Customs and Excise" side of the new HMRC.

23–09   Advisors were well acquainted with the difference in outlook of HM Inspectors of Taxes on the one hand and the Customs and Excise section on the other. The former were characterised by an attempt to reach agreement, with prosecution being the last resort. The latter were characterised by a more robust approach. Since the merger of the two branches in 2005, the Revenue Special Compliance Office (SCO) and the law enforcement investigation section of Customs have been combined into a new HMRC office, Special Civil Investigations (SCI).

They employ a new civil investigation of fraud (CIF) procedure. Frighteningly, there are also teams of specially trained officers formed by HMRC in local and national compliance who will also use the new CIF procedure for smaller cases. A new Code of Practice reflects the new CIF procedure and applies to all investigations commenced post September 1, 2005. However, the most significant change is the removal of the underlying threat of prosecution, which was an integral part of the former investigations carried out by SCO. Where HMRC decide to investigate using the CIF procedure, the executor will be advised immediately that HMRC will not seek a prosecution for the tax fraud being investigated. Accordingly, SCI interviews will not be held under caution, nor will they be tape recorded.[6] There is also to be a single meeting under CIF to discuss both direct and indirect tax matters. It is

---

[5] Jonathan Levy, "Not a civil affair", *Taxation Magazine*, June 2008.
[6] As was previously the case with SCO interviews.

unlikely that the practitioner or the executor will be involved in a "fraud" case. It is important that the practitioner is aware of the problem and the need to seek specialist advice.

As stated, dishonesty differentiates tax evasion from tax avoidance. There is, however, a crucial distinction between the two. Tax evasion is unlawful and the essential key difference is dishonesty on the part of, say, the executor (and/or his advisor under certain circumstances).

The executor is free to attend the interview or not, but the best advice **23–10** should be that he does, because of the seriousness of the investigation and the background possibility that, if the executor fails to co-operate, HMRC will consider a criminal prosecution.

HMRC will also be seeking, in addition to tax lost and interest, penalties. The new regime, introduced by the FA 2007, applies to direct and indirect taxes for returns in respect of any period commencing on or after April 1, 2008, which are completed on or after April 1, 2009. Until then the old regime will apply.

HM Revenue & Customs will give guidance on what constitutes "taking reasonable care". Particular consideration will be taken of systems in place which, if followed, could reasonably be expected to produce an accurate basis for the calculation of tax due but, despite this, inaccuracies have arisen, resulting in mis-statements.

Attention!!

HMRC regard the dishonest advisor as a "centre of infection"; if it can be proved that the advisor has acted untruthfully, e.g. by holding back information germane to the report from HMRC, the matter may be referred to the Revenue and Customs Prosecution Office for consideration of criminal proceedings. The case of R v Cunningham, Charlton, Wheeler and Kitchen *[1996] S.T.C. 1418 illustrates the criminal sanctions that can be imposed when a tax advisor does step over the line. This is a specialised area of work where the advisor needs to tread carefully.*

THE SCOTTISH LEGAL COMPLAINTS COMMISSION

The Scottish Legal Complaints Commission took over on October 1, **23–11** 2008, the Law Society of Scotland's responsibility to receive complaints against solicitors and to consider inadequate professional service. However, complaints about the professional conduct of solicitors under the Legal Profession and Legal Aid (Scotland) Act 2007 as well as the new category of complaint, which falls short of professional misconduct, namely unsatisfactory professional conduct, will still to be dealt with by the Society. By contrast, more serious allegations of professional misconduct will continue to be referred to the Scottish Solicitors' Discipline Tribunal (SSDT).

It is difficult to escape the conclusion that the legal profession has a bad press and legislators see electoral mileage in this and indeed to find yet another excuse for setting up yet another *quango* at the expense of the professions! Indeed the general public and our legislators seem to be obsessed with complaints against solicitors in Scotland despite the less than infinitesimal percentage of complaints upheld as against the incredible and overwhelming volume of work carried out satisfactorily! As evidence of this it should be noted that the system for handling complaints against solicitors has undergone several changes in recent years, including the most recent spectacular one. The new Commission is to act as a channel or gateway for all complaints against lawyers, and by mediating, resolving or determining complaints about service and sifting out those that are frivolous, vexatious or without merit. Current evidence suggests that these will be the majority! Conduct matters will be passed on to the professional organisations, though the Commission will supervise the way conduct complaints are handled.

The Commission has also taken over the Scottish Legal Services Ombudsman's current overseeing powers.

As previously stated, the Commission will only consider complaints about service where the business was instructed after October 1, 2008. The Law Society continues to deal with service complaints about business instructed before October 1. There is to be a one-year time limit for making complaints.

Please note, the Law Society still deals with professional misconduct matters, with prosecutions before the independent Scottish Solicitors' Discipline Tribunal.

Unsatisfactory Professional Conduct

23–12   A new category of complaint has also been created. It is known as "unsatisfactory professional conduct". The Law Society have the right to investigate and decide upon this new category of transgression, which falls short of professional misconduct. It has its own sanctions, namely, a mandatory censure and (potentially) a fine of up to £2,000, compensation to the "successful" complainer of up to £5,000 or an order to undergo training, or a mixture of these.

It cannot be emphasised strongly enough that as the Law Society must continue to deal with service complaints where the business was instructed before October 1, 2008, their panel reporters will still have a role to play in handling those cases. For complaints regarding conduct, in respect of work instructed after October 1, 2008, the Law Society in-house complaints investigators will investigate and report thereon to the Professional Conduct Committee.

A spokesperson for the Law Society stated:

> "Making findings of unsatisfactory professional conduct will be a particular challenge for the Society as we have no precedents or case law, so we will have to start from scratch and build up our jurisprudence. We will look at the particular circumstances of the case when judging unsatisfactory conduct. The decisions taken by the Professional Conduct Committee and on any appeals to the SSDT will help to mould the process."

23–13   The Law Society has instituted an updated system of investigators to replace the volunteer reporters. However, a new unit has also been formed to liaise with the Commission and to offer information and advice to solicitors and the public. The spokesperson continues:

"The new regulation liaison team will provide a particularly valuable service for solicitors in the new regulatory landscape. It will give information and advice to the profession at every stage of the complaints process and about how the Commission works. We know it might be confusing when there are suddenly two organisations to deal with, but we are there to help. In fact, we will be able to do everything short of representing the solicitor—we cannot do that because of the possibility of a conduct complaint arising out of the service complaint."

In liaising with the Commission, the new team will be responsible for dealing with any correspondence and issues that arise, for instance how to go about investigating a hybrid complaint with elements of both service and conduct. The spokesperson continues further:

"Solicitors and clients will have to get used to the new process—all complaints going initially to the Commission, the transfer of the Ombudsman's powers to the new body, appeals heard before the Court of Session, and so on. But whatever the issue, we will do everything possible to help out. The Commission staff are gradually getting up to speed and we are working constructively with them. There has been some uncertainty during recent months and years but we know what we must do and are ready for the challenges that lie ahead."

ABOLITION OF CODE OF CONDUCT

As if matters were not confused enough, the Law Society introduced, **23–14** with effect from January 1, 2009, new Standards of Conduct Practice Rules.[7] The Code of Conduct, which was introduced in October 1989, has been abolished. In an article entitled "Setting the standards" in the *Journal of the Law Society*,[8] Bruce Ritchie, co-author of the article, stated:

"The main differences from the provisions in the Code of Conduct are as follows: The interests of the client Paragraph 3 in the Schedule of Standards deals with the interests of the client, and includes a requirement to be fearless in defending clients' interests regardless of the consequences (including, if necessary, incurring the displeasure of the bench). However the rule adds that the clients' best interests require solicitors to give honest advice, however unwelcome that may be. The duty to the client is only one of several duties which solicitors must strive to reconcile."

---

[7] Solicitors (Scotland) (Standards of Conduct) Practice Rules 2008 dated November 28, 2008, made by the Council of the Law Society of Scotland under s.34(1) of the Solicitors (Scotland) Act 1980 and approved by the Lord President of the Court of Session in terms of s.34(3) of the said Act.

[8] P. Yelland and B. Ritchie, "Setting the Standards" (2009) 54(1) J.L.S. 28.

> *Danger Warning!!*
>
> *The rules contain no power to the Council to grant a waiver, and—as these are rules passed under s.34 of the Solicitors (Scotland) Act 1980—breach of them may be treated as professional misconduct or unsatisfactory professional conduct.*

CLAIMS POTENTIAL

23–15   As mentioned, examples of failure could include, in the context of tax, the failure to actually prepare a tax return deed at all, the failure to follow the instructions given by the client, the failure to advise that a tax return needed to be made, to take reasonable steps to ascertain the wishes as regards the estate, and to see that time limits have been observed and documentation has been complied with. It may well be that proper advice has not been given on the tax effect of the transferred nil-rate band. However, the duty may not extend to other estates to which the testator may be entitled, or to tax savings schemes in respect of them. The damages, of course, will be mitigated or restricted by the usual rules for damages as to remoteness, etc.

Certain factors can be identified in recognising an increase in claim "potentialability". There is also a culture of blame and claim.[9]

The attitude of the different professional bodies can play an important role in defining what conduct is claimable.

CULTURE OF LITIGIOUSNESS

23–16   There can be no doubt that we live in a time when clients are more ready to question the judgments of professional persons. It is sometimes argued that this emanates from the US. There is some merit in the argument that people *should* challenge and question advice rather than, as perhaps in the past, being more ready to accept advice from a professional. Paradoxically, the "difficult" client is the one to cherish as this is the one who may draw your attention inadvertently to a mistake which has been made.

It is alleged that society has developed a culture of "blame and claim", although lawyers naturally resent this assertion and point to contrary evidence.

INCREASED SPECIALISATION

23–17   In days gone by there was little if any specialisation in the legal profession. Solicitors routinely appeared in the courts in the morning and dealt with chamber practice in the afternoon. There may have been specialisation into court and chamber practice. Now there is a bewildering list of 24 specialisations, including private client tax. Indeed the Law

---

[9] Mark McLaughlin and David Coldrick, "Blame and Claim?—Personal Injury and Disabled Trusts", *Taxation Magazine*, November 11, 2004, p.158.

Society of Scotland operates a well-developed and mature accreditation scheme, which was established in 1990. The exceptional quality and skill of accredited specialists under the scheme is recognised by practitioners throughout Scotland. Entry to the scheme is difficult and there are only about 400 accredited specialists out of over 10,000 solicitors in Scotland. Reference is made to the excellent article "Making a specialism pay" by Iain Talman.[10]

While solicitors will see accreditation as a way of developing their skills and career, the qualification assures clients that they are having access to specialist advice of the highest standard. This is particularly important in difficult cases.

The problem is that solicitors, for various reasons, continue to take on work for which they are not really qualified, lack the necessary experience or have no one in their firm (especially where it is a small or medium-sized one) to consult. They may wish to retain a client or it may be that a client who trusts them may not speak to anyone else. Unless the solicitor is prepared to pass the work on to someone more qualified or to take detailed advice from a more experienced colleague or counsel, he runs the risk of making a costly and expensive mistake.

COMPETITION FOR LEGAL SERVICES

There is now much more competition for what was traditionally legal **23–18** work from outside the profession. The legal profession in Scotland has shown itself to be singularly skilful in losing vast areas and trenches of work to other professions or quasi professions. Accountancy, tax work, and town and country planning law are just the tip of the iceberg. If there is added to this financial planning, financial services, employment law, and trust and executry work, a more realistic picture can be seen. The problem here is that, by losing this work, solicitors do not build up the expertise in that type of work, and when they take it on or are consulted, it is likely to be the difficult case!

LAW SOCIETY OF SCOTLAND

It may seem to members that the Society is more concerned with **23–19** protecting the interests of the public than championing the interests of solicitors! The Society would probably accept this to a limited extent. This changed drastically as the Society had its overall "policing" power of complaints against practising lawyers face major changes as a result of the recently formed Scottish Legal Complaints Commission (SLCC) to handle service complaints against lawyers. According to the Society's website:

> "This announcement followed the Society's decision to call for an independent body for service complaints in order to increase confidence in the system. That decision was reached despite the many improvements made to the Society's own complaints system

---

[10] I. Talman, "Making a specialism pay" (2007) 52(2) J.L.S. 20.

since 2003. The Society's view is that many criticisms are based on perception rather than reality."

In a recent statement, Deputy Justice Minister Hugh Henry said the bill would provide:

> "Greater consumer choice, increase public confidence in the justice system . . . [and that] consumers [clients!] are right to expect high standards of service, and the time is now right for this culture change in our society to be extended into Scotland's legal system."

23–20 This Commission is to deal with all complaints against practising lawyers. Any complaints, which relate to professional misconduct, or a new category of unsatisfactory conduct, will still be referred to the Society or Faculty of Advocates to investigate. The Society retains its power to prosecute before the Scottish Solicitors Discipline Tribunal. If the complaint concerns inadequate professional services, the Commission will decide that it is eligible, that is to say, not frivolous or vexatious, and not premature in that no attempt has been made to resolve it at source. The Commission may offer mediation but both sides have to accept.

Needless to say the Commission will have much stronger financial powers than the Society. In addition to ordering a refund of fees, or action at the practitioner's own expense to remedy matters, it is to have power to order compensation of up to the staggering amount of £20,000. It is unlikely that there will be a right of appeal from the Commission.

It is also to have a supervisory role over the professional bodies' handling of conduct complaints, with power to award up to £5,000 in compensation for loss, inconvenience or distress, plus costs, to a complainer if an investigation has been badly handled.

23–21 All solicitors will pay a flat-rate annual levy, set by the Commission and collected by the Law Society, to fund its work (£275.00 for 2009). It does seem slightly bizarre that in addition a further levy will be made as a result of the number of complaints made. This could rise at an ever-increasing rate with greater and greater numbers of complaints made, whether or not the complaint is upheld. Somewhat unsportingly, complainers will not be expected to pay even if their complaint turns out to be frivolous. Indeed solicitors in practice are to pay a sum each year to underwrite the cost of this body.

The Society is to have power to censure, fine up to £2,000 and award compensation up to £5,000 for unsatisfactory professional conduct, defined as conduct beyond inadequate professional services but falling short of professional misconduct. A right of appeal will be provided to the Discipline Tribunal.

While the public should be protected it does seem that there is an element of a "sledgehammer to crack a nut" about the whole process given the tiny number of complaints as a proportion of the millions of pieces of work undertaken satisfactorily by solicitors every year.

INDEMNITY POLICY, AKA THE MASTER POLICY FOR PROFESSIONAL INDEMNITY INSURANCE

23–22 Taking a cynical view of matters there is little point in raising complaint or negligence actions against those "who do not have pockets deep enough to satisfy claims". The present legal aid system allows a legally-aided pursuer great advantages to raising proceedings against those who do not qualify for legal aid since in the event of their failure it is unlikely that any award of expenses will be made against them! Solicitors working in private practice have professional indemnity insurance cover for claims against them. The Master Policy is the compulsory professional indemnity insurance arrangement, which covers all Scottish solicitors working in private practice. The Society arranges the Master Policy for Professional Indemnity Insurance. Claims are handled by the Master Policy insurers. The limit of indemnity is £2 million for each and every claim. The self-insured amount (the excess) is £3,000 per partner with a 15-partner cap. Any excess may be doubled for matters such as the supposed riskiness of certain types of work, such as conflict of interest matters, non-standard undertakings, certain time-bar matters, inadequate professional service awards (on or after April 1, 2005) and where a settled claim arises from a conveyancing transaction carried out where the cause is because the practice charged the client a low fee. The problem is that this may encourage clients to make specious (and sometimes spurious) claims in the belief that there are deep pockets or that the solicitor himself may not be liable since it is not "him who is paying but the insurer"!

Effect of Foreign Attitude

Anecdotal evidence suggests that the influence of foreign practices **23–23** almost solely from North America initiating proceedings is contributing to an increasing number of claims in this country.

Duty of Care: What is it?

What Indeed?

As already mentioned, the basic problem for professional negligence is **23–24** to define what standards the law will require of a professional person and what standards provide protection for the consumer. It may be that the new Commission will provide answers to that question in the course of time.

The problem of the duty of care has bedevilled courts not only in Scotland but elsewhere and a full discussion of the scope is outwith the scope of this text.

Financial Services

The Financial Services Authority is the principal regulator for invest- **23–25** ment business in the UK. It came into operation on December 1, 2001 and its powers are set out in the Financial Services and Markets Act 2000.

This provides that no individual or firm may carry on a regulated activity unless that individual/firm is authorised by the FSA. From December 1, 2001 to October 31, 2004 the FSA's regulatory regime was confined to the conduct of investment business. However, with effect from October 31, 2004, the FSA's regulatory regime is extended to incorporate mortgage business and with effect from January 14, 2005, the regime is extended to include general insurance business.

Solicitors may carry out certain regulated activities and be exempt from the requirement to be authorised by the FSA if they are licensed by the Law Society regime, known as the "Incidental Financial Business (IFB) Regime". This allows solicitors to carry out certain activities, which would otherwise require FSA authorisation. It is paramount that these activities are integral to other business, e.g. trust administration, and must not under any circumstances be advertised as "stand-alone" activities.

23–26   If the correct authorisation is not held solicitors are vulnerable to a claim. It is important to realise that a breach could occur very easily. For example, if the solicitor passes on a copy of the stockbroker's letter recommending the sale of certain shares to pay off the loan taken out to pay IHT and an executor asks the solicitor what he thinks; if the solicitor were to voice an opinion he might well have contravened the terms of his firm's incidental business authorisation.

It may difficult in the future for bodies such as the FSA to have any credibility given the quite bewildering behaviour of (particularly) Scottish banks and others under their oversight. Cynics might take a jaundiced view of an entity which insists on seemingly minute regulation of small legal firms while allowing some larger financial institutions to so order their affairs that they record enormous losses.[11]

THIRD PARTIES

23–27   Until the decision in the case of *Holmes v Bank of Scotland*,[12] it was probably the law that a disappointed beneficiary had no claim for negligence against the solicitors who had caused them to lose their inheritance. In this case, relatives sought damages from a bank, for losses caused by the bank's failure to have the will executed. Lord Kingarth held that the principle in *White v Jones*,[13] a leading English case, would be followed in Scotland and that an intended beneficiary would be allowed a remedy; that the duty alleged was a matter for evidence, and prima facie the loss, which was reasonably foreseeable, was the loss of the legacies to be provided. This case may open the floodgates by disappointed beneficiaries.

INCREASE IN STANDARDS/EXPECTATIONS

23–28   All of the foregoing, it is suggested, may give rise to an increase in the expectations of clients and this may have a "knock-on" effect on claims.

AVOIDING CLAIMS—GENERAL

23–29   There is no special magic for avoiding claims. It almost goes without saying that keeping up to date with the law and practice is vital; reference to publications such as the *Journal of the Law Society of Scotland* and *Taxation Magazine* are relevant. There are a number of

---

[11] The Royal Bank are reported to be posting over 25 billion of losses in 2008!
[12] 2002, G.W.D. 8–269.
[13] [1995] 2 A.C. 207.

discussion "forums" such as the Trust Discussion Forum.[14] The Trusts Discussion Forum[15] is dedicated to discussion by practitioners of topics relating to the "drafting and administration of trusts, wills and other private client issues including taxation". The forum was founded by James Kessler, Q.C., TEP in 1998 and is now moderated by Richard Vallat, TEP and Sarah Dunn, TEP of Pump Court Tax Chambers. It is administered by STEP (The Society of Trust and Executry Practitioners) and is open to members and non-members. They have an extremely useful archive section.

The phenomenon of tax blogs, of which there are probably now many thousands, may be another source of keeping up to date; some should have a "health warning" as they can turn into vehicles for "rants" by disaffected taxpayers! There was a useful article in *Taxation Magazine* on October 19, 2006 on these: "The Online Soapbox" by Allison Plager.

Generally speaking, the methods of avoiding claims will fall into seven tried and tested groupings as follows:

1. Taking full particulars;
2. A letter of engagement;
3. Observing and including realistic time scales;
4. Use of checklists and styles;
5. Keeping in regular contact with the client;
6. Responding to and trying to resolve complaints;
7. Security of records; and
8. Reviewing the foregoing and the files.

1. Full Particulars

This of course includes a full client information sheet. Think of the **23–30** problems which could arise if the executor took instructions from an impostor. Of course, knowing your client is now a matter which is covered by Law Society regulation.

There is no substitute for taking full particulars at the outset of the executry. A checklist is appended for executries. The matters which are particularly relevant to executry tax, are shown in bold. Frequently, obtaining instructions is rushed. There are often good reasons for this, for example, obtaining information from beneficiaries who have only a limited amount of time, but this type of excuse will not save liability. It is as well to be as prepared as possible, looking out title deeds, copies of the will and cash records (as regards clients) and other papers which are available, and studying these in advance. In estates of any complexity, e.g. where it is likely inheritance tax will apply or where there is heritable property or another difficulty it would be as well to leave aside *a whole morning or afternoon* for this purpose. The notes should be extended as soon as possible and letters sent out at the same time as the letter of engagement or as soon as possible thereafter. This should be carried out before any letters are written to banks, building societies or others.

It seems obvious that file entries should be made for telephone and face-to-face instructions and that these are regularly maintained.

---

[14] Available at *http://www.trustsdiscussionforum.co.uk* [accessed April 29, 2009].
[15] Details of ow the forum works is shown in the Appendix.

The following may prove helpful. It was produced by the Law Society some years ago.

First meeting checklist—new clients

Have you clear instructions?	no			**Do not proceed**
Yes				
Do you have experience of the work?	no	refer to a more experienced solicitor		**Do not proceed**
Yes				
Do you have full names and addresses?	no	Can you obtain and verify?	No	**Do not proceed**
Yes		Yes		
Have you copy documents on file?	no	Agree deadline for production obtained		
Yes	Yes	obtained	no	**Do not proceed**
Terms of Business explained and accepted?	No	**Do not proceed**		Yes
Client finance—				
employment details?	no	self employed	other categories	no
				Do not proceed
yes		yes	yes	no
				Do not proceed
note fully—income streams Assets/ borrowings		note fully— income streams Assets/ borrowings	no	**Do not proceed**
Yes		Yes		
Note and clarify unusual aspects		of finance or business proposed	no	**Do not proceed**
Yes		Yes		
commence acting and		Issue Terms of business.		

2. Letter of Engagement

23–31

> "Getting terms of engagement right is one of the principal ways of avoiding client claims. During more difficult economic times, when clients may be more inclined to dispute fees and challenge the service provided, it is particularly important to ensure that clients are absolutely clear about the scope of the executor engagement for the particular transaction and the terms on which services are being provided."[16]

At the commencement of an instruction (and throughout), it is vital to be focused on what is and is not your responsibility. Where there are

---

[16] Alastair Sim, "The year that crunched" (2008) 53(12) J.L.S. 48.

other advisors involved this is crucial. Agreement on the scope of your responsibilities is extremely important and correspondingly making crystal clear that this is reflected in your terms of engagement letter.

It is vital to define what the practitioner's responsibilities are at the *outset and during*.

The letter of engagement, a style of which is shown in the Appendix, should also be sent out. It is important that extreme care should be given to this and that where, say, work is to be carried out by another professional, e.g. a chartered accountant in connection with tax, that this is expressly specified. Where another professional or professionals are involved, the risk of confusion arising about who is responsible for doing what increases exponentially!

If the practitioner is agreeable to accepting instructions by email he **23–32** should specify that, for example, emails are only checked say twice a day. In these days when there are considerable difficulties as regards financial services and otherwise it would be as well to spell out exactly what the firm's responsibility is under this heading also.

The Law Society, under The Solicitors (Scotland) (Client Communication) Practice Rules 2005, makes it compulsory for practically all types of business to issue a letter containing terms of engagement. It is vital to use the letter as a means of stipulating what the practitioner's obligations are to be. Many firms (regrettably) run these off from their word processing software package, merely having changed the names. This is a mistake at many levels. It ignores the practitioner's opportunity to protect himself against certain matters, e.g. if the inventory has been drafted on the basis that the practitioner has not seen original documents or if the deceased's previous year's tax return has not been forthcoming.

The other important aspect is that this is the actual *contract between the practitioner and the executor client*. It may be useful to have provision to take a payment to account before the end of the executry, say after confirmation has been obtained.

It is also advisable to have the client sign and return a copy of the letter as acceptance of the terms.

3. Timescales/Diaries

By far the most effective tool in preventing claims is an efficient and **23–33** regular diary service and bring/forward system. It does not really matter whether this is a handwritten diary or other commercial product or the most sophisticated online diary system, which the computer can produce, but it is essential that this is prepared. It is suggested that there is incorporated in the diary system all the relevant critical dates.

If all of these three steps are carried out and the position and the diary checked and progress made then it is likely that 95 per cent of possible claims will be avoided. There are many diary systems on the market of an electronic nature; one that is useful is the Time and Chaos one. However, Microsoft Outlook is equally good and there are other ones on the market, which can be secured for a modest outlay.

4. Use of Checklists and Styles

23–34 A checklist is printed in the Appendix. The list is by no means
exhaustive. Others can be found in other publications, such as *Ensuring
Excellence*.[17] An exhaustive list of styles for executries is outwith the
scope of this work but the practitioner should build up his own "bank"
of styles from Barr, Elder Diploma notes, CPD notes, *John Kerrigan's
Drafting for Succession*, etc.[18] It may be permissible to "steal" styles from
other practitioners. Some find it very flattering to see something "stolen"
from them.

It is important to mention to the client at the outset the question of
timescales. In an extremely helpful article, "Trust and competence",[19]
subtitled "Case studies and risk management points based on the
experience of claims under the Master Policy in the areas of trust and
executry work", the author, Alistair Sim, deals inter alia with some
aspects of executry work and states that:

> "While some claims arising out of trust and executry practice are
> down to getting the law wrong or other technical errors or omissions
> (application of inheritance tax rules to charitable bequests is one
> example), more arise as a consequence of communication failures,
> misunderstandings or administrative mistakes or oversights. In
> common with other areas of work, risk awareness, risk assessment
> and practical risk controls have a significant part to play in
> avoidance of claims. A review of the experience of trust and
> executry claims confirms that being clear about the scope of the
> work, communicating effectively with the client, identifying and
> managing critical timescales and addressing 'loose ends' at the
> conclusion of the work are all essential to minimising claims in this
> practice area. All of this is well illustrated by case studies based on
> the experience of claims."

One of the case studies quoted is extremely relevant to the question of
timescales:

> "Case study—'delay' in administration
> Allegations of delay are a regular feature of recent claims arising in
> relation to executry administration. Actual delays are capable of
> causing loss to the estate or to beneficiaries but there are instances
> where the allegation of delay is down to a genuine, but unjustified,
> perception of the executor or beneficiary rather than actual
> tardiness.

---

[17] A.J. Spencer, Professor A.D.M. Forte and A.J. Sim, *Ensuring Excellence, even better
practice in practice: A handbook on practical Risk Management for Solicitors in Scotland*
(Sedgwick, 1998).

[18] Certain styles may be culled from the author's text, *Scottish Drafts: A drafting guide*
(Edinburgh: W. Green, 2006) and from the *Scottish Trusts and Succession Service*
(Edinburgh: W. Green).

[19] Alistair Sim, "Trust and competence" (2008) 53(2) J.L.S. 36 (case studies and risk
management points based on the experience of claims under the Master Policy in the areas
of trust and executry work by Alistair Sim).

Swift & Co had acted for Mr Bigg for several years. An extremely demanding client, he produced regular work for the firm. When Mr Bigg's aunt died, the client partner promptly introduced one of his trust and executry colleagues, assuring Mr Bigg that his aunt's estate was in good hands.

The client partner was shocked when, months later, he received an email from Mr Bigg with a veritable tirade about the length of time it was taking to wind up his aunt's estate. The email concluded "If it takes the firm six months to wind up a simple estate, I have to question the firm's ability to handle my other business properly."

Risk management points
This scenario illustrates the importance of addressing clients' expectations and managing those expectations. The administration of even a "simple" and modest estate may well take longer than six months to complete and there are sound reasons why ordinarily the estate will not be (fully) distributed before the expiry of six months from the date of death. However, the beneficiary's expectations may be entirely different and client care, if not claims avoidance, justifies taking trouble to explain the minimum and potential timescales and the external, uncontrollable factors liable to make a difference to these timescales."

5. Keeping in Regular Contact with the Client

This may be the last thing the practitioner may want to do but the opportunity should not be lost to keep in regular contact with executors/beneficiaries. Do not let too long a period go past without some form of communication. The opportunity to speak will often alert the practitioner by "reading between the lines" to something worrying a client and to give the executor early warning of a client.   **23–35**

6. Responding to and Trying to Resolve Complaints.

As far as solicitors in Scotland are concerned a firm's designated client relations partner is an increasingly important role. The Law Society has been trying to liaise with the SLCC to ensure that the operational arrangements between the Society and the SLCC are reasonable to complainants and the solicitors against whom complaints are made. It is thought that there is likely to be many complaints, which will be regarded as premature. The SLCC can consider a service complaint from any party who appears to them to have been directly affected by inadequate professional services. The legislation which covers this is the Legal Profession and Legal Aid (Scotland) Act 2007. Section 4 states that where complaints are received by the Commission, it must not act on them until the solicitor has a reasonable opportunity to deal with the complaint. The SLCC does not have discretion; if it receives a complaint which alleges professional misconduct, unsatisfactory professional conduct or inadequate professional service then the solicitor named in the complaint must be given the opportunity of resolving that complaint. This applies whether or not the complainer is a client of the solicitor.   **23–36**

The process

23-37 The complainer is advised that the complaint is premature and to make it to the solicitor, who, by this time, will have been notified directly.

When receiving complaints, the solicitor must reply and investigate. The SLCC appreciates that a reply to a non-client may be brief because of the solicitor's duty of confidentiality.

Danger Warning!!

If the solicitor fails to deal with the complaint then it may lead to a further complaint, which, if made to the SLCC, is within its jurisdiction to investigate. It may even refer the complaint to the Society as a conduct complaint. Please note that the SLCC will notify only the solicitor named in the complaint that a premature complaint has been received, not the client relations partner of the firm.

This is a marked change from current practice; the regulations actually create a situation where the practitioner must consider and act on complaints from parties to whom they are giving no service. Taking a positive stance, the SLCC considers this as an opportunity for what it describes as "self-regulation and improvement".

7. Security of Records

23-38 At a time when well-publicised HM Revenue & Customs records are being "lost" it is worthwhile pausing to consider that all electronic records are "backed up" and that these backup records are kept securely, preferably in another premises. If the data is not backed up then it should be! Consider how valuable these records are, i.e. the chargeable hours which have been expended in compiling the original data. Unfortunately it seems that these backup tapes are often left on reception desks in public areas, in cars or worse still are never taken off-site at all. *Backup tapes and CDs need to be taken off-site, handled securely and carefully all the way.* They may be needed! Please remember also that laptop theft is rife. If possible the information should be encrypted and backed up.

8. Reviewing the Foregoing and the Files

23-39 While the executor's inclination may be to throw the files out the window there is no substitute for reading the file and especially the notes of the original interviews and checking that all matters raised have been addressed. It might be worth taking a copy of this and keeping it beside the file as the practitioner reads through it.

A Happy New Fiscal Year!

23-40 At the risk of being considered fanciful, would it not be a good idea for all those involved in tax matters (including taxpayers themselves) to make some resolutions? For example, reviewing their accounting and record-keeping arrangements. The reason many resolutions fail is because of lack of incentive. However if incentive is lacking, on April 1, 2009 the new penalty regime will come into force!

It is always stated that prevention is better than cure. There is no shame in not giving the forces of confusion even a sporting chance to upset matters! It may be possible to avoid incurring penalties by reviewing record-keeping systems now and making any relevant improvements.

Attention!!

If an inaccuracy in any tax return is discovered, disclose it to HMRC as soon as possible; this might be the only way to avoid or reduce a penalty.

Avoiding Claims—Particular

In a sense, this whole text is a manual for avoiding claims! However, it is **23–41** important to take a firm grip on tax matters at the earliest opportunity. The first priority is to frame the tax return to date of death. To accomplish this it is necessary to begin the gathering of information process as soon as possible. If the practitioner does not have the skill to "crack the tax code", it is well worth acquiring this as it may enable the practitioner to form a quick view as to whether or not there is likely to be a repayment, perhaps going back several years. The actual processing of the repayment claim should be addressed and it should be determined what form the return is to take and the appropriate time limits.

During the executry, i.e. the administration period, the practitioner must always be on the lookout for untaxed income, knowing the beneficiary's circumstances, with a view to timing payments and identifying if inheritance tax has been paid on accrued Income.[20]

Certification of income if appropriate must be made to the beneficiary as soon as possible after April 5.

When considering realising shares or other assets which may generate **23–42** a capital gain the practitioner should first consider if there is a charity involved in the residue and, if there is a loss, to remember to advise on the time limits for loss relief.

During and AFTER THE ADMINISTRATION PERIOD, the practitioner should be considering the advisability of a deed of variation in general but in particular to ascertain if it can be utilised for inheritance tax and/or capital gains tax saving. The possibility of setting up a trust by way of variation should be fully canvassed with executors and beneficiaries and/or their agents.

An extremely relevant case where the duties of the executor were discussed is *Robertson v Inland Revenue Commissioners (No.2)*.[21] It may be that this matter should be considered under the inheritance tax section of the text but is dealt with here since it impacts on the duties of an executor who was also the solicitor dealing with winding up the estate. It is also a salutary lesson in why professionals should not act as executors. The Revenue (as HM Revenue & Customs were then known)

---

[20] Income and Corporation Taxes Act 1988 s.699.
[21] *Robertson v Inland Revenue Commissioners* [2002] S.T.C. (S.C.D.) 182; [2002] W.T.L.R. 885; [2002] S.T.I. 766.

initiated proceedings before the special commissioners alleging negligence by an executor of a will, Mr Robertson, a solicitor in practice in Scotland. They alleged that in delivering the inventory of the deceased's estate by entering estimated values of a deceased, who died in 1999, he had grossly undervalued these. It seems that Mr Robertson was concerned (rightly) that the Scottish property should be sold as soon as possible to avoid the inevitable deterioration and also while the market was slow. For obvious reasons, not least of which was that there was no title, Mr Robertson did not advertise executry properties for sale until confirmation of the executors' title had been applied for. Perfectly properly, he lodged an inventory with estimated values for both properties with a view to obtaining confirmation (and title to act) as soon as possible. When accurate valuations were subsequently obtained, an additional sum of inheritance tax was found to be due. The Capital Taxes Office advised Mr Robertson that in their opinion the obligations under the Inheritance Tax Act 1984 s.216(3) had not been satisfied, i.e. to make the fullest enquiries reasonably practicable in the circumstances to ascertain values for the properties.

23–43   The present form of the relevant part of s.216[22] of the IHTA 1984 is as follows:

> (3A) If the personal representatives, after making the fullest enquiries that are reasonably practicable in the circumstances, are unable to ascertain the exact value of any particular property, their account shall in the first instance be sufficient as regards that property if it contains—
>
> (a) a statement to that effect;
> (b) a provisional estimate of the value of the property; and
>   (c) an undertaking to deliver a further account of it as soon as its value is ascertained.

A penalty of £9,000 was to be imposed under s.247. Mr Robertson was absolutely outraged; he considered that the penalty was excessive and understandably refused to accept this penalty. It was held:

> "Declaring that R [Mr Robertson] was not liable to any penalty, that R had made the fullest enquiries that were reasonably practicable in the circumstances and was therefore not liable to penalties. It had been prudent to lodge the inventory so that the Scottish house could be sold as soon as possible; to have obtained professional valuations in the circumstances would have caused considerable delay. R had acted in accordance with accepted practice and the Revenue had failed to show what a prudent executor would have done in the circumstances."

It is difficult to understand why the Revenue took the case to the Special Commissioners, but it may have been because of ignorance of Scottish

---

[22] It was slightly different in 1999.

Commissary Practice. The sequel to this was that Mr Robertson sought his expenses, which by this time were considerable! The Revenue claimed that the Special Commissioners were entitled to award expenses only in circumstances where they considered that the claim had been brought unreasonably.[23] However, the Special Commissioners found in favour of Mr Robertson. He was entitled to the expenses of and incidental to the hearing!

> "The proceedings ought not to have been brought against R. Further, on the facts there was no rational basis on which the proceedings ought to have been brought. The Revenue's evidence had not addressed the question of 'negligence' in the presentation of the return. Had it done so, the Revenue ought to have realised that the claim was without foundation."

DIVISION OF RESIDUE BETWEEN EXEMPT AND NON-EXEMPT

In the context of exempt and non-exempt beneficiaries the practitioner **23–44** should "take a step backward" to see if he has correctly dealt with the division of the estate and the allocation of inheritance tax on the different shares.

Discharge

Although strictly not necessary there may be some merit, particularly **23–45** where there has been a history of difficulty with a client or the beneficiaries, to have a discharge prepared and signed. If there is to be difficulty it is as well to have it aired before funds are distributed.

Something along the following lines may be appropriate:

I, MRS. GLADYS ELIZABETH RAGWEED, residing at Calle Wingstem, Alicante, Spain, being entitled to a one-third share of the residue of the executry estate of the late DAVID WILLOW HERB who resided at One hundred and twenty nine Wister Row Road, Glasgow and who died at Hope on the First January Two thousand and six, hereby acknowledge to have received from WINTER & CRESS, Solicitors, Glasgow the sum of ONE HUNDRED and FIVE THOUSAND SEVEN HUNDRED AND NINETY POUNDS SEVENTY EIGHT PENCE which sum, with interest accrued to date of close, and that in full settlement thereof being the balance due to me, in terms of the Account of Charge and Discharge which has been exhibited to me, the terms of which I approve; therefore I hereby approve of the said Account of Charge and Discharge and of the actings of and I Herby Discharge ELLIOT WILLOW HERB residing at of One hundred and twenty nine Wister Road aforesaid, and GORDON HIGHLANDER residing at Aster Cottage, Near Jedburgh, Roxburghshire, as Executors of the late David Willow Herb and Messrs. Winter & Cress aforesaid being the law agents employed by them of their intromissions with the executry Estate; And I declare that I am satisfied with everything they

---

[23] Under the Special Commissioners (Jurisdiction and Procedure) Regulations 1994 reg.21.

have done. And I all agree that these presents shall be binding and effectual IN WITNESS WHEREOF

Mitigation

23–46 The opportunity to mitigate any claim should not be missed; if the practitioner can keep his head or seek quick advice from another practitioner, e.g. if the practitioner misses the date to claim loss relief for sale of shares, which have shown a catastrophic loss after death the practitioner, he can be advised to vary the will to include this as a legacy to a charity. There will be some cost but at least the inheritance tax can be reclaimed!

The psychology of the final

23–47 Often when we think repeatedly about concluding a particular task, usually a long drawn out matter, our subconscious mind will "tick it off" as actually having been done. This is known as the "the psychology of the final". Obviously this can be disastrous in connection with legal work.

When this concept is mentioned to those unfamiliar with it their reactions border on disbelief. However, if we pause to reflect on some task of the above kind how often will we think to ourselves: "I thought I had done that!"

The end of the executry is an extremely difficult part. Sometimes the practitioner will become like a "Watership Down" rabbit standing in the centre white line of a busy road. Disaster will occur with any movement sideways. Our instinct for self-preservation compels us to stand still. While this may often be good practice it is difficult with executors and beneficiaries breathing down the practitioner's neck. With executries this often means that the file is put back in the cabinet, while more pressing matters are dealt with. In a busy practice there is always pressing work to do.

23–48 A former partner of the author's said the reason he particularly liked new work was that it gave him a good excuse for not dealing with "old stuff".

The important thing is to structure the final procedure—that time between sending out the account of charge and discharge and paying out beneficiaries when there is A LAST CHANCE TO CORRECT OR PUT MATTERS RIGHT. It is important to read and review the files and checklists against the particulars.

If this and all the other matters are faithfully done them the practitioner can cut down drastically the chances of the forces of confusion having even a minimal chance of coming back to haunt him.

Contributory Negligence

23–49 The possibility of the client having caused the loss in whole or in part should not be overlooked. This is unlikely but a more hopeful line may be to see if another professional could be involved, e.g. a surveyor or accountant.

Attention!!

ONE-YEAR TIME BAR FOR COMPLAINTS AGAINST SOLICITORS

The time limit for members of the public who have a complaint against their solicitor is to be halved from two years to one.

The changes, introduced as part of the Legal Profession and Legal Aid (Scotland) Act 2007, follow the concerns of consumer groups about the self-regulation of the profession.

The reduced time limit is to improve the transition of complaints from the Law Society of Scotland to the new Scottish Legal Complaints Commission, which opens on October 1, 2008.

Chapter Twenty Four

FUTURE TRENDS

"Please proceed more carefully . . . take your time, take your time."[1]

24–01   There is a constant stream of tax legislation. The tax rewrite programme will gather impetus. The problem is that it will create its own internal momentum for change and we may well have separate sets of changes, one for that tax legislation which is covered by the tax rewrite project and one for that which is not.

It is difficult not to take a somewhat jaundiced view of the future of tax change. If anything it places more responsibility on professionals to assimilate changes and be in a position to explain them clearly and concisely to clients, who are understandably bemused not to say befuddled by the rate of change, not to say the changes themselves.

There may be pressure from the Scottish Executive for tax raising powers. It is unlikely that the main political parties will readily accede if at all to this demand.

Changes in the law of succession are likely. As outlined in Chapter Two, the law of intestate succession in Scotland lays out the rules for the distribution of assets from a person who dies intestate. The most recent statute, namely the Succession (Scotland) Act 1964, is regarded by many as outdated and not in touch with family relationships today, even though it has been amended substantially. The Scottish Law Commission has been actively involved in reviewing the area for 20 years. It is likely that there will be significant changes proposed to the rules relating to intestate succession.

Under the current rules, where a person dies intestate and is survived by a spouse or civil partner, that spouse or civil partner is entitled to rights to the matrimonial home together with its contents and a cash sum, variable depending on whether or not there are any children involved. The surviving spouse and any children take their "legal rights", which can extend between one-half and two-thirds of the deceased's moveable estate. As previously stated, the remaining one-half or two-thirds of the moveable and any remaining heritable property (other than the value of the house taken as "prior rights") is then divided amongst near relatives in a defined order of priority; i.e. children, grandchildren, or if there are none, parents and siblings, who effectively take preference over the widow due to their blood ties with the deceased. It seems that many people and experts consider this to be out of gear with current public thinking, highlighting the social changes which have occurred over the last 40 years.

---

[1] *Gently, Johnny*, Popular Song, Toomey Wise/Weisman.

The Scottish Law Commission are of the view that the law should be **24–02** reformed here, so that in cases where there are no children, *the surviving spouse should inherit the whole of the estate*. Where there are children, it is proposed that the surviving spouse be entitled to a fixed, index-linked sum together with one-half of the residue; the other half being shared amongst the children.

The Scottish Law Commission's proposals are still far from being enshrined in law and its proposed amendments to intestate succession will not meet every individual's wishes for the distribution of their estate on death. This uncertainty as to the law, the Commissions final recommendations and, more importantly, what the Government will choose to legislate thereon surely underlines the need for people to make wills.

The other matter, if nothing else, which will make it essential to make a will occurs in the case of a person dying who is in a "cohabiting" relationship. The uncertainty of the position and the profligate cost involved in actions under ss.28 and 29 of the Family Law (Scotland) Act 2006 emphasises this. This has already been mentioned in Chapter Two but it is something which will run. The statutory provisions are reproduced below:

Financial provision where cohabitation ends otherwise than by death

28.—(1)Subsection (2) applies where cohabitants cease to cohabit otherwise than by reason of the death of one (or both) of them.

    (2) On the application of a cohabitant (the "applicant"), the appropriate court may, after having regard to the matters mentioned in subsection (3)—

        (a) make an order requiring the other cohabitant (the "defender") to pay a capital sum of an amount specified in the order to the applicant;

        (b) make an order requiring the defender to pay such amount as may be specified in the order in respect of any economic burden of caring, after the end of the cohabitation, for a child of whom the cohabitants are the parents;

        (c) make such interim order as it thinks fit.

    (3) Those matters are—

        (a) whether (and, if so, to what extent) the defender has derived economic advantage from contributions made by the applicant; and

        (b) whether (and, if so, to what extent) the applicant has suffered economic disadvantage in the interests of—

            (i) the defender; or

            (ii) any relevant child.

    (4) In considering whether to make an order under subsection (2)(a), the appropriate court shall have regard to the matters mentioned in subsections (5) and (6).

    (5) The first matter is the extent to which any economic advantage derived by the defender from contributions made by the applicant is offset by any economic disadvantage suffered by the defender in the interests of—

(a) the applicant; or
(b) any relevant child.

(6) The second matter is the extent to which any economic disadvantage suffered by the applicant in the interests of—

(a) the defender; or
(b) any relevant child,

is offset by any economic advantage the applicant has derived from contributions made by the defender.

(7) In making an order under paragraph (a) or (b) of subsection (2), the appropriate court may specify that the amount shall be payable—

(a) on such date as may be specified;
(b) in instalments.

(8) Any application under this section shall be made not later than one year after the day on which the cohabitants cease to cohabit.

(9) In this section—
"appropriate court" means—

(a) where the cohabitants are a man and a woman, the court which would have jurisdiction to hear an action of divorce in relation to them if they were married to each other;
(b) where the cohabitants are of the same sex, the court which would have jurisdiction to hear an action for the dissolution of the civil partnership if they were civil partners of each other;

"child" means a person under 16 years of age;
"contributions" includes indirect and non-financial contributions (and, in particular, any such contribution made by looking after any relevant child or any house in which they cohabited); and
"economic advantage" includes gains in—

(a) capital;
(b) income; and
(c) earning capacity;

and "economic disadvantage" shall be construed accordingly.

(10) For the purposes of this section, a child is "relevant" if the child is—

(a) a child of whom the cohabitants are the parents;
(b) a child who is or was accepted by the cohabitants as a child of the family.

Application to court by survivor for provision on intestacy

29.—(1)This section applies where—

(a) a cohabitant (the "deceased") dies intestate; and
(b) immediately before the death the deceased was—

(i) domiciled in Scotland; and

(ii) cohabiting with another cohabitant (the "survivor").

(2) Subject to subsection (4), on the application of the survivor, the court may—

    (a) after having regard to the matters mentioned in subsection (3), make an order—

        (i) for payment to the survivor out of the deceased's net intestate estate of a capital sum of such amount as may be specified in the order;

        (ii) for transfer to the survivor of such property (whether heritable or moveable) from that estate as may be so specified;

    (b) make such interim order as it thinks fit.

(3) Those matters are—

    (a) the size and nature of the deceased's net intestate estate;

    (b) any benefit received, or to be received, by the survivor—

        (i) on, or in consequence of, the deceased's death; and

        (ii) from somewhere other than the deceased's net intestate estate;

    (c) the nature and extent of any other rights against, or claims on, the deceased's net intestate estate; and

    (d) any other matter the court considers appropriate.

(4) An order or interim order under subsection (2) shall not have the effect of awarding to the survivor an amount which would exceed the amount to which the survivor would have been entitled had the survivor been the spouse or civil partner of the deceased.

(5) An application under this section may be made to—

    (a) the Court of Session;

    (b) a sheriff in the sheriffdom in which the deceased was habitually resident at the date of death;

    (c) if at the date of death it is uncertain in which sheriffdom the deceased was habitually resident, the sheriff at Edinburgh.

(6) Any application under this section shall be made before the expiry of the period of 6 months beginning with the day on which the deceased died.

(7) In making an order under paragraph (a)(i) of subsection (2), the court may specify that the capital sum shall be payable—

    (a) on such date as may be specified;

    (b) in instalments.

(8) In making an order under paragraph (a)(ii) of subsection (2), the court may specify that the transfer shall be effective on such date as may be specified.

(9) If the court makes an order in accordance with subsection (7), it may, on an application by any party having an interest, vary the date or method of payment of the capital sum.

(10) In this section—

"intestate" shall be construed in accordance with section 36(1) of the Succession (Scotland) Act 1964 (c.41);

"legal rights" has the meaning given by section 36(1) of the Succession (Scotland) Act 1964 (c.41);

"net intestate estate" means so much of the intestate estate as remains after provision for the satisfaction of—

(a) inheritance tax;

(b) other liabilities of the estate having priority over legal rights and the prior rights of a surviving spouse or surviving civil partner; and

(c) the legal rights, and the prior rights, of any surviving spouse or surviving civil partner; and

"prior rights" has the meaning given by section 36(1) of the Succession (Scotland) Act 1964 (c.41).

24–03   There are understood to be a number of issues about to be raised but few have actually been raised. No decisions of any real guidance have been reported but the case of *Chebotareva v Khandro*[2] turned on the question of domicile.

The case of *Savage v Purches*,[3] heard on December 19, 2008 before Sheriff Arthurson at Falkirk Sheriff Court, is the first reported case to deal with the substantive issues. It is noteworthy for several reasons but primarily because it arose out of a "same sex" relationship. The Sheriff found that the pursuer had co-habited for a continuous period from October 4, 2004 until April 28, 2007 with the deceased who died intestate and without issue. The deceased's only relative was a sister of the half blood, namely the defender. He was unmarried, had never been married, and had not entered any civil partnership with any person.

The case was also interesting because the pursuer received the sum of £124,840, being a half-share of the lump sum death benefit payable from the deceased's BT pension scheme at the discretion of the trustees of the said scheme. The pursuer also received an adult dependant's pension from the BT pension scheme of £9,530.40, index linked. The pension did not form part of the deceased's estate, being payable at the sole discretion of the trustees of the BT pension scheme. This was valued at £298,900. The defender was the sole beneficiary of the deceased's net intestate estate in terms of the Succession (Scotland) Act 1964. Apart from the s.28 claim, she would be entitled to the whole of the deceased's net intestate estate.

24–04   The Sheriff dealt with the situation where if in terms of ss.8 and 9 of the Succession (Scotland) Act 1964, the parties had been civil partners. Then, the pursuer would have been entitled to the whole value of the deceased's net intestate estate by the exercise of: (a) prior rights in terms of s.8 to the dwellinghouse in which they lived and to the furniture therein to a maximum value of £324,000 including any secured lending;

---

[2] *Chebotareva v Khandro*, 2008 Fam. L.R. 66; 2008 G.W.D. 12–231.

[3] *Savage v Purches*, 2009 G.W.D. 9–157.

here the equity of the dwellinghouse and the furniture; and (b) prior rights in terms of s.9 in the deceased's remaining net intestate estate to financial provision on intestacy to a maximum of £75,000, would have covered the residue. Apparently, a future civil partnership was never discussed between them.

> "The issue of life insurance policy or cover was never discussed between them. The issue of future wills was never discussed between them. The Pursuer elected to change his career path in the course of the relationship by moving into his current self-employment, was supported therein, and was accordingly fully dependant on the deceased for a period of at least a year. It took about a year to 18 months before the Pursuer could take a salary from his new self-employment as he sought to build the business up. The deceased had a loving relationship with the Pursuer, which lasted approximately 2 years 8 months. The deceased also had a loving and life long relationship with his half sister. They had a very troubled childhood and lived together with their mother for the first 11 years of the deceased's life ... The Defender personally scattered the deceased's ashes on a beach subsequent to his funeral."

The Sheriff observed that the deceased had a previous 15–year long cohabiting relationship. The deceased had named his former partner as a beneficiary in a prior will, which he destroyed. The pursuer and the deceased at no stage discussed their testamentary intentions. However, the deceased had completed an "Expression of Wish" form in respect of the BT pension scheme in favour of his previous cohabitant but did not do this for the pursuer.

The Sheriff accordingly found that the pursuer and the deceased, being co-habitants in terms of s.25 of the Family Law (Scotland) 2006, the deceased having died intestate and immediately before death having been domiciled in Scotland and co-habiting with another co-habitant (the pursuer), the pursuer was entitled to a right in relation to succession on the estate of the deceased in terms of the said Act, but that having regard to the provisions of s.29(2)(3)(4) and (10), the quantum of the said claim is assessed at nil. It seems that the Sheriff was unimpressed with the pursuer and the time and quality of the relationship. He laid stress on the generosity of the deceased and the closeness of the deceased with his half sister.

This case will be of considerable guidance to those involved in executry tax practice and should be studied closely.

WHAT WILL CONSERVATIVES DO?

Their proposal to be funded according to the Shadow Chancellor Mr **24–05** George Osborne, who has pledged to fund the IHT move through a £25,000 levy on "non-domiciled" wealthy individuals, is for £2 million as the limit for married couples to leave to their relatives, which is more than three times the current threshold for the unpopular duty. This is also double the £1 million the party famously pledged last year, which undermined Gordon Brown's plans for a "snap" general election.

The threshold would be made up to £2 million because the Conservatives would allow couples to transfer a spouse's £1 million allowance on their death to the surviving partner. It is understood that around 9 million families would escape paying inheritance tax if this proposal were enacted.[4] As regards income tax, Mr Cameron has recently stated that he wants to abolish income tax on all savings for those paying basic rate tax while at the same time raising the tax allowance for pensioners by £2,000. This move mirrors the success of the proposal to increase the inheritance tax threshold to £1 million announced in September 2007, which arguably helped spoil Gordon Brown's early election plans. In effect, every savings account would become an unlimited ISA for basic rate taxpayers.

LEGAL SERVICES

24–06 The Scottish Government is actively considering the whole question of provision of legal services and the Law Society and others are in communication with it.

It was mentioned in the Preface that there was an application by Chartered Accountants in Scotland to carry out "probate" work in England and Wales. The position in Scotland is slightly different. It is possible for non-solicitors or advocates to have rights of audience under the Law Reform Miscellaneous Provisions (Scotland) Act 1990. However, application requires to be made to the Lord President. It is understood that an application has been or will be made to the Lord President by the Institute of Chartered Accountants in Scotland. They require to satisfy the Lord President that they have a scheme for dealing with matters such as training, complaints and so forth. If they are able to satisfy the Lord President and the Scottish Government then it may well be that they will be given authority to carry out inter alia "probate work" in Scotland.

As stated it may be that they will not be granted full rights of audience but it may be that the Scottish Government will consider granting rights to carry out certain aspects of "legal work" such as the grant of confirmation and so forth under the ambit of the umbrella of the whole position regarding legal services. While accountants may not receive the full right of audience they and other professions may be allowed to carry out confirmation work in Scotland.

SCOTTISH PARLIAMENT

Taxation Powers

24–07 The Scottish Parliament's main source of finance is the block grant[5] from the Treasury which is calculated under the "Barnet Formula".[6] This covers funding for Scotland, such as health and education. Because of the "Barnet Formula", Scotland apparently receives a proportionally

---

[4] HMRC website.

[5] Currently, the Scottish Parliament is funded via a block grant of £30 billion.

[6] Named after the Treasury Minister who devised it in 1979.

greater share of the money available than the share received by the regions of England.

The Scotland Act 1998, which drew up the conditions of devolution, granted the Scottish Government some tax raising powers. This would allow the Government to vary income tax by plus or minus three pence in the pound. If there were to be an increase in income tax in Scotland this would give the Government much more money with which to finance its spending. It would discourage "immigration" probably out of all proportion to its size and needless to say would be incredibly unpopular with some of the electorate. A reduction in income tax on the other hand would be another story.

Currently, the Scottish Parliament is funded via a block grant of £30 billion. An expert group, led by leading economist Professor Anton Muscatelli, argues strongly that Holyrood must be made more accountable by having greater powers to raise taxes.

The First Minister Alex Salmond has called for greater tax-raising powers for the Scottish Parliament.

However, the Commission on Scottish Devolution ("the Calman Commission") has published its interim report entitled: *The Future of Scottish Devolution within the Union: A First Report*, December 2008.

The remit of the Commission was: **24–08**

"To review the provisions of the Scotland Act 1998 in the light of experience and to recommend any changes to the present constitutional arrangements that would enable the Scottish Parliament to serve the people of Scotland better, improve the financial accountability of the Scottish Parliament."

The Commission in its interim report of December 2008 states:

"We believe that the present funding arrangements have undoubtedly got the Scottish Parliament off to a good start. But as the Independent Expert Group notes, those arrangements have strengths and weaknesses, especially in relation to accountability.

But any system of funding involves trade-offs between equity, efficiency and accountability. We agree with the Independent Expert Group that these can conflict, and that choosing among them requires us to have a view on the sort of Union we are looking for. The balance between conflicting principles should be determined not by technical considerations, but by the constitutional objectives that the funding system is designed to support.

18. The Commission recognises that there are three generic mechanisms that may be used to fund the Scottish Parliament—the assignment of tax revenues, the devolution of taxes and block grant from the UK Government. The mix of funding mechanisms to be used will be determined by the balance between the conflicting principles, and so, ultimately by the sort of Union, which Scotland forms with the rest of the UK.

19. We have given preliminary consideration to how the individual funding mechanisms might be used in Scotland, and to the question of borrowing powers for the Scottish Parliament. We regard the maintenance of an economic Union in the UK as in the

interests of Scotland, we have looked at the effect of each of them on the free flow of trade inside this integrated single market. This has led us to seek further views and evidence, for example in relation to some aspects of tax devolution.

20. So our consideration of finance follows from our discussion of the nature of the Union. As well as being an economic Union, the UK has a shared social citizenship. Greater tax devolution would be associated with less shared social citizenship, while high dependence on grant funding implies some common expectations about the need for welfare services like health and education. We have not reached a view on the appropriate point in what is a spectrum of possibilities, but we do recognise that this must reflect the expectations of the Scottish population. In the next phase of our work, with further help from the Independent Expert Group, we will identify the possible combinations of the funding mechanisms and their implications for the nature of the Union.

21. We have come to no conclusions on these issues and are seeking further representations and evidence."

It does not appear that there is likely to be any change within the foreseeable future.

PROFESSIONAL CONDUCT

24–09 The setting up of The Scottish Forum for Professional Ethics, a voluntary association of professional bodies and interested individuals in Scotland whose aim is to sustain inter-professional dialogue and exchange on the ethical basis and dilemmas of professional life, may provide an opportunity for "refocusing" on questions of professional conduct. This non-party political organisation intends over the three-year period to work with the Centre for Ethics and Legal Philosophy at the University of Glasgow, where the administrative base of the Forum is located. According to their website:

"The activities of the Forum are currently overseen by a Planning Group, which has been in existence for almost a year. It made a successful bid for funding from a charitable organisation that does not seek publicity. It has also attracted financial support from three leading professional bodies in Scotland, the General Medical Council, the Law Society of Scotland, and the Institute of Chartered Accountants of Scotland. These funds will enable us to establish the Forum and to arrange a series of seminars and conferences on inter-professional themes, which we hope, will be of wide interest amongst the professional communities in Scotland."

AND FINALLY

24–10 It is important to finalise all matters up to the date of death. The deceased's responsible officer should always do this.

BIBLIOGRAPHY

Adler, M. *Clarity for Lawyers—The Use of Plain English in Legal Writing* (The Law Society, 1990)

Barlow, J.S. et al. *Wills, Administration and Taxation Law and Practice*, 9th edn (Thomson Sweet & Maxwell, 2008)

Barr, A.R., Biggar, J.M.H., Dalgleish, A.M.C. and Stevens, H.J. *Drafting Wills in Scotland* (Butterworths Ltd, 2009)

Currie, James G. *The Confirmation of Executors in Scotland*, (W. Green, 1965)

Cusine, Professor D. J. *Greens Practice Styles* (W. Green)

Doonan, E. *Drafting* (Cavendish Publishing Ltd, 1995)

Galbraith, H. Reynold. *Scottish Trusts and Succession Service* (W. Green)

Gowers, Sir E. *The Complete Plain Words* (Her Majesty's Stationery Office, 1986)

Henderson, C. *Candlish Henderson on Vesting* (W. Green, 1938)

Hiram, Hilary. *The Scots Law of Succession* (Butterworths, 2002)

HM Revenue & Customs. *Self Assessment Tax Returns Guide* (April 6, 2008 to April 5, 2009)

Jones, M. and Mackintosh S. *Revenue Law in Scotland* (Butterworths Ltd, 1986)

Kerrigan, J. *Drafting for Succession* (Thomson W. Green, 2004)

Laidlow, P. *Tolley's Tax Planning for Post-Death Variations* (Tolley, 1993)

The Law Society of Scotland. *Procedures and Decisions of the Scottish Solicitors' Discipline Tribunal* (The Law Society of Scotland, 1995)

Macdonald, D.R. *Succession*, 3rd edn (W. Green, 2001)

Meston, Professor M.C. *The Succession (Scotland) Act 1964* (W. Green, 1993)

Morley, M.F. *Accounting for Scottish Executries and Trusts* (Law Society of Scotland, 1984)

Philips, A. *Professional Ethics for Scottish Solicitors* (Butterworths Ltd, 1990)

Reid, K.G.C. and Gretton, G.L. *Conveyancing* (Avizandum Publishing Ltd, 2006)

Rennie, Professor R. *Solicitors Negligence* (Butterworths, 1997)

Scobbie, Eilidh M. (ed.). *Currie on Confirmation of Executors*, 8th edn (W. Green, 1995)

Scott, C.A. *Trust Accountancy* (Oliver and Boyd, 1950)

Sedgwick Ltd. *Ensuring Excellence: even better in practice; a handbook on practical risk management for solicitors in Scotland* (Sedgwick Ltd for the Law Society of Scotland, 1998)

Tax Faculty of the Institute of Chartered Accountants in England and Wales. *Tax Guide 6/08 Engagement Letters for Tax Practitioners* (Tax Faculty, August 2008)

Thomson, Prof. J. *Family Law Reform* (W. Green, 2006)

Thurston, J. *Estate Planning for the Middle Income Client* (Tottel, 2005)

Wilson, W.A. and Duncan, A.G.M. *Trusts, Trustees and Executors* (W. Green, 1995)

Law Society of England and Wales Publications

- *Solicitors' Code of Conduct 2007*, 1st edn
- *Companion to the Solicitors' Code of Conduct*
- Hopper, Andrew, Q.C. and Treverton-Jones, Gregory, Q.C. *The Solicitor's Handbook 2008*

USEFUL WEBSITES

http://www.absolvitor.co.uk
http://www.adviceguide.org.uk/index/life/tax/tax-
exempt_and_taxable_income.htm
http://www.baili.org
http://www.darhsolicitors.co.uk
http://www.fergusonsca.co.uk
http://www.hmrc.gov.uk
http://www.hmrc.gov.uk/CTO/customerguide/page1.htm
http://www.hmrc.gov.uk/poa
http://www.hmrc.gov.uk/trusts/
http://www.journalonline.co.uk
http://www.lawscot.org.uk
http://www.mencap.org.uk
http://www.nsandi.com
http://www.opsi.gov.uk/http://www.plainenglishcampaign.com
http://www.scotcourts.gov.uk
http://www.taxresearch.org.uk/Blog
http://www.taxuk.co.uk

Useful Email Addresses

marymcgowan@lawscot.org.uk
phillipyelland@lawscot.org.uk

SDLT CONTACT DETAILS

To contact the Stamp Taxes Helpline telephone 0845 603 0135
Open 8.30am–5.00pm Monday to Friday (12.00pm–2.00pm is a quieter period, therefore the practitioner may wish to telephone during this time.)
(For enquires relating to a specific SDLT1 the executor must have the Unique Reference Number (UTRN) available.)

Stamp Taxes (posting payments, returns and writing)
Stamp Duty Land Tax (SDLT) Transaction Return submissions including payments.
HMRC Stamp Taxes, Comben House, Farriers Way, Netherton L30 4RN
or

DX: Rapid Data Capture Centre
DX 725593 Bootle 9

General correspondence and Stamp Duty:
Birmingham Stamp Office, 9th Floor City Centre House, 30 Union Street, Birmingham B2 4AR
DX: 15001 Birmingham 1

SDRT Fax: 0121 633 3921

Scottish Solicitors only may send Scottish transactions/documents to Edinburgh Stamp Office, Grayfield House Spur X, 4 Bankhead Avenue, Edinburgh EH11 4BF

DX: ED 543303 Edinburgh 33
Tel 0131 442 3191
Fax 0131 442 3038

Legal Post from Scottish Solicitors only
Stamp Taxes/SDLT
LP18
Edinburgh 2

APPENDICES

Appendix 1

THE TWO PICASSO CARTOONS

A Cautionary Tale[1]

Setting: The present.

Patrick Bateman, a young wealthy merchant banker, died unmarried and without issue on January 1, 2007. There are therefore three tax years to contend with:

- From January 1, 2007 to April 5, 2007
- From April 6, 2007 to April 5, 2008
- From April 6, 2008 to April 5, 2009

In his Will he left the residue of his estate, which includes two small authenticated signed Picasso cartoons, the Inventory value of which is and has been agreed with HMRC at £100,000 each, equally to his fiancée, Evelyn Williams (aged 50) and a former friend, Courtney Rawlins, who is 70 years of age. Miss Williams is a recently discharged bankrupt. Although she calls herself "Miss Williams", she was married and widowed many years ago. Her impecunious spouse Captain Micawber left her penniless. Courtney Rawlins, although extremely wealthy, is shortly to give up employment and resign his Directorships and other lucrative consultancies. Courtney's solicitors and accountants are in the course of preparing a complicated scheme, which will mean that the bulk of his fortune is gifted to his wife and children and he will be left with a small annuity. Substantial amounts of his estate will also go to charity. It is likely that these schemes will reach fruition in two or three months' time, i.e. sometime early in 2010.

The income from Patrick's estate is substantial, consisting of taxed interest and dividends. The shares which he held were sold shortly after Confirmation was obtained and so there are no dividends to speak of since date of death; the income after taking into account relief for inheritance tax loan interest and management expenses is £20,000 in the year to April 5, 2007, £30,000 in the year to April 5, 2008 and £70,000 in the year to April 5, 2009. The income for the year to April 5, 2010, or earlier if the estate is finalised before then, is likely to be even higher! The estate is dragging on principally because of some difficulties with Patrick's former involvement as a Lloyds Underwriter.

The beneficiaries are becoming quite tiresome in requesting payments and in fact, for reasons which are not altogether clear to the executor in retrospect, nothing has been paid to them.

---

[1] This is a fictitious case study, which the author used to amuse and illustrate during the seminars which he had presented to students, and during CPD courses. It has been updated and is included in the hope that the reader will find it useful and amusing and will forgive the author's self-indulgence in including it!

In particular, Rawlins, who at the best of times is a bit of a "whinger" has been nagging on at the executor for some time and has received shortly before April 5, 2009 one of the Picasso cartoons. When she heard this, Miss Williams nagged on at the executor and eventually the executor arranged for her to be handed over the other Picasso cartoon; this was on April 7, 2009. Rawlins received his on April 4, 2009. The executor expects to conclude the estate next year.

However, somewhat out of the blue you receive the letter on the following page:

Messrs Grabbit & Sue
1 Cheetham Row
LONDON
EC3

12th June 2008

Dear Sirs

Our Clients: Mr Courtney Rawlins and Miss Evelyn Williams
Patrick Bateman's Executry

On behalf of and as instructed by our clients, Miss Evelyn Williams and
Mr Courtney Rawlins, we hereby intimate a claim against the executor
for loss sustained by our clients arising out of failure to schedule
payments to account of residue from the estate of the late Patrick
Bateman, in which you are acting as Agents for the executors.

We are still quantifying the amount of our clients' loss and will let you
have a note of this as soon as possible. In the meantime, please
acknowledge receipt of this letter.

We would respectfully suggest that you should report the matter to your
professional indemnity insurers.

As stated above, we are presently quantifying the estate but reckon it will
be in the order of £25,000.00 at this stage.

  Yours faithfully

How has this Come About?

There had been something nagging at the back of your mind and
eventually you trace the reference which is in fact to s.701(12) of the
Taxes Act 1988 which provides that references to sums paid (to
beneficiaries) "are transferred or are appropriated by a personal representative to himself, and to debts that are set off or released".

The executor realises that the transfer of the Picassos have indeed
constituted exactly this and that the capital and the value of the Picasso
cartoons represents a payment to account of the beneficiaries up to the
amount of their assumed income entitlement from the Executry!

SUMMARY OF RESIDUARY INCOME

FOR THE PERIODS FROM:

JANUARY 1, 2007 (DATE OF DEATH) TO APRIL 5, 2007

APRIL 6, 2007 TO APRIL 5, 2008

APRIL 6, 2008 TO APRIL 5, 2009

	£Net			£Tax			£Gross	
2006/07	2007/08	2008/09	2006/07	2007/08	2008/09	2006/07	2007/08	2008/09
Non-Savings Income (rent)								
Nil	Nil	Nil	Nil	Nil	Nil	Nil	Nil	Nil
Non Dividend Savings Income (interest)								
20,000	30,000	70,000	5,000	7,500	17,500	25,000	37,500	87,500
Dividend Income								
N/A	Nil	Nil	N/A	Nil	Nil	N/A	Nil	Nil

Allocation

Courtney
Rawlins one half

10,000	15,000	35,000	2,500	3,750	8,750	12,500	18,750	43,750

Miss Evelyn
Williams one half

10,000	15,000	35,000	2,500	3,750	8,750	12,500	18,750	43,750

ASSUMED INCOME ENTITLEMENT

	COURTNEY	**EVELYN**
2006/07	Carried forward	Carried forward to next year
Net Income	10,000	10,000
Distributed	Nil	Nil
	10,000	10,000
2007/08		
Net Income	15,000	15,000
Add		
Carried forward from		
Previous year	10,000	10,000
Total	25,000	25,000
Distributed	Nil	Nil
Carried forward	25,000	25,000
2008/09		
Net Income	35,000	35,000
Carried forward from		
Previous years	40,000	40,000
Total	60,000	60,000
Distributed	100,000[2]	Nil
Carried forward	40,000(A)	60,000(B)
Period to April 5, 2010		£60,000

Comment

(A) *At this stage the payment to account represented by the cartoon is in excess of Courtney's assumed (aggregated) entitlement.*

(B) *For Evelyn her AIE is now a staggering £60,000 which is equivalent to £75,000.*

---

[2] The cartoon is worth £100,000.

PRELIMINARY QUANTIFICATION OF MISS WILLIAMS' CLAIM

Miss Williams has lost the benefit of three years' Personal Allowances:

2006–2007	£5,035
2007–2008	£5,225
2008–2009	£6,035
	£16,295

£16,295 @ (say) 20% = £3,259

She has also lost the benefit of the Starting Rate Income Band of 10 per cent for the three Fiscal Years as follows:

2006–2007	£0–£2,150	= £215.00
2007–2008	£0–£2,230	= £223.0
2008–2009	nil	= nil
		£438.00

Total to date therefore is £3,697 (£3,259 + £438)

As if that was not bad enough she has actually been pushed into the Higher Rate Tax Band for 2009–2010 as follows:

In the year 2008–2009 Evelyn has an assumed income entitlement of at least £60,000. She may indeed receive other payments during the year which shall add to the problem but if the assumed income entitlement is grossed up at 20 per cent it becomes £75,000 which is the amount of the payment made to her.

The transfer of the property counts as transfer of cash.

As soon as the £60,000 is grossed up at 2009–2010 Rates (assumed to be 20 per cent), i.e.

NET	£60,000
TAX	£15,000
GROSS	£75,000

Tax Calculation

The rates for 2009–2010 are not yet fully known but are estimated.

	2009–2010 GROSS	TAX
Non savings rate		
Personal	Nil	Nil
Executry	Nil	Nil
Savings Rate		
Executry	£75,000	£15,000
Deduct PA (estimated)	£ 6,475	
	£68,525	

Tax due as follows:-

LRB	@ 10%	nil (assumed lost because over the limit)
	37,400 @ 20%	£ 7,480.00
	31,125 @ 40%	£12,450.00
		£19,930.00
Less paid		£15,000.00
Due to be paid		£ 4,930.00

Comment

The claim on behalf of Miss Williams, in the tax year 2008/2009 to date is therefore *at least* £8,627 made up of £3,697 as before plus £4,930 higher rate tax which could have been avoided had payments been scheduled to her over the years.

NOTE: It could be argued that the benefit of the personal allowances should actually be shown as at 40 per cent.

In addition there is bound to be more income in the year to April 5, 2010 which may have to be deferred still later to allow Miss Williams to have the benefit of personal allowances and lower rates of tax!

Preliminary Quantification of Courtney's claim

The analysis for Mr Courtney Rawlinson's claim is as follows. The amount he has received (by way of the cartoon) amounts to £100,000. At this time at the end of the tax year 2008–2009, he has received his payment in the year 2008–2009 of £60,000 net. This is grossed up at 20 per cent, i.e. £75,000. Because his income is so high, all of his payment suffers tax at an extra 20 per cent, i.e. £15,000.

Comment

Had the payments been staggered to him after his income position changed next year or even the following year a great amount of this could in fact have been saved. How could the matter have been avoided?

Summary
Courtney's claim   = £15,000
Miss Williams' claim   = **£ 8,627**
                                  £23,627

How could the Claims have been Avoided?

It is suggested that some attempt should have been made in advance to know the beneficiary and for some prediction to be attempted as to the tax rate in advance to the end of the fiscal year. A sustained attempt should be made to ascertain the beneficiaries' personal circumstances either directly if they are existing clients (or at least not someone else's clients) or indirectly through their own solicitors or other professional advisors. A questionnaire letter is printed below.

If some kind of exercise had been carried out, it is likely that the personal circumstances of both beneficiaries would have been ascertained and some attempt at scheduling could have been made.

At the least, they would have been given the option for some stage payments to be made. The small additional fees involved in the above could be more than justified by the beneficiaries' gratitude!

Comment

It could be argued that the practitioner only has a duty to the executors. They are, after all, his clients. The above matters relate to the interests of beneficiaries. It is likely that the terms of engagement letter may have made this clear. However, it may well be that one or more of the executors may be a residuary beneficiary as well. In these circumstances the role of the executor/beneficiary may be clouded in the minds of the individual client/executor/beneficiary. This may not avoid a complaint being made. The present structure operates unfairly in that even if a complaint is made and thrown out sooner or later, the practitioner will certainly be involved in hours of work supplying records, not to say hours of angst while the complaint is being processed!

Danger Warning!!

It is important that no suspicion of unethical approaching of a beneficiary should be possible and for this reason, it is important to include a paragraph to indicate that if the beneficiary has separate representation the letter should be passed to their advisor.

Appendix 2

STATEMENT OF RESIDUARY INCOME FOR THE
YEAR TO APRIL 5, 2009 TEMPLATE

	NET £	TAX £	GROSS £

Non-Savings Income ("NSI")

RENTAL INCOME (3.20–3.42)

Savings Income ("SI")

TAXED BANK AND BUILDING SOCIETY INTEREST

(where no tax has been deducted) (9.1)

(where tax has been deducted) (9.2–9.4)

NATIONAL SAVINGS INTEREST (9.8–9.11)

OTHER INTERESTS (GILTS) (9.12–9.14)

ACCRUED INCOME (8.39)

Dividend Income ("DI")

INCOME BEARING NON REPAYABLE

UK DIVIDENDS (9.15–9.17)

UK UNIT TRUSTS (9.18–9.20)

UK SCRIP DIVIDENDS (9.21–9.23)

FOREIGN INCOME DIVIDENDS (8.24–8.26)

SUMMARY

	NSI Total	SI	DI
NET INCOME	Nil		
LESS	Nil		
RELIEFS (9.1–9.3)			
MANAGEMENT			
EXPENSES (12.4)			
NET RESIDUARY INCOME	Nil		

ALLOCATION

BENEFICIARY ONE
BENEFICIARY TWO
TOTAL

ASSUMED INCOME ENTITLEMENTS

	ASSUMED INCOME ENTITLEMENT	
	BENEFICIARY ONE	**BENEFICIARY TWO**
Tax Year	Carried forward to next year	Carried forward to next year

Net Income
Distributed

Tax Year

Net Income
Add
Carried   forward
from
previous year
Total
Distributed
Carried forward

Tax Year

Net Income
Carried   forward
from
previous years
Total

Distributed

Period to April 5, 2009

BENEFICIARY ONE
Brought forward 2006–07
Net Income 2007–08
LESS
Distributed 1996/97
Carried forward 1997/98

BENEFICIARY TWO
Brought forward 1995/96
Net Income 1996/97
LESS
Distributed 1996/97
Carried forward 1997/98

Appendix 3

CHECKLIST

A general executry checklist is printed for reference. Before taking instructions, it is important to take full details. The consequences of not taking these and the matters which might be overlooked should be carefully considered.

The questions which may be uppermost in the client's mind, such as how long will all this take and how much it will cost, should be addressed before the client raises them.

There is no special magic about the checklist which follows. Checklists are a vital tool in preventing or at least lowering the chances of a complaint or claim. They should be kept up to date and revised as time, experience and changes in the law dictate. In the executry checklist which follows those matters which have particular reference to tax **are shown in bold**.

It goes without saying that a terms of engagement letter will have been sent out and proper identification vouched in advance of the meeting.

It is suggested that this checklist together with the replies be typed up and stapled inside the front cover of the file (and removed to the inside front cover of subsequent files!).

1. **Funeral Arrangements.** Headstone. Disposal of ashes. Expenses to be refunded.
2. **Domicile—domicile of spouse/civil partner restricted IHT exemption.**
3. **Death Certificate**
4. **Will or Intestacy any legal rights claims or claims by cohabitants.**
5. **Any Codicils or informal writings.** Holograph Will—Affidavits.

   - Intestacy—who is to petition for appointment as Executor-dative? **Was the deceased in a relationship, which might qualify for a claim by cohabitee?**
   - Name and Address of executors.
   - **Bequests free of tax or bearing their own tax, check and identify any exempt and non exempt bequest in residue.**
   - Names, current names addresses and ages of family.
   - **Beneficiaries (any predeceasing family members?) special references to charities and beneficiaries living abroad for CGT exemptions.**

6. **Foreign assets. Check if Scottish will covers heritable property. Has foreign IHT or similar been paid? Investigate possibility of relief on UK IHT for this and foreign legal fees. Pay particular attention to ensuring rates of exchange are correct, e.g. may be a different rate for date of death value and date of payment of foreign death duty.**

7.   House—obtain valuation. CONSIDERATIONS OF VALUE VERY IMPORTANTHERE BECAUSE THIS VALUE MAY BE TREATED BY HMRC AS BASE FOR CGT. FOR EXAMPLE, IF THE ESTATE IS WELL BELOW THE LIMIT THEN IT SHOULD BE EXPLAINED TO EXECUTORS THAT THEY SHOULD HAVE REGARD TO CONSEQUENCES OF INCLUDING A LOW VALUE. APART FROM THE OBVIOUS CONSEQUENCES OF GIVING A FALSE RETURN TO HMRC, E.G. PENALTIES, ETC. THERE IS ALSO THE QUESTION OF THE BASE VALUE FOR IHT.
8.   Value. Sale. Title Deeds. (**Survivorship destination? Remember it may be possible to alter this by deed of variation.**) Any Loan.
9.   **Insurance policy assigned in security? Impact of this on legal rights calculation and surviving spouse/civil partner exemption.**
10. Arrangements for gas, electricity, telephone. Insurance (House and Contents). Possible debts to be deducted from estate.
11. Any other heritable property?
12. Value. Was it let?—**If so lease required/details of tenancy. Is tax on heritable property to be paid by instalments? Was it the subject of a specific legacy? Tax consequences of lease continued by executors after death.**
13. Joint Property.
14. Details of joint property—date when joint ownership began and names of other joint owners—by whom and from what source was joint property provided—how was income (if any) dealt with—how does joint property devolve on deceased's death?
15. Timeshare in UK or abroad.
16. **Furniture and personal effects—have them valued—remember gifts of jewellery for IHT.**

   - Valuation. Jewellery. (Any claim for exemption?)

17. **Motor Car** (number plates). Value Sell/Retain. Insurance. Any items rented (T.V.).
18. **Cash in house.**
19. **Bank Accounts.** Building society accounts. Credit card accounts. Standing orders or direct debit authorities? **Be thinking at this time of ingathering information to produce tax return to date of death—try to get information as early as possible to enable framing of deceased's tax return to date of death.**

Remember to mark "deceased" on passbooks, etc.

   - **PEP}**
   - **TESSAs} remember tax due after the date of death**
   - **ISAs?}**

20. **Stock and Shares.** Who holds certificates? Held on CREST? Stockbrokers.

   - **Valuation 1/4 up.**
   - **Unit Trusts lower of two prices.**

- OEICs **price on date of death.**
- PEPs.
- Private Company shares—Valuation—company auditors.
- Foreign Property.
- Accrued Income Scheme **note for future.**

21. **National Savings**

   - Premium Savings Bonds. National Savings Certificates. Other.
   - National Savings products **try to identify any untaxed interest and remember to pay tax on it later.**

22. **Life Assurance Policies.** Obtain details of bonuses—valuation.

   - Case of unit linked policies.
   - Retain copies of policies in case required by HM Revenue & Customs. Were any of the policies effected in conjunction with, or at the same time as, any other policy or annuity?
   - **Any chargeable events on death?**

23. **Pension arrears** (state and private). Pension Book. Be thinking at this time of ingathering information to produce tax return to date of death.

   - National Insurance Number.
   - **Superannuation Pensions (exempt?) or lump sum payments.**
   - **Annuities.**

24. **Funeral Payment** from Social Fund. Widow's pension.
25. **Money due from Trusts.** Interest in possession. Name of Agents. Ask agents for tax certificates.
26. Was deceased a trustee or executor? Name of Agents.
27. **Has deceased inherited any assets to which quick succession relief might apply? (i.e. tax paid within five years.)**
28. **Gifts**

   - **Details of all transfers made within seven years of the deceased's death (viz. capital and other lifetime transfers chargeable when made).**
   - **Unless covered by the annual/small gifts exemptions or unless made to UK domiciled spouse it will be necessary to provide details of the following if made by the deceased within seven years of his death; gifts, settlements or other transfers of value; dispositions for the maintenance of a relative; disposition in favour of a relative whether for consideration or not; payments of a premium on a life assurance policy not included in the Inventory. (It may then be necessary to go back seven years from the date of any transfers chargeable on the death of the deceased in order to establish the rate of tax on these transfers.) Any other gifts such as failing to claim legal rights.**
   - **Potentially Exempt Transfers may now be chargeable and additional IHT may be payable on lifetime transfers chargeable when made.**

- Gifts with Reservation—Did the deceased on or after March 18, 1986 make any gift with reservation?
- Remember to investigate whether any gifts may be regarded as out of income/normal expenditure.

29. Business interest, e.g. Interest in Partnership. 100 per cent or 50 per cent relief.

- Any asset used in the business but owned by the deceased?
- Name of accountants. Payment of tax by instalments.
- Obtain partnership agreement and any other writings relating to partnership; also accounts to date of death or last set of accounts prepared prior to death.

30. Tax affairs. Who dealt with them? Copy of last return.

- Who is to lodge return to date of death?
- What income tax liabilities were due as at date of death?
- Any repayments of income tax due to the deceased?

31. Debts. Funeral Account. Remember to claim mournings in IHT200 or IHT400.

- Household Accounts. Wages to employees? Rates.
- Medical Accounts. Any BUPA—type of cover.
- Were any of the debts prescribed? Are all of the debts properly evidenced and legally enforceable?
- Any contingent liabilities, e.g. guarantees. What rights of reimbursement had the deceased? (A contingent liability will be deductible for inheritance tax only to the extent that reimbursement cannot be obtained—IHTA s.162(1).
- Any Deeds of covenant (but any outstanding payments will not be deductible for Inheritance Tax—they were not incurred for consideration in money's worth—IHTA s.5(5)).
- Finance Act 1986 s.103 may limit the deductions from the deceased's estate if the creditor has received property from the deceased at any time in his or her lifetime (this applies to debts incurred on or after March 1986).

32. **Immediate cash requirements** of dependants.
33. **Bank loan for IHT—Consumer Credit Act?**

- Bear in mind that all possible exemptions should be claimed in the Inventory to keep the overdraft to a minimum. Watch out for bequests to charities! Remember that there is an option to pay tax by instalments on, say, heritable property even if the decision is subsequently changed and payment is made in a lump sum. The first instalment may not be due before the Inventory is lodged, which will mean an even smaller loan. If time allows investigate the possibility of the bank transferring funds to pay IHT.

34. **Legal Rights—Are they to be claimed/discharged?**

- If they are to be discharged it should be in writing and within two years from the date of the deceased's death—s.142 IHTA.
- Are there any children under 16 entitled to legal rights? What funds are to be set aside to meet possible claims by them? Keep in view IHTA s.147.

35. Disclaimer of legacy or residue—What to take? Deed of Variation—raise this at earliest opportunity explain time frame.
36. Fees—Possible early agreement with executors to refer to the Auditor of Court for fixing of fees.
37. Financial Services Act—include this in Terms of Business Agreement?
38. Make diary entries for tax:

- Final deadline for submitting paper entries, also intimate any executry income and/or capital gains—September 31
- Final deadline for submitting income tax returns online—January 31
- Final deadline for elections under POT regulations (to have gift with reservation regulations applied)—January 31
- From January to Mid March—consider making payments to residuary beneficiaries.
- As soon after April 5 as possible prepare and send R185 (Estate Income) forms to beneficiaries to enable them to submit their returns by paper.
- Before the expiry of six months after death prepare and submit IHT forms even though estimates may be required.
- Prepare fee notes.
- Have accounts of charge and discharge prepared and approved.
- Have discharges or receipts prepared and signed by the beneficiaries.
- Arrange to make payment of all sums due, including interest to close.
- Take instructions re titles and other papers.
- Prepare document to deal with death of spouse to facilitate claiming transfer of nil rate band if appropriate.
- Send file to store.

Appendix 4

TERMS OF BUSINESS

"The importance of an engagement letter for tax work is to define the terms and limitations of the engagement and to agree these with the client."[1]

This letter can be altered as required. One of the problems is that this type of letter can be extremely long and perhaps somewhat intimidating for clients, particular elderly clients. The length of these letters is becoming a cause for concern for not only the legal profession but other professions as well. As can be seen the basic letter (without making the small print too small!) is at least seven pages long. However much regard is given to presentation, etc. it is still a lengthy document for clients to read and absorb! Some thought may be given to splitting it up into several documents, e.g. one for the basic information for all clients, time of openings, taxation of fees, client identification complaints and so forth; one for the basic facts for this type of work—what is being done—investigating estate and obtaining confirmation; and a third one for the fee rates and time to be taken together with what is not being done. Without wishing to appear cynical, this last one is what most people are principally interested in.

Alternatively, the letter could consist of one sheet with the least information on it and a reference could be made to terms and conditions on the firm's website. **This can only be done if it is known that the client has access to the internet**.

Mrs. Heather Mellow
12 Berkeley Square
EDINBURGH

Dear Mrs. Mellow

Your late Mother's Executry
Terms of Business Letter

We thank the executor for the Death Certificates and other papers. We are proceeding to investigate the estate and the debts and will thereafter proceed to obtain Confirmation of your mother's estate from the Sheriff Court and ingather and distribute the estate. We note that we are to receive instructions from you on behalf of your sister and yourself.

As Solicitors in Scotland, our dealings are regulated by the Law Society of Scotland. We carry appropriate professional Indemnity Insurance and we subscribe to the Solicitors' Guarantee Fund.

---

[1] Tax Faculty of the Institute of Chartered Accountants in England and Wales, *Tax Guide 6/08 Engagement Letters for Tax Practitioners* (Tax Faculty, August 2008).

We refer to the executor's instructions to Mr Hemlock and are pleased to confirm that we are acting in the winding up of the executry of your late Mother's estate.

The solicitor who will be dealing with your work on a day-to-day basis is Mr Hemlock.

We will advise you at regular intervals regarding the progress of our work and keep you informed of all significant developments. If you are uncertain about what is happening at any time, please ask Mr Hemlock.

We would take the opportunity of drawing certain matters to your attention.

The Terms of business apply unless otherwise agreed in writing. Often we may have to move quickly to safeguard your interests, possibly before full consideration of these terms. In such cases we will take it that, unless you notify us immediately in writing to the contrary, you agree these Terms retrospectively.

Contacting Us

The business will be conducted by our Mr. Hemlock and other colleagues. Our office hours are Monday to Friday 9.15a.m. to 12.30p.m. and 1.45p.m. to 5p.m. Consultations outwith the office hours are available by arrangement.

How Long Will It Take?

The nature of the work and the variables makes it difficult to estimate precisely in many cases how long something will take to complete. **Often, however, the speed which we can complete a piece of work is directly affected by the co-operation we receive from other people outwith our control**. In addition, other factors can affect the timescale. For example winding up an estate which involves the sale of a house when the market is low moving can cause delays. It is in our interest as much as yours to complete the work as quickly and efficiently as possible. If you have not heard recently from the person dealing with your work, then please contact us.

Confidentiality

Information passed to us is kept confidential and will not be disclosed to third parties except as authorised by you or required by law, e.g. by order of the court. You should be aware that not all of our advice to you is confidential. Our Client Relations Partner, Mr Nice, will be happy provide you with further details if you ask.

Conflict of interest

We will carry out this work with the highest professional standards and integrity. We will contact you immediately if we become aware of any conflict of interest with a view to resolve matters.

Fees

The basis upon which our fee will be charged will depend on the time spent carrying out the work. Mr Hemlock's rate of payment for this work will be at the rate of £140.00 per hour plus outlays including VAT. Clients sometimes prefer to have a percentage charge made for the work and if so this would be of the order of 2.5%. If the work turns out to be more complex than normal, we may require to increase our estimate to take account of this. We will inform you as soon as possible about any such increase.

The Auditor of Court or the Auditor of The Royal Faculty of Procurators in Glasgow is always available to provide a complete independent assessment of a fair fee for a piece of legal work carried out. In certain instances to ensure that a file has been correctly charged, we may voluntarily send the file to the Auditor. Unless agreed with you beforehand, we will pay the Auditor's fee. Should you at any time wish to dispute or challenge the amount of a fee charged by us then you are entitled to ask to have the Auditor calculate the fee independently. This process is known as "taxation". In that case, both sides are bound by the fee as fixed by the Auditor. If the Auditor reduces the amount of the original fee, we will only charge that reduced amount and we will pay the Auditor's costs. If he confirms that our fee is correct or undercharged, then you will be responsible for the Auditor's costs.

Interim Accounts

We may render its fee at the end of a matter or may render interim accounts as may be agreed with you. In matters, which are likely to continue for longer than 3 months, we will expect to render interim accounts. It is practice to issue an interim fee after confirmation has been obtained.

Outlays and Expenses

You authorise us to incur on your behalf such outlays and expenses, such as search dues, copyright dues, confirmation dues, as we consider necessary, which you will be required to reimburse to us from executry funds. You may place a limit on the amount of fees and/or outlays and expenses, which may be incurred without your prior approval, provided that the limit is realistic. If you wish to do so, please tell us in writing.

Money Laundering/Client Identification—Proceeds of Crime

You have complied with this. OR

The Money Laundering and Client Identity Regulations require us to be satisfied as to the identity of our clients and as to the source of any funds passing through our hands. In order to comply with these Regulations, we may need to ask you for proof of identity and other information in relation to these matters. We reserve the right to withdraw from acting for you if you fail to provide us with the information requested of you and required in connection with our Money Laundering Procedures.

Before we can proceed to act on your behalf, we require to comply with the Regulations. Below are two lists detailing forms of identification, which are sufficient for this purpose. In this regard, we would be grateful if you could provide **one item** from each of the lists below: We confirm that it will be returned to you as soon as possible.

List A	List B
A current signed passport	Telephone Bill
Current UK photo card/driving licence	Gas Bill
Current full UK driving licence	Water Bill
Pension or child benefit book	Electricity Bill
Inland Revenue notification	Credit Card Statement
	Bank/Building Society Statement
	Pension Book

Please provide us urgently with two of the items specified in this list, one from List A and one from List B.

Financial Services

We only hold an incidental financial business certificate from the Law Society. In effect this does not allow us to give advice but only to pass on any instructions from clients **where this is incidental to other business conducted by us**. The specific Incidental Financial Business undertaken by this firm will be the sale of shares through stockbrokers on your instructions. The firm has limited its incidental financial business activities to arranging the purchase and sale of shares given the limited scope of activities allowed under the Incidental Financial Business regime. We are licensed by The Law Society of Scotland to carry on incidental financial business under the Solicitors (Scotland) (Incidental Financial Business) Practice Rules 2004. We are not authorised by the Financial Services Authority under the Financial Services and Markets Act 2000. The firm has professional indemnity insurance under The Law Society of Scotland's master policy. The current level of indemnity on the master policy is 1.25 million pounds per claim. The firm is also covered by the Scottish Solicitors Guarantee Fund which is a fund established by Section 43 of the Solicitors (Scotland) Act 1980 to compensate persons who suffer loss by reason of dishonesty.

We have to tell you that we are obliged to report certain matters, including possibly confidential information, under the Proceeds of Crime Act 2002, the Money Laundering Regulations 2003, and the Terrorism Act 2000 and related Statutory Instruments, to the authorities. We may not be be allowed to tell you of such a report.

Ownership of work product / papers

Work which we carry out, whether or not in writing, and all documentation (including working papers), during the course of the work carried out for you will be our property. We are of course happy to store title deeds, usually without charges, for you by prior agreement.

Clients' Funds

If we receive any monies for the executry, which are not required to meet legacies debts or our fees and outlays, these monies **must be held separately from our own funds in designated client accounts**. We will credit the account with interest in accordance with the Rules of the Law Society of Scotland. We operate The Royal Bank of Scotland Global

Investment Scheme which enables us to obtain interest on deposit sums held for clients at a rate which will frequently be in excess of the interest individually obtainable for such sums. As stated we will, where appropriate, endeavour to utilise The Royal Bank of Scotland Global Investment Scheme.

We do not charge for the collection of interest on clients' deposits. Although the current financial situation has made this next provision somewhat irrelevant, in happier times we would be entitled to retain commission paid to us by the relevant bank, which commission will not exceed 1.5 per cent of the global sum invested.

Accounts

We will issue our Account of Charge and Discharge at the end of the matter.

Restrictions

We would point out that while say suggestions may be made by Mr Hemlock, the work carried out may impact on other taxes, e.g. income tax, capital gains tax, pre-annual assets tax and stamp duty.

We shall incur no liability to you if we are unable to carry out your instructions as a result of any cause beyond our reasonable control. In such circumstances, we shall notify you as soon as reasonably practical in order that you can decide whether to terminate or amend our instructions. We shall not be responsible for any failure to advise or comment on any matter which falls outside the scope of our engagement or your specific instructions.

Website

Our terms and conditions can be found at our website on *www.thistlesolicitors.co.uk*. This is updated from time to time.

Your Co-operation

When we request papers or deeds sent for signature, it goes without saying that it would be helpful to have these back at your earliest convenience. In addition, it would be helpful if you are able let us have, also at your earliest convenience, all relevant information and paperwork. It is important for us to be fully informed to enable us to carry out your work, and any further information which we reasonably request. In providing us with information and/or when instructing us, you should assume that we have no knowledge of any relevant factual matters or background, even if the same information has been given to us previously in connection with other matters.

Holidays—if you are to be on holiday perhaps you could let us have a note of the dates and a contact number or e-mail address. By the same token if moving house please let us have a note of any time you are incommunicado. This may be the time at the date of entry when BT terminates your service at the precise moment we are trying to contact you urgently!

COMMUNICATION

We are happy to communicate by letter, fax or email. As regards email we point out that we are not "logged on" all through the day and may not receive this until later in the day or the next morning.

We shall communicate with you and with any relevant third parties and take instructions from you by telephone, post, facsimile or e-mail. It is understood that communications are not always secure but we will use all reasonable procedures to check for the most commonly known "viruses".

Finally

our aim is to provide a service which is satisfactory in every respect. However, if you have any concerns about the manner in which work is being carried out on your behalf, please contact our Client Relations Partner (Mr Nice) who will be happy to discuss your concerns. You have a right to complain in respect of work instituted before October 1, 2008 to The Law Society of Scotland, 26 Drumsheugh Gardens, Edinburgh EH3 7YR (website address: *www.lawscot.org.uk* and telephone 0131 226 7411) and after work commenced after October 1, 2008 to The Scottish Complaints Commission.

Yours sincerely

The following is a more abbreviated letter and refers to the firm's website:

October 16, 2008

Mrs Pansy Parsley
22350 Finity Street
CALIFORNIA 21345
USA

Dear Mrs Parsley

YOUR LATE MOTHER'S ESTATE
TERMS OF ENGAGEMENT

We refer to recent instructions to us. We are required by The Law Society to set out our terms and conditions for the work, which has been instructed, namely the winding up of your late mother's estate.

Broadly speaking our terms are as follows:

1. *As Mr Thistle may have mentioned we are accepting instructions from the executors through yourself.*
2. *Mr Thistle's rate of payment for this work will be at the rate of £xx per hour plus outlays plus VAT. Clients sometimes prefer to have a percentage charge made for the work and if so this would be of the order of 2.5%*
3. *Our terms and conditions can be found at our website on www.darhsolicitors.co.uk.*
4. *You have confirmed to us that you have access to the internet.*

   Yours sincerely

A yet even shorter letter follows.

Dear Mr Primrose

The time charge for carrying out the winding up of your late mother's estate is £140 per hour plus VAT and the usual outlays such as Confirmation dues. The name of the Client Relations Partner is Mr Nice who may be contacted should you have cause for dissatisfaction at any time. We understand that we are to take instructions in connection with the Executry direct from yourself and we confirm having received confirmation of your identity etc.

Yours sincerely

Appendix 5

KNOW THE BENEFICIARY: STYLE OF LETTER TO BENEFICIARY (TO BE SENT IN DUPLICATE)

Dear Mrs. Houghton

Your late mother's executry

We refer to previous correspondence. Recent changes in the law allow the executors some limited scope for income tax planning which may be of benefit to you. To enable us to explore this we require some prediction of your tax position for the end of this fiscal year and the next one or two fiscal years.

If you are willing to supply this, the information needed is undernoted. Specific figures need not be given. General indications on the enclosed copy will be sufficient.

[Under existing law the Revenue will allow variations and discharges of entitlements under wills or on intestacy provided these are made timeously. There may be tax benefits by way of inheritance and capital gains tax if these variations are made. However, to secure these benefits it is essential that decisions are made <u>at the earliest opportunity</u>. We shall be happy to discuss these.]

If you are being separately advised on this matter please pass this letter to your advisors.

Yours sincerely

Note referred to:

Date of Birth: (if over 64)
Gross income from all sources, for current year ending 5/4/2009 (2010)
Capital Gains expected/not expected* to exceed £9,600
Tax Prediction for following year to 5/4/2010
Present personal circumstances relating to tax allowance, i.e. married/ single/single parent/widow(er)*
Any lifetime changes, e.g. retirement, divorce, insolvency.

---

* delete if inapplicable

Appendix 6

TEXT OF LETTER FROM CAPITAL TAXES OFFICE EXPLAINING THEIR VIEWS ON GIFTS WITH RESERVATION FOR IHT PURPOSES

(18 MAY 1987)

GIFTS WITH RESERVATION

The following is the text of a letter from the Inland Revenue to the Law Society.

Following our discussions on the inheritance tax matters raised in the Society's Reform Memorandum I am now able to write to you about the points concerning the provisions on gifts with reservation (GWR).

As we previously explained, it does not seem realistic to think in terms of precise and comprehensive guidance on how the GWR provisions will be interpreted and applied since so much will turn on the particular facts of individual cases. However, as the provisions are similar to those adopted for estate duty, the relevant estate duty case law and practice provide a helpful guide to the interpretation and application of the inheritance tax legislation. That said, may I turn to your specific concerns.

G of land

1. Consistent with the assurance given last year by the Minister of State in Standing Committee G (HC Deb, June 10, 1986, col 425) the estate duty practice on the treatment of gifts involving a share in a house where the gifted property is occupied by all the joint owners including the donor will apply. The donor's retention of a share in the property will not by itself amount to a reservation. If, and for so long as, all the joint owners remain in occupation, the donor's occupation will not be treated as a reservation provided the gift is itself unconditional and there is no collateral benefit to the donor. The payment by the donee of the donor's share of the running costs, for example, might be such a benefit. An arrangement will not necessarily be jeopardised merely because it involves a gift of an unequal share in a house.

2. In other cases the donor's occupation or enjoyment of the gifted land will only be disregarded if the occupation is for full consideration in money or money's worth as provided in paragraph 6 (1) (a) of Schedule 20 to the Finance Act 1986 (or if it is by way of a reasonable "care and maintenance" provision within para 6 (l)(b)). Whether an arrangement is for full consideration will of course depend on the precise facts. But among the attributes of an acceptable arrangement would be the existence of a bargain negotiated at arm's length by parties who were independently advised and which followed the normal commercial criteria in force at the time it was negotiated.

3. You raised the possibility that a donor might give his house subject to a prior lease created in his own favour. Consistent with the principles established in the case of Munro v Commissioners of Stamp Duties (New South Wales) [AC 61, we would not normally expect the donor's retention of the lease to constitute a reservation, assuming that the creation of the lease and the subsequent gift of the property subject to that lease are independent transactions. The application or otherwise of the decision in Re Nichols [1 WLR 534 concerning a (donee) landlord's covenants would be a matter for determination in the light of all the facts at the time of the donor's death.

Gifts involving family businesses or farms

4. A gift involving a family business or farm will not necessarily amount to a GWR merely because the donor remains in the business, perhaps as a director or a partner. For example, where the gift is of shares of a company, the continuation of reasonable commercial arrangements in the form of remuneration for the donor's ongoing services to the company entered into before the gift will not of itself amount to a reservation provided the remuneration is in no way linked to or beneficially affected by the gift. Similar considerations will apply in the case where the gift is into trust which empowered a trustee, who may be the donor, to retain director's fees, etc. for his own benefit.

5. The "Munro" principle will also be relevant in determining the tax treatment of gifts affecting family farms where the donor and the donee continue to farm the land in pursuance of arrangements entered into prior to and independently of the gift. In cases where this principle does not apply, the test of "full consideration" for the purposes of paragraph 6 will need to be satisfied with regard to the donor's occupation of the land. In applying that test we shall take account of all the circumstances surrounding the arrangement including the sharing of profits and losses, the donor's and the donee's interests in the land, and their respective commitment and expertise.

Gifts of chattels

6. You referred to potential difficulties in determining what amounts to "full consideration" for the donor's continued enjoyment of gift chattels, particularly pictures and paintings, for the purposes of paragraph 6 of Schedule 20. These may not be insuperable, as appears from the recent case of *IRC v MacPherson*, and in any event it would be difficult to overturn an arm's length commercial arrangement entered into by parties who were independently advised.

Settlor's retention of reversion

7. In the case where a gift is made into trust, the retention by the settlor (donor) of a reversionary interest under the trust is not considered to constitute a reservation, whether the retained interest arises under the express terms of the trust or it arises by operation of general law, e.g. a resulting trust.

Finally, we have no objection to your publishing this letter in the Society's Gazette. I am copying the letter to the Law Society of Scotland, the Institutes of Chartered Accountants (England and Wales, and Scotland) and the Institute of Taxation who may also wish to bring it to their members' attention.

INDEX